## ADVANCE PRAISE FOR
## THE WORLD'S NEWEST PROFESSION

"If you use consultants, or claim to be a consultant, you should read this book." – Charles Wilson, CEO, Booker Ltd.

"This book should be required reading for everyone who teaches at a business school, as well as for all MBA students. I recommend it to anyone interested in the upheavals around corporate governance and professional ethics that marked the turn of the 21st century." – JoAnne Yates, Sloan Distinguished Professor of Management, MIT Sloan School of Management

"McKenna has unearthed the distinctly American origins of modern consulting in the evolution of financial market regulation – surprisingly and convincingly." – John Clarkeson, Co-Chairman of the Board, The Boston Consulting Group

"Witch doctors or miracle workers? Whatever your view of management consultants, it pays to understand how the world's leading consulting firms have become so influential. McKenna's superb history reveals how one crucial piece of U.S. legislation – the 1933 Glass-Steagall Act – and one vibrant American city – Chicago – spawned an industry that has transformed the face of global business and national government in the 20th century." – Martin Giles, Managing Director, The Economist Group, North America

"Fascinating, frightening, and perfectly timed – McKenna's sweeping survey shines a brilliant light on a profession that has always preferred to keep outsiders in the dark." – Martin Kihn, author of *House of Lies: How Management Consultants Steal Your Watch and Then Tell You the Time*

"McKenna opens the private world of management consulting to his keen analytical eye, providing a rich, absorbing accounting of the rise and expansion of this profession and a sharp critique of consulting's role in shaping the strategies of the world's largest corporations. This is a fascinating, revealing book about a profession that has received little serious, sustained scholarly attention." – Walter W. Powell, Professor of Education & Sociology, Stanford University

"This history of management consulting analyzes an important stream of the history of modern business itself. Today's managers can put its insights to practical use when engaging – or deciding not to engage – consultants." – Tony Tyler, Chief Operating Officer, Cathay Pacific Airways

"McKenna's book does a superb job of exploring the role that this industry played in transforming (not always for the better) a variety of different types of organizations – from businesses to religious and charitable associations to government agencies – and through them much of the fabric of modern life." – Naomi Lamoreaux, Professor of Economics & History, University of California, Los Angeles

"History is not bunk. With Glass-Steagall repealed and the aftershocks of the Enron scandal by no means over, the timing of *The World's Newest Profession* could hardly be more fortuitous. McKenna's breadth of scholarship and clarity of argument will undoubtedly sit, like Banquo's ghost, at the consulting banquet for years to come." – Fiona Czerniawska, *Consulting to Management*

"McKenna offers a lively look at a profession that has often been shrouded in secrecy and shows how it has become enormously lucrative – although not always as a result of the quality of advice being doled out. Interesting and provocative, McKenna's book offers a lens to understand the development of the modern corporation." – Jon Housman, Managing Director, *The Wall Street Journal Europe*

# THE WORLD'S NEWEST PROFESSION

In *The World's Newest Profession*, Christopher McKenna offers a history of management consulting in the twentieth century. Although management consulting may not yet be a recognized profession, the leading consulting firms have been advising and reshaping the largest organizations in the world since the 1920s. This groundbreaking study details how the elite consulting firms, including McKinsey & Company and Booz Allen & Hamilton, expanded after U.S. regulatory changes during the 1930s; how they changed giant corporations, nonprofits, and the state during the 1950s; and why consultants became so influential in the global economy after 1960. As they grew in number, consultants would introduce organizations to "corporate culture" and "decentralization" but they faced vilification for their role in the Enron crisis and for legitimating corporate blunders. Through detailed case studies based on unprecedented access to internal files and personal interviews, *The World's Newest Profession* explores how management consultants came to be so influential within our culture and explains exactly what consultants really do in the global economy.

Christopher D. McKenna is University Lecturer in Strategy at the Saïd Business School, Fellow of Brasenose College, and a founding member of the Clifford Chance Centre for the Management of Professional Service Firms, all within the University of Oxford.

CAMBRIDGE STUDIES IN THE EMERGENCE
OF GLOBAL ENTERPRISE

*Editors*

Louis Galambos, *The Johns Hopkins University*

Geoffrey Jones, *Harvard Business School*

*Other books in the series*

*National Cultures and International Competition: The Experience of Schering
AG, 1851–1950*, by Christopher Kobrak, ESCP-EAP, European School
of Management

*Knowledge and Competitive Advantage: The Coevolution of Firms,
Technology, and National Institutions*, by Johann Peter Murmann, Australian
Graduate School of Management

# The World's Newest Profession

## MANAGEMENT CONSULTING IN THE TWENTIETH CENTURY

### Christopher D. McKenna

Saïd Business School and Brasenose College, University of Oxford

CAMBRIDGE
UNIVERSITY PRESS

CAMBRIDGE UNIVERSITY PRESS

Cambridge, New York, Melbourne, Madrid, Cape Town, Singapore, São Paulo

Cambridge University Press
40 West 20th Street, New York, NY 10011-4211, USA

www.cambridge.org
Information on this title: www.cambridge.org/9780521810395

First published 2006

Printed in the United States of America

*A catalog record for this publication is available from the British Library.*

*Library of Congress Cataloging in Publication Data*

McKenna, Christopher D.
The world's newest profession : management consulting in the twentieth century /
Christopher D. McKenna.
p.   cm.
Includes bibliographical references and index.
ISBN 0-521-81039-6 (hardcover)
1. Business consultants – United States.   2. Consulting firms – United States.   I. Title.
HD69.C6M395   2006
011 – dc22          2006002824

ISBN-13  978-0-521-81039-5 hardback
ISBN-10  0-521-81039-6 hardback

*For Mara, who assures
me that money and power
are sexy.*

# Contents

# Series Editors' Preface

In the past century, the United States has made many important contributions to the global economy – in technology, in business practices, and in organizational structures. Few of these innovations, we believe, have been more significant than the subject of Christopher McKenna's book on the rise of management consulting in the twentieth century. In an era of tumultuous organizational transformations, of giant cross-border mergers and acquisitions, and of decisive transitions in public and nonprofit organizations as well as corporations, management consultants have become ubiquitous agents of organizational change, deeply embedded in all of the developed economies.

McKenna digs into the history of the leading management consulting firms and provides his readers with the best available account of the business' origins and early years. Basing his study on internal documents, interviews, and government reports, he is able to chart the evolution of this new form of professional advice over a long century of decisive change in global capitalism. As he demonstrates, transitions in the governmental context as well as in the private and nonprofit sectors had dramatic impacts on the markets and performance of the management consultancies in America and abroad.

This is a study that speaks to a variety of audiences: to all those who want to understand current problems in the corporate sector, including in particular the Enron scandal; to researchers interested in business strategy and corporate reorganization; to readers who want a better grasp of the history of modern business, of politics in the twentieth century, and of the sociology of organizations. It is, in that sense, an impressively multidisciplinary study. We are proud to include Christopher McKenna's *The World's Newest Profession: Management Consulting in the Twentieth Century* in our series, *Cambridge Studies in the Emergence of Global Enterprise*.

Geoffrey Jones
Harvard Business School

Louis Galambos
The Johns Hopkins University

# Acknowledgments

This book has been more than a decade in the making and during the intervening years I have incurred a great many debts to family, friends, institutions, and associations. I want to begin, however, by thanking a series of wonderful teachers who continue to inspire me in my own teaching at Oxford. At Amherst College, where I first encountered economic history, the late Hugh Aitken served as a model of how an eminent scholar and a charismatic teacher could also be a sympathetic advisor. I am sorry that I am not able to show Hugh this book, for I owe a great intellectual debt to both his early analysis of Taylorism and his later conception of "translators" in my own academic work. After I left Amherst, when I was despairing of Wall Street's corporate culture, Hugh suggested that I study with another wonderful scholar, David Hounshell, then at the University of Delaware. In particular, David helped me to make the transition from thinking like an economist to writing like a historian. He was no less remarkable for helping me to jump, only shortly after I had first begun to study with him, to a Ph.D. program under the supervision of Louis Galambos in the history department of The Johns Hopkins University. At Hopkins, Lou was an ideal doctoral supervisor, always willing to support my decision to pursue interdisciplinary and comparative work even when I questioned my own eclecticism. Professors Ron Walters and Bill Leslie, both at Johns Hopkins, also generously supported me throughout my time in Baltimore and remain wonderful colleagues. At three different institutions, in three very different settings, I was blessed with the very best teachers that I could imagine.

Extensive financial support made my long tenure as a graduate student if not lucrative, at least not dispiriting. The history departments at the University of Delaware and The Johns Hopkins University provided me with graduate fellowships as well as travel and book allowances. When money for graduate education seemed to be drying up, generous dissertation fellowships from the John Rovensky Foundation at the University of Illinois, the Newcomen Society in Pennsylvania, the Memorial Fund at Amherst College, and from the Dean's Teaching Fellowship at Johns Hopkins provided invaluable assistance. During the final two years of my graduate study, Daniel Raff, a fellow business historian and strategist, kindly secured me a position as a lecturer in the Management Department of the Wharton School at the University of Pennsylvania and gave me the opportunity to discuss my work with scholars and students in strategy and organizational theory. I would also like to thank the following institutions for fellowships and travel grants toward my doctoral research: The Fulbright Commission of Rome; John D. Rockefeller 3rd Fellowships, Program on Non-Profit Organizations, Yale University; Andrew Mellon Research Fellowship, Virginia Historical Society; Herbert Hoover Presidential Library; Harry S. Truman Presidential Library; Alfred D. Chandler, Jr., Travel Fellowship Fund, Harvard Business School; and the Center for the History of Business, Technology, and Society, Hagley Museum and Library.

While in Oxford, I have had extensive support for my research from a variety of institutions. First and foremost, I would like to thank Professor Anthony Hopwood, the Dean of the Saïd Business School, for encouraging me to pursue the publication of this book and for supporting my continuing research in business history. Travel and research funds from both the Saïd Business School and Brasenose College provided crucial support and, most recently, I have received extensive support from the Clifford Chance Centre for the Management of Professional Service Firms based in the Saïd Business School. Tim Morris, the first Director of the Clifford Chance Centre and Laura Empson, the current Director, provided supplementary funding for research and editorial assistance to finish this book, but even more important, they provided crucial intellectual support for my academic research. For their unwavering support of the Centre, I would also like to thank Stuart Popham, the Managing Partner of Clifford Chance, and the many partners and staff at Clifford Chance, all of whom have been exceptionally generous patrons of academic scholarship on professional service firms.

Just as important as financial support were the thoughtful discussions I had about my work with other academics, with their home institutions, in many cases, covering my costs for travel and accommodation. These generous institutions include: the International Institute for the Sociology of Law, Onati, Spain; the Andrew Hook Centre for American Studies, University of Glasgow; University of Paris, Sorbonne; the University of Toulouse; the Society for Business History, Frankfurt; the Economic History Seminar, All Souls College, Oxford; the Business History Unit, London School of Economics; the Carlson School of Management, University of Minnesota; the Business School, Columbia University; the Sloan School of Management, MIT; the Rothman School of Business, University of Toronto; ESSEC School of Management, Paris; The Wharton School, University of Pennsylvania; London Business School, University of London; Kellogg School of Management, Northwestern University; the American Studies Workshop, The Pennsylvania State University; The Tuck School, Dartmouth College; the Stern School of Business, New York University; The Chemical Heritage Foundation, Philadelphia; the Centre for International

Business History, University of Reading; University of Michigan Business School; Center for Interdisciplinary Studies (ZiF), University of Bielefeld; Center for the History of Business, Technology, and Society, Hagley Museum and Library, Wilmington; and the Centre de Sociologie, Ecole des Hautes Etudes en Sciences Sociales, Paris. In several other cases, organizers of academic conferences provided funds to cover my attendance, including the Business History Conference, the Academy of Management, the University of Bologna, the Management History Research Group, and the European Studies Association.

As the preceding acknowledgments suggest, I have received an extraordinary amount of assistance from academic institutions, but my debts to corporate, nonprofit, government, and professional institutions are just as numerous. Good institutional history requires the willingness of individuals and organizations to open themselves to outside scrutiny and I have been overwhelmed by the generosity of the many institutions from whom I sought assistance. Beyond the many university and academic archives I consulted in the course of my research, these institutions included: A. T. Kearney & Co.; American Cancer Society; Arthur Andersen & Co.; The Association of Management Consulting Firms (USA); the Bank of England, The Boston Consulting Group, Booz Allen & Hamilton; Consultants News; IBM; The Management Consultancies Association (UK); McKinsey & Company; Mount Sinai Hospital; NASA; The Navy Historical Center; The New York Philharmonic; The Philadelphia Museum of Art; The Presbyterian Church of the USA (Northern); RCA, Sears Roebuck & Co.; Stone and Webster, Inc.; Towers Perrin; The United Negro College Fund; and the World Bank. Although many people in these institutions supported me, I would particularly like to thank the late Marvin Bower of McKinsey & Company, Bill Price, also of McKinsey, and Ted Buswick of The Boston Consulting Group for their support of my scholarship by allowing me unfettered access to their archival collections.

Just as remarkably, many old friends were willing to house and feed me when I was visiting archives and conferences, without getting much in return except personal relief that they were no longer peripatetic students themselves. So, let me take this opportunity to thank: Jamie and Nathalie Schofield, Russ Covey, Larry Platt and Ruth Diener, Paul Tarr and Alicia Brooks, Margie Rung, Christine Skwiot and Larry Gross, Jordy Kleiman, Jon Rottenberg and Laura Reilly, and Matthias Kipping, for their generosity during my national and international archival tours.

One of the great joys of being an academic is the network of colleagues who become friends as you pursue your scholarship. They remind you that the academic world remains a generous place. For their assistance, counsel, and support over the years, I want to thank Bruce Kogut, Chick Perrow, David Sicilia, Geoff Jones, Giuliana Gemelli, Dick Sylla, Eric Guthey, Ludovic Cailluet, David Kirsch, JoAnne Yates, Andy Hargadon, Steve Usselman, Lars Engwall, Les Hannah, Marina Moskowitz, Teresa da Silva Lopes, Lisa Berlinger, Matthias Kipping, Mauro Guillèn, Naomi Lamoreaux, Patrick Fridenson, Peter Hall, Phil Scranton, Sally Clarke, Roger Horowitz, Marie-Laure Djelic, Will Hausman, Jonathan Zeitlin, Antti Ainimo, Bernie Carlson, Charles Booth, Woody Powell, Royston Greenwood, Mike Lounsbury, John Wilson, Avner Offer, Glenn Porter, and Meg Graham.

Let me also thank my many friends in Oxford, both in Brasenose College where the Fellows have been particularly welcoming to their inaugural Fellow in"management"and also in the Saïd Business School where my colleagues are building a truly international and intellectual business school. In particular, let me thank Colin Mayer, Steve New, Owen Darbishire, Roy Westbrook, Robert Pitkethly, Mari Sako, Victor Seidel, Eric Thun, Marc Ventresca, Richard Whittington, Steve Woolgar, Tarun Ramadorai, Alan Morrison, Thomas Powell, Steve Rayner, Simon Evenett, and Maike Bohn. In Brasenose, I want to thank Vernon Bogdanor, Sos Eltis, Fergus Millar,

Martin Ingram, Laura Herz, Richard Cooper, Stefan Vogenauer, Ed Bispham, Nick Barber, Bill Swadling, Harry Judge, Jonathan Jones, Robin Sharp, William James, George Bitsakakis, Abigail Green, Thomas Krebs, Roger Cashmore, Robert Gasser, and Tony Courakis. My students, both in Brasenose College and in the Saïd Business School, have made thoughtful suggestions on my research and for their help I want to express my continuing appreciation. Similarly, in the last stages of the project, Nick Brown provided invaluable assistance in guiding me through the intricacies of case law in Britain and America.

Camilla Stack, who serves as the Administrator of the Clifford Chance Centre, has read every sentence of this manuscript more times than either of us would care to admit. If any split infinitives remain, it is not due to Camilla but because I was too pigheaded to dutifully remove them from the final text. I should also acknowledge both the remarkable editorial advice from Lou Galambos and the thoughtful, if sometimes terse, advice from Frank Smith at Cambridge University Press. Both Frank and Lou have shown remarkable support and patience for this project. Ken Karpinski of Techbooks did a wonderful job reassuring a first-time author about the production process. Ruth Diener, who designed the book's cover, has been a good friend for many years and never fails to impress me with her sense of style.

In a more familial vein, I owe a deep gratitude to my parents, Elizabeth McKenna and the late John McKenna, talented academic historians, who always set events in historical context at home and encouraged a broad, eclectic perspective on the outside world. As a contemporary historian who was raised by medievalists, I learned from them that modern institutions must always be understood in a comparative fashion. Similarly, my brother, Ted McKenna, a journalist in Washington, D.C., has always provided thoughtful encouragement and interesting suggestions to broaden my perspective.

My in-laws, Fred and Anita Keire, have been remarkably generous and welcoming; indeed without the extended use of their home in Connecticut for archival visits to New York, much of the research for this book would never have been possible. Their support for my academic career, despite my decision to spirit their only daughter away to Britain, has been a testament to their own rich intellectual lives.

Finally, I come to my greatest debt. Mara Keire, while working on her own (and much more fascinating) scholarship on the history of the world's oldest professional, has always encouraged me to find my own voice. Mara's intellectual rigor, her humor, and her continued support for this project were essential to its completion. This book is dedicated, with much love, to her.

# Making a Career of Consulting

Soon after I began teaching strategy at the University of Oxford's Saïd Business School, one of the MBAs whom I supervised came to talk with me. The economic downturn in 2000 had left most of the business school students scrambling to find jobs when only a year before they would have been considering offers from several well-known employers. The student began by describing his work experience; he had served as a general manager both in his family business and also in another traditional company before he decided to pursue an MBA. The man, in his mid-twenties, explained that he was having a difficult time finding a job in either a management consulting firm or in an investment bank because neither group of professional service firms was hiring during the current recession. Did I have any suggestions or contacts that I could offer him?

My initial response was simple and reasonable, or so I thought. Given his work experience and the fact that he was so clearly a superb general manager, why wasn't he looking for a challenging job within an industrial company that would suit his newly acquired "Master of *Business Administration*" degree? The student smiled at me and indulged my naïveté by replying that if he had really wanted another job in industry, why would he have spent all that time and money to acquire an MBA? The MBA, after all, was the *de facto* qualification for an elite position within a professional service firm and, therefore, a job in general management was obviously a waste of the potential value of his hard-earned degree.

I soon recognized both how common this perspective is among business school students and how the faculties in business schools persist in deluding themselves that their central purpose is to train MBAs to enter large industrial corporations.[1] By the late 1990s, at a time when the career placement services within the leading business schools were mostly helping students to enter either management consulting or investment banking firms (to be fair, some students also wanted to work in high-technology startups, venture capital firms, and hedge funds), traditional management theorists like Peter Drucker no longer had any illusion that the faculties in business schools still believed that they could make management a "true profession."[2] Instead, business school degrees had come to certify that these quasi-professionals were qualified to advise corporate executives on their strategy (management consultants), their financial structure (investment bankers), or both (venture capitalists). Although business school faculty may originally have hoped to create a new "profession of business," by the end of the twentieth century, the leading professional service firms had first captured, and then redirected, the elite business schools to serve the specialized needs of their own quasi-professions.[3] Where the American reformer Louis Brandeis had once argued that business would ultimately become its own profession, now the self-regulated, business professionals saw their MBA as the most effective way to distance themselves from direct competition with the nonprofessionals who actually managed the large corporations.[4]

In 1999, just before the decade-long expansion in management consulting was about to crash, cultural critic Nicholas Lemann mused in *The New Yorker* about what he called an extraordinary "development" in the history of Western culture. As Lemann argued, the United States had decided, "in effect, to devote its top academic talent to the project of streamlining the operations of big business," by directing its best and brightest students into management consulting.[5] Just as perplexing, in Lemann's words, was the fact that "if the old disrepute of business in elite universities is now suddenly gone, then why shouldn't young graduates just go all the way, and work in actual companies instead of consulting firms and investment banks?"[6] Lemann's question cut to the heart of my exchange with the graduate student in Oxford: just how had it come to pass that nearly one-third of the top MBA graduates and one-sixth of all elite undergraduates (whether at Oxford or Yale) now began their working lives as management consultants?[7] What explained the remarkable dominance of the world's newest profession?

Nicholas Lemann's own answer to the question of why management consulting had come to assume such importance in American society was less theoretical than pragmatic. In Lemann's view, the best students were drawn to jobs in the elite consulting firms because these firms offered students, "that odd upper-meritocratic combination of love of competition, herd mentality, and aversion to risk."[8] Where law (in America) or accounting (in Britain) had once been the means further to burnish the credentials of those graduates who were uncertain of what to do next, management consulting now fulfilled that role. In other words, for those students who couldn't yet decide what to do with their lives, but did not want to appear directionless, management consulting promised the credentialed path to future glory.[9]

To be fair, however, students were following the advice of career surveys that showed that management consulting offered a relatively secure way to achieve corporate success. In August 1999, only two months before Lemann's critique appeared, *Fortune* magazine ran a feature comparing the relative success of General Electric and McKinsey & Company in training chief executive officers (CEOs) to lead other organizations. The "CEO Super Bowl," as *Fortune* named their imaginary competition, resulted in a tie for the stock performance of the five companies led by the alumni of the two institutions but *Fortune's* calculations also demonstrated that the partners at McKinsey & Company produced many more CEOs, and far more quickly, than the executives in General Electric, which was then the world's largest corporation.[10] The differences were even starker if one focused on the details of specific CEOs, for although General Electric had trained the future leaders of Allied Signal, Stanley Works, and Owens Corning, by 1999, former consultants from McKinsey ran IBM, Morgan Stanley, American Express, Delta Airlines, and Polaroid to name only the very best-known organizations.[11] As *Fortune's* charts illustrated, the total market capitalization of the five companies managed by CEOs who had started at General Electric was less than 15 percent of the value of the five companies controlled by former consultants from McKinsey & Company.[12] Not coincidentally, by 1997, surveys showed that in both America and Europe, management consulting had become the top career choice for graduates and that a position within McKinsey was considered the dream job on both continents.[13] By the end of the twentieth century, an entry-level position in a management consulting firm was not only a safe job to accept after completing a university degree, but a partnership within one of the elite management consulting firms had become the preferred path for promotion to the very highest executive positions throughout the world.[14]

Of course, neither Nicholas Lemann nor the journalists at *Fortune* argued that management consulting had always been so powerful a force in Western societies. Indeed, either implicit or explicit in the journalists' analysis was the question of just how this relatively new group of quasi-professionals – generally less well understood than other business professionals such as lawyers, accountants, and investment bankers – had come to command such prominence within such a short period of time. Less than forty years earlier, in 1962, the managing partners of the top management consulting firms had felt that it was necessary to explain to the MBAs at the Harvard Business School just why they would want to join one of the leading consulting firms and just what, more precisely, was actually involved in pursuing a career in management consulting.[15] As Marvin Bower, then the Managing Director of McKinsey & Company, explained in the Harvard Business School's *Career Guide*, "management consulting firms – which are rapidly emerging as members of one of the newer professions – help top management executives of businesses, governmental units, institutions, and other organizations solve their major management problems."[16] All of the other leading consultants who contributed to the 1962 Harvard *Career Guide* – Richard Paget, D. Ronald Daniel, Leonard Spacek, and Bruce Henderson – echoed Marvin Bower by declaring that this new profession would continue to grow rapidly in the years ahead.[17] For those who became consultants, whether in the 1960s or the 1990s, the future seemed particularly bright even if no one knew just how this had happened quite so quickly.

It was no coincidence that Marvin Bower of McKinsey & Company described management consulting as "one of the newer professions" when he addressed the MBAs at Harvard in 1962. In particular, Bower was a leading advocate of the ongoing professionalization of management consulting and professional status was a constant topic of concern as consultants gained economic and cultural status. Yet management consulting never achieved full professional status during the twentieth century. The *double entendre* in this book's title, "The World's Newest Profession," plays off both the longstanding perception that consulting is an emerging profession and also the widespread public apprehension that the advice proffered by consultants constituted little more than corporate pandering. Both elements, as I argue throughout this book, were long-standing concerns in the evolution of management consulting firms and in consultants' continuing quest for both autonomy and respect. In particular, as long as both insiders and outsiders to consulting accepted that the profession was still young, management consultants could dismiss any perceived ethical failings as symptomatic of the profession's adolescent development.

If immaturity shielded consultants from direct criticism, however, consulting's "newness" could not assuage the public's recurring concern over the particular role of consultants; a question of whether consultants primarily offered their clients legitimacy or some more tangible form of knowledge. The importance of legitimacy and knowledge varied from assignment to assignment and from decade to decade, with the two sometimes in harmony and sometimes in opposition. For example, in America during the 1930s and the 1990s, the legitimating function became consulting's most important role, often exceeding the importance of knowledge transfer, while in Europe, during the 1960s, legitimacy and knowledge transfer generally went hand in hand as consultants carried new organizational structures to European corporations. The oscillation of these two functions, as they varied in importance over time, continually shaped the historical development of management consulting during the twentieth century.

But before consultants could worry about their reputation or role, they first had to create markets for their services and to defend those new markets from rival professional groups. The historical explanation for the dominance of management consulting, as it turns out, was not to be found in the pragmatic choices of university graduates, but in a set of regulatory changes in America during the 1930s, the 1950s, and the 1980s that were bolstered by the strategic development of new markets by the leading management consulting firms. American antitrust regulation shielded early consultants from competition from rival professionals even as entrepreneurial firms created new lucrative practices by concentrating on particular market segments, like nonprofits or the state, or by installing specific organizational techniques, like the multidivisional form or information technology. This regulatory history helps to explain why most of the leading management consulting firms in the world are American in contrast to the other business professions, like law or accounting, where state regulation did not favor one geographic market over another. Remarkably, the regulatory history returned to haunt management consulting firms at the end of the twentieth century because corporate board members had come to rely so heavily on professionals to reduce their corporate liability. Throughout the twentieth century, state regulation, as much as institutional innovation, first shaped and then reshaped the evolutionary path of management consulting.

The historical answer to Nicholas Lemann's implicit question – "just how had the leading management consulting firms come to achieve such a dominant economic and cultural position?" – is the subject of this book. In the early twentieth century, before management consulting even existed, there was a need for management advice and a nascent professional setting in which that counsel was offered. The first chapter, then, is a "theory of management consulting" that is both consistent with modern economics and yet rooted in historical institutions. Before I can explain how consultants came to exert such enormous influence on the modern world, I must first answer the question of why management consulting firms even came to exist. We turn to that question now.

# ONE

# Economies of Knowledge

## A Theory of Management Consulting

In 1930, *Business Week* introduced its readers to a new professional service: management consulting. As the writers at *Business Week* explained, the existing system of business professionals had become so complicated that, according to James McKinsey at the University of Chicago, a new type of professional was "increasing in numbers and influence...the advisor that tells business what other advisors to use and when."[1] Although *Business Week* would go on to chronicle the rise of management consulting over the next seventy years, consultants struggled to explain to the public what service they performed, particularly as the world's newest profession kept expanding faster than the wider American economy.

Since the 1930s, observers have repeatedly been surprised by the growth of management consulting.[2] In 1965, *Business Week* commented with astonishment that there was one consultant for every hundred salaried managers. By 1995, the ratio stood at one for every thirteen.[3] "Will the growth of consulting finally stop," people were prone to ask, "when every manager employs their own personal consultant?" The sheer number of consultants nowadays may be striking, but their relative increase is particularly interesting when one wonders, following Peter Drucker's lead: "Why management consultants" at all?[4] In other words, why should executives routinely employ outsiders to advise them on administrative issues about which they, presumably, are themselves the experts? Or, following the language of economists, why do executives employ external advisors to span the boundaries of the firm?

Analysts trying to explain the phenomenal growth of management consulting have traditionally tied the field's expansion to the overall growth in the American economy, the impact of international competition, and the complexities of modern management. Their interpretation is not wrong – consultants have prospered during periods of economic expansion and suffered during economic recessions.[5] But generalizations about increasing global competition and the complexity of management cannot fully explain the relative growth of consulting over other administrative roles. Consider, for example, a leading consultant's explanation of the growth of consulting: "You have to be bullish about consulting. It thrives on change and this is an era where change is accelerating."[6] Many consultants would have agreed with this explanation of the growth of consulting in 1999, but the statement was also true in 1969, when the consultant uttered those words. And a similar description would also have been true thirty years before that when, in 1939, Marvin Bower refounded McKinsey & Company. How else could McKinsey & Co.'s phenomenal growth be explained (an average 47 percent increase in profits per year between 1939 and 1944), if not through the accelerating need for consultants to help executives in an increasingly complex world?[7] As these examples suggest, any explanation of the growth in management consulting must be sensitive to exogenous changes in the economy and to the impact of global competition, but scholars cannot explain the remarkable run of management consulting solely through economic complexities and global change. Instead, in order to understand their growing influence on the national and international economy, we must first understand why consultants exist and how consultants outmaneuvered their professional rivals. Subsequent chapters in this book will build on this approach, charting the institutional impact of the rise of management consulting during the twentieth century. Before I describe the widespread influence of consultants, I must first set out why it is that outside advisors exist.

Peter Drucker's question, "Why management consultants?" echoes economist Ronald Coase's famous question, "Why are there firms?"[8] The two questions parallel one another because, at their heart, they challenge the traditional view of economists, "that firms might be envisaged as islands of planned coordination in a sea of market relations."[9] Because the two questions are so similar, it is not surprising that their explanations are also interconnected.[10] Ronald Coase's answer to his own question is that entrepreneurs create firms in order to reduce transaction costs (defined by economists as the cost of the administration of contracts and other relationships between separate firms). This partly helps to explain why executives are so willing to hire outside consultants.[11] As Coase argued, long before the widespread acceptance of management consultants, not only do firms routinely face the decision of whether to "make or buy" their physical goods, but "we can [also] imagine a system where all advice or knowledge [is] bought as required."[12] Like the process that drives manufacturers to buy materials from lower cost vendors, suppliers of management information enjoy substantial "economies of knowledge" that are, in turn, passed along to their customers.[13] Within the transaction cost framework, an executive decision on the margin to purchase advice from a consultant is no more outlandish than the decision to purchase machine tools rather than fabricate them internally.[14] The nature of the firm, it turns out, defines the nature of the consultant.[15]

## The Utility of Outside Advisors

Administrators have employed outside advisors for thousands of years, but their counsel has traditionally been political, not commercial. As Sir Francis Bacon wrote in 1597, there has been an "inseparable conjunction of counsel with kings."[16] Yet if political advisors, sanctified in the form of the king's confessor, were commonplace, so too were warnings by political philosophers, from Aristotle to Erasmus, that it was dangerous to invest too much trust in outsiders.[17] Writing in defense of political advisors, Thomas Hobbes argued that it was a mistake to punish the counselor for the actions of the king, but Machiavelli, always the realist, devoted a chapter of his *Discourses* to "the Danger of Being Prominent in Counseling any Enterprise."[18] Political theorists, including Francis Bacon in his essay "On Counsel" always conceded that despite the inherent danger in employing outsiders, external advisors offered a valuable sounding board for untested ideas.[19] This pattern of pragmatic acceptance of the value of advisors, twinned with persistent concerns over their intensely political nature, has characterized the perception of professional and administrative expertise for more than 400 years.[20] Most recently, in postwar America, state-sponsored experts proliferated as successive Presidents created national advisory councils like the Atomic Energy Commission, the National Security Council, and the Council of Economic Advisors, despite widespread misgivings that these experts served their own interests, and not those of the public.[21] For better or for worse, government officials, nonprofit managers, and corporate executives came to depend on this new "mandarin" elite and, although suspicious of the advisors' motives, grudgingly accepted the utility of these experts.[22]

Executives have accepted the merits of advisors because specialists have proven themselves able to master, manipulate, and extend novel realms of complex knowledge. Economists, ever since Adam Smith's analysis of the specialization of labor in *The Wealth of Nations*, have understood the economic benefits that flow from the specialization of knowledge.[23] By concentrating on one task, or by focusing on a single canon, those who specialize can enjoy personal economies of scale. These economies are evident in even the classical professions, despite fears of overspecialization, as specialists within bureaucratic organizations have gradually replaced generalists. Indeed, it is ironic that those critics most likely to clamor for the return of generalists have often themselves been the most highly specialized professionals.[24] In this context, it is not their specialization that sets consultants apart but their continuing independence from the corporation.

It has not been the function, therefore, but rather the *form* of outside counsel that commentators have found so perplexing. Critics have not, in general, asked why executives need to employ experts in administrative reorganization, information technology, or corporate strategy, but instead why these experts remain external, not internal, to the firm. In part, this concern reflects the long-standing presumption, in the words of management theorist Joseph Badaracco, that "firms have boundaries and that they should be kept sharp."[25] But even as companies have gradually formed business alliances that blur the traditional boundaries of the firm, the growing use of outsiders has confounded the expectation (widely predicted during the 1970s) that large bureaucratic organizations would internalize management consulting.[26] Instead, as the use of external advisors has grown, the demand for internal consultants has withered.[27] Management consultants have flourished primarily because they have remained outside the traditional boundaries of the firm.

In contrast to political advisors, the earliest management consultants, from the 1880s to the 1950s, served not as confessors, but as subcontractors to business.[28] Outside advisors brought specialized knowledge, not otherwise available, into organizations that faced problems that internal staff members could not easily resolve.[29] In particular, executives decided whether or not to employ external advisors based on two distinct preconditions. First, that the underlying problem be brief, specialized, and nonrecurring, thus making the alternative – an internal analysis of the topic – both slow and costly. Second, that the potential consultants had experience with similar cases through previous assignments in the industry, either because of the consultants' knowledge of a functional specialty, or, most often, because the consultants had performed a similar study for a competitor.[30] Thus management consultants were, in this first incarnation, idea- or knowledge-brokers who solved administrative problems, not through their innovative solutions to unusual questions, but rather through the application and reformulation of existing knowledge to known problems.[31] As studies of management consultants and their clients, from the 1930s through the 1950s, invariably concluded, clients primarily chose among rival consultants based on the consultants' reputation in the industry and their experience with similar assignments.[32] In 1958, for example, Jock Whitney, the financier and diplomat, selected McKinsey & Company over Booz Allen & Hamilton to reorganize *The New York Herald Tribune*, primarily because his business partner assured him that McKinsey "had extensive experience in newspaper work" through its studies of the *Los Angeles Times* and a large newspaper chain in Michigan.[33] Through their intrinsic "economies of knowledge," which were necessarily predicated on their status as outsiders, management consultants provided their clients with a cost-effective means to acquire managerial skills, techniques, and processes at a lower cost than the equivalent internal studies of the same problems.

Consultants flourish where the benefits from economies of knowledge outweigh the costs of external contracting. In each case, an executive's decision about whether to use consultants or to tackle problems internally depended on the consultant's incremental expense: an estimate of the relative transaction costs.[34] Executives faced a "make-or-buy" decision, forcing them to weigh the scale advantages of outside vendors against the contractual efficiency of internal administration.[35] As economist Oliver Williamson has argued, following Coase, organizations are created and maintained, in large part, because the reduced transaction costs from internalizing production offset the potential returns from buying products from outside contractors.[36] If the large modern corporation can best be understood as an organizational adaptation that minimizes transaction costs, then consultants represent the converse – an institution that has prospered despite high contract costs.[37]

Transaction costs, therefore, define the very livelihood of the consultant. Consultants, in effect, prosper on the razor's edge of the managerial/transaction-cost calculus. From the perspective of institutional economists, consultants' incremental sale of external expertise is a particularly efficient economic outcome as those who possess better knowledge can easily "sell [their] advice or knowledge" without "themselves actively taking part in production."[38] Moreover, because, in economist J. M. Clark's words, "knowledge is the only instrument of production that is not subject to diminishing returns," the sale of knowledge to one party does not necessarily diminish, and may actually increase, its competitive value.[39] The repeated transmission of managerial best practices within a single industry may be relatively inexpensive for consultants, but it is of priceless strategic value to competitors.[40] One might therefore, given the substantial advantages inherent in employing outsiders, reverse Peter Drucker's original question, "Why management consultants?" and wonder, in turn, why most firms choose *not* to subcontract all of their managerial problems to outside experts.[41]

The immediate answer to why corporations do not subcontract the production, administration, and transmission of all managerial knowledge is that unique knowledge is the single best way for firms to gain a competitive advantage in their attempt to differentiate themselves in the market.[42] Differentiation in knowledge, now hailed as the most valuable corporate asset in the evolving "knowledge economy," is a necessity.[43] But there is also a related explanation as to why firms do not subcontract all of their managerial knowledge that is, perhaps, less obvious: most firms also serve as implicit, and sometimes explicit, consultants to their customers, selling crucial knowledge along with their physical products. Firms do not subcontract all of their knowledge production to consultants, because companies, in turn, often act as consultants. Thus, the same "economies of knowledge" on which consultants depend in order to serve their corporate clients are also employed by manufacturers when they license new technology to their rivals, teach retailers how to market their goods, or educate customers about their products. Indeed, Charles Merrill's recognition that the stockbrokers at Merrill Lynch really sold knowledge, not simply shares, and the decision by executives at Seagram's to educate retailers in the proper marketing of spirits, are both examples of large companies that sold a tangible product by combining it, in part, with intangible advice.[44] Corporate executives, like the consultants they hire, understand that knowledge is not simply an internal resource, but also an external product.

In recent years, the reconstruction of large manufacturing and service firms in the image of consultants has been all the rage. Whether corporate executives have followed McKinsey & Company's emphasis on a shared corporate culture, Accenture's skill in knowledge management, or The Boston Consulting Group's expertise in teamwork, management theorists have hailed consultancies as the ultimate institutions in the evolving knowledge economy.[45] In particular, Wall Street analysts have praised companies like IBM and EDS, which have created successful consulting divisions, for adapting to the new global economy where manufactured products have become commodities, and knowledge is now the prized product.[46] This corporate transformation, however, begets further questions. If analysts now better understand why executives employ consultants as knowledge brokers, they seem less clear why consultants, in particular, have come to dominate this crucial economic function. If external information can be transmitted through any number of institutional conduits, including industry associations, government trade groups, the business press, think tanks, and professional networks, all of whom enjoy "economies of knowledge," why was it consultants that triumphed in the new knowledge economy?[47]

### Consultants as the Preeminent Knowledge Brokers

Ronald Coase's explanation of the nature of the firm as a solution to transaction costs provides the conceptual base for a general theory of management consulting, but transaction costs alone cannot directly answer the question, "why consultants?" While the transaction-cost framework explains the underlying demand for outside knowledge, it does not account for the institutional network through which the knowledge must be transmitted.[48] Indeed, corporate executives have always gathered external information through a variety of institutional arrangements, including strategic alliances, geographic clusters, government trade groups, and university partnerships.[49] Since almost all external providers of knowledge exhibit substantial "economies of knowledge," transaction costs on their own do not explain why consultants have expanded more rapidly than their rivals. Instead, we must look beyond economics to the law to understand the institutional success of consulting firms. The institutionalization of management consulting in the United States, as Ronald Coase might have suspected, was not simply the inevitable outcome of ever-increasing transaction costs, but an unintended consequence of American legislation in the 1930s aimed at restricting the flow of collusive information between firms.[50] By comparison, in Japan and Germany, where legislators never outlawed alternative institutions for the transfer of organizational knowledge, management consultants never assumed the same degree of influence within the corporate economy.[51] The long-standing tradition of anti-monopolism in America led, unintentionally, to an institutional reliance on management consultants.[52]

The rise of management consulting as a distinct professional field occurred as a direct result of Congressional passage of the

Glass-Steagall Banking Act in 1933.[53] Before the Glass-Steagall Act, which separated commercial and investment banking, commercial bankers often supervised the work of accountants and engineers who performed the "investigations" later conducted by management consultants.[54] The Banking Act of 1933 not only forced commercial banks to abandon underwriting and stockbroking, but the legislators also outlawed the consultative and reorganizational activities previously performed by banks. Concurrently, the Securities Act of 1933 required that "any financing be preceded by the exercise of due diligence," which Wall Street lawyers interpreted to mean that all subsequent deals required, "the investigation of the subject firm by a firm of competent [management] consultants."[55] Moreover, the Securities and Exchange Commission (SEC) required the large accounting firms to restructure their professional practices around corporate audits in order to maintain the professional "independence" of accountants and to avoid potential conflicts of interest.[56] Well-known accounting firms, like Arthur Andersen & Company, which had previously specialized in "industrial and financial investigations," restricted their practices to performing limited (although lucrative) financial audits.[57] In a complicated and not always fully anticipated fashion, the Banking Act and the SEC prohibited rival professional groups, like lawyers, engineers, and accountants, from continuing to act as consultants, and promoted the rapid growth of independent management consulting firms during the 1930s.[58]

Management consulting did not grow through a gradual process of linear evolution, but instead emerged from a competitive equilibrium shattered by regulatory change in the early 1930s. It was no coincidence that economist Joel Dean would declare in 1938 that "unheralded, almost unnoticed, professional management counsel has become an important institution in our business world."[59] For, as sociologist Andrew Abbott has explained, "professions develop when jurisdictions become vacant."[60] The federal government, through regulations requiring bankers to perform due diligence on management, and through rules preventing accountants and lawyers from engaging in activities that posed potential conflicts of interest, emptied the field of corporate investigations of any competitors except for management consultants. As a result, relatively young consultants like George Armstrong, James McKinsey, and Edwin Booz responded to this remarkable opportunity and within only a few years had succeeded in institutionalizing the field of management consulting.

The jurisdictional reconfiguration of expert advice that occurred after passage of the Glass-Steagall Act was personified in the career of George Armstrong. Armstrong was a Vice-President in charge of industrial investigations at National City Bank (now Citibank) between 1921 and 1932.[61] During the 1920s, National City Bank retained Armstrong to conduct a study of the bank's troubled loans to Anaconda Copper, an analysis of the proposed merger of Palmolive, Kraft, and Hershey, and, at J. C. Penney's personal request, Armstrong drew up a comparison of the relative expense ratios of the Penney chain stores.[62] In 1932, however, with inside assurances from his uncle that Franklin D. Roosevelt intended to break apart commercial and investment banking, Armstrong resigned from National City Bank to found his own consulting firm in 1933. Armstrong's new firm, George S. Armstrong & Company, was immediately successful. The consultancy was employed by a series of investment banking firms during the 1930s, investigating such corporate giants as Jones & Laughlin, Seagram's, Birds Eye Frozen Foods, and Philip Morris. Thus, George Armstrong profited from the transition from banker supervision of organizational studies to the institutionalization of management consulting, even though the types of studies that Armstrong performed did not change. George S. Armstrong & Co. grew rapidly, not because it offered a new form of organizational advice, but because Armstrong had founded an independent firm that conformed to the new regulatory requirements.

The story was much the same at both James O. McKinsey & Company (the forerunner of McKinsey & Company and A. T. Kearney & Company) and Booz Allen & Hamilton: the Glass-Steagall Act dramatically boosted business in what had been a relatively stable, but slow-growing field. In 1926, after twelve years in business, Edwin Booz still employed only one other consultant, but by 1936, Booz Allen & Hamilton had eleven consultants on staff.[63] Similarly, James O. McKinsey and Company, which McKinsey founded in Chicago in 1926, had, by 1936, expanded to more than twenty-five employees and had a second office in New York.[64] Both consulting firms profited from the tight connection between banking and their organizational studies. Marvin Bower, who joined McKinsey's consultancy in 1933, wrote that these surveys resembled the corporate reorganizations for bondholders' committees that Bower had previously overseen as a young lawyer at the law firm Jones Day.[65] Indeed, because investment bankers so often hired consultants during the 1930s, the partners at James O. McKinsey & Company came to refer to their work as "bankers' surveys."

Management consultants quickly forgot how important the regulatory changes in the 1930s were to the growth of their profession. Because these Federal laws did not directly govern their activities, but instead outlawed potential competition from their professional rivals, consultants easily overlooked the direct consequence of indirect legislation.[66] What consultants forgot, moreover, was not simply the chronology and the evolving structure of consulting as a professional field, but the emergence of consultants as the legal conduits for the exchange of potentially "anti-competitive" information.[67] The Glass-Steagall Act was, after all, the culmination of extensive congressional investigations, spurred on by widespread public fears, into what contemporaries had called the "Money Trust."[68] The public had long worried that Wall Street bankers, epitomized by J. P. Morgan & Company, not only controlled the flow of capital, but that they also oversaw a maze of anticompetitive cartels and associations through the bankers' seats on the boards of the largest industrial companies.[69] When Congress devised the New Deal legislation regulating financial markets, of which the Glass-Steagall Act was a central part, the politicians not only broke apart commercial and investment banking, but they also installed curbs on the transmission of anticompetitive information by bankers.[70] In the late 1930s, following the rejection of several price-fixing stratagems, including the "open-price" movement, banker-led cartels, and the National Industrial Recovery Act, consultants became the distinctly American solution to the intrinsic needs of executives to share certain forms of "inside" information.[71] As sociologist Neil Fligstein has pointed out, the American government forced companies to adopt alternative means to share knowledge, "by foreclosing the possibility for monopoly and collusion between firms."[72] Corporate executives, aware that the New Deal laws prohibited them from employing trade associations, industry cartels, or bankers to create industry benchmarks and to learn about administrative innovations, turned instead to management consultants as their primary source of interorganizational knowledge.

Antitrust regulation not only institutionalized management consulting during the 1930s, it also shaped the development of computer consulting during the 1950s. Just as management consulting was a byproduct of Depression-Era antitrust regulation, information technology consulting was a byproduct of postwar antitrust regulators who sought to limit the power of monopolies and redirect the transmission of organizational knowledge. If accounting firms like Arthur Andersen & Company were the losers during the 1930s when officials in the SEC decided that management consulting represented a conflict of interest with corporate auditing, then accountants were symbolically repaid during the 1950s when the U.S. Department of Justice prohibited IBM from offering computer consulting advice. The decision by the President of IBM, Thomas Watson, Jr., to settle a long-standing antitrust suit by the federal government in 1956 meant that IBM would, *de facto*, cede the emerging field of information technology consulting to the large accounting firms.[73] Ironically, not only would the partners at Arthur Andersen, the information-technology consulting giant, later wonder why their accounting firm had exited from the field of management consulting in the 1930s, but these same partners would fail to recognize why Andersen's entry as consultants on computer systems had been so easy during the 1950s.[74] By recognizing that antitrust regulation was at the heart of the emergence of information technology consulting during the 1950s, we can better understand why Andersen did not face more competitors and why IBM remained outside such a potentially lucrative field for so long before its entry with great fanfare in the early 1990s.

Arthur Andersen, in particular, profited because in 1956 the government excluded IBM from offering professional advice on installing and using computers. Although Arthur Andersen & Company had offered "financial investigations" to investment bankers in New York and Chicago during the 1920s, after Glass-Steagall they focused instead on corporate audits. Andersen would not reenter the field of management consulting until the 1950s, and only then through a narrow specialty that initially seemed far removed from the organizational concerns of the elite management consultancies: the installation of electronic computer systems.[75] In the 1950s, convinced that electronic computers would revolutionize internal cost accounting and billing, the partners at Arthur Andersen & Company began to offer their business clients advice on how to install and use computers.[76] Their counsel was a logical outgrowth of Arthur Andersen's own accounting practice, because executives hoped to use electronic computers to speed up the production of accounting information, but Andersen's advice was innovative, because, prior to 1953, only scientists and the military had used electronic computers. In 1953, however, Arthur Andersen & Company oversaw the installation at General Electric of the first computer used

specifically for business purposes and soon began marketing themselves as experts in the installation of electronic computer systems
in business.

IBM, under Tom Watson's leadership, might have quickly quashed
Arthur Andersen & Company's entry into computer systems consulting, had the federal government allowed IBM to enter the field of
consulting advice.[77] International Business Machines had, after all,
always employed specialists who advised IBM's clients on the installation, maintenance, and utilization of IBM punchcard and tabulat-
ing machines.[78] As historian Robert Sobel observed, "IBM-trained
technicians would install the equipment, accompanied by a service
representative who would be on call if anything went wrong, and
would offer advice on how best to alter or add machines as the business changed."[79] There were very few consultants who advised on
the purchase or installation of IBM tabulators because the salesmen
at IBM made sure that their customers did not have any questions.[80]

IBM's oligopolistic power, however, had a downside, as both of
the Watsons (father, and later, son) had to manage the firm under
the constant threat of antitrust action by the U.S. Department of
Justice dating back to the 1930s.[81] In 1956, however, Tom Watson,
Jr. convinced his father to settle with the Department of Justice and
to accept a consent decree.[82] That decree, which limited IBM's competitive ability for thirty-five years, not only required IBM to sell,
and not lease, its machines, and to make IBM's proprietary technology available to the company's competitors, but also prohibited
IBM from offering advice on the purchase and integration of computer systems.[83] The Department of Justice forbade IBM from offering
what we now understand as information technology consulting services, because the lawyers presumed that IBM would recommend its
own equipment over its competitors. In pursuing antitrust regulation,
the Department of Justice divided the sale of IBM's organizational
knowledge and physical products. With IBM, the leading computer
manufacturer, barred from the consulting field, Arthur Andersen &
Company soon established its jurisdictional dominance in the

area of information technology. Andersen's "Management Advisory Services" division steadily grew from just a few accountants in the early 1950s to tens of thousands of consultants by the 1990s.[84]

Ironically, IBM's monopoly power may have been indirectly responsible for the rise of independent information technology consulting, but it was the weakening of this power that drove the rapid growth in the field. As IBM's market share declined during the 1970s and 1980s, and the market for computing equipment expanded to every corporate desktop, the need for consultants to integrate these systems increased dramatically. Although IBM would win the first of several pyrrhic victories when the Department of Justice dropped its long-standing antitrust case in 1982, the firm would remain bound to the last remnants of the 1956 consent decree until 1991.[85] When IBM finally succeeded in having the consent decree lifted, the company, then led by Lou Gerstner (a former consultant from McKinsey), immediately created an information technology consulting group.[86] By 1996, only four years after IBM had inaugurated its consulting subsidiary, the IBM Consulting Group had annual revenues of $11 billion, nearly one-fourth of its total revenues, and it had already become a significant competitor to Andersen Consulting.[87]

In the late 1990s, American banking regulators and the U.S. Congress largely eliminated the Glass-Steagall Act, paving the way for bankers once again to serve as management consultants reconstituted in novel institutional forms.[88] Most consultants, although acutely aware of the impact the repeal of Glass-Steagall had on the recombination of insurance, commercial banking, and Wall Street, have little sense of the strategic implications this change might have for their own firms. Without a working knowledge of the past, consultants cannot foresee how old rivals like J. P. Morgan & Co., or international competitors like Deutsche Bank, might once again pose a competitive threat.[89] And, without any institutional memory of how consulting emerged as a distinct professional field, the large management consulting firms could find themselves competing against the same professional rivals they defeated through an accident of legislation more than sixty years ago.[90]

## Conclusion

In 1962, the consultant George Armstrong began his autobiography, *An Engineer in Wall Street*, with the hackneyed quotation from Santayana that "those who cannot remember the past are condemned to repeat it."[91] Unwilling to leave well enough alone, Armstrong also added an epigraph from the old Courthouse in Vicksburg, Mississippi that, "those who forget the past have no future..." Armstrong, it seems, believed that he knew something important from the early history of management consulting that future generations of consultants needed to know. Strangely enough, he was right.

Armstrong knew that his role as a consultant was not to devise novel organizational designs or experimental strategies, but to reconfigure the organizational knowledge around him to suit the needs of his corporate clients. As he had learned while working for National City Bank, George Armstrong was a knowledge broker and the reason that executives turned to him was that consultants gave managers access to crucial organizational knowledge through their previous consulting assignments. Although the term "transaction costs" postdates George Armstrong's autobiography by a decade, Armstrong would have readily agreed that his consulting business depended on economies of knowledge, for he served as a central figure in the information network that ran through the corporate economy in the middle of the twentieth century.[92]

In his autobiography, George Armstrong was not, however, trying to explain to consultants the underlying economic rationale for their job, but rather to warn them about their slumbering competitors. For he knew that economies of knowledge might explain why executives chose to purchase external knowledge, not simply create it themselves, but this "make or buy" analysis could not explain why businesses had favored the growth of consultants over alternative sources of information. In particular, Armstrong remembered the fact that the widespread employment of consultants was an unintended consequence of anti-monopoly legislation, dating from the 1930s, which institutionalized the use of consultants and prohibited rival professional groups, particularly bankers, from supplying similar services. Consulting might represent only one of many potential solutions for the institutional transfer of best practices, but in the United States, most of the other modes were illegal.[93] Management consultants offered an alternative, legal method to transfer knowledge between rival organizations without incurring regulatory sanctions.

In the end, Armstrong recognized that his own history demonstrated an important lesson for future generations of consultants. George Armstrong had prospered, in large part, by following his uncle's advice and founding his own consultancy to profit from politically-driven changes in the banking laws. The development of both management and information technology consulting did not emerge from consultants' purposeful manipulation of antitrust regulation, but rather from them taking advantage of a jurisdictional void in professional services created by government prohibitions.[94] With hindsight, we can see how Armstrong's experience, profiting from regulatory change, might provide a valuable lesson for subsequent generations of consultants. When IBM could not offer expert advice on computer installations, Arthur Andersen picked up the slack; but once the Department of Justice lifted the consent decree, IBM reemerged as a leading provider of consulting services, despite Andersen's head-start of more than thirty years. Without regulations prohibiting bankers from offering consulting services, Armstrong's old employer, Citibank, might well become an important competitor in consulting once again; or at least until the next radical shift in the regulatory environment.

# TWO

# Accounting for a New Profession

## Consultants' Struggle for Jurisdictional Power

When the editors of *Fortune* magazine published, in 1944, a feature on the increasing importance of management consulting, the article included a perfunctory description of the field's origins. As the *Fortune* writer explained, "its development in the U.S. started with Frederick W. Taylor, Henry L. Gantt, Harrington Emerson, and other pioneers of scientific management."[1] This first popular magazine article profiling management consulting in America set the presumed genealogy. Subsequent journalists, historians, and consultants would all presume the same lineage, pointing out that the early efficiency engineers "pioneered the use of scientific management principles" and, more generally, that the craze for scientific management predated the general rise of management consulting as a distinct subject.[2] This presumed lineage, however, was based on circumstantial evidence and was misleading.[3]

Instead of evolving from Taylorist firms, from the 1930s on, the leading management consultancies in the United States had little or no connection with scientific management.[4] If the staff at *Fortune* had investigated the backgrounds of the eleven leading consultants whom they profiled in their 1944 article, they would have noticed that only one, Wallace Clark, had any ideological or institutional ties with Taylorism and, not coincidentally, only Wallace Clark & Company among those profiled had largely forsaken the United States, by the 1940s, to pursue clients in Europe.[5] Although there was a connection in the United States between the modern form of management consulting and the development of Taylorism through their mutual involvement in cost accounting, that institutional legacy was less direct than casual observers have routinely presumed.

This error in establishing the genealogy of management consulting would not have mattered had it not misdirected academics and practitioners away from the important implications of consulting's rapid growth during the 1920s and 1930s. In recent years, for example, academics have lamented the sudden disappearance of American cost accountants during the late 1920s. Sociologist Andrew Abbott has described how the struggle over cost accounting was "without question the most heavily contested information jurisdiction in American history." Yet Abbott was unable to uncover "who the early members of the National Association of Cost Accountants (founded 1919) were or what profession they thought themselves members of."[6] Subsequent generations of business people, however, would remember the leading American cost accountants of the 1920s, academics like Arthur Andersen and James McKinsey, not as cost accountants but as consultants. Not surprisingly, at the same time that the leading cost accountants seemed to vanish with the founding of the early "management engineering" firms, theoretical advancement within cost accounting also began to stagnate. As accounting historians H. Thomas Johnson and Robert S. Kaplan have argued, "Organizations became fixated on the cost systems and management reporting methods of the 1920s."[7] The cost accounting systems of the 1920s, once stuck in time, simply "lost relevance," as financial auditors favored inappropriate financial controls over better cost accounting measures. The point is important because with a better understanding of consulting's true genealogy, we can see that the cost accountants did not cease their investigations. They simply shifted their professional jurisdiction from monitoring costs as accountants to lowering costs as consultants.

In the same vein, the recent critique of the American structure of corporate governance – a critique stressing the primacy of professional managers over either banker or stockholder interests – has overlooked the particular influence of consultants within the American institutional framework.[8] Both legal historian Mark Roe and institutional sociologist Neil Fligstein, for example, have charted how the regulatory politics of antitrust, as much as the drive for economic efficiency, shaped the American system of corporate governance in the middle of the twentieth century.[9] Yet it was the impact of American management consultants, first as cost accountants behind the associational movements of the 1920s, and subsequently as arbiters for SEC-mandated "management audits" during the 1930s, which provided the institutional infrastructure for American-style corporate governance.[10] In the United States, management consultants, as much as lawyers, engineers, and accountants, became central figures in the intricate structure of bureaucratic professionals who ultimately superceded the powerful bankers.[11]

The professionals who defined the field of management consulting were intensely pragmatic entrepreneurs. Management engineers sought to supply existing knowledge not immediately available within the executive suite. It is therefore ironic that consultants should have benefited from the anti-monopolism of the 1930s, for as professional accountants and as engineers, like the managers to whom they reported, consultants had worked to consolidate the giant American oligopolies from the 1890s onward.[12] Ultimately, as George Armstrong's career suggests, the industrial engineers and cost accountants who benefited the most from the New Deal reforms of the 1930s were not trying to recast, but rather to promote, the growth of big business.[13]

The previous chapter described how U.S. federal regulation during the 1930s, and particularly anti-monopolism embedded in the

Banking Acts, led to the emergence of management consulting as an integral part of the American system of corporate governance. This chapter will extend that account by tracing how engineers and accountants struggled to define the jurisdictional boundaries of consulting. In particular, this chapter will explain why the early Taylorist consultants ultimately ceded control of the emerging field to cost accountants, why many of the leading cost accountants abandoned accounting to move into consulting, and why Chicago, not Boston or New York, emerged as the center of the consulting industry. The story of consulting will begin at the end of the nineteenth century not in Chicago, home to the leading consultancies, nor in New York, where the largest corporations were headquartered, nor even Philadelphia, where Frederick Taylor first developed scientific management. It begins, instead, in Boston, where the electrochemical engineers at the Massachusetts Institute of Technology (M.I.T.), who spearheaded the second industrial revolution, first founded independent consulting engineering firms.

## The Electrochemical Revolution

From the 1870s on, as the second industrial revolution took shape in the United States, geologists, chemists, physicists, and their more practical brethren in civil, electrical, and chemical engineering, took occasional jobs as consultants with the emerging manufacturers clustered around the "science-based" industries.[14] Because the traditional pattern of research and development involved both independent inventors' commercializing their patents and the defensive purchase of external innovations by existing manufacturers, the traditional boundaries of the firm were extremely porous in corporate research and development.[15] After generating remarkable returns on their initial investments, and, perhaps even more importantly, monopoly yielding patents on the production processes, executives at Standard Oil, General Electric, and AT&T soon realized that by employing engineers, either as short term consultants or as long-term research staff, they could control the pace of innovation within their science-based industries.[16] Thus it was no accident that the most technologically advanced companies, like DuPont and Eastman Kodak, which were also the most dependent on proprietary technology, quickly forged close ties with the staff, students, and administrators of the leading engineering schools, particularly M.I.T., at the turn of the century.[17] The experiences of these companies during the first decades of the twentieth century would, in turn, become the model for subsequent generations of executives trying to manage innovation within their own companies.[18]

Nowhere else was the success of industrial engineering more obvious than in the rapid growth of two consulting engineering firms founded in Boston during the 1880s by M.I.T. alumni. Within a decade of founding their eponymous consultancies, Arthur D. Little, a chemical engineer who had dropped out of M.I.T. before his senior year in 1884, and Charles Stone and Edwin Webster, two electrical engineers who had both graduated in the M.I.T. Class of 1888, were working with the largest industrial companies on cutting-edge technologies and advising State Street financiers on their investments in high technology. Although many engineers founded consulting firms throughout the United States at the turn of the century (most notably Ford, Bacon & Davis in New York), the Boston-based firms of Arthur D. Little, Inc. and Stone & Webster were particularly successful because of their strong connections with the faculty at M.I.T. and Harvard and the preeminence of the Boston banks in financing industrial companies prior to 1900.[19] Both firms, moreover, used their personal connections – Louis Brandeis was Arthur D. Little's lawyer, and Edwin Webster's father ran Kidder Peabody's Boston office – to secure important clients.[20] These similarities, however, are less important in understanding their success than the radically different paths each firm took.

Although both Arthur D. Little, Inc. and Stone & Webster received their first commissions from paper mills (Little for the chemical analysis of paper pulp and Stone & Webster for the design and construction of a hydroelectric plant) the two firms soon pursued strikingly different business models as consulting engineers. While Stone & Webster focused on transferring engineering solutions among their clients within a single industry, Arthur D. Little boasted of solving problems that others could not handle including his now infamous demonstration that he could turn a "sow's ear into a silk purse" by spinning gelatin made from a sow's ears to create artificial silk that was then woven into a purse.[21] Arthur Little's decision to specialize in the most difficult and unique problems – and never doing the same thing twice – was a reversal from his career prior to founding his consultancy, since his initial experience managing the first sulfite paper mill in Rhode Island and his subsequent design and operation of pulp mills in North Carolina and Wisconsin had made him an expert in the routine transfer of established best practices.[22] Although Little would go on to earn a fortune as an engineering consultant, seven years elapsed before the profits from his professional firm matched his salary managing the paper mill in Rhode Island.[23]

Arthur Little preferred, however, to wrestle with a succession of novel engineering puzzles rather than concentrate on a single specialty as an engineer and manager; following Isaiah Berlin's famous distinction, Arthur Little was a fox, not a hedgehog.[24] It is perhaps not surprising then, that Little generally shunned assignments that tended toward the "management" side of consulting rather than the "engineering" side of consulting, even though the two were frequently, and necessarily, intertwined. Arthur Little's aversion to management may also explain why he repeatedly declined membership in the Association of Consulting Management Engineers and, conversely, why he was delighted to help General Motors (G.M.) set up its own research and development laboratory in 1911.[25] As the

company historian recounted years later, Little explained his decision to teach G.M. how to manage its in-house research laboratory,
because '"the more research they have, the more they'll need me."'[26]

In contrast to Arthur D. Little's unflinching emphasis on contract research, the founding partners at Stone & Webster began
by offering to solve technical questions about electrical engineering, but, by the 1920s, had transformed their partnership into an
electrical utility holding company.[27] Although the partners' first
assignments involved the installation of electrical generation facilities, within only three years of their founding, J. P. Morgan &
Co. had hired Charles Stone and Edwin Webster to evaluate the
economic prospects of utilities acquired by General Electric during
the 1893 recession.[28] During one investigation, when Charles Stone
believed more strongly than J. P. Morgan that a utility in Nashville
would recover quickly from the downturn, Morgan suggested that, as
Charles Stone later recalled, "... if I felt so confident about the future
of these things, he thought I ought to buy them."[29] For $60,000, most
of it borrowed, Stone & Webster purchased the utility company,
managed it, and subsequently resold it for $500,000.[30] As Charles
Stone remembered twenty years later, "that half million looked like
the biggest thing I had ever seen in my life, and I still have never seen
anything quite so big."[31] Lured by the potential for substantial profits
from the amalgamation of management, engineering, and financing,
by 1906, Stone & Webster was providing these services "to twenty-
eight independent power, light, gas, and traction utilities throughout the United States."[32] Moreover, because the utilities that they
served required a significant infusion of capital in order to meet surging demand for electrical power, the partners at Stone & Webster
worked closely with Boston-based investment firms to market utility
securities.[33] By 1933, Stone & Webster controlled an array of companies that, in sum, generated more than 2 percent of all the electricity
in the United States.[34]

From 1915 to 1920, approximately thirty years after they had left M.I.T., Charles Stone, Edwin Webster, and Arthur Little returned to M.I.T. to transform their alma mater. Little joined the board of visitors for the Chemistry Department, raised money for the university, and, when the university decided to move to Cambridge in 1916, he purchased land close to the new campus for his new corporate headquarters, christened "M.I.T. East" by his corporate clients.[35] In contrast, the construction division of Stone & Webster actually built the new M.I.T. campus, financed by George Eastman, along the Charles River in Cambridge. It was a sign of the times, however, that Charles Stone's son, Whitney, Edwin Webster's son, Edwin, Jr., and Arthur Little's nephew (his adopted son), Royal, all graduated from Harvard (not M.I.T), even if they all went on to work, if only briefly, for their family firms.[36] No less successful than their predecessors, Edwin Webster, Jr. used his family money to refound Kidder Peabody in 1931, Royal Little rebuilt Textron, a bankrupt New England textile company, into the first American conglomerate, and Whitney Stone went on to succeed his father as president of Stone & Webster.[37]

Neither Arthur D. Little, Inc. nor Stone & Webster, however, ultimately became the archetype for management consulting. Arthur D. Little, Inc., remained linked, both in the public eye and in the boardroom, with research and development; the consultants at Arthur D. Little were engineers not *of* the corporation, but *for* the corporation. In contrast, Stone & Webster both captured, and were captured by, the electrical generation industry. Like other management consulting firms that specialized in a single industry, most notably Kurt Salmon Associates, that specialized in textiles, Stone & Webster's institutional evolution became intertwined with the particularities of the electrical power industry.[38] The partners at Stone & Webster went on to create their own investment bank when utilities needed money for expansion, become a holding company when the rest of the industry was consolidating, and develop expertise in atomic power when uranium became the cutting-edge fuel source.[39] Because the underlying expertise that management consultants generally offered was not specialized knowledge, but general managerial "know-how," neither Stone & Webster nor Arthur D. Little, Inc. would dominate the mainstream of the emerging field of management consulting.[40] The Boston-based consulting engineers would follow, not lead, the success of "management engineering."

If firms like Stone & Webster and Arthur D. Little, Inc. came to represent the triumph of engineering counsel at the turn of the century, then they did so in contradistinction to the public face of general management counsel epitomized by J. P. Morgan and Frederick W. Taylor. As the last chapter argued, prominent commercial bankers like J. P. Morgan & Company ultimately lost control of the market for corporate advice during the 1930s when regulators decreed that providing both consulting and banking represented a potential conflict of interest.[41] Just as remarkable was the precipitous decline of Taylorism as a commercial venture by the middle of the 1920s, even though "efficiency engineers" would continue to dominate the public perception of consulting for another half century.[42] Despite Taylorism's success in America prior to the First World War, these early consultants perished, like allegorical "Neanderthals," just as management engineers conquered the evolving professional field.

## How "The One Best Way" Became a Professional *Cul-de-Sac*

Frederick Taylor began his career as an engineer in 1874, roughly a decade before Arthur Little, Charles Stone, and Edwin Webster finished their university training.[43] Although Taylor's public career as an engineer was contemporaneous with the careers of the Boston-based engineers, Taylor's hands-on-training as an apprentice machinist in Philadelphia had more in common with the nineteenth-century tradition of shop-floor education than the professional training of the M.I.T. engineers.[44] It was not simply

Taylor's education as a machinist, however, that would set him apart from the Boston consultants, for Frederick Taylor eventually became far more famous than his Boston rivals by consulting not on research and development in the emerging electrochemical industries but on the productivity of labor in more traditional industries like iron and steel.

Taylor believed that by carefully studying each component of a job and by devising novel bonus systems, engineers could dramatically increase worker productivity and eliminate purposeful "soldiering" (slowing the pace of work) among industrial workers. Although Frederick Taylor had been recognized among his peers as a leading expert on "task management," Taylor became internationally famous when Louis Brandeis, the legal reformer, testified against rate increases before the Interstate Commerce Commission in 1910 by arguing the American railroads could save "a million dollars a day" through the installation of Taylor's system of "scientific management."[45] Soon after Brandeis had popularized the term "scientific management," many of the prominent efficiency engineers, including H. L. Gant, Frank Gilbreth, and Harrington Emerson, published books detailing their research on scientific management.[46] It was Taylor's extended essay from 1911, "The Principles of Scientific Management," however, that would secure him a place in history as the "first management guru," and, by affinity, as the "first management consultant."[47]

In retrospect, Frederick Taylor developed his system of motion study and wage incentives to solve a problem that was specific to the development of manufacturing at the turn of the twentieth century: the need to speed up shop-floor workers who would not otherwise be paced by the continuous flow of the industrial assembly line. It is no coincidence that Taylor happened to be a foreman of the most skilled workers – the machinists – within the Midvale Steel Works.[48] As economic historian Hugh Aitken explained, Taylor's initial experiments in perfecting chromium-tungsten steel for high-speed machining created a series of unforeseen problems, since Taylor's ability to increase the speed of machines led to bottlenecks in the handling of materials, which in turn led to a renewed focus on job analysis and time study.[49] As a result, from the 1880s onward, Frederick Taylor alternated his attention between mechanical innovations designed to increase the speed at which factory machines operated and organizational innovations aimed at increasing the pace with which the factory workers used those machines. Taylor's research specifically focused on those workers whose jobs could not be paced by the assembly line – the highly-skilled machinists who operated the machine tools and the low-skilled laborers who lugged the pig iron on the factory floor.

Thus Taylor's system, often conflated with Henry Ford's system of mass production, was always intended to work alongside, not overlap, the assembly line.[50] As Henry Ford's ghostwriter would argue in Ford's famous 1926 entry in the *Encyclopedia Britannica*, Taylorism was fundamentally different from Fordism because, "the efficiency experts…did not see that another and better method might be devised," like the assembly line, which could truly automate production.[51] Taylorism and Fordism together, like adjoining pieces in a jigsaw puzzle, sought to simplify tasks and pace industrial workers through employing piece-rate bonuses in the first instance and the assembly line in the second instance. Taylorism, in contrast to Fordism, however, was ultimately more powerful in its impact as an ideology than in its impact as an industrial practice.[52]

More than 100 years after Frederick Winslow Taylor first began publicizing his methods to speed up factory production, Taylorism remains emblematic of the struggle between industrial efficiency and inhumane automation.[53] In large part, Frederick Taylor assured himself of lasting fame (and public vilification) by refusing to accept any middle ground between the extreme surveillance of motion study and the ad hoc individualism of craft labor.[54] There was, as Taylor's followers liked to say, just "one best way" to produce anything and "scientific" managers were the best equipped to decide the most efficient path.[55] Indeed, Frederick Taylor insisted that his system, although itself characterized by the systematic breakdown of manual operations into constituent parts, simply could not be installed piecemeal. Scientific management, as Taylor didactically explained to representatives of the U.S. Congress in 1912, required a "total mental revolution" in order to succeed in the workplace.[56]

If Frederick Taylor resisted differentiating the building blocks of scientific management, his contemporary followers and subsequent academics were far more willing to identify Taylorism's constituent parts. There were at least four distinct research strands within mainstream scientific management – worker psychology, workplace and tool design, wage systems, and cost accounting – and only cost accounting, perhaps the least recognized element of Taylor's system, would connect the early efficiency engineers with the modern consultants who followed them.[57] Instead, efficiency engineers, with their stopwatches and motion studies, would come to epitomize the public image of Taylorism.[58] In 1911, for example, when a foundry worker at the Watertown Arsenal in Massachusetts refused to work while an engineer timed him with a stopwatch, the Arsenal's workers walked off the job and precipitated the Congressional hearings at which Taylor would subsequently testify.[59] And, by 1936, when Charlie Chaplin sought to parody industry in "Modern Times," even before he showed the iconographic Fordist laborers working along assembly lines in a factory, Chaplin began with an opening image of a clock.[60] Time and motion study, not cost accounting systems, would spark the public imagination and come to define scientific management.

All of this publicity, of course, meant the possibility of lucrative consulting contracts for Taylor's followers, an observation hardly lost on the self-trained engineers who quickly came to represent the movement. Between 1901 and 1915, the well-known promoters of scientific management in America, including Frank Gilbreth, Harlow Person, Morris Cooke, Henry L. Gantt, and Harrington Emerson, "introduced scientific management in nearly 200 American businesses," and their corporate solutions, as much as Taylor's theoretical pronouncements, defined the subject.[61]

It is striking, however, that the majority of these well-known consultants did not operate within firms, but rather as individual advisors.[62] Frank Gilbreth, for example, worked alongside his wife Lillian and routinely employed assistants, but despite accepting international assignments and operating a construction company, neither Frank nor Lillian institutionalized their professional practice.[63] And, those few Taylorists who did institutionalize, like Charles Bedaux and Wallace Clark, increasingly turned to international assignments in the 1920s and 1930s to keep their practices afloat. Outside the United States, Taylorist firms throve into the 1960s, but within the United States they gradually withered away.[64]

One of the best-known Taylorists to institutionalize his consulting practice was Harrington Emerson, whose firm, the Emerson Company (subsequently the Emerson Engineers), performed hundreds of surveys in the United States between its founding in 1907 and the withdrawal of Harrington Emerson from his firm in 1925.[65] Harrington Emerson's success, however, was the exception that proves the rule, for despite surviving through the 1980s, Emerson Engineers, like Emerson himself, soon abandoned any pretext of prescribing "one best way" and, instead, offered a variety of services, few of which had any relationship to the rigid precepts of scientific management.[66] Harrington Emerson himself, by the late 1920s, no longer preached the gospel of efficiency but rather the value of corporate counsel to Wall Street investment houses like Dillon, Read & Co.[67] Emerson, like his former partners at Emerson Engineering, preferred the pragmatism of securing contracts over the ideological principles espoused by Frederick Taylor.[68] For the few Taylorist consulting firms that survived into the 1920s, managers and workers' antipathy toward scientific management foreclosed it as a saleable product. Frederick Taylor's – or, alternately, Frank Gilbreth's – "one best way," would ultimately become a professional cul-de-sac.[69]

In contrast to the commercial limitations of scientific management, cost accounting systems, as historian Sharon Hartman Strom has argued, ultimately proved more valuable than either motion study or wage incentive systems to industrial manufacturers.[70] Frederick Taylor and his followers had developed better tool steels to improve the throughput of machining, piece-rate incentive systems to overcome the tendency of workers to "soldier," and psychological tests to weed out less effective personnel, but the overall costs involved in operating manufacturers' multiple product lines remained exceedingly difficult to calculate. Manufacturers faced the problem of how to allocate overhead, variable demand, and depreciation when they were selling not just final but also intermediary products. To solve this problem, engineers in tandem with accountants created costing systems that not only distinguished between fixed and variable costs, depreciation, seasonal fluctuations, and variable labor rates, but also offered a way to compare costs between different manufacturers within a single industry. Thus it was the development of cost accounting, not scientific management, that would provide the bedrock for the foundation of the first successful management consulting firms in the United States.

## Cost Accounting and the Engineering of Associationalism

In both the United States and in Britain, engineers and cost accountants worked in tandem to develop the general principles of cost accounting from the turn of the century on. Indeed, by the 1890s the distinction between the two sets of professionals had become increasingly difficult to discern; in the words of a contemporary cost accountant, "the increasing use of statistics, budgets, estimates, and forecasts, which require both engineering and accounting methods, have broken down the dividing lines between the two until one can hardly distinguish them any more."[71] If pressed, however, knowledgeable executives were able to distinguish between those engineers and accountants involved in cost accounting and the more traditional members of the two professions. As accounting historian S. Paul Garner described those engineers involved in cost accounting:

> the profession of cost accounting developed out of the attention which was shown in the subject by early industrial engineers, if that term is used to refer to the group of engineers who showed interest not only in the technical engineering problems of industry, but also in the more skillful management of manufacturing enterprises.[72]

If those engineers most likely to be involved in cost accounting were readily distinguished from other engineers by their interest in management, so too were the cost accountants differentiated from traditional auditors by their overriding interest in devising ways to minimize production costs. Indeed, so different were cost accountants' views on accounting for industrial costs from the conventional measures used by financial accountants that cost accountants would be driven from the mainstream of accounting. As a result of their ideological differences, cost accountants would be forced to create a new and distinct professional identity.

The disagreement between the traditional accountants, who were concerned with company audits, and the cost accountants, who wanted to devise precise manufacturing benchmarks, centered on their respective definitions of interest payments on commercial loans. The question, simply put, was whether or not interest represented an inherent cost of manufacturing.[73] The prominent cost accountants, led by Hamilton Church, argued that interest, because it constituted one of the expenses incurred in production, should be included in all cost calculations.[74] These cost accountants, backed up by economists, argued that in order to manufacture a product companies had to borrow money and that the substantial cost of this debt was a very real cost.[75] In direct opposition, the leading auditors, who dominated the professional associations and journals, argued that interest should never be included as a cost because it violated their general principle of not including "profit" within manufacturing costs.[76] As one auditor asked,

Where will it all end? Are we to reach some advanced economic stage in which the "industrial engineer's" art will enable the tired business man to sell "at cost" and still receive a return on investment?[77]

Moreover, as a "Special Committee" of the American Institute of Accountants ultimately concluded, the cost of interest not only varied over time, but from region to region, thus making year-on-year comparisons impossible.[78] After a series of increasingly contentious debates, the auditors stood firm and ruled that interest could not be included in any accountant's calculation of cost.

This decision resulted in a cleavage between the auditors who made up an increasingly prosperous arm of the profession (President Wilson's introduction of income taxes, after all, had assured tax accountants a very secure market for their services) and the cost accountants who, because of their links with engineering, were quickly moving toward the fringes of the accounting profession. In 1919, led by Clinton Scovell, the cost accountants seceded, forming their own professional group, the National Association of Cost Accountants (NACA). Over the next two decades, NACA's journal would provide the leading cost accountants with a place to argue over the central tenets of the new field. The authors of the articles on cost accounting would read like a virtual "Who's Who" of management consulting in the 1920s and 1930s – including Arthur Andersen, James McKinsey, Charles Bedaux, Charles Stevenson, Carle Bigelow, and J. P. Jordan. The leading cost accountants of the 'teens would evolve into the leading management consultants of the 'thirties.

Cost accountants did not, however, immediately transform themselves into management consultants. The transition between cost accounting and management consulting, instead, would run through the most important current in American industrial policy during the

1920s – the rise of "associationalism."[79] As historian Ellis Hawley and others have described, when Herbert Hoover assumed control of the Commerce Department during the 1920s, the "Great Engineer" sought not only to standardize sizes of screws and bolts, but also to create a commonality of interest between the government and the leading manufacturing associations.[80] So broad were Hoover's ambitions that his friend Mark Sullivan wrote that Hoover perceived himself as a "consulting engineer" reorganizing the structure of American business.[81]

At the heart of Herbert Hoover's associative movement was the hope that by eliminating ruinous competition, yet forestalling anti-competitive cartels and monopolies, the federal government could promote business without suppressing innovation.[82] Such a program, however, required industrial competitors to be able to judge each other's operating costs without legally binding themselves within a price-setting cartel.[83] Cost accountants, it turned out, offered the perfect solution – standardized, industry specific measures of costs, tailored, as the auditors had suggested in a less positive manner, to allow the "business man to sell 'at cost' and still receive a return on investment."[84] The leading cost accountants, in conjunction with Herbert Hoover's technocratic engineers, could solve the problem of excessive competition without government intervention. Prominent cost accountants, now recognized as transitional management consultants, like Charles Stevenson of Stevenson, Jordan & Harrison, would quickly declare their support for the associational cause.[85]

By the middle of the 1920s, the cost accountants who formed the core of the rapidly professionalizing management engineers provided two distinct, but related, services to their clients. For open-price associations, and their members, cost accountants offered costing information and for commercial and investment bankers they provided "management audits" on the soundness of corporate executives and their decisions.[86] Both of these functions, moveover, were discussed in the articles within the cost accountants' professional journal, *The NACA Bulletin*, where the partners in the leading management engineering firms reported their research in specific industries like dressmaking, silver plating, and railroads, as well as their more general conclusions on potentially useful management methods.[87] Eventually, however, regulators would come to view both the cost accountants' role as arbiters of standardized costs and their role as providers of due diligence surveys as promoting unfair competition among financiers and industrialists. The regulators' solution was to turn cost accounting on its head and employ these professionals, who had provided the institutional infrastructure for American oligopolies, as the *de facto* monitors of unfair competition.

## Management Consulting as the Regulatory Solution to Monopoly

Ironically, management consultants would achieve their institutional success with the death of their associational agenda. Herbert Hoover's associationalism of the 1920s crescendoed with Franklin D. Roosevelt's creation of the National Recovery Administration (NRA) in 1933.[88] Roosevelt created the NRA to organize federally supervised trade associations that planned production, quality, prices, distribution, and labor standards for each industry in order to counteract excessive competition during the Great Depression in America.[89] In 1935, the Supreme Court declared that the National Recovery Act was unconstitutional, but the Glass-Steagall Act, which involved a similar extension of federal powers, was allowed to stand. The institutional entrepreneurs, like Edwin Booz and James McKinsey, who founded management engineering firms, were on both sides at that point, and they did not worry about the ideological inconsistency of their shift from promoting associationalism to interposing themselves within the flow of information to limit cartel-like behavior. Steady assignments were all that mattered.

President Roosevelt and his advisors had created the NRA in order to stabilize the depressed economy and avoid ruinous competition. Fundamentally corporatist, under the watch of the Blue Eagle (the symbol of the NRA), each industry, in turn, drew up codes of fair competition assisted by the cost accountants who acted as the monitors of industrial costs.[90] Cost accountants rejoiced, for it seemed that they had secured a stable market for their services and only a few months after Roosevelt had signed the National Industrial Recovery Act into law in June of 1933, cost accountants began reporting on their attempts to enforce the new codes.[91] The associationalist triumph, however, was short-lived and "the NRA began to self-destruct almost from the moment it began operations."[92] By the time that the Supreme Court ruled, in May of 1935, that the NRA was unconstitutional, Roosevelt's attempt at New Deal associationalism had failed miserably. By this point, however, most management engineers, in a remarkably serendipitous coincidence, had begun serving as the token regulators of corporate oligopolies. The "management audits" mandated by the Securities and Exchange Commission rapidly replaced associational code setting as the major management-engineering firms quickly added partners to handle the extra work.[93] From 1933 on, cost accountants assumed jurisdictional control over a professional field in which they could build their institutional power.

The new institutional arrangements in banking opened up a vacuum into which the consultancies rushed. The contrast between the old and new institutional order was particularly evident in Ford, Bacon & Davis's reorganization of U.S. Steel between 1935 and 1938. In 1901, J. Pierpont Morgan had personally supervised the initial organization of U.S. Steel, but in 1935, U.S. Steel's Chairman, Myron Taylor, asked his college friend, George Bacon, to oversee the reorganization of the largest industrial firm in America.[94] As Taylor reported to the stockholders of U.S. Steel in 1938,

> In 1935 we retained the firm of Messrs. Ford, Bacon & Davis to go through all of our properties, methods, personnel and markets and, in collaboration with our engineers and executives to formulate definite recommendations.[95]

Ford, Bacon & Davis's study took three years, cost 3.2 million dollars, and eventually included 203 separate reports produced in collaboration with five different subcontracting consulting firms, including McKinsey and Stevenson, Jordan & Harrison.[96] It was the largest study ever done by management engineers, and the recommendations that Ford, Bacon & Davis made on the organization, strategy, and operations of U.S. Steel influenced the company's investment, labor, and administrative policies through the 1950s. In labor relations, for instance, the 1937 accord reached with workers overturned a long-standing antagonistic relationship endorsed by the Morgan Bank, an adversarial position that could have immobilized U.S. Steel in the tight labor markets of the Second World War.[97]

The net result of the disintegration of the NRA at the same time as the success of the SEC was that management engineers moved from one regulatory sphere to another, hardly pausing to mourn the loss of the first market as they rushed into the second. Their triumph, however, did come at a substantial cost for some firms. The larger accounting firms, those which offered both auditing and cost accounting services, had to choose between remaining auditors and becoming management engineers. Like the choice, after the passage of the Glass-Steagall Act, by merchant bankers who had to decide between reverting to purely commercial banking or becoming investment banks, cost accountants could either offer financial auditing services or management auditing services, but not both.[98] Generally, the smaller and more specialized cost accounting firms, like James O.

McKinsey & Company and Stevenson, Jordan & Harrison, chose to pursue management consulting while others, like Peat, Marwick, Mitchell & Co. and Arthur Andersen & Company, decided to remain accountants.[99] The leading accounting firms, notably Arthur Andersen & Company, eventually reentered the market for administrative advice roughly twenty-five years later, but by then management consultants regarded accountants not as their traditional competitors, but as interlopers, within the professional field.[100]

In hindsight, Arthur Andersen & Company's decision to exit the field of management consulting is particularly remarkable both because of the firm's influence within the field during the 1920s and its subsequent reemergence as the world's largest consulting firm by the 1990s. Arthur Andersen & Company had been an influential accounting firm, particularly in cost accounting, since the firm's namesake, Arthur E. Andersen, founded his Chicago-based partnership in 1913.[101] The accountancy grew quickly during the 1920s, and by 1930, Arthur Andersen & Company had offices in Chicago, New York, Washington, Kansas City, Los Angeles, San Francisco, Detroit, and an affiliate in London.[102] At the firm's height in the 1920s, investment bankers in New York and Chicago frequently hired Arthur Andersen & Company to perform "financial investigations," like the studies also performed by fellow cost accountants Charles R. Stevenson at Stevenson, Jordan & Harrison (the leading New York cost accounting firm) and James O. McKinsey at James O. McKinsey & Company (Andersen's main rival in Chicago).

Andersen's tax practice, however, was so substantial that the partners chose to remain auditors in the 1930s, giving up their substantial management engineering practice, much to the confusion of subsequent generations of partners who forgot why Arthur Andersen & Company had been forced to choose between auditing and consulting after regulators loosened demands for their continued independence.[103] The loss of leading competitors like Arthur Andersen coupled with the withdrawal of bankers from the provision of management engineering services, however, represented a remarkable opportunity for a handful of firms, largely based in Chicago, that had institutionalized their practices prior to the passage of the Glass-Steagall Act.

## Chicago and the Institutionalization of Management Consulting

When seven leading management engineering firms met in Pittsburgh in 1929 to found the Association of Consulting Management Engineers (ACME), there was no clear geographic center within the field of management consulting: consulting, like law or engineering, did not appear to favor geographic concentration.[104] But the Glass-Steagall Act changed all that, for the sudden jurisdictional shift gave Chicago-based firms the edge over their New York-based rivals.[105] By the early 1950s, the leading firms would all have their roots in Chicago, to the chagrin of subsequent generations of management consultants from New York. As the former managing director of Arthur Andersen reminded interviewers many years later, "you see, most of the management engineering firms originated in Chicago – Cresap, Booz Allen, McKinsey, George Fry, all of them ..."[106] In management consulting, Chicago, the infamous "second city," had come out first.

The extraordinary success of Chicago's consulting firms can be explained, in large part, by the relatively small size of Chicago's investment banking community before the Second World War. Because they did not have many employees in Chicago, New York and Boston financiers had been forced to hire Chicago consultants to analyze the management of the midwestern companies in which they planned to invest. These "financial investigations," for example, were the basis of much of Arthur Andersen & Company, Booz Surveys (as Booz Allen & Hamilton was then known) and James O. McKinsey & Company's work during the 1920s and early 1930s.[107]

As McKinsey himself reminded his New York employees, "the New York staff should give special attention to the development of a technique for handling surveys for investment banking firms."[108] Later, after the Banking Acts precluded banks from using internal investigators, like George Armstrong, as consultants, Wall Street bankers began to hire the leading Chicago consulting firms to study East Coast companies and by the 1940s, the consultants from Chicago dominated their national rivals. Chicago based consultancies dominated the market for management consulting services not so much because it was intrinsically difficult to found these new consulting firms, but because the Chicago consultants had institutionalized first.[109]

In particular, the history of James O. McKinsey & Company illustrates what happened after the passage of the Glass-Steagall Act. During the 1930s, James McKinsey, an accountant from the University of Chicago and the author of the best-selling accounting textbook in history, *Accounting Principles*, worked to systematize the complicated process of soliciting new clients and conducting management engineering surveys. To secure new clients, McKinsey methodically cultivated contacts throughout the financial community. He claimed to have taken every important banker in Chicago or New York to lunch and, in return, "'...nearly every one at one time or another has given me some work...'".[110]

Perhaps James McKinsey's greatest contribution to the institutionalization of his Chicago firm, however, was his "general survey outline," which he drafted in December 1931, to give young, inexperienced consultants a model to follow, when, as McKinsey specified, they were asked to prepare a complete study of a company that was in financial difficulties.[111] Indeed, the general survey outline survived in modified form in McKinsey & Company's training manuals into the 1960s, more than twenty-five years after his death.[112] These "bankers surveys" as they were known within McKinsey became their hallmark, for they not only gave them access to the most important executives in the organization but they also paved the way for more specialized studies.[113] As early as the 1930s, James O. McKinsey & Company was profiting from the external imposition of banking and finance regulation, a transition the firm was well equipped to exploit while the consultancy also profited from its internal systematization of client contact and report writing.

These internal arrangements allowed the successor firms, McKinsey & Company and A. T. Kearney & Company, to overcome the limitations of novice consultants and variable economic conditions as they expanded. This became particularly important after James McKinsey resigned from his original firm in 1935 to run Marshall Field & Company and subsequently died less than two years later.[114] Contrary to most accounts, James McKinsey was an innovator not because of his particular skills in cost accounting, extensive as they were, but because he institutionalized his professional practices.

By the early 1960s, the three leading consulting firms in the United States – McKinsey & Company, Booz Allen & Hamilton, and Cresap, McCormick and Paget (another spin-off from Booz Allen) had all followed their corporate clients and moved their headquarters to New York. The roots of management consulting, however, remained in Chicago. Although the most prominent consulting firms are now international organizations, management consulting was born in Chicago, when New York, struggling under the sudden imposition of banking regulations during the New Deal, turned to Chicago-based consulting firms to provide independent counsel. Once engaged, the prominent Chicago consultancies never ceded control of the professional field, they simply expanded into new markets.

## Conclusion

Modern management consulting has its origins in the 1920s and 1930s. Contrary to popular assumptions, Taylorism was not the predominant influence on the development of consulting firms. Instead, early management engineers drew on the practices of accountants and engineers to offer CEO-level studies of organization, strategy, and operations. The major change in this emerging quasi-profession took place in the 1930s and was primarily a product of political developments coming out of populist anti-monopolism aimed at Wall Street and institutionalized in the New Deal Banking Acts and through the curtailment of the associationalist agenda of the NRA. Before the 1930s, cost accountants had worked to promote associationalist goals while merchant bankers had coordinated the "engineers" who performed management audits. In the 1930s, however, the Glass-Steagall Act and SEC disclosure regulations forced commercial and investment bankers to abandon internal management consulting activities even as regulators mandated that they commission outside studies. These required studies, combined with the curtailment of the associationalist agenda, propelled the rapid growth of consulting firms from the 1930s onward. New Deal legislation and firm-level systemization catalyzed the development of this particularly American form of professionalized corporate counsel.

From the late 1880s until the late 1930s, over a span of roughly fifty years, engineers and accountants in the United States fashioned a new professional jurisdiction through institutional entrepreneurship and a series of fortuitous regulatory interventions. As a result of consulting's eclectic background and its legislative monopoly, management engineers, by the late 1930s, exerted significant influence within the boardrooms of the largest American companies. That influence would grow increasingly more powerful in the postwar period when consultants used their professional authority to reshape the corporate, government, and nonprofit sectors to reflect their often self-serving opinion of the most "efficient" organizational forms. And when, in the late 1950s, consulting firms expanded overseas, they disseminated these particularly American solutions for corporate governance among their international clients. The next five chapters describe how American consulting firms reshaped organizations in a variety of institutional settings throughout the world.

THREE

# How Have Consultants Mattered?

## The Case of Lukens Steel

Since the 1920s, management consultants have reorganized the largest institutions in the world, including IBM, The University of California, Shell Oil, Congress, Westinghouse, and the Bank of England. Listing their important clients, however, sidesteps the obvious question: "how have consultants mattered?" The case of Lukens Steel, which was purchased by Bethlehem Steel in 1997, is a particularly useful case-study of the efficacy of management consultants, because executives at Lukens corresponded with, and hired, many of the best-known consulting firms from 1912 through 1970.[1] These consulting firms included: Harrington Emerson & Company; International Bedaux Company; Arthur D. Little, Inc.; Robert Heller & Associates; Arthur Andersen & Company; and Booz Allen & Hamilton.[2] Using Lukens's internal records, this chapter will analyze the continuing influence of management consultants on a medium-sized industrial firm that was always better known for its traditional production than for rapid changes in its organization or technology.[3]

## A Brief History of Lukens Steel

Lukens, founded over 170 years ago in Coatesville, Pennsylvania traditionally produced one major product: plate steel. Throughout the twentieth century, Lukens trailed the two largest manufacturers of plate steel, U.S. Steel and Republic Steel. U.S. Steel and Republic, both nationally known, vertically integrated steel producers, made a range of plate steels. But the two industrial giants focused on high volume, low-cost steel. Lukens, by contrast, remained a specialty competitor focused on high quality, batch production with consistently higher costs than the market leaders.[4] Lukens, led by family members up through the 1960s, used many of the same rolling mills, albeit with ongoing technical improvements, from the turn of the century until its sale to Bethlehem Steel in 1997.[5] The company's workforce was just as stable: throughout the twentieth century extended families followed previous generations into the steel mills.[6] In administration, product, capital stock, geography, labor, technology, and profitability, Lukens remained remarkably steadfast, changing very little throughout the twentieth century.[7]

Although Lukens was never a market leader in steel production at any point in the twentieth century, and the gulf between the largest steel manufacturers and Lukens only increased over time, historian Phillip Scranton would remind us that flexible production in eastern Pennsylvania had its own advantages.[8] When the market for locomotive boilers derailed after World War I, Lukens began supplying plate steel for ships, and when the shipbuilding industry foundered in the 1920s, the new executives at Lukens turned to selling prefabricated and specially-clad steels. Thus, Lukens survived market changes. In an era marked by the consolidation and conglomeration of the largest integrated steel producers, Lukens maintained its independence long after most of its competitors had sold out and the company remained the third largest domestic plate steel manufacturer until 1997.[9] Lukens also did well financially. Throughout the

1940s and 1950s, Lukens's profits represented a lower average percentage of sales than the larger, integrated steel producers, but their returns on equity were 20 percent higher than Republic Steel, which also specialized in plate steel.[10] Despite, or perhaps even because of, steady increases in invested capital, Lukens Steel earned over 12 percent annually, on average, on its retained earnings in the 1940s and 1950s. Lukens's specialization in prefabricated plate steel products and specialty steels clad in noncorrosive nickel – high quality, batch lot jobs – enabled it to prosper during the century of "big steel."

Consultants mattered to this stable, medium-sized firm – one whose basic product, location, and means of production never changed – because they leveled the playing field of knowledge. At Lukens, and in other large industrial firms, consultants acted as the transmitters – or, as technological historian Hugh Aitken called them, the "translators" – of managerial ideas developed in other organizational settings.[11] Lukens, bound by its traditional, centralized management structure, and limited in its dealings to long-established customers, used consultants to supplement existing knowledge developed within the company or brought in by new employees. Consultants transmitted contemporary theories of management from the Taylorist work practices disseminated by industrial engineers in the 1910s and 1920s to the organizational structures, marketing theories, and operational techniques transmitted by management consulting firms from the 1930s onward. At Lukens, and in many other medium-sized companies, outside consultants introduced a stream of incremental changes so that dramatic managerial revolutions were not necessary.[12] If the "visible hand" of corporate management gave a marked advantage to the corporate giants who could internalize the functions of the market, then the many invisible hands of management consultants worked to equalize the advantages of size as they disseminated managerial techniques developed in big businesses among medium-sized organizations like Lukens.[13]

## Scientific Management at Lukens

Taylorism, of course, had its roots in the steel industry. Frederick Taylor's experiments on increasing efficiency at Midvale Steel in the 1880s and Bethlehem Steel in the 1890s were the source of both his research on the use of high-speed cutting tools and his better-known theories on speeding up the shop floor.[14] The large scale production of steel required large numbers of workers, but unlike the mass production of textiles, automotive manufacturing, or chemical production, steel workers could not be regulated by continuous-flow machinery or the constant pace of assembly lines.[15] So it is not surprising that some of the earliest outside consultants to Lukens Steel were proponents of wage-incentive systems designed to increase productivity through piece-rate rewards.

In May 1912, the year after Frederick Taylor had published *The Principles of Scientific Management*, Suffern & Son, an accounting and engineering firm from New York City, contacted Lukens to see if they could apply wage-incentive systems to the workers in Lukens's boiler rooms in the mill.[16] Efficiency engineers from Suffern & Son reported that workers at Lukens were not interested in generating "the required steam with the minimum amount of fuel" as they were paid a day rate with "no incentive to induce better results." If hired by Lukens, Suffern & Son promised that:

> A scientific study of the conditions of firing and cleaning of the boilers and producers and proper training of the men ... will result in a saving of 5% to 8% of the total fuel now used and possibly even more. Based on the working of the plant during the year 1911, this saving would amount to approximately $20,000 a year for fuel alone.[17]

But there was a catch. The engineers needed to make many time studies: for a start, the central steel mills, the flange fabrication department, and the storage yard. Engineers from Suffern & Son needed to improve clerical systems so that storeroom losses could be eliminated and Lukens's executives could instantly access the status of their orders. For only $500 a month, one of their engineers, under the supervision of the manager of the engineering department in the New York office (at an additional $25 a day plus expenses), could proceed with the studies. This, Ernest Suffern assured in his letter, was "an unusually low rate for such services." Furthermore, if, in any month, the value of their services was not "at least as great" as Suffern & Son's charges, the management at Lukens could reduce the bill.[18] To the modern ear, their sales pitch has a timeless sound.

The pitch worked. Charles Lukens Huston, vice-president and manager of the works at Lukens Steel, and a member of the same family that had controlled the company since the middle of the nineteenth century, accepted Ernest Suffern's offer to show them how to reduce fuel costs. In the tradition of Frederick W. Taylor's appeal to share the cost savings from scientific management with the workers, Huston pointedly stipulated that Suffern & Son provide management at Lukens with: "a permanent system of records and reports...so that our General Superintendent can keep supervision of the current results and arrange for the extra compensation of the Boiler Room men to give them a suitable share of the savings affected."[19] But, despite Charles Huston's good intentions, by September 1913 the relationship between Lukens and Suffern & Son had turned antagonistic. When Huston refused to pay the past bills, arguing that Suffern & Son's engineering services had not proven that the savings were worth the efficiency engineering firm's charges, Suffern & Son first disagreed with his reading of the contract and then, two months later, threatened to pursue legal action.[20] In December 1913, Huston summarily refused to pay the back bills and referred all further correspondence to Lukens's attorney in Coatesville.[21] Although no evidence survives of the final legal resolution, we can assume that the first relationship between Lukens and an outside industrial consulting firm ended on a sour note.

Lukens's experience was not unusual. Many of the companies that hired Taylorist engineers to introduce scientific management techniques to their plants were disappointed with the results.[22] Even when workers did not strike as they had at Joseph & Feiss Company in 1909 or at the Watertown Arsenal in 1911, companies like E. I. DuPont deNemours & Co. (DuPont) were often unable to find significant savings by applying scientific management techniques to their shop floors.[23] The hard sell was also not unusual. As historian Judith Merkle has written, "Taylor's system was an entrepreneurial scheme for selling organizational methods as science."[24] The leaders in the scientific management movement, like Harrington Emerson (founder of Emerson Consulting), were constantly deluging prospective clients, like Lukens, with promotional pamphlets and trial offers. Even if executives at Lukens or DuPont were interested in the potential savings that industrial consultants touted, once burned by an unsuccessful attempt to "rationalize" their factories, it was years before company executives were willing to let Taylorist consultants into their plants for a second try.[25]

In November 1919, seven years later, Charles L. Huston again began interviewing prospective industrial engineers. The possible savings in the mill from efficiency engineering continued to intrigue Huston. Despite worrying that workers at Lukens would oppose "any system imposed on the men from above," Huston wrote to past clients of Miller, Franklin, Basset & Company and L. V. Estes, Inc. to ask their opinion of the two Taylorist firms' work in production engineering and industrial relations.[26] After interviewing three different firms, and working hard to convince the Board of Directors to employ an efficiency engineering firm, Huston eventually hired L. V. Estes, Inc. in November 1920 to install industrial relations and wage incentive systems.[27] The methods that L. V. Estes, Inc. promised to install at Lukens were virtually identical to those that Suffern & Son had tried to introduce in the boiler rooms, with abysmal results, eight years earlier.

L. V. Estes, Inc. worked at Lukens for more than four months. Estes' consulting engineer on the site, S. B. Schlaudecker, submitted weekly reports to Huston from November 17, 1920, through March 1, 1921, on his reorganization of the mill's operation. Schlaudecker's first step was to draw an organizational chart of the manufacturing division specifying the lines of authority from Huston's position as "Director of Manufacturing" down to the workers on the shop floor and to have it posted throughout the mill.[28] When the chart was ignored, and a Second Helper in the Open Hearth Department complained directly to Huston, bypassing his supervisor's authority, Huston grudgingly admitted that Lukens's written "Industrial Representation Plan" needed to be clearer so that workers could express their grievances through the proper channels.[29] This case was not only typical of Huston's heavy-handed supervision of Schlaudecker's ongoing review but it also reflected the clear ambivalence that Huston felt in systematizing the mill and removing himself from the paternalistic-style management that had always characterized Lukens's labor relations.[30] Although Charles Huston liked many of Schlaudecker's individual suggestions, calling them "excellent" and "very good," he refused to embrace Taylorist ideology or accept that companies needed to install scientific management as a complete system.[31] Frederick Taylor had warned against applying his system in a piecemeal fashion without accepting the "fundamental principles of scientific management" and the extensive changes the system required, but Huston was like many executives who wanted both fast results and control over the changes in the organization of the factory.[32]

In fact, Huston accepted modifications of the existing system at Lukens more easily than the core changes that L. V. Estes's version of scientific management required. The addition of suggestion boxes, daily inspections in the mill, and multicolored carbon forms were all warmly received by Huston, but not the considerable expense of weighing the raw materials, calculating standardized times for steel production, or classifying the many individual intermediary products.[33] The fifty separate measurements that

Schlaudecker needed in order to systematize production controls involved not only considerable expense and supervision, but also stable production volume. Indeed, Schlaudecker spent most of his time perfecting production standards that subsequently failed when new products, special orders, or variable economic conditions altered the "standard" work rhythm.[34] The Materials Superintendent at Lukens, in charge of the inventory of raw materials, complained not only about the increasing costs due to bureaucratic "red tape," but also of decreasing efficiency because of "too much routine."[35] He was right that the mill could not be routinized: Lukens custom-tailored work could not be "Taylorized." The production controls that L. V. Estes introduced allowed managers like Huston to gauge production costs, but the enormous variance that these measures found was a necessary byproduct of Lukens's flexible, specialized production. The consultant from L. V. Estes learned that the Taylorist methods developed for continuous, high fixed-cost steel production in vertically-integrated mills like Bethlehem were difficult to adapt to the variable needs of smaller batch producers like Lukens Steel.

Not only were L. V. Estes's and Suffern & Sons' methods similar, but so were the unhappy terms on which they parted company with Lukens. In mid-March of 1921, four months into their work for Lukens, L. V. Estes, Inc. and Charles Huston began a two-month disagreement over the back bills. As Huston understood the contract (and like his agreement with Suffern & Son some eight years earlier), if the consulting firm's services did not show clear results, he was under no obligation to pay; not surprisingly, L. V. Estes disagreed.[36] Eventually, despite his sense that the shutdown of the mill during the 1921 recession had made any measurement of cost savings meaningless, Huston settled with L. V. Estes.[37] This encounter, like Huston's experience with Suffern & Son, left Lukens even more knowledgeable about scientific management and even more wary of hiring efficiency engineering firms.[38] When Miller, Franklin, Basset & Company solicited work from Lukens in 1923, Huston apologized that, despite their valuable suggestions during an initial interview, "our Executive Committee is so strongly opposed to any further attempts at efficiency service that it would be impossible for me to overcome their objections."[39] In 1923, just as in 1912, the board at Lukens Steel was adamant that it would not give efficiency engineers another chance. As of 1925, with the retirement of Charles Lukens Huston from the daily management of the mill to a seat on the board of directors, Huston's long-standing interest in Taylorism would have less direct influence.

Besides, by 1923, the craze for scientific management had died down in America in contrast to Europe where Taylorism had become the first great "post-war" technical assistance program from America. After World War I, leaders in war-torn Germany and Russia seized on scientific management as the best means to restore their industrial sectors. While managers at Lukens preferred Miller, Franklin, Basset & Company over Walter N. Polakov & Company in 1923 because the firm was "not likely to be addicted to theories and isms," Soviet planners were attracted to Polakov's explicit Taylorist ideology.[40] In the mid-1920s, after both Lenin and Trotsky had proclaimed Taylorism the solution to Russia's problems, Soviet planners brought in Walter Polakov, "to draw up Gantt production charts for the entire Five-Year Plan."[41] As the popularity of scientific management declined in the United States, European Taylorists increasingly took over the ideological charge. In the 1920s, these same European Taylorists founded consulting firms that survived as the production-oriented "management consultancies" in Britain and France.[42]

The new president of Lukens, Robert Wolcott, acknowledged European leadership in scientific management when he hired the International Bedaux Company in 1930.[43] By the 1930s, the international reputation of Charles E. Bedaux, a French-born, American trained follower of Taylor and Gantt, equaled the fame of his mentors.[44] Although Lukens, like DuPont, remained wary of industrial engineering firms that promised to install a complete "system," both Lukens and DuPont hired the International Bedaux Company in the early 1930s because Bedaux's wage incentive system "did not demand new investment, radical changes in management systems, or a long transition."[45] The Bedaux system, in comparison to L. V. Estes's elaborate inventory controls, focused exclusively on wage incentives. Lukens and DuPont were among the 200 North American companies that hired Bedaux before 1934; other well-known clients included General Electric, Standard Oil, Dow, Eastman Kodak, Swift, and, importantly, American Rolling Mill, one of Lukens's main competitors.[46]

The wage incentive system that Bedaux engineers installed at Lukens was almost immediately successful. As President Robert Wolcott wrote to Charles L. Huston ("Uncle Charlie") in August 1930,

> this, as you will see from the report, is working out in a most satisfactory manner...the men in the mills are responding to it with a very good spirit, and the fact that we have actually paid them more than they received before, has been a tremendous incentive, and we are now having demands from all over the plant to install this system.[47]

By the end of 1931, the Bedaux engineer, R. C. Cooper, had brought almost all of the shop floor workers under the Bedaux System – only electrical repairmen and "Chippers and Grinders" were not paid by their output of "B's" or standard Bedaux labor units.[48] By September 1932, Cooper estimated that the total net savings to date topped $132,000 despite International Bedaux's fees of over $40,000 and an additional $20,000 in increased plant costs.[49] If, as Robert Wolcott believed, Lukens could expect $215,000 in annual savings, and a 20 percent increase in average hourly earnings, the efficiency engineers had earned their high fees. These savings were probably realistic because the National Industrial Conference Board found an average 20 percent decrease in unit costs and 20 percent increase in average hourly wages among the companies that it surveyed using the Bedaux System.[50] By comparison with its competitors, the Bedaux system was good, but not great. The so-called Halsey Plan, which offered workers a piece-rate bonus if they increased their productivity, but did not use time-motion study or try to correct for worker "soldiering," also produced a 20 percent increase in average hourly wages and a 20 percent decrease in unit costs.[51] By 1938, an accountant at Lukens had altered the Bedaux system, based on similar changes at American Rolling Mill, so that employees could easily figure out their pay rates. At the same time, they dropped the Bedaux name from the wage-incentive system at Lukens.[52] Workers at Lukens and elsewhere accepted the bargain of higher wages for increased effort whether they were measured by a stopwatch or by average productivity.

In the 1930s, Lukens installed scientific management in its plant. After three attempts over twenty years, an outside efficiency engineering firm finally succeeded in introducing wage incentives. It seems that the cost savings from Bedaux's Taylorist innovations more than offset the firm's high fees. Yet, despite Charles Huston's interest in scientific management since 1912, it took a two-year commitment of $60,000 in the early 1930s before consultants could successfully introduce an individual productivity bonus to all the shop floor workers.[53] Ironically, with this success, the efficiency engineering firms lost Lukens' business – International Bedaux was the last Taylorist firm that Lukens hired. Direct labor costs made up a declining percentage of total production costs after the 1930s.[54] As a result, potential savings through reducing costs, although easier to calculate, had less potential impact than increased sales, new products, or new markets for existing products. Like DuPont in the 1910s and 1920s, as the family-controlled management at Lukens moved away from direct supervision of the shop floor, executives like Robert Wolcott became more concerned with the financial, sales, and organizational innovations than with industrial relations and production engineering systems. Following the increasing tendency of corporate board members to focus on administrative and legal matters over productivity and industrial relations, external managerial advisors shifted their focus to aiding executives. The legal and institutional changes of the 1930s, twinned with executives' growing need for advice on best practices, would propel the rapid emergence of a new form of external consulting – that would eventually become "management consulting" – during the 1930s.

## The General Survey

From the 1920s on, a new type of consulting service evolved that focused on controlling the white collar bureaucracy of large companies, not their line workers. In contrast to Taylorist consultants, management engineering firms specialized in restructuring the boardroom, not the shop floor. They provided "business surveys" for companies interested in learning new methods of cost accounting and departmental organization. Unlike the self-taught engineers who led the scientific management movement, the university-trained accountants, engineers, and lawyers who founded the leading management engineering firms – Stevenson, Jordan & Harrison and Ford, Bacon & Davis in New York, and Booz Allen & Hamilton and James O. McKinsey & Company in Chicago – offered executive-level advice on administration and organization. Management engineers helped not only large corporate clients but also their bankers by restructuring troubled companies, merging rival firms, or analyzing possible acquisition targets.[55] In the 1930s and 1940s, management engineering firms, now better known as management consulting firms, proved themselves useful to American corporations.[56] As a result, between 1930 and 1940, in the midst of the Great Depression, the number of management consulting firms grew, on average, 15 percent a year from an estimated 100 firms in 1930 to 400 firms by 1940, and, during the 1940s, the number of new firms continued to grow at nearly 10 percent a year so that by 1950 there were an estimated 1,000 management consulting firms in existence.[57] In the late 1930s and the early 1940s, contemporary observers, from both the academic and the business world, perceived that this rapid growth of management engineering was distinct from the scientific management movement – eschewing the ideology of Taylorism, management engineers studied the top of the organizational pyramid, not its base.[58]

Although consultants performed thousands of management engineering studies for hundreds of different clients in dozens of industries during the 1930s, steel companies remained an important market for consulting firms. If Bethlehem Steel (long before its purchase of Lukens) was the proving ground for Taylorism, then Ford, Bacon & Davis' study of U.S. Steel between 1935 and 1938 (described more fully in the last chapter) represented the triumphant success of management engineering firms in the 1930s. At U.S. Steel, where Taylorists had previously investigated the shop floor and J. P. Morgan & Company had controlled the boardroom, by the mid-1930s, management consultants from Ford, Bacon & Davis were reorganizing its management structure from top to bottom.[59] And at Republic Steel, the other great plate steel manufacturer, the investment banking firm of Kuhn, Loeb & Company hired James O. McKinsey & Company in 1934 to analyze their proposed merger of Republic Steel with Corrigan-McKinney, another steel manufacturer.[60] McKinsey concluded that the proposed merger made sense because of the companies' complimentary strengths and the potential savings that would result.[61] The giant steel companies, hard hit by the Depression, used management engineering firms to rationalize, consolidate, and reorganize their plants, hoping to gain an edge on their competitors and survive the brutal price wars of the 1930s.

Lukens was just as savvy as Republic Steel and U.S. Steel in its strategic use of management engineering firms. In 1927, Ford, Bacon & Davis surveyed Lukens Steel, making a detailed inspection and inventory of the land, buildings, and equipment at their Coatesville, Pennsylvania, New Orleans, Louisiana, and New Castle, Delaware locations.[62] Since 1922, when Ford, Bacon & Davis had discussed the proper amortization schedules for equipment at Lukens, the consultancy had been one of several management engineering firms offering to perform a mix of accounting and engineering services for Lukens. Even as Lukens was employing the International Bedaux Company in the early 1930s to install wage incentives in order to lower production costs, executives at Lukens had begun turning to management engineers to rationalize their white collar workforce and increase sales.

Between 1936 and 1937, at the same time that consultants were reorganizing both Republic Steel and U.S. Steel, the Philadelphia-based management engineering firm of Day & Zimmerman, Inc. conducted eleven separate surveys at Lukens Steel. Day & Zimmerman's influence at Lukens extended into the boardroom: Lukens elected W. Findlay Downs, the president of Day & Zimmerman, to its board of directors in 1933.[63] When, in December 1937, Robert Wolcott decided to stop using Day & Zimmerman because of the severe downturn in the economy, Wolcott and Charles L. Huston (now in his eighties) began a systematic review of Day & Zimmerman's studies for Lukens from 1936 through 1938. In a preliminary review of the management engineers' work at Lukens, Wolcott concluded that: "to sum up all of the above work, Day & Zimmerman has been most satisfactory and helpful. I can state without fear of contradiction that it has meant considerable savings to our company."[64] Yet, as Charles L. Huston reported, economic conditions were so bad that even labor unions were pessimistic about a recovery in the steel industry for six months or more.[65] Wolcott and Huston were right to be pessimistic. The mills were virtually shut down in 1938 (just as they had been in 1921) and Lukens Steel suffered a yearly loss of over a quarter of a million dollars in the 1938 financial year.[66]

Although Findlay Downs, the President of Day & Zimmerman, acknowledged that the downturn at Lukens was severe, he was still upset with Lukens's "summary treatment" in discontinuing their services. He asked that the newly formed manufacturing committee review the Day & Zimmerman studies of Lukens over the preceding two years.[67] These reviews generally supported Robert Wolcott's preliminary conclusion that the management engineering firm had done good work – as Wolcott had pointed out, their recommended changes to the sales department resulted in estimated savings that more than covered Day & Zimmerman's fees of $27,337.60 for four different studies in 1937.[68]

Day & Zimmerman's work for Lukens alternated between engineering consulting and organizational counsel. As civil engineers, Day & Zimmerman recommended that Lukens switch to natural gas to decrease their fuel costs and that Lukens's executives negotiate a special rate with the Philadelphia Electric Company.[69] As management engineers, Day & Zimmerman evaluated the organization and incentives in the sales department and restructured the budgeting system at Lukens. Many times the two roles merged, as they did when Day & Zimmerman proposed capital improvements in July 1936. In 1936, Day & Zimmerman estimated that nearly $2 million in capital improvements, primarily to the steam and electrical power system in the two largest mills, would bring in nearly $800,000 dollars in annual savings – a 40 percent return on Lukens's investment in the first year.[70] Charles Huston objected to the expenditures arguing that their plan, although technically sound, did not accurately project gross sales.[71] Lukens went forward with the improvements, but Charles Huston was proven right by the continued downturn in 1938. As Stewart Huston, the corporate secretary, wrote at the beginning of 1938, Day & Zimmerman had predicted that sales would increase nearly 75 percent between 1936 and 1938, but sales actually declined over the same period.[72] Yet, Charles Huston was sympathetic toward Day & Zimmerman's error admitting that Lukens' board of directors could hardly have predicted the severe downturn themselves.[73]

Despite the depression, the increased debt obligations due to Day & Zimmerman's suggestions, and the virtual shutdown of the mills, the executives at Lukens all concurred that the management engineering work performed by Day & Zimmerman had been beneficial. Lukens suspended its management engineering work only because the mills were virtually shut down by the disastrous economy in late 1937.

The organizational and engineering advice that Day & Zimmerman offered to Lukens was typical of the assignments that early management engineers performed. Both Stevenson, Jordan & Harrison and Ford, Bacon & Davis in New York were originally engineering firms and both continued to offer civil engineering counsel in addition to management engineering advice in the 1930s.[74] For example, when Arthur Little founded his engineering firm in Boston in the 1880s he provided chemical analysis, but by 1911, Arthur D. Little, Inc. was advising General Motors on how to manage its new Research and Development Laboratory.[75] As one staff member later described the transformation: "'You don't get big fees by doing chemical analyses. You get them by giving advice to a C.E.O.'"[76] Despite being well known for cost accounting innovations, James O. McKinsey & Company also found it worthwhile to link itself with the perceived authority of engineering knowledge.[77] In 1932, James O. McKinsey & Company changed its letterhead from "certified public accountants" to "accountants and engineers" even though the firm did not employ any licensed engineers.[78] Like Day & Zimmerman, whether licensed as accountants or engineers, management engineering firms combined traditional professional roles with the more distinctive organizational skills of management engineering.[79] Management engineering firms emphasized their ability to perform both technical work, like engineering and cost accounting studies, and general surveys of corporate organization for their corporate clients.

Management engineering firms used their principal tool, the general survey, to identify and solve organizational problems. The general survey was a detailed overview of a company's organizational structure and, as Stevenson, Jordan & Harrison described it in 1934, "such a survey appraises the effectiveness of the management, checks the organization procedures, the nature of records, the standards, budgets, quotas, and the like."[80] At James O. McKinsey & Company, as at Stevenson, Jordan & Harrison, the general survey was the preferred means of studying a company, and staff consultants first performed a general survey before tackling specific organizational problems.[81] This "holistic" approach to corporate problems helped the consulting firm in two ways. First, such a complete survey was likely to uncover many problems that were not immediately evident when executives first hired the consulting firm – endearing them to the executives in the company and simultaneously increasing the potential for additional work. Second, because a general survey required the assistance of the top executives in a company, consultants gained instant recognition, access, and respect from a cadre of potential clients.

The wartime economy of the 1940s created new opportunities for consultants. By the mid-1940s, no management engineering firm had a larger reputation than Robert Heller & Associates. Heller's reorganization of Congress during World War II alongside his corporate work for the Radio Corporation of America (RCA), The Baltimore and Ohio Railroad, Continental Can, Standard Brands, and his status as one of the subcontractors on the U.S. Steel study, made Robert Heller & Associates perhaps the best-known and respected management engineering firm in the country.[82] Continuing Lukens's pattern of hiring the leading consulting firms, in 1945 Robert Wolcott hired Robert Heller & Associates to perform a general survey of Lukens Steel, which began in August 1945 and ended one year later at a cost of nearly $120,000.[83]

To describe the conclusions of the Heller survey, however, a little backtracking is necessary. Shortly after Robert Wolcott became President of Lukens in 1925, he established two separate companies – not divisions, but separate legal companies – under the control of Lukens Steel Company. First, Wolcott founded the By-Products Steel Company in 1927, which produced prefabricated parts, like engine blocks, for corporate customers who did not want to build them from scratch. The second company, Lukenweld, which Wolcott founded in 1930, specialized in designing and building prefabricated structures using arc welding. Both companies, although Taylorized by Bedaux engineers and reorganized by Day & Zimmerman, remained legally and organizationally distinct from Lukens for the next fifteen years although it was widely known that Lukens owned them.

In 1945, Robert Heller & Associates worked to convince Wolcott to fold Lukenweld into Lukens Steel while simultaneously establishing an interlocking managerial structure between By-Products Steel Corporation and Lukens Steel Company. This tighter corporate connection, Heller argued, would eliminate intercompany rivalries, reduce accounting overhead, and spur sales as "weldments" became a direct product line of Lukens Steel.[84] Executives at Lukens agreed and, by April 1946, Wolcott had consolidated the operating and sales organization so that the general mill superintendents, general fabricating superintendents, and production control managers of both By-Products and Lukens Steel reported to the same corporate vice president of operations.[85] Similarly, both companies' sales managers reported to the same vice president of sales in the parent company. In 1947, Lukens folded Lukenweld into the main company, completing the recommended consolidation of the three separate companies into a single, flexible plate steel manufacturer with three separate divisions.

This consolidation was one of dozens of recommendations contained in the eighteen reports submitted by Robert Heller & Associates covering administrative matters as diverse as reducing product defects, improving sales controls and incentives, and establishing a market research department.[86] One legacy of the studies performed by both Day & Zimmerman and Robert Heller & Associates was the increasing power of the sales and finance departments over the product people. Despite an attempt by Robert Heller & Associates to adjust pay levels in the sales department, Lukens continued to pay veteran salesmen in excess of the established ranges and Robert Wolcott, a former salesman, refused to consider cutting them.[87] Management engineers, focused on reorganizing the structure of corporations, emphasized that manufacturing costs represented a decreasing percentage of overall corporate costs. As the cost of sales, marketing, public relations, plant supervision, finance, and research and development (R&D) came to dominate the overall cost structure of the modern bureaucratic firm, shop floor productivity became a less important arena for improving performance than organizational efficiency and control.

Robert Heller & Associates reorganized Lukens's thin managerial layer into an organization of divisional managers led by senior executives focused on strategic concerns. Consultants at Robert Heller & Associates worked to reconstruct Lukens as a modern multidivisional corporation, not the centralized, single-product manufacturer it had always been. Although Robert Heller & Associates' proposals fell far short of a full decentralization of Lukens (consultants, for example, actually worked to centralize the sales function among the three divisions) the management consulting firm began to move Lukens toward the decentralized organizational form. The multidivisional form that the large, multinational corporations ultimately adopted may have been developed in the 1920s within Sears, DuPont, General Motors (G.M), and Standard Oil, but it was management consultants who disseminated it among American businesses in the 1940s and 1950s and, later, it was the consultants who carried the organizational form with them to Europe in the 1960s.[88] Examples of the institutional transfer of this organizational device abound, including the experience of Cresap, McCormick and Paget, which brought the decentralized organization to Westinghouse in 1949 and Booz Allen & Hamilton, which introduced it to IBM in

1956.[89] Although Robert Heller & Associates did not fully decentralize Lukens, when Lukens began to diversify the company in the early 1960s, its executives did not have to alter the company's organizational structure to add new operating divisions parallel to the three already in place by 1947.

At Lukens, as in many companies, management engineers worked in the 1930s and 1940s to establish themselves as close advisors to top management. When Robert Wolcott described Day & Zimmerman's work for Lukens in 1937, he explained that not only had he employed them for specific studies but also for their general advice during weekly conferences on Lukens' "day by day operations."[90] During the 1940s, Lukens's comfort in retaining consultants continued to grow and by the time that Wolcott hired Robert Heller & Associates in 1945, the board routinely approved hiring outside management consulting firms, in sharp contrast to their case-by-case review of Taylorist consulting firms a quarter-century earlier. In the postwar era, management consultants came to be the accepted institutional conduits for organizational advice not immediately available to the executives in Lukens.

## The Institutionalization of Management Consulting

The rapid growth of management consulting firms in the 1930s and 1940s eventually posed a problem for this expanding professional field. Even if executives saw the value of management consultants, by the early 1950s, consultants had already reorganized many of the large companies in America. Like the earlier Taylorist efficiency engineers, management consultants were rapidly working themselves out of a job as they moved through corporate America. The Association of Consulting Management Engineers (ACME), the professional association of management consulting firms, estimated that by 1950 there was one management consultant for every 154 salaried managers in the United States, and the ratio was continuing to narrow.[91] Consulting firms quickly saw that the solution to their problem was a simple one – instead of selling general surveys, management consulting firms decided to offer increasingly specialized studies to their clients. General management consulting firms like McKinsey & Company offered to make detailed studies of specific departments, products, and markets for companies whose organizations had already been "surveyed."[92] In effect, this frequent use of consultants for smaller surveys made their presence less ad hoc and more a part of the corporate routine, institutionalizing the role of management consultants in the ongoing management of companies.

At Lukens, the size of management consulting studies decreased even as their number and frequency rose. Rather than have one organization such as Day & Zimmerman or Robert Heller & Associates coordinate several simultaneous studies, Lukens hired many different consulting firms for discrete projects. In 1958 alone, Lukens hired four different management consulting firms to reorganize its central office, research possible uses for new alloys, increase quality control, and provide advice on industrial engineering.[93] When Lukens needed a management consulting firm to evaluate the management reports prepared by their Controller's Division, they hired Scovell, Wellington & Company, a consulting firm that still had accountants on staff.[94] In contrast, when Lukens needed a marketing survey of its existing product line, it hired Cresap, McCormick and Paget, one of the three leading consulting firms in America.[95] By the mid-1950s, Lukens's budget for "Consulting and Outside Service Expense" routinely exceeded $75,000 per year and the process of hiring management consulting firms had become so institutionalized that Lukens's Board of Directors no longer requested periodic reviews of their effectiveness.[96]

Unlike the direct solicitation commonly practiced by efficiency engineering firms, and used by a few of the early management engineering firms, the code of ethics of ACME, of which both Scovell,

Wellington & Company and Cresap, McCormick and Paget were members, discouraged mass mailings and other forms of "unprofessional" behavior.[97] Instead, management consulting firms were urged to build up their clientele through social contacts and professional referrals – for example, executives at Lukens probably met the management consultants from Cresap, McCormick and Paget through their mutual work for the Second Hoover Commission (which is described in greater detail in the next chapter).[98] Consultants from McKinsey & Company, Booz Allen & Hamilton, and Arthur D. Little, Inc. also used frequent articles in the *Harvard Business Review* and other prominent business publications to promote themselves to top executives.[99]

As management consulting evolved, the reputations of the leading firms became more important than the prominence of individual consultants to the growth of the profession. By the late 1950s, a distinct hierarchy had emerged led by McKinsey & Company, Booz Allen & Hamilton, and Cresap, McCormick and Paget. Although all three firms worked across the American economy, McKinsey & Company was best known for decentralizing international corporations, Booz Allen & Hamilton for its work with U.S. government agencies, and Cresap, McCormick and Paget for its Institutional Division that advised universities, museums, and other nonprofits on their structure and operations.

The increasing specialization of management consulting firms, particularly firms specializing in computers and strategy, eventually cracked this oligopoly. As we saw earlier, during the 1950s, the accounting firm of Arthur Andersen & Company began offering its clients advice on how to install and use computers for billing, accounting, and cost control.[100] Their counsel on information technology was a logical outgrowth of Arthur Andersen's own accounting practice, because businesses were attracted to electronic computers as a means to speed up the generation of accounting information. In 1953, Arthur Andersen & Company oversaw the installation at

General Electric (GE) of the first computer used specifically for business rather than scientific or military applications. The Univac I that Arthur Andersen & Company installed in Louisville, Kentucky, handled the entire payroll for the 15,000 workers in the factory and kept track of the inventory at the plant.[101] Although some companies chose not to use outside consultants, and intentionally developed internal expertise in electronic computer systems and software, executives at many large companies called in management consultants to advise them on the adoption and use of these multi-million dollar systems. As the Manager of General Electric's plant in Louisville recounted in an influential article in the *Harvard Business Review*:

> because of the pioneering aspect of the program, we found it wise to employ an independent management consultant firm (Arthur Andersen & Co., Chicago), experienced in computer logic and developments. This firm has been particularly helpful in assisting the company group in training personnel, arranging management orientation meetings, and planning for conversion of initial applications.[102]

The executive specifically recommended that companies first "employ a competent consultant" before trying to install the new technology. For many companies, that consulting firm was Arthur Andersen & Company.[103]

Lukens was very intrigued by the possible use of electronic computers and, in September 1956, only three years after the first commercial installation of an electronic computer, Lukens hired Arthur Andersen & Company to study the economics of installing a computer to handle order processing, production control, shipping, and billing.[104] The report by Arthur Andersen & Company found that Lukens' enthusiasm for computers far exceeded the company's needs. The volume of transactions at Lukens was too low and the total cost too high to justify a computer even if the volume of orders at Lukens was to increase by 50 percent. Not only was its volume too low, but the specialized nature of Lukens's production and the company's "individual attention to orders" precluded easy automation by computers.[105] As consultants had found before, Lukens's flexible production defied the simple transmission of managerial techniques to Lukens. In this case, the management consultants from Arthur Andersen & Company mattered as much for the path that they warned Lukens's executives not to take as for any new ideas that they introduced in the company.

But neither the cost of the systems nor the cost of the consultants could keep the executives in Lukens away from computers for long. Although a computer system at Lukens might not have been cost effective in 1957, management reopened the question in 1964. By July 1965, when Lukens hired Booz Allen & Hamilton to evaluate the installation of a computer, Booz Allen's consultants estimated that the recurring savings from a computer system would exceed $1 million annually, offsetting in a single year the nonrecurring planning and installation costs.[106] The projected costs, however, increased as Booz Allen & Hamilton continued to study the problem – by June 1966, less than one year later, Booz Allen estimated that the initial installation would cost more than $2 million [107] At $15,000 to $17,000 per month for nearly twelve months, the consultants were not cheap, but the consultancy's $185,000 fee was less than one-tenth of the overall cost to install the computer system. Wages for Lukens personnel to plan and implement the data processing, run parallel accounting systems during the conversion, and build new facilities added up rapidly.[108] The one relatively inexpensive component in the entire installation was the computer itself – a new $167,500 IBM System 360 Model 30.[109] In the end, half of the $1.5 million in annual savings that Booz Allen & Hamilton estimated would accrue from the computer installations, were not reduced costs, but $750,000 in additional "value" to management from the improved information system.[110] Booz Allen & Hamilton increasingly justified installing a computer system not on its own merits, but in comparison to the operating cost of Lukens' current system of accounting: "during the next five-year period, about $21,000,000 will be spent by Lukens for information gathering and processing (at $4,160,000 per year) whether or not the BIS ["Business Information System"] is implemented."[111] The "modern" computer system that Lukens finally installed may well have produced cost savings, but as Booz Allen & Hamilton sharpened their estimates, and the projected start-up costs grew larger, the management consultants came to justify the installation of a computer at Lukens less on lower costs than on the increased capabilities that the system offered.

While computer systems were a lucrative and fast-growing market for management consulting firms in the 1960s, no specialty grew faster than "strategy" consulting. The Boston Consulting Group, best known for its concept of the "growth share matrix," pioneered these expensive, boardroom-level studies of business strategy in 1962 just as the demand for the organizational studies provided by the older consulting firms began to slow.[112] By focusing not on reorganizing the structure of a company but on rethinking its corporate strategy, The Boston Consulting Group and, later, Bain & Company showed their clients which businesses were "dogs," which were "cash cows," and which were "stars" so that they could expand into new, and presumably more profitable, markets.

With this new focus on strategy, the work of management consultants began to parallel that of investment bankers because consultants recommended that their clients divest themselves of divisions that were "dogs" and buy existing companies that were "stars," a choice made possible by their common decentralized structure.[113] For example, the management consulting firm of McKinsey & Company provided detailed advice for clients like Sun Oil on what companies to acquire and how to integrate the acquired company into their existing decentralized organizational structure.[114] Management consulting firms thus helped to feed the merger and acquisition boom in the 1960s, advising their clients on how to diversify their business lines. Some companies quickly came to resemble the rapidly growing conglomerate corporations like Textron that were all the rage.

Beginning in 1959, executives at Lukens began to diversify the steel company, first by acquiring a manufacturer of small pleasure boats as an outlet for the mills' light plate steel and, again in 1968, by buying Natweld Steel Products, Ltd., a Canadian plate steel fabricator similar to Lukens's own Lukenweld division.[115] There is no evidence as to whether executives at Lukens hired management consultants to advise them on the purchase of these two companies, but soon after the acquisition of Natweld in 1968, Lukens hired the consultants at Cresap, McCormick and Paget to prepare a long-term plan to further diversify its business line through a program of corporate acquisitions.[116]

The diversification plan that the consultants from Cresap, McCormick and Paget prepared for Lukens concluded that the company would best be served by diversifying horizontally into "precision metal products fabricated of special materials," which were indirectly linked to their traditional strength in steel production.[117] From their initial survey, Cresap, McCormick and Paget chose companies in five product categories as possible acquisition targets: (1) mechanical fasteners, (2) precision ball bearings, (3) specialty metal tubing, (4) testing instruments and equipment, and (5) custom quality alloys.[118] After comparing price/earnings (P/E) ratios, corporate management, and industry growth rates, Cresap, McCormick and Paget recommended in 1969 that Lukens acquire one of two companies producing rivets, bolts, and screws.[119] By their May 1970 report, Cresap, McCormick and Paget had narrowed their recommendation to the H. M. Harper Company as Lukens's $17 million acquisition would yield a return of 11.5 percent per year based on Harper's predictable earning stream.[120] A dependable if not fast growing company, H. M. Harper would have been described by the consultants from Boston Consulting Group as a "cash cow." The reports that the consultants produced resembled investment banking studies in their use of Wall

Street terminology and the emphasis on the financial aspects of the transaction. For Lukens, Cresap, McCormick and Paget's recommendation represented the company's first step in their diversification away from Lukens's traditional business of producing and custom fabricating plate steel.

Lukens never bought an industrial fastener manufacturer, but executives at Lukens, who were no longer part of the Lukens-Huston dynasty after 1974, continued to diversify the company away from steel production.[121] Under the presidency of Robert Wilson in the 1980s, Lukens bought several other non-steel businesses and dropped the word "Steel" from its corporate title, renaming itself "Lukens, Inc.," in order to deemphasize its links with the steel industry.[122] But, as the fashion for diversification passed in the 1990s, a new president, R. W. Van Sant, began selling off the unrelated businesses and reemphasizing steel production at Lukens to the delight of stock market analysts who had by then turned against diversification.[123] By 1995, Lukens once again described itself as "a leading North American specialty steel manufacturer whose subsidiaries supply carbon, alloy, and clad plate steels; and stainless steel sheet, strip and plate products."[124] While management consultants were no doubt responsible for the installation of Lukens's "total quality management" (TQM) system in the mid-1990s, and no doubt aided managers at Bethlehem Steel in merging the two companies after Lukens was acquired in 1997, Lukens' position as the leading manufacturer of high-quality plate steel had remained unchanged for the eighty years preceding the company's merger with Bethlehem Steel.

Although management consultants would continue to follow the latest fads and fashions in management, by the time that Cresap, McCormick and Paget had completed its work for Lukens in the 1970s, the institutional path for management consulting had largely been set.[125] Management consulting firms, from the 1970s onwards, would generally fall into two camps: those who provided advice on corporate strategy, like BCG, Bain, and McKinsey, and those who provided advice on information systems, like Andersen (subsequently Accenture) and later IBM. Even as demand for consultants rocketed during the 1990s, this distinction within the profession would remain fairly constant and the consultants' focus on serving boards of directors seldom wavered.

The U.S. market for management consulting services now totals more than $100 billion a year, and Wall Street analysts expect that even after a sharp decline in demand in the early part of the twenty-first century, corporate demand for consultants' services will continue to grow.[126] Large companies not only accept the institutionalization of management consulting, but openly acknowledge their dependence on the consulting firms – recent C.E.O.s of IBM, American Express, and Westinghouse were all former consultants at McKinsey & Company.[127] Whether in computer systems, strategic counsel, organizational design, or corporate acquisitions, management consulting firms have become, and continue to be, a crucial institutional solution to executives' ongoing need for outside information.

## Conclusion

The question then remains: how have consultants mattered? Although management consultants often introduced new techniques, frequently saved Lukens more money than they cost, and repeatedly restructured the company, external consultants did not do anything that company insiders could not have done given time, personnel, or thoughtful deliberation on insiders' suggestions. Twice, people in power at Lukens implicitly asked whether or not outsiders were really necessary. The first was the production manager who, when asked his opinion about hiring a Taylorist firm in 1922, suggested that "we, in ourselves, could ultimately attain to just as great an efficiency...."[128] The second was the president of Day & Zimmerman, a Lukens board member, who asked why the company did not perform a marketing study internally instead of hiring the outside management consulting firm of Coverdale & Colpitts in 1943.[129] Why was Lukens, both men asked, not able to use its own personnel to solve these problems? The answer was that consultants offered Lukens economies of knowledge. Or, to quote the production manager in 1922, "...even at the [high] price you pay for these people for their service, it would be cheaper in the end and attained in a great many months' less time."[130]

Consultants mattered at Lukens by extending the range of abilities and knowledge already available to the executives who ran the company. The small cadre of family executives who controlled Lukens through 1974 could not keep up with the current literature on Taylorist work incentives, organizational theories, marketing, computer applications, or corporate acquisition models without outside help. Management consultants kept Lukens Steel competitive with larger plate steel manufacturers by giving it access to organizational innovations. At a cost of less than 2 percent of Lukens' annual net income, management consultants represented a cost-effective means to guard against the serious structural, strategic, and technological changes that might have otherwise blind-sided the firm and its executives.[131] Lukens's periodic checks of the consulting firm's effectiveness and concurrent cost-benefit calculations showed that consultants were worth their high fees. At Lukens, consultants permitted a small, flexible manufacturer to remain competitive in a cutthroat industry over a sixty-year period by acting as the institutional conduits for new ideas.

# FOUR

# Creating the Contractor State

## Consultants in the American Federal Government

One of the distinguishing characteristics of the American federal government since 1945 has been its amalgamation of administrative capabilities with professional expertise, a combination that historian Brian Balogh has labeled "the prominstrative state."[1] Federal bureaucrats and independent professionals, although initially wary of one another, united during the postwar era to take on emerging technological and administrative challenges. Government officials in concert with professional experts promoted commercial nuclear power through the Atomic Energy Commission, oversaw advances in medical research through the National Institutes of Health, and worked to stabilize the economy through the Council of Economic Advisors.[2] Balogh has described how these internal experts, however, eventually lost political power in the 1970s as grassroots organizations entered the political fray with their own "independent" experts, challenging the entrenched authority of professionals employed within the bureaucratic agencies of the American state.

This description of the prominstrative state is extremely useful, but it overlooks a crucial paradox of the federal government in the postwar era: its remarkable lack of growth during a time of constantly expanding responsibilities. Although the number of state and local government employees in the United States more than tripled from a postwar base of 3.8 million in 1947 to 12 million in 1975, the number of federal civilian employees rose less than 50 percent from 2 million to 2.9 million over the same period.[3] Even as the federal government added supervision of atomic energy, medical research, and aggregate economic activity to its already long list of official responsibilities, the U.S. Congress and government administrators held back the increase in the number of federal employees. Following a series of legislative amendments in the early 1950s by Congressman Jamie Whitten, President Harry Truman and his successors shifted the bulk of federal employment from the permanent civil service to temporary contractors.[4] Instead of enlarging the standing bureaucracy, officials in the executive branch self-consciously reconstructed the administrative state in the image of American corporate structures as they increasingly employed outsiders in place of additional federal personnel. By the early 1970s, the professional advisors who guided the affairs of the prominstrative state were as likely to be employees of external consulting firms as employees of the federal government.[5] These external contractors served as the government's own "independent" experts, enabling the "hollowed-out" structure of the prominstrative state to continue providing highly technocratic services and command authority even as professionals directly employed by the government lost political clout.[6]

External management consultants oversaw the restructuring of the federal bureaucracy and encouraged the use of outside contractors from the 1940s onward. In the process, the extensive use of management consulting firms in government assignments fundamentally reshaped the administrative state into the contractor state. Through their reorganization of Federal departments and agencies, management consultants institutionalized a reliance on outsiders to solve organizational problems rather than permanently adding federal employees – an ongoing policy that political scientist Francis

Rourke has labeled "adhocracy."[7] This use of outside contractors, particularly management consulting firms, represented a particularly American solution to the conundrum of keeping the number of federal personnel low even as the central government took on ever greater administrative responsibilities.[8] The extended use of outside consulting firms to stand in for government bureaucracy became a hallmark of American administration – both a cause and a result of the growth of the proministrative state.

This chapter traces the extensive use of management consulting firms by the federal government in the construction of the contractor state beginning in 1940 when the leading management consulting firms first helped to organize and then to reorganize the state. This chapter will focus on three high-profile assignments: (1) surveys for the Navy during World War II by consultants from Booz, Fry, Allen & Hamilton, (2) the reorganization of the Executive Branch for the Hoover Commission in the late 1940s by Cresap, McCormick and Paget and Robert Heller & Associates, and (3) the initial organization of NASA in 1958 by McKinsey & Company.[9] In each case, the consulting studies represented a new milestone in the use of management consulting firms in Washington. By the mid-1960s, their influence had become so great, yet so diffuse, that critics charged that the leading management consulting firms represented a virtual "shadow government" in America.[10] Long before that happened, however, consultants had begun to provide their services to the military during the Second World War.

## Organizing for War

World War II presented the American public with tangible evidence of the potential of the proministrative state. Atomic energy graphically demonstrated the rewards of government-funded science, the rapid development of penicillin showed the benefits of federal involvement in modern medicine, and the massive wartime deficit confirmed that Keynesian economists could indeed manage the American economy with government support. These dramatic examples of what could be accomplished through the alliance of professionals and the administrative state publicized "the potential that this partnership offered to postwar America."[11] The initial postwar growth of the prominstrative state would flow from the wartime success of professionals and government administrators during the 1940s.

Management consultants, no less than physicists, engineers, and economists, made themselves indispensable to the war effort. While government agencies often hired consulting firms, many of these firms' senior partners also volunteered their individual services. Robert Heller, founder of the leading management consulting firm in Cleveland, Robert Heller & Associates, spearheaded the wartime reorganization of the U.S. Congress.[12] Tom Kearney, a senior partner in James O. McKinsey & Company, and the subsequent head of A. T. Kearney & Company, helped reorganize the War Production Board after serving as its regional director in Chicago.[13] Marvin Bower, one of the three founding partners of McKinsey & Company, spent more than half his professional time on organizational studies for the Air Corps.[14] The contributions of Robert Heller, Tom Kearney, and Marvin Bower would later position their consulting firms to receive plum government assignments after the war, including Robert Heller & Associates' organization of the newly formed Department of Defense.[15]

During the war, it was the consultants from Booz Allen & Hamilton who received many of the best consulting assignments for the Army, Navy, and War Production Board. In the Spring of 1940, Frank Knox, then Secretary of the Navy, hired Booz, Fry, Allen & Hamilton to survey the Navy's East Coast shipyards.[16] Knox, the former publisher of the *Chicago Daily News* and the 1936 Republican nominee for Vice President, knew Edwin Booz from their years in Chicago prior to Knox's appointment to the Navy. Although Booz's initial jobs, like estimating office space needs and rerouting the internal postal system for the U.S. Navy, were relatively unimportant, more significant studies, like the reorganization of the Office of Naval Operations, soon followed America's entry into the war.[17] Although several staff members contributed to these surveys, Edwin Booz personally oversaw all of his firm's work in Washington; in 1942 he wrote to his brother that the pressures of the government surveys had left him without a single day off in nearly two years.[18] Booz's hard work during the war would pay off in later years as Booz Allen & Hamilton grew to be the most influential management consulting firm in the public sector.

It was not easy for the consultants to sell their services to the military. Many military officials remained dubious that the use of outsiders was the best means to solve their organizational problems. Lieutenant General Thomas B. Larkin, Director of Logistics, for example, complained as late as 1949 that, "I do not see where it helps to pay outside firms to tell the Army how to organize."[19] Instead, the Army and Navy set up their own internal management engineering departments to perform "industrial surveys." But to do so they had to use former staff and administrative advice from the leading management consulting firms![20] The Army promoted Mark Cresap, a former Booz Allen employee and a captain in the U.S. Army Reserve, to serve as colonel in charge of Administrative Management, a staff position that reported directly to the Commanding General of the Army Service Forces. Similarly, the Navy hired Richard Paget, who had previously overseen Booz, Fry, Allen & Hamilton's survey of the Navy's telephone system, to be Management Engineer of the Navy supervised by the Secretary of the Navy.[21] Cresap and Paget, together with Willard McCormick, who served as the Assistant Management Engineer of the Navy under Richard Paget, would found their own management consulting firm shortly after the war ended.[22] In the meantime, their industrial surveys for the Army and Navy would demonstrate both the advantages and disadvantages of internalizing the expertise of management consultants.

The potential gains from internalizing the role of management consultants, as with the scientists employed by the military, appeared to be enormous. By hiring outside consultants as internal staff, the military could simultaneously eliminate the high fees of professional firms, exercise greater administrative supervision of sensitive documents, and better disseminate the final results of the surveys. The military's creation of an internal consulting staff was a massive experiment. As Ewing (Zip) Reilley, a partner at McKinsey & Company, recounted his own experience as an internal consultant attached to the Quartermaster Corps of the Army, "before the war only a few very progressively managed business and government agencies had a staff to perform [general surveys] for the chief executive and other members of top management."[23] Now the military was leading the way in the hope that internal consultants could provide high quality management consulting services without the disruption associated with outsiders.

As the military discovered, ultimately, the use of an internal consulting staff to replace the services of outside consultants was both useful and not. In the Navy, under the direction of Richard Paget, the Organization Planning and Procedures Unit surveyed and reorganized more than ten Navy Yards from Portsmouth, New Hampshire, to Pearl Harbor, Hawaii, paralleling Booz, Fry, Allen & Hamilton's assignment four years earlier.[24] Paget's survey of the naval yards concluded that too many Navy departments had supervision of the naval shipyards, a situation that promoted inefficient management. Paget's solution was to centralize authority for the shipyards in the Bureau of Ships, and to decentralize operational control to the commanding officer of the individual shipyards.[25] As a commander in the Navy, Paget had the rank, procedural knowledge, and contacts to ensure that the Chief of Naval Operations implemented the consultant's recommendations. The problem, however, was that circumstances and tradition restricted the potential scope of Paget's work to the civilian operations operated by the Navy including the shipyards.[26] Thus the Navy would not allow Richard Paget or other internal consultants to investigate Naval Operations, as Edwin Booz had, but instead limited Paget's purview to industrial facilities that lay outside the Navy itself. In this and other cases, internal consultants lacked the professional authority that they needed to get the job done – because they were not themselves in command!

The military learned that the professional authority of management consultants derived, in large part, from their "outsider" status. Ironically, Richard Paget, a commander in the Navy, had less impact on the internal administration of the Navy once he left Booz, Fry, Allen & Hamilton and joined the Navy. Whereas Commander Paget may have had high enough internal clout to reorganize the naval yards, he did not possess sufficient rank or status to implement changes that might disrupt the turf of high ranking naval officers. One lesson learned from the military's experience was that internal staff consultants were best at handling external investigations while external firms of management consultants were most effective in solving internal administrative problems. Management consultants would play a powerful role in the growth of the prominstrative state after the war ended, but they would have to function as the external agents of adhocracy, not employees within government agencies. The prominsitrative state could not internalize all forms of professional expertise.[27]

If World War II offered management consultants a dramatic showcase for their professional expertise, the immediate postwar era gave the leading consulting firms an opportunity to institutionalize their presence in the federal government. Just as the rapid expansion of the military during the war necessitated organizational change, the rapid reduction in federal employees after the war required a similar structural adaptation. Although the military shed its excess personnel quickly, dropping from 12 million active personnel in 1945 to 1.6 million in 1947, Federal civilian employment also shrank nearly 50 percent from 1945 to 1947.[28] Many Americans worried, however, that the federal government was still too large at two million employees, for it had employed less than one million civilians as late as 1939. There was pressure for further reductions in the government's scale and scope. One congressional response to the political pressure was to create the Hoover Commission to reorganize the federal government. The Hoover Commission, in turn, attempted to solve the organizational dilemma by doing just what corporate executives would have done – hiring management consulting firms to restructure the Executive Branch.

## The Hoover Commission

In 1947, partly to embarrass Harry S. Truman, the incumbent Democratic President, the Republican-controlled Congress created the Commission on the Organization of the Executive Branch of Government and charged it with making the federal government more efficient. Truman responded to this openly partisan maneuver with remarkable political savvy – he immediately appointed former President Herbert Hoover, the last Republican president, to head the task force.[29] During the twenty years since Hoover's presidency, through Depression-era employment programs and wartime mobilization, annual, nominal federal expenditures had increased from $3.6 billion to over $42 billion and the number of federal administrative units had increased from less than 500 to over 1,800.[30] By any measure, Herbert Hoover's attempt to reorganize the postwar federal government was a Herculean task.

Guided by his conception of the "associative state" and his training as an engineer, Hoover responded to the challenge by bringing "business methods" to bear on the organization of the Executive Branch: Hoover created twenty-three separate task forces, led by dozens of different business executives who were, in turn, supported by outside management consulting firms. The Hoover Commission's task forces surveyed everything from the management of the Office of the President to the organizational structure of the U.S. Post Office.

The Commission's recommendations, including a unified Department of Defense, centralized federal purchasing through the newly created General Services Administration, and the creation of the job of White House Chief of Staff, are at the foundation of the modern American Executive Branch.[31]

To translate management ideas developed for large business organizations to fit the needs of the Executive Branch, the Hoover Commission contracted fifteen of its thirty-four policy studies to research and consulting firms.[32] Among those hired, the Trundle Engineering Co. surveyed the U.S. Department of Veterans Affairs, Robert Heller & Associates looked for cost savings in the U.S. Post Office, and the newly founded Cresap, McCormick and Paget recommended new procedures for federal personnel management.[33] Although different in their structure and purpose, these three management consulting studies all recommended decentralizing the government's organizational structure. And, unlike studies conducted by the other task forces, management consultants produced concrete estimates of the savings from their suggested changes ranging from a low of $75 million in Veterans Affairs to a high of $256 million in federal personnel management.[34] The Hoover Commission represented a highly public use of management consulting firms by the federal government and the potential for favorable publicity from the assignment was not lost on the management consulting firms. Each of the firms, in varying degrees, gained prestige and future clients from its work for the Hoover Commission.

### Staffing the Hoover Commission

The Hoover Commission was only one in a long series of commissions created by the U.S. Congress in an ongoing effort to streamline the administration of the Executive Branch. Earlier commissions included the Cockrell Committee (1888), the Dockery Commission (1893), the Taft Commission (1910), and the Brown Commission

(1920).[35] In 1936, a decade before the Hoover Commission, Congress created the Committee on Administrative Management, the Brownlow Commission, to reduce the number of administrative agencies and improve efficiency in Roosevelt's administration.[36] But congressional restrictions on Roosevelt's ability to restructure the executive branch, and public fears that the changes would promote excessive presidential power, hampered the Brownlow Commission's attempt to restructure the government.[37] In contrast, when Congress established the Hoover Commission in 1947, both President Truman and ex-President Herbert Hoover emphasized the Commission's bipartisan leadership and downplayed any association with earlier reorganizations in order to mobilize popular support for the new commission's recommendations.

Hoover's most dramatic innovation was not improved public relations, but his insistence that administrative experts drawn from the private sector staff the new commission. Like his reorganization of the U.S. Department of Commerce more than twenty-five years earlier, the former president saw the Hoover Commission not only as a way to "reduce wasteful overlap and unwise expenditures," but also as a means to promote his vision of an "associative state" in which business and government would voluntarily collaborate to solve technocratic problems.[38] Instead of former government officials, the bulk of the 300 task force members Hoover selected were business executives.[39] Active corporate executives, however, could not reorganize the federal administration without staff assistance so, instead of using federal employees, Hoover agreed to hire outside management consulting firms to produce the initial studies and make preliminary recommendations to the commissioners. Hoover saw management consultants as the natural translators between the organizational needs of the commission and the business experience that he considered crucial to making government more efficient.

When James Webb at the Bureau of the Budget first considered, in 1946, who should be on an advisory committee for the reorganization of the Executive Branch, Webb included, "a man with private management engineering experience," among the proposed "industrial executives" and "well-known educators."[40] It is striking that Webb included a consultant on his proposed advisory committee, because management consultants were still less common than professional accountants, lawyers, or engineers, even if by 1946, management consulting firms were becoming increasingly accepted by the business community – the 1930s and 1940s, after all, was the period when the number of management consulting firms grew more than 10 percent annually, on average, for more than two decades.[41] By the mid-1940s, Hoover Commission members could comfortably debate the relative merits of different management consulting firms even if they remained hesitant about the professional qualifications of these firms.[42]

The members of the Hoover Commission agreed that using management consultants was the most cost effective way to prepare the task force reports. Although Hoover and the other commissioners initially worried about the high fees charged by the leading consulting firms, Clarence Brown, a Republican congressman from Ohio, pointed out that in comparison with the $5 million Congress had budgeted for the reorganization of the War Department, the commission's $750,000 budget was modest.[43] Relieved, and perhaps encouraged, the Commissioners tried to use management consulting firms whenever they could to eliminate the need for additional federal personnel and to lighten the load for the task force members. As Commissioner George Mead, the owner of a leading paper products company, noted when he explained his initial selection of Robert Heller & Associates to reorganize the Post Office: "I approached [the problem] from a business standpoint."[44] Hoover agreed with Mead's analogy and quickly agreed to hire Robert Heller & Associates. As the Stanford-trained engineer Hoover replied: "The Post Office is a commercial business – is it not a fact? – and it needs that type of

investigation. . . . "[45] Mead based his selection of Robert Heller &
Associates to reorganize the Post Office not only on Heller's work for
U.S. Steel, RCA, and the Baltimore and Ohio Railroad, but also on
the firm's strong reputation on Capital Hill following Heller's reorganization of Congress in 1945.[46]

Hoover Commission members chose Robert Heller & Associates
and Cresap, McCormick and Paget because these firms had previously served both the federal government and private industry.
Mark Cresap, Richard Paget, and Willard McCormick had, from the
moment they founded their consulting firm after leaving the military,
announced their intention to serve "government officials" along with
more traditional business clients.[47] It was not Cresap, McCormick
and Paget's rising reputation in the business world that brought them
to the attention of the Hoover Commission, but their previous work
for the military.[48] When committee members began debating the
merits of different management consulting firms, the firm's experience weighed heavily. The Secretary of the Navy, James Forrestal,
recalled that they were "good men."[49] Little more than a month later,
the head of the task force on personnel met with Richard Paget to
negotiate the firm's contract with the Hoover Commission.[50]

### Reorganizing the Post Office

Robert Heller & Associates' reorganization of the U.S. Post Office
was not without precedent. As early as 1908, the Penrose-Overstreet
Commission had recommended that the federal government decentralize the Post Office by breaking it down into regional administrative units. Yet, in 1948, the Post Office was still so centralized that
postal administrators supervised all of the 42,000 local postmasters
in the United States directly from their Washington headquarters.[51]
Not only was the nineteenth-century patronage system that saddled
the Post Office with over twenty thousand political appointees still

in existence, but the lack of managerial continuity between executive appointees remained a long-standing problem.[52] In the twenty-five years before 1948, the average tenure of the six Postmaster Generals dropped to only four years.[53] Although Congress created the Post Office as a self-supporting, independent agency, by 1947 the yearly deficit had reached nearly 20 percent of its $1.3 billion in revenues, resulting in an annual shortfall of $263 million.[54] Prevented by Congress from increasing postal rates and controlled by an inefficient, centralized bureaucracy, the Post Office was pictured in newspaper editorials and cartoons as a lumbering dinosaur of "antiquated business methods" in the modern managerial age.[55]

Consultants at Robert Heller & Associates agreed with this widespread perception that the U.S. Post Office, although generally efficient in the physical distribution of the mail, was poorly managed as a business. At the root of the problem, the consultants argued, was a tension between the tendency of Congress to use postal subsidies and jobs to curry political favors and the expectation that the Executive Branch should efficiently manage "one of the largest business operations in the world."[56] The consultants believed, however, that this dilemma could be solved, in their words, "by adapting to Government use the principles of organization and operation found in large commercial and industrial enterprises."[57] By embracing modern business methods of decentralization, cost accounting, and personnel administration, the Post Office could be managerially "responsible to the executive branch and adequately accountable to the legislative."[58] The first step in reforming the Post Office, the consultants agreed, would be to reestablish the Post Office as a revolving fund agency (instead of being dependent on annual congressional appropriations) whose administration and operation would be closer to that of a business than to a federal department.

Second only in importance to amending the Post Office charter, Robert Heller & Associates recommended that the Post Office decentralize its administration. As the consultants put it: "the need for decentralized, close-at-hand direction of operations in this gigantic, country-wide business enterprise is apparent to anyone who has studied the operation in the field."[59]

Decentralization, of course, was not a novel solution to managing large, national bureaucracies, but was, instead, the governing principle of the largest corporations in America. Big businesses like Sears, Standard Oil, and A&P developed the decentralized administrative form in the 1920s and 1930s to manage their national, multiproduct companies.[60] By the 1940s and 1950s, management consulting firms like Booz Allen & Hamilton, Robert Heller & Associates, and Cresap, McCormick and Paget were the primary disseminators of the multidivisional form to public and private organizations across the United States.[61]

Robert Heller & Associates argued that the decentralization of the Post Office into fifteen regions would allow regional directors to better administer field activities, coordinate the postal service between interdependent geographical regions, and rapidly disseminate improved managerial practices.[62] It would also allow Congress to assign to the Postmaster General, in the consultants' words, "responsibility only for matters of a departmental and public policy nature thus relieving him of day-to-day operating duties."[63] Robert Heller & Associates hoped to install in the postal service the same decentralized line and staff system regularly used by the largest industrial companies in the 1940s.

Even though the management consultants at Robert Heller & Associates might have convinced corporate executives of the wisdom of their proposed decentralization, the politicians turned out to be a difficult audience. Unlike business, where the chain of command descends directly from the CEO, neither Herbert Hoover as head of the Hoover Commission nor President Truman could enact Robert Heller & Associates' proposals without congressional approval. And, unfortunately for the consultants' plan, the acting U.S. Postmaster General actively opposed decentralization, arguing that the management of the Post Office was "the most efficient...service in the world."[64] Without the support of the Postmaster General, the Hoover Commission could push through eight of its nine major recommendations to Congress, but not decentralization.[65]

## Rethinking Federal Personnel Management

The report by the task force on federal personnel management, in contrast to the Commission's work for the Post Office, was not the exclusive work of a single management consulting firm. Hoover selected John Stevenson, President of the Penn Mutual Life Insurance Company, to lead a sixteen-member task force that included such prominent figures as Vannevar Bush of MIT, Senator Harry F. Byrd of Virginia, and David Lilienthal of the Atomic Energy Commission (AEC), in addition to five prominent corporate executives.[66] Like the head of the Post Office task force, John Stevenson made it clear that he did not have much time available and, therefore, he hired Cresap, McCormick and Paget to create the agenda of the task force, and to draft the initial report.[67]

Like the Post Office report, the study of federal personnel policies was seen by the commission members as one of the Hoover Commission's most important subjects.[68] In the late 1940s, with the rapid upsurge in civilian wages, the federal government was losing many of its talented employees to private industry.[69] By 1948, the number of federal employees leaving their jobs had reached 3 percent per month or nearly half a million workers a year.[70] Surveys conducted by Cresap, McCormick and Paget underscored the federal government's difficulty in attracting new employees – only one quarter of all college students were interested in a career in government and the most talented of the students were convinced that the Civil Service offered lower salaries and less opportunity for advancement than private industry.[71] From the outset of the study, task force members believed that their most important challenge was, in the words of Stevenson's assistant, "attracting qualified supervisory and top level personnel into the government."[72] The solution that the consultants from Cresap, McCormick and Paget offered was simple – increase the speed of recruitment, make federal salaries competitive with industry, and decentralize the hiring process.[73]

The decision to decentralize federal hiring was no more radical than decentralizing the Postal Service – in Cresap, McCormick and Paget's initial meeting with John Stevenson, the consultants were told that "there is some indication that Mr. Hoover is likewise interested in decentralization of personnel administration."[74] Indeed, by the time that Cresap, McCormick and Paget had prepared its preliminary report on procurement policies and practices, the consultants had begun to see decentralization as a central tenet of the Hoover Commission itself. As Cresap, McCormick and Paget's preliminary report concluded:

> Speed of procurement in the government necessitates a high degree of decentralization. This is borne out by the experience of World War II and is the keynote of the program of modernization now being developed by the Commission.[75]

The management consultants at Cresap, McCormick and Paget saw decentralization not only as a common solution to administrative problems in the federal government but as a systematic answer to the Hoover Commission's inquiries. This was a solution that acquired almost ideological overtones within the commission. Not surprisingly, the final report of the Hoover Commission recommended that personnel administration be reorganized to create a decentralized administration under the centralized oversight of the Civil Service Commission.[76]

Unlike the Postal Service, personnel administration could be decentralized by presidential decree so there were no delays due to disputes over congressional legislation.[77] By October 1950, all but one of the Hoover Commission's twenty-nine recommendations had been enacted.[78] Within a year of the commission's report, the Executive Branch was benefiting from Cresap, McCormick and Paget's recommendations for higher salaries, speedier hiring, and decentralized personnel administration.

Harry Truman later remembered the Hoover Commission as one of the great triumphs of his presidential administration.[79] Perhaps he was right, because political scholars often trace the origins of the modern administrative state to the reforms instituted by the Hoover Commission. If so, the pattern that the Hoover Commission adopted, of using institutionalized management consulting firms to marry Herbert Hoover's conception of the "associative state" with the managerial power of a strong Executive Branch, owes a considerable debt to the extensive use of management consulting firms. Consultancies like Robert Heller & Associates and Cresap, McCormick and Paget promoted their vision of a decentralized, corporate bureaucracy in the federal government by acting as the standing agents of adhocracy.

### Gilt by Association

In his memoirs, Dean Acheson tells the story of overtaking Herbert Hoover while walking home in New York shortly after the Hoover Commission had disbanded. "Mr. President," Acheson called out from behind, "it would greatly improve my financial and social standing if I might be seen walking with you." "Anything I can do," Hoover replied, "short of a loan."[80]

Hoover was also careful with the commission's money. Although their fees from the Hoover Commission were not insubstantial – the commission spent $146,000 on Robert Heller & Associates' study of the Post Office and nearly $100,000 on Cresap, McCormick and Paget's survey of personnel management – the management consulting firms gained more from the prestige that the assignment brought than from the studies' fees.[81] Knowing how much publicity he got reorganizing Congress in 1945, Robert Heller first volunteered his firm's services for free to the Hoover Commission, but the commissioners, of course, declined this offer.[82]

In August 1948, soon after Robert Heller & Associates had submitted its final draft of the report on the Post Office, Robert Heller wrote to Herbert Hoover to ask for a signed photograph to display in his new offices in Cleveland.[83] Within a year, the Secretary of Defense had hired Robert Heller & Associates to organize the newly formed Department of Defense even while the management consulting firm was reorganizing *Time* magazine's circulation department based, in part, on its work for the Post Office.[84] Robert Heller & Associates used its association with the Hoover Commission to keep up the firm's reputation during the rapid expansion of rival management consulting firms.

Although Cresap, McCormick and Paget could count the Pennsylvania Railroad, Georgia-Pacific, Revlon, and Filene's among its clients by 1949, it was through its work for the Hoover Commission that the firm gained a national reputation.[85] In 1950, only one year after the commission disbanded, Cresap, McCormick and Paget published a summary of the Commission Report, which the firm mailed to leading politicians and executives in order to capitalize on its work.[86] Of course, with so many executives serving on the commission, Cresap, McCormick and Paget did not have to go too far afield to find work – in 1950, the consultancy worked for the Pure Oil Company, whose Chairman, Rawleigh Warner, also served on the Hoover Commission Task Force on Federal Personnel Management.[87] The consulting firm repeated this pattern in the mid-1950s when it worked for the Task Force on Military Procurement during the Second Hoover Commission right before starting an assignment for the Lukens Steel Company, both of which were chaired by Robert Wolcott.[88] By the late 1950s, partly because of its work for the Hoover Commission, Cresap, McCormick and Paget was widely seen as one of the top three management consulting firms in the United States along with McKinsey & Company and Booz Allen & Hamilton. Cresap, McCormick and Paget's work for the Hoover Commission served as a marketing tool through the end of the 1950s as the firm emphasized the continuity of its work in corporate, government, and nonprofit institutions.

## Uniting with the Proministrative State

The pattern that both Robert Heller & Associates and Cresap, McCormick and Paget set for the use of management consultants by the federal government continued long after the Hoover Commission finished its work. In 1950, Truman allocated $1 million for management consulting studies following on recommendations made by the Hoover Commission. Immediately after the first Hoover Commission disbanded, the Federal Field Service, covering nearly 90 percent of all civilian employees, hired George Fry & Associates to reorganize its executive administration, the U.S. Coast Guard hired Cresap, McCormick and Paget to rethink its personnel administration, and the Veterans Administration hired Booz Allen & Hamilton to restructure its organization.[89] Of course, Truman was not the only President who employed consultants; upon being elected in 1952, Eisenhower called in McKinsey & Company to advise him on possible political appointees for the Executive Branch in addition to having the consulting firm plan the initial organization of the White House staff.[90] In the 1950s, Federal agency officials increasingly turned to management consulting firms to solve their administrative problems creating, in effect, temporary adhocracies to reform their long-term organizational structures.[91]

The reorganization of federal agencies and departments by management consulting firms soon became a common pattern. McKinsey & Company, for example, worked for Nelson Rockefeller's ad hoc committee on the organization of the Department of Defense in 1953; a restructuring that followed Robert Heller & Associates' initial organization of the Department of Defense and Cresap, McCormick and Paget's survey of the Army, both completed in 1949.[92] In the Executive Branch, Cresap, McCormick and Paget reorganized both the Civil Aeronautics Administration and the Department of Housing, Education, and Welfare in 1954, while McKinsey & Company worked in 1955 for the McKinney Committee of the AEC documenting the potential commercial applications of nuclear power.[93] These extensive connections gave the leading consulting firms an edge in securing assignments as administrators moved from one federal agency to another. McKinsey & Company's work for the AEC, for example, introduced them to Keith Glennan, then one of the five AEC commissioners and the president of the Case Institute of Technology.[94] When Glennan went on to serve as the first administrator of NASA in 1958, he immediately hired McKinsey & Company to organize the newly founded agency.[95]

Administrators' familiarity with the various consulting firms gave government officials an increasingly sophisticated understanding of the best ways to use consultants' specialized talents in government assignments. In the late 1940s and early 1950s, the government's increased use of consultants allowed federal officials to gauge the particular strengths of the individual management consulting firms. For example, when the chairman of the Department of Defense Management Committee, General McNarney, selected Robert Heller & Associates to organize the Department of Defense in 1949, the Secretary of the Army asked McNarney whether Heller's survey of the Department of Defense would emphasize organizational change, like Cresap, McCormick and Paget's work for the Army, or operational procedures, like Heller's previous assignments for the Air Force.[96] Such a technical question required experience with studies performed by several different management consulting firms. McNarney's reply was just as knowledgeable: the Department

of Defense expected Robert Heller & Associates' survey to identify short-term cost savings, not long-term organizational problems.
General McNarney contrasted Robert Heller & Associates with
other leading management consulting firms, explaining that Heller
& Associates was "a firm which believes in progressively implement-
ing things as they go along rather than completing a survey, making a report, and leaving it to somebody else to implement."[97] This
response satisfied the other members of the management committee
and they readily agreed to hire Robert Heller & Associates. By the
late 1940s, the members of the Department of Defense Management
Committee, like the members of the Hoover Commission, were comfortable discussing the relative merits of individual consulting firms
and their particular approaches to management problems both inside
and outside the federal government.

As government officials gained a more sophisticated understanding of management consulting studies, the selection process became
more bureaucratic and less based on past relationships. Federal
administrators, familiar with previous consulting assignments, could
better estimate the probable cost of a survey and solicit competing bids. For example, in 1949 the Department of Defense received
twenty-one bids by consulting firms for an advertised survey of the
military's job classification scheme. The Department of Defense narrowed the initial list down to seven firms that they investigated carefully before selecting the consulting firm of Rogers & Slade above
Booz Allen & Hamilton based on the perceived quality of their contract proposal and staff.[98] After Robert Heller questioned the officer
in charge of the military's selection process, Heller grudgingly admitted that the Department of Defense had done a thorough job estimating the survey's probable cost, rating the professional standing of
the consulting firms, and drafting a tight contract.[99] By 1952, the
General Accounting Office (GAO) routinely published standardized requirements for hiring management consulting firms, including a preapproved list of acceptable firms.[100] Consultancies like Booz

Allen & Hamilton that specialized in work for the federal government benefited from the increasing sophistication of government
officials and the use of standardized bids; however, the systematization of management consulting contracts narrowed the profit margin of assignments in the public sector. These lower profit margins,
in turn, would drive consulting firms like A. T. Kearney & Company and McKinsey & Company from the technocratic government
assignments that came to dominate consulting assignments within
the federal government.[101]

By the time that happened, however, government officials, with
the assistance of the major management consulting firms, had constructed the long-term framework for the proministrative state.
Although the number of organizational studies performed by consulting firms declined during the 1960s, general surveys, like McKinsey
& Company's work for NASA in the late 1950s and early 1960s,
further institutionalized the use of outside contractors by the federal
government. McKinsey & Company's work for NASA was, therefore, representative of management consulting assignments from the
1950s and 1960s and, simultaneously, a catalyst for the emerging contractor state.[102]

## Organizing for the Space Race

Long term institutional developments were on occasion influenced
dramatically by unanticipated events. The Soviet Union's surprise
launch of Sputnik in 1957, for example, set the United States on a
campaign to catch up with the Soviets in aerospace development.[103]
The American government's most enduring response, other than
the education of a generation of "rocket scientists," was the establishment of the National Aeronautics and Space Administration
(NASA) in 1958. NASA, which absorbed the preexisting National
Advisory Committee for Aeronautics (NACA), already had an
annual budget of $100 million and a workforce of eight thousand

employees when President Eisenhower installed Keith Glennan as its first administrator in October 1958.[104] The U.S. Congress, anxious to beat Soviet accomplishments in space, immediately tripled NASA's budget to $300 million for 1959 and more than doubled the agency's annual appropriation to $615 million in 1960.[105] Given the space agency's rapid growth, and Keith Glennan's prior experience with McKinsey at the AEC, it was not surprising that Glennan's first official act at NASA was to hire McKinsey & Company to organize the fledgling agency.[106]

McKinsey's initial organizational survey of NASA, in the autumn of 1958, largely confirmed the need for the decentralized structure proposed by NACA employees the previous summer.[107] Robert Rosholt, NASA's administrative historian, would later write that McKinsey & Company's organizational study resulted in very few structural changes, but "satisfied the need felt by Glennan for an outside point of view."[108] Indeed, Keith Glennan overruled consultant John Corson, head of McKinsey's Washington office, on their only point of disagreement – the appointment of a "general manager" to oversee daily operations. John Corson may have been the organizational expert, but Keith Glennan had a keen vision of what he wanted to accomplish at NASA.[109] Although McKinsey & Company's initial organizational survey of NASA did not alter the agency's overall structure, the consulting firm's inaugural assignment would lead to eight other studies within NASA worth $232,000 in fees, a staff position for a former McKinsey consultant within NASA, and, most importantly, a crucial voice for the consultants in the promotion of the contractor state.[110]

Glennan's decision to employ a management consulting firm had ideological as well as functional overtones. An engineer of the proministrative state both literally and figuratively, Glennan wanted to shift technical expertise from "in-house" employees to external institutions because he hoped "to avoid excessive additions to the federal payroll."[111] Glennan described in his private diary how this philosophy ran counter to NACA's earlier organizational culture that had emphasized internalizing the agency's technical needs.[112] NACA, like the Manhattan project, had been a product of the wartime integration of professionals into the prominoistrative state while NASA, in comparison, was representative of the emerging "hollowed-out" structure of the contractor state. When Keith Glennan resigned from office in January 1961, twenty-eight months after assuming control of NASA, roughly 85 percent of NASA's nearly $1 billion budget "was spent out-of-house by contract."[113] From NASA's establishment, the organizational structure that Glennan and the consultants from McKinsey & Company devised for the space agency promoted the use of outside contractors over building internal expertise.

## NASA: Prototype for the Contractor State

In December 1959, more than a year after McKinsey's initial work for NASA, Keith Glennan and John Corson agreed, over lunch, to have consultants from McKinsey & Company survey NASA's contracting policies.[114] Corson's preliminary proposal for the McKinsey study noted that several other surveys of military contracting, including a collaborative Harvard Business School/Rand Corporation study of weapons acquisition and a Brookings Institution study of government contracting for research and development, were already underway.[115] NASA, like the military, was finding it extremely difficult to oversee its contracts for high technology services because of the intrinsic complexity of the projects. As historian Walter McDougall has described the process, building a rocket required:

> the administrative art of conceiving a whole, breaking it into subsystems, nursing along the R & D, testing, and evaluation of each like a cook with six dishes on the stove, and finally making sure that each "interfaced" properly with all the others when the time came to put the meal on the table.[116]

With billions of dollars at stake, and national honor in the balance, Keith Glennan hired McKinsey & Company to reappraise the contracting policies and procedures that NASA had "inherited from the armed services."[117] The consultants from McKinsey believed that this would be NASA's last chance to reevaluate the agency's emphasis on outside contractors, an issue, it turned out, that would be a recurring concern within NASA.[118]

McKinsey & Company's survey of contracting policies – itself the product of a detailed, single-spaced, six-page contract worth $65,000 – pointed out just how difficult it was to create single-use space technology.[119] Although military contracts often involved intricate systems as complex as NASA's technology, private contractors generally anticipated that successful military prototypes would lead to multi-billion dollar orders. In contrast, executives at NASA regularly treated even successful space designs as one-off orders. Thus, NASA was even more reliant than the military on close working relationships with its external suppliers, since private contractors could neither anticipate extended production runs nor could they economize by lowering their engineering standards without jeopardizing mission safety.

The solution to NASA's contracting problems, the consultants from McKinsey argued, lay not only in using sophisticated cost control systems – like PERT (Program Evaluation and Review Techniques), for instance – developed for the military, but also, paradoxically, in deemphasizing NASA's internal, technological expertise.[120] The management consultants, with the support of Glennan, argued that NASA needed to retain only enough in-house engineering capabilities to (1) conceive of innovative space-flight projects, (2) develop technical specifications for private subcontractors, and (3) supervise contractors to ensure high reliability missions.[121] Beyond the bare minimum of internal technical expertise, however, the McKinsey consultants argued that America's "free enterprise society dictates that industry should be given as extensive a role as possible."[122] McKinsey & Company's final report approvingly quoted the chairman of General Electric, Ralph Cordiner, explaining that "space research and industrial research mutually support each other" in order to defend the consultants' ideological emphasis on outside contractors.[123] NASA's problem, therefore, was not preventing excessive numbers of contractors from decreasing the agency's efficiency, but deciding how few internal experts NASA could employ to coordinate their efforts effectively.

McKinsey & Company's report concentrated on deciding "what is the bare minimum of internal expertise necessary for NASA to function effectively?" The consultants' explicit answer, for NASA to "contract for the bulk of the research and development services needed," may have dismayed the agency's engineers, but the response cheered NASA administrators.[124] Consultants proposed that each of NASA's three major centers (the Jet Propulsion Laboratory, the Marshall Space Flight Center, and the Goddard Space Flight Center) retain only enough internal design, fabrication, assembly, and testing staff to create a single advance launch vehicle. NASA, the consultants from McKinsey argued, needed these internal experts in order to understand the potential problems faced by outside contractors. Consultants argued that even the conceptual and preliminary design elements, however, once the exclusive domain of internal NASA engineers, " . . . should be supplemented extensively through the use of study contracts."[125] NASA would then, in this schema, become an administrative shell coordinating the design, fabrication, assembly, and testing of space vehicles.[126] NASA, the federal agency described by Brian Balogh as the exemplar of the promin, also became, according to Paul Light, the "premier example" for the contractor state.[127]

As NASA's budget grew, the percentage of funds the space agency spent on outside contractors continued to increase. Indeed, by 1964, 90 percent of NASA's $5 billion budget went to private contractors.[128] In terms of personnel, however, NASA's transformation during the 1960s was even more dramatic. In 1960, NASA's external contractors employed 36,500 staff, more than three and a half times the 10,200 personnel employed within the agency. By 1964, NASA's internal personnel had more than tripled to 32,500 employees. NASA's outside contractors, however, employed nearly 350,000 people, or more than ten times NASA's internal staff.[129] NASA's administrators had indeed heeded the management consultants' plea "for a persistent and positive effort to contract out."[130] The space agency did little more than coordinate the activities of its contractors – internal engineers from NASA may have pushed the button for lift-off, but it was most likely that outside contractors from Martin Marietta or Lockheed had installed the switch.

## The Hollowed-Out State

Glennan's decision, with the consultants' assistance, to employ external professional institutions instead of building technical expertise within NASA, paralleled the concurrent growth of contracting within the federal government. By 1962, approximately 10 percent of the federal government's annual $80 billion budget went to external contractors for research and development.[131] Throughout the 1960s, despite occasional notes of caution, including the Bell Commission's warning about the " . . . government's 'increasing reliance' on private contractors to do the research and development work of government," the federal government continued to contract for 80 percent of its research and development needs.[132] For management consultants, however, the rise of the contractor state did not immediately translate into more engagements; indeed during the 1960s many of the leading management consulting firms saw their assignments for federal clients decline.

The routine use of consultants by the federal government in the 1950s, ironically, drove the more general management consulting firms like McKinsey & Company, A. T. Kearney & Company, and Cresap, McCormick and Paget away from federal assignments in the

1960s. Government officials tightened the terms of contracts and broke down larger management consulting jobs into smaller assignments that favored consulting firms with specialized, technical skills like Arthur D. Little, Inc. and Booz Allen & Hamilton. While McKinsey & Company continued to conduct general organizational surveys of agencies like the Department of the Interior, the Department of Labor, and the Office of the Secretary of Defense, these surveys experienced dramatic fluctuations in demand unlike narrower, technical studies that had a more predictable contracting cycle.[133] As a result, the general management consulting firms, like McKinsey & Company, Cresap, McCormick and Paget, and Robert Heller & Associates, never generated a significant portion of their revenues from the federal government. In the late 1960s, for example, the receipts from McKinsey's Washington office only equaled those from McKinsey's regional office in Cleveland.[134] The form of the proministrative state was solidifying: the contractor state expanded and technocratic consulting contracts replaced organizational studies as the primary source of consulting assignments within the federal government.

In the late 1960s and early 1970s, the federal government increasingly turned its focus from the administration of bureaucratic departments to the creation and promotion of legislative standards. The Bureau of Solid Waste Management set guidelines for the demolition of railroad freight cars, the U.S. Maritime Administration searched for further opportunities for American shippers, and the Urban Mass Transportation Administration devised the specifications for city transit systems.[135] All of the preceding tasks, however, were performed not by federal employees, but by personnel from management consulting firms. Federal agencies increasingly contracted out these routine, and not so routine, administrative reports to management consulting firms instead of expanding the federal bureaucracy. Federal agencies even hired management consultants to help them understand how recent legislative changes would affect their own departmental programs. Thus the Department of Health, Education, and Welfare hired Booz Allen & Hamilton in 1971 to survey how individual states chose to purchase their social services following revisions to the Social Security Act, while, that same year, the Department of Transportation had Arthur D. Little, Inc. analyze how the National Environmental Policy Act would change the legislative mandate of the Transportation Department.[136] If, as Brian Balogh argues, the growth of expertise outside the federal government threatened the authority of the proministrative state, federal administrators learned quickly how to respond to the threat: hire external consulting firms to replace internal expertise. By the mid-1970s, management consulting firms were as likely as internal bureaucrats to conduct the special surveys and the routine reports for federal agencies like the Office of Technology Assessment, the Environmental Protection Agency, and the Department of Energy.[137] Management consultants had filled in the core of the "hollowed-out" state, and in the process consultants became central to the everyday administration of the contract state.

## Conclusion

When lawyers Daniel Guttman and Barry Willner first described the rising influence of management consultants in the federal government, they entitled their exposé "the shadow government."[138] Recent critics, however, have worried less about this lack of public accountability (what political scientist Donald Kettl has called "government by proxy") and more about the "hollowing out" of public service as a result of this transformation.[139] In the United States, federal organizations like the Environmental Protection Agency and the Department of Transportation now routinely contract ongoing projects to management consulting firms. One of the largest consulting firms in the world, Booz Allen & Hamilton, relocated its corporate headquarters to the Washington area specifically so that it could be near its largest client, the federal government. If, as political scientists argue, the federal government has increasingly favored impermanent organizational structures over long-term bureaucracy, then management consultants have actively worked to become central actors in these adhocracies, shaping their structures and capabilities to fit the opportunities created by the situation.

To understand the evolution of the proministrative state as first the rise and then the decline of internal expertise within the American federal government understates the enduring importance of external institutions. If the Manhattan Project, through its development of atomic weaponry, was the first great symbol of the powerful potential of the proministrative state, then historians should not underestimate the role of contractors in the development and construction of the atomic bomb. From the extraction of uranium isotopes by DuPont in Hanford, Washington, to federal contracts with the University of Chicago, neither the Manhattan Project nor the Atomic Energy Commission ever sought to build a formidable area of expertise.[140] Instead, the growth of the proministrative state went hand in hand with the development of the contractor state, each demonstrating the potential for federal administrators to reconceive of the state as an administrative shell.

Management consulting firms actively participated in the construction and supervision of the contractor state. Whether in their efficiency work for the armed services in WWII, the restructuring of the Executive Branch after the war, or the creation and design of NASA, consultants self-consciously carried business techniques into government agencies. Moreover, the consultants' ideology that the federal government favor outside contractors over internal bureaucracy consistently resonated across party lines. We have continued to see this process at work in the political platforms of recent American presidents – both Democrat Clinton's declaration of the end of "big government" in 1996 and in Republican Bush's pledge to substitute contractors for half of the remaining federal civilian workforce in 2002.[141] Both projects could only be contemplated because a new set of intermediaries – management and technical consultants – had emerged. Ultimately the "hollowed-out" structure of the American contractor state owes its form not only to pragmatic public concerns about the growth of federal bureaucracy, but also to the long-term influence of management consultants.

# FIVE

# Finding Profit in Nonprofits

## The Influence of Consultants on the Third Sector

In the 1950s, only two groups – management consultants and the American Internal Revenue Service (IRS) – viewed "nonprofits" as a distinct sector of the economy, and both hoped to find profit in these nonprofits.[1] While the IRS worried that federal tax receipts would decline because of the rapid growth of these tax-exempt institutions, management consultants from Cresap, McCormick and Paget worked to create a niche for the sale of their organizational advice by targeting what they labeled for the first time in 1955, in a promotional brochure, "nonprofit organizations."[2] By the time they published their brochure, Cresap, McCormick and Paget, one of the three leading U.S. management consulting firms, had reorganized dozens of nonprofit organizations including St. Paul's School (1948), the New York Public Library (1949), Yale University (1950), the Republican Party (1951), the Presbyterian Church of the U.S.A. (1952), the Rockefeller Institute for Medical Research (1953), the American Civil Liberties Union (1954), and the Metropolitan Museum of Art (1955).[3] Although these organizations did not yet see themselves as a unified "third sector" of the American economy, the consultants at Cresap, McCormick and Paget understood that this was a distinct sector of the economy – one with growing power and substantial potential profits for consultants.

The management consultants at Cresap, McCormick and Paget had good reasons for focusing on nonprofit institutions in the 1940s and 1950s. Despite the relatively small size of the sector at that time, no portion of the American economy was growing faster than nonprofits during the immediate postwar era. While total business employment rose by 32 percent between 1940 and 1960, the number of people working in the nonprofit sector quietly surged by 121 percent over these same two decades.[4] In 1954, Cresap, McCormick and Paget estimated that the potential demand by nonprofits for consulting studies, then approximately one-twelfth of total demand, would increase by a factor of ten, eventually comprising a quarter of all demand for their services.[5] The nonprofit sector's explosive growth in institutional numbers, organizational size, and employee budgets represented a remarkable opportunity for management consultants – after all, organizational problems tended to accompany such rapid institutional growth, and consultants offered nonprofit institutions ready-made answers for their administrative headaches. In the process, management consulting firms introduced specific business models, like decentralization and sophisticated forms of cost accounting, originally developed in large private companies, to the rapidly growing nonprofit sector.[6]

Sociologists trying to analyze the increasing similarity of the structures of nonprofit and for-profit institutions have frequently invoked the bureaucratic models of Max Weber and the structural-functionalism of Talcott Parsons to explain the convergence of structural forms among private enterprise, government, and philanthropic associations in the postwar era.[7] This similarity, I argue, is due less to a teleological drive toward a single, rational, bureaucratic model shared by all large organizations than management consultants' intentional sale of business structures and techniques, first developed for corporate giants, to the burgeoning nonprofit sector.

Indeed, organizational sociologists call this process, "mimetic institutional isomorphism" and describe the process in virtually identical terms: "large organizations choose from a relatively small set of major consulting firms which, like Johnny Appleseeds, spread a few organizational models throughout the land."[8] The work of management consulting firms, then, helps to explain why bureaucratic institutions in the nonprofit sector adopted similar managerial styles despite initial organizational differences.

Cresap, McCormick and Paget's work was most influential among colleges and universities ranging from Yale University to the University of California, so the analysis of the firm's work for academic institutions will occupy a disproportionate share of this chapter. Bear in mind, however, that the consulting firm also conducted many important studies of cultural institutions, nonprofit associations, religious orders, and hospitals.[9] As Cresap, McCormick and Paget carried crucial business techniques into the nonprofit sector in the 1950s and 1960s, the consulting firm's recommendations changed these influential institutions and created a more homogeneous nonprofit sector.

## The Growth of Cresap, McCormick and Paget

When its three partners founded Cresap, McCormick and Paget in 1946, the young firm entered a rapidly growing field already dominated by a handful of management consulting firms, like Booz Allen & Hamilton and McKinsey & Company, that promoted themselves to business executives as experts in bureaucratic organization, operational techniques, and cost accounting.[10] By the 1930s, hundreds of chief executives of large corporations including Armour, U.S. Steel, Kroger, Carrier, Johnson Wax, and the occasional nonprofit organization like the University of Chicago Medical School and the American Red Cross, had hired "management engineering" firms to rethink their strategy, structure, and financial performance.[11] While the large management consulting firms did not reject jobs from large nonprofits, neither did they focus on marketing themselves to the nonprofit sector.

Cresap, McCormick and Paget grew rapidly in the immediate postwar years by looking beyond the business sector to the government and nonprofit sectors of the growing American economy. As the last chapter described, both Mark Cresap and Richard Paget had previously worked for the consulting firm of Booz Allen & Hamilton before they resigned to join the military during World War II. Richard Paget and Willard McCormick worked together in the Navy as management engineers, while Mark Cresap served as a colonel in charge of administrative management for the Army.[12] By February 1947, only one year after forming their partnership, Cresap, McCormick and Paget was a thriving management consulting firm with six young consultants on staff and Smith Barney, Champion Paper, United Air Lines, and Ford Motor Company among its first-year clients.[13] Nevertheless, despite all their success in securing important business clients and in the publicity that came from their work for the Hoover Commission, it would be the partners' decision to market Cresap, McCormick and Paget to the nonprofit sector that would secure the firm's national reputation for the next two decades.

The trustees of the major nonprofit organizations, many of whom worked for large corporations in New York, hoped that management consultants could solve the administrative problems of the prestigious nonprofit institutions that were growing so rapidly in the late 1940s. Initially, it was the trustees from the most elite, national, nonprofit institutions, like St. Paul's School, Yale University, and the Colonial Williamsburg Foundation, who hired the consultants from Cresap, McCormick and Paget because the leading institutions had access to both the networks of professionals and the financial resources that the less powerful nonprofits lacked.[14] As a result, the firm of Cresap, McCormick and Paget, worked backward from the most elite institutions to the less prestigious organizations in its conquest of the nonprofit sector. The consultants from Cresap,

McCormick and Paget's began their conquest of the nonprofit sector by working for the prestigious East Coast educational institutions whose trustees represented New York's corporate elite.

### Rethinking Educational Institutions

As Merle Curti and Roderick Nash pointed out in 1965, the influence of business executives on higher education "grew phenomenally" in the immediate postwar years as corporations became an important source of revenue and businessmen assumed greater influence on the boards of American colleges and universities.[15] As Cresap, McCormick and Paget wrote in a 1954 internal review of their work in the nonprofit sector:

> Work in the [nonprofit] field has important values beyond the immediate assignments. The boards of trustees of universities, for example, are made up of top business men, some of whom are on the boards of Cresap, McCormick and Paget client firms. This relationship builds better public relations for the firm as a whole.[16]

It is not surprising, then, that Cresap, McCormick and Paget's first nonprofit assignment was for St. Paul's School, a preparatory school that C. Wright Mills identified with the handful of boarding schools that produced the "power elite" in the 1950s.[17] Indeed, over the next twenty years, educational institutions would remain the largest market for Cresap, McCormick and Paget in the nonprofit sector and, mirroring the rest of the firm's work in the sector, the most prestigious educational institutions hired management consultants first. Eventually, Cresap, McCormick and Paget's success with colleges and universities prompted the firm to print brochures on their work for educational institutions, and their reputation led to the firm's few international assignments in the nonprofit sector.[18]

In June 1948, Charles Dickey, the treasurer of St. Paul's School and a partner of J. P. Morgan & Company, began negotiating with

Richard Paget for Cresap, McCormick and Paget "to make a study of some of the business problems" at his boyhood alma mater.[19] The trustees of St. Paul's, a boarding school in Concord, New Hampshire, hired the management consulting firm to reduce the school's projected budget deficit of over $100,000, but specifically excluded the consulting firm from considering academic efficiency. As Cresap, McCormick and Paget's report put it, in typically stilted prose, "the Trustees desire the same effectiveness as would be expected in an effective business organization."[20] How Charles Dickey and Reeve Schley, a St. Paul's trustee and vice-president at Chase National Bank, came to select Cresap, McCormick and Paget is not clear, but both Dickey and Schley were bankers in New York and commercial bankers often recommended management consultants to their clients in need of organizational advice.

Cresap, McCormick and Paget's survey of St. Paul's School, completed in December 1948, recommended drastic cuts in the school's nonacademic staff in order to save $72,100 annually.[21] The consultants noted that in comparison with thirty other prep schools, St. Paul's had the "most costly" dining halls, despite having already replaced their waitresses with student workers.[22] By cutting the overall food bills, consolidating the kitchens, and "eliminating dishwiping," consultants estimated that St. Paul's could cut its costs by $24,600 or 22 percent of its annual deficit. Cresap, McCormick and Paget's other recommendations included reductions in the janitorial staff ($18,500 in savings), eliminating several health service employees (to save $9,800), and reducing the overall use of utilities (for $6,000 in savings). As trustee Reeve Schley wrote after reading a first draft of the report, "we could really obtain some substantial savings in operations but [we] will have to put the knife in pretty deep."[23] The trustees and Henry Kittredge, the headmaster of St. Paul's, decided to use the knife. They found the report "admirable" and agreed to put most of its forty-six separate recommendations into effect.[24]

In the winter of 1949, only a few months after Cresap, McCormick and Paget submitted their final report, St. Paul's fired thirty people including "janitors, kitchen-workers, dormitory maids, and power-house and shop employees, in addition to members of the Infirmary, commissary, and housekeeping staffs."[25] According to the school's headmaster, these changes produced "no perceptible jolts or jars" and got off to an "auspicious start."[26] Clearly Charles Dickey, the trustee responsible for bringing Cresap, McCormick and Paget to St. Paul's School, was satisfied with the consulting firm's suggestions since only one year later he arranged for the consultants at Cresap, McCormick and Paget to perform an organizational survey of Yale University, his other alma mater.[27]

Cresap, McCormick and Paget's emphasis on reducing staff wages, speeding up their work, and cutting the cost of utilities at St. Paul's School was, in a sense, a return to some of the older Taylorist practices of "scientific management." By the 1940s, efficiency engineering firms like Harrington Emerson & Company and Miller, Franklin, Basset & Company, which promised to cut costs through stop-watch studies and wage incentives on the shopfloor, had largely been supplanted by "management engineering" firms, like McKinsey & Company, which focused on reorganizing the structure of large, bureaucratic organizations from the top down.[28] Because St. Paul's limited Cresap, McCormick and Paget's survey to "the whole question of maintenance – heat, food, bookkeeping and the like," their study focused on identifying excessive operating costs such as the repair of vandalized postboxes by students who forgot their keys.[29] Although Cresap, McCormick and Paget could easily locate tangible savings in the process, the firm's survey of St. Paul's did little to alter the structural causes for the school's long-standing problems. Perhaps realizing its own strengths and weaknesses, in subsequent studies of educational institutions, Cresap, McCormick and Paget tended to emphasize long-term structural change over itemized cost savings.

Cresap, McCormick and Paget continued to work for elite prep schools like Andover and Exeter Academies, but it was the firm's work for colleges and universities that grew most rapidly in the immediate postwar years. In 1950, following a trial survey of Colgate University in 1949, the Carnegie Corporation offered to pay half the cost of administrative surveys at several leading universities including Johns Hopkins and Vanderbilt.[30] As Charles Dollard, the head of Carnegie at the time, later remembered the foundation's experiment:

> We got a little sick of hearing trustees say that the colleges and universities wouldn't need so much money if they were well managed, so we decided to see how well managed they were.... [Management consultants] didn't solve anybody's problems, but they did seem to demonstrate that the colleges were about as well managed as most businesses.[31]

The Carnegie Corporation's interest in outside surveys was a tremendous boost for Cresap, McCormick and Paget. By underwriting the cost of outside consulting studies, the foundation almost single-handedly created a new market for "college management surveys." As Dollard later said: "that turned out to be sort of path-breaking, because a great many colleges then undertook to have these studies done. Cresap, McCormick and Paget finally set up a whole division that did nothing but academic studies."[32] As a further boost for the young consulting firm, the Carnegie Corporation recommended Cresap, McCormick and Paget as the management consulting firm best qualified to work with academic institutions in the letters that it sent to universities proposing to underwrite half of the cost of an outside survey.[33]

In 1951, the trustees of the Johns Hopkins University negotiated with the Carnegie Commission to split the cost of a $25,000 survey of "the business operations and administration" of the university's main campus, a study which Cresap, McCormick and Paget would perform.[34] The consulting firm's voluminous study of Johns

Hopkins's arts and sciences campus, Homewood, took seven months, during which six management consultants visited Johns Hopkins under Richard Paget's supervision. Cresap, McCormick and Paget studied virtually every administrative unit of the university except the Medical School, and included in its survey the library, the bookstore, the administration, student aid, the athletic program, the university press, and outside contracting through the Advanced Physics Laboratory. The final report, hundreds of pages long, suggested 115 changes that Cresap, McCormick and Paget estimated would save $127,000 annually.[35] Just as trustees of St. Paul's had agreed with Cresap, McCormick and Paget's proposals for saving money, so too did the trustees of Johns Hopkins conclude that the survey of Homewood was "most acceptable" and urged the university administration to put the firm's cost-saving proposals into effect "with enthusiasm and without delay."[36]

Cresap, McCormick and Paget's survey of Johns Hopkins was a mixture of cost-cutting recommendations and suggested changes to the university's organization, and it was the latter, not the former, that university administrators believed were the most successful. Hopkins officials accepted Cresap, McCormick and Paget's advice about structural changes but balked at the consulting firm's detailed suggestions on how to cut costs. Thus, although Johns Hopkins's board of trustees readily adopted a more egalitarian committee system and its president revised the organizational structure of the university, there was resistance to cost-cutting. The director of the Johns Hopkins Press wrote a scathing response to Cresap, McCormick and Paget's report labeling it "of no value." The University Librarian dismissed the study as "a terrible waste of time, theirs and ours, a profligate waste of money, and a flagrant misuse of information."[37] The organizational changes did not put the knife in as deeply as the suggested cost-cutting measures in the library and press. The university provost concluded that, "the value of the report diminished rapidly in those areas where it came closest to affecting the academic program. Its least valuable – and most controversial – sections were those relating to the Library and the Press."[38] He wryly noted that, "the results you obtain from management engineers are likely to be related closely to the quality of the personnel assigned to the job. We were generally fortunate in this respect, but the quality of the team of six or seven which visited us was not uniform throughout."[39]

This was a problem that none of the management consulting firms could avoid entirely. Firms like Cresap, McCormick and Paget wanted their nonprofit clients to believe that they were buying a "uniform" product, but the individual parts of the survey were necessarily performed by different consultants with varying amounts of experience or skill. In the case of Cresap, McCormick and Paget's study of Johns Hopkins, consultant John Draper performed both the survey of the library and the university press, while John Batchelor, the project supervisor, wrote the sections on the organization of the university and its related institutional divisions.[40] As Johns Hopkins's provost, Stewart Macaulay, concluded in his evaluation of the survey, a university had to buy "the package" the consultants had to offer. By hiring a consulting firm, not an individual consultant, the university was assured of a minimal level of quality, but neither a university nor an industrial corporation could ensure that the results would be uniform.

University administrators consistently agreed that Cresap, McCormick and Paget was most effective in giving organizational advice; yet these same administrators were hesitant to admit that outside surveys were a necessity. Both President A. Whitney Griswold of Yale and President Lowell Reed of Johns Hopkins responded with muted praise to confidential inquiries from President Wallace Sterling of Stanford and President Harold Dodds of Princeton about Cresap, McCormick and Paget's work.[41] Even more damning was Dwight Eisenhower's description of an $80,000 consulting report on Columbia University as, "the most expensive and least read book the university ever acquired."[42] According to Stewart

Macaulay, the provost of Johns Hopkins, the value of the surveys was not in the recommendations that they put forward but in their tendency to "stir things up," forcing employees to reexamine their practices and "eliminating complacency."[43] President Everett Case of Colgate agreed, arguing that Cresap, McCormick and Paget's study of Colgate had been helpful because the management consultants put forward "a series of concrete propositions" that served to "stimulate and accelerate the search for still more effective answers."[44] On the other hand, trustees may have been less interested in the "process" of the outside survey than they were in the final results. Provost Stuart Macaulay thus felt the need to prepare a lengthy report for the Johns Hopkins trustees describing his administration's response to the consultants' proposals, often justifying at length his decision not to follow Cresap, McCormick and Paget's suggestions.

Cresap, McCormick and Paget's surveys of Johns Hopkins and Yale, both university-wide surveys of the nonacademic activities of East Coast research universities in the early 1950s, showed remarkable similarity in both the organization of the reports and in their conclusions. Cresap, McCormick and Paget patterned their organizational studies for nonprofits after their surveys of large businesses and, as a result, the consulting firm argued that very clear lines of authority were crucial within all organizations. Of course, academic institutions traditionally operated with a greater degree of informality than large corporations; but in both surveys, Cresap, McCormick and Paget pointed out in their section on "administrative organization" that neither Yale nor Hopkins had a formal organizational plan.[45] Indeed, Cresap, McCormick and Paget constructed the two reports in such a parallel fashion that the consulting firm made this identical point on the same page in the same section (section III, page 4) of both surveys. Cresap, McCormick and Paget's solution in both cases was to create an organizational chart to represent the current administrative structure and then to create a second chart to illustrate their suggested changes. These organizational charts, as

Cresap, McCormick and Paget devised them, would not have looked out of place in the boardroom of most American corporations.

Yale and Johns Hopkins had different structural problems, yet Cresap, McCormick and Paget identified many similarities. Hopkins, because of its reliance on military contracting, received only 10 percent of its revenues from student tuition, while Yale depended on its students for 45 percent of its income.[46] Despite this and other differences, the two universities' shared certain problems – overburdened provosts, excessive staff decentralization, and conflicting committee structures. Many of Cresap, McCormick and Paget's suggested changes for the two institutions were thus virtually identical. For example, Cresap, McCormick and Paget recommended that both Yale and Johns Hopkins create the position of Dean of Students under the Provost to oversee the directors of student health, the registrars office, athletics, and admissions. Although Cresap, McCormick and Paget would have argued that functional needs entirely explained this proposal, the degree of uniformity in the plans appears to have gone beyond what could be explained functionally. Instead, I believe the management consultants had in mind a preconceived model of the appropriate organizational structure for any research university. It is easy to understand why administrators worried that Cresap, McCormick and Paget's studies might be overreliant on these preformulated ideas. As President Harold Dodds of Princeton voiced his concern: "when it came to the administrative job of deans, assistant deans, and departmental organizations, that sort of thing, I felt that they had a formula and that these formulas were dangerous things to live with."[47] University administrators wanted the outsider perspective and insider knowledge that management consulting firms like Cresap, McCormick and Paget promised, but they feared that consultants would impose a generic organizational model on their unique institutions.

Ironically, it was precisely these "formulas" that made Cresap, McCormick and Paget so valuable to the universities. The templates provided the university and it administrators with a perspective that they would not otherwise obtain. Norman Sidney Buck, the Master of Branford College at Yale, acknowledged that he could only acquire Cresap, McCormick and Paget's knowledge of other institutional practices "by the expenditure of an inordinate amount of time," and even if he could acquire their perspective, an identical "plan recommended by Paget would and should carry much more weight" with Yale's trustees.[48] It was their experience with other institutions, and organizational models, that made management consultants so valuable to the trustees.

### Selling Decentralization to Universities

In the 1950s and 1960s, management consultants repeatedly recommended that large organizations adopt the decentralized model, an organizational "formula" that came to dominate American industrial companies: by 1967, 86 percent of the 500 largest companies in America had adopted the decentralized organizational model.[49] Executives from large corporations like General Motors, Sears, and DuPont developed the decentralized, or "multidivisional," form during the 1920s in order to manage their national, multiproduct companies.[50] Other executives who wanted to install the same structure in their companies learned more about it from Peter Drucker's 1946 best-seller, *The Concept of the Corporation*, which described how General Motors decentralized by dividing its product lines (Chevrolet, Buick, Cadillac, etc.) into autonomous divisions that competed against one another yet were ultimately responsible to the chief executive officer.[51]

As historian Alfred Chandler has written, even if corporate executives recognized the form of the multidivisional model, they generally hired the leading management consulting firms to help them install it in their companies.[52] Consultants from Booz Allen & Hamilton decentralized IBM in 1956, Cresap, McCormick and Paget divisionalized Westinghouse in 1951, and McKinsey & Company installed the multidivisional structure in Chrysler in the 1950s.[53]

Management consultants thus believed in the virtues of decentralized organization and, in the words of DiMaggio and Powell, "like Johnny Appleseeds," they spread it among the institutions for whom they worked, including those in the nonprofit sector.[54]

Like many of the large businesses that wanted to divisionalize in the 1950s, the University of California system hired Cresap, McCormick and Paget to help it decentralize its administration of local campuses.[55] "The establishment of new campuses and the enlargement of existing campuses," the president of the University of California explained in 1959, "will increase the need, already apparent, for decentralization of the University's administration."[56] In their survey of the university's organization, Cresap, McCormick and Paget found that although administrators agreed that decentralization was a good idea, and they had already begun the transfer of authority to the local campuses, many of the smaller campuses remained unprepared for their new administrative duties and their lines of authority remained muddled.[57] The management consulting firm's solution was to prepare a statement of "basic organizational principles" that clearly defined the fundamental tenets of decentralized authority (for example: "No person should be responsible in a line capacity to more than one supervisor") and Cresap, McCormick and Paget devised generic organizational plans for large and small campuses, like the one illustrated here, that could be superimposed on both existing and future branches of the university.[58] These model campuses encouraged administrators to rapidly enlarge the University of California system in the early 1960s.

The generic organizational charts that Cresap, McCormick and Paget devised for the individual campuses at the University of California in 1959 resemble the plans that the firm developed for Yale and Johns Hopkins in the early 1950s, while the consulting firm's plan for the central administrative organization of the University of California system looked much like the decentralized structure that McKinsey & Company installed at Shell Oil in 1959 (see Figure 5.1).[59] Indeed, the university president's

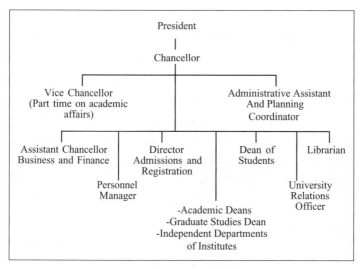

Figure 5.1. Chart of Proposed Organization for University of California System Campus (1959).

description of the advantages of decentralization could even have been lifted from Shell's corporate manual: with divisionalization, "the Vice-Presidents and other state-wide officers can concentrate their attention on development of University policy and on review of performance; and that the day-to-day operating decisions will be made close to the campus which they concern."[60] Administrators at the University of California, like those at Shell Oil, could focus on the strategic direction of the university system while still overseeing campuses as geographically and administratively diverse as Berkeley, Riverside, and Davis. The consultants from Cresap, McCormick and Paget grafted the decentralized structure of an industrial company onto the main branches of American higher education.

The college and university practice at Cresap, McCormick and Paget thrived through the 1960s, yet the firm faced a continuing problem in the market for management consulting services. Even though Ivy League institutions, like Cornell and Columbia, and public universities, like the University of Toronto and the University of Washington, continued to hire Cresap, McCormick and Paget in the 1960s, the firm had reason to be worried about the future.

It was focusing almost exclusively on the administrative organization of universities.[61] Once the firm had restructured a university, the administrators rarely called the consulting firm back a second time. Indeed when Norman Sidney Buck, master of Branford College, suggested in a letter to A. Whitney Griswold that they bring Cresap, McCormick and Paget back to advise Yale University on its fundraising techniques, President Griswold noted in the margins that Buck had missed the point: "we don't want to commit ourselves to Paget in advance – merely to find out all he knows about practices elsewhere...."[62] Although management consultants, particularly The Boston Consulting Group, had preempted this problem with their corporate clients by successfully convincing business executives of the value of "strategy consulting," as the demand for organizational consulting dried up in the 1960s, the consultants found it hard to do this with colleges and universities. Unfortunately colleges and universities hardly ever hired consultants to advise them on their long-term planning.[63] McKinsey & Company's domination of the European market for structural advice in the late 1960s had a similar problem. Because Cresap, McCormick and Paget had reorganized so many educational institutions in the 1950s and 1960s, the firm simply ran out of potential clients. The twenty year boom in higher education had begun to slow down. In the meantime, the consultants at Cresap, McCormick and Paget began to look elsewhere for new clients and turned to what might appear the most unlikely consumers of innovative management methods: religious denominations and churches.

### Religious Denominations

If Cresap, McCormick and Paget wanted access to the power elite in the United States, the consulting firm could hardly have done better than to work for St. Paul's School, Yale University, or the Presbyterian Church in the 1950s.[64] Headquartered in New York City in the 1950s, the Presbyterian Church included in their congregation one-fourth of the "metropolitan 400" (the most elite urban families in Manhattan), and a disproportionate share of the leading business executives.[65] Like the consulting firm's work in the rest of the non-profit sector, the Presbyterian Church was an organization associated with wealth and power, yet intently concerned with lowering its expenses by using outside consultants.

American Presbyterians have been remarkably open to organizational change throughout their history – an observation that led the religious historian Richard Reifsnyder to entitle his study of the Northern Presbyterians "The Reorganizational Impulse."[66] Since they founded the American Presbyterian Church in 1788, Presbyterian leaders have restructured the church five times (in the 1830s, 1870s, 1920s, 1950s, and the late 1960s [this includes Cresap, McCormick and Paget's survey of the church's administration in 1952]). In the twentieth century, Presbyterian leaders pressed the church to adopt organizational techniques originally developed by corporate managers to remake its administration in the image of a modern corporation.[67] For example, at the height of the scientific management movement in 1912, the church's executive commission recommended that the Presbyterian General Assembly employ an "efficiency expert" to "devise the very best methods of conducting our church business in the manner most efficient and economical."[68] Of course Presbyterians were not the only religious denomination to borrow models from the corporate world in the twentieth century. Indeed all of the major American Christian denominations including the Episcopalians, Baptists, Congregationalists, Methodists, Lutherans, and Catholics adopted corporate models during the twentieth century to coordinate their finances and church administration.[69] By the time that Northern Presbyterian administrators brought in Cresap, McCormick and Paget in June 1951, the Presbyterian Church of the USA was already a highly bureaucratic, centralized institution modeled after the business world.[70]

Cresap, McCormick and Paget's survey of the "business methods" in the Presbyterian Church found very little to criticize in the administration of the Office of the General Assembly in New York.[71] The management consultants estimated that their thirty-seven suggestions would produce only $10,000 a year in net savings. The Stated Clerk of the General Assembly, the highest administrative office in the Northern Presbyterian Church, agreed, pointing to the underpaid staff and antiquated offices as signs of an extremely budget-conscious administration.[72] The management consultants from Cresap, McCormick and Paget believed that improved organizational control and employee morale would result from adding new equipment and furniture. The benefits the consultants cited, however, were more closely related to improved organizational efficiency than lower administrative costs. If Chairman of the Budget and Finance Committee Samuel Slaymaker, who commissioned the survey, hoped that the study would cut expenses, he must have been disappointed. The fees for Cresap, McCormick and Paget's survey of the church no doubt exceeded the annual savings from the firm's recommendations.[73]

University administrators at Johns Hopkins and Yale had argued that the benefits of an outside survey by consultants flowed from the internal process of self-examination, not the specific suggestions of the consulting firm. From this perspective, Cresap, McCormick and Paget's survey of the Presbyterian Church was a resounding success. Presbyterian administrators took Cresap, McCormick and Paget's suggestions very seriously, poring over them "with a view to their possible applicability to the Board's organization and procedures."[74] Of the thirty-seven recommendations made by Cresap, McCormick and Paget (only thirty-three of which fell within the purview of the New York administration) the executive board eventually accepted eleven, rejected six, and indefinitely postponed their decision on the remaining sixteen.[75] Whether it was the number of annual reports to print, centralizing their finances through a single bank in New York, or the installation of a common phone system, Presbyterian administrators debated the proposed changes at length.[76]

Cresap, McCormick and Paget did not do another study of a religious denomination for fifteen years. Although such outside surveys of religious organizations were not widespread – after all, the Southern Presbyterian Church also hired a management consultant to help them reorganize in 1947 – they did not become common until the late 1960s.[77] In the meantime, Cresap, McCormick and Paget advertised that they were "experienced in solving the management problems of churches," but the consulting firm did not believe in the mid-1950s that surveys of religious organizations would ever bring in even a small percentage of their revenues.[78]

All this changed in the late 1960s, however, when the major religious denominations responded to widespread dissatisfaction with their missions by launching internal self-examinations. Like Vatican II in the Catholic Church, these efforts were designed to make the churches rethink their structure and purpose. Frequently, the denominations hired management consultants to guide them through the process of creating a new organization to match their new goals. The Episcopal Church, for example, hired Booz Allen & Hamilton in 1967 "to make recommendations about structural and personnel changes," the Society of Jesus (the Jesuits) used consultants from Arthur D. Little, Inc. in 1968, to help them conduct a study of the future development of "manpower and financial resources" in their Chicago Province, and the U.S. Catholic Conference hired Booz Allen & Hamilton in 1967 to rethink its social and religious mission.[79]

Cresap, McCormick and Paget also worked for a variety of religious denominations in the late 1960s, and its studies, like the ones performed by the other large management consulting firms, focused on the changing mission of the denominations. Consultants from Cresap, McCormick and Paget studied the organization and mission of the Mennonite Board of Education, recommending that the church expand its educational programs to include voca-tional and technical training.[80] In contrast, consultants from Cresap, McCormick and Paget suggested that the School Sisters of Notre Dame close down several schools because of the predicted staff short-falls in the aging Catholic sisterhood.[81] In both cases, the consultants evaluated the market for education in light of the religious denom-ination's changing mission – as one newspaper article described Cresap, McCormick and Paget's work with Sacred Heart convents in New York and Chicago: "now, after almost 200 years of catering to the upper crust, they're leaping into the ghetto."[82]

Consultants pointed out that religious organizations frequently entered other nonprofit industries, like education or health care, for valid reasons, but over time became swamped by the economics of these other auxiliary industries, a development that drained the coffers of the religious order in the process. For example, Cresap, McCormick and Paget's 1974 study of the hospitals managed by the Church of Jesus Christ of Latter-Day Saints (the Mormons) rec-ommended that "the church disassociate itself from hospital own-ership and operation" by spinning off the hospitals into a separate nonprofit corporation and relieving the Mormons of further capital expenditures.[83] Cresap, McCormick and Paget argued that a separate nonprofit organization could accept funds from the federal govern-ment and enter into relationships with other hospitals like the Medi-cal School at the University of Utah, with fewer administrative prob-lems. This study of a hospital system within a religious organization illustrated the very real economic decisions that nonprofit admin-istrators faced as they competed with rival institutions both within and outside of the nonprofit sector.

## Cultural Institutions

In cultural institutions, as in for-profit businesses, when the board of trustees appointed a new chief executive, the installation of a new executive was often accompanied by the employment of external management consultants. There were two ways that such a transition in leadership might lead to a management consulting study. Sometimes the overseeing board hired a management consulting firm, as happened in the New York Philharmonic in 1956, to report on existing practices to the incoming executive.[84] For example, the Presbyterian Church hired Cresap, McCormick and Paget for precisely this reason in 1951 – the General Council had just appointed a new Stated Clerk of the General Assembly and they wanted to make sure that existing office practices were cost-effective.[85] In other cases, incoming presidents hired consultants to restructure the organization to reflect their management style. This was rarely the case for new nonprofit administrators, but new executives in business and government often used consultants to this end. Both Thomas Watson, Jr., who became president of IBM in 1956, and Robert McNamara, who took over the World Bank in the early 1970s, immediately hired management consultants to reshape their organizations to reflect their vision for the proper direction for those institutions.[86] At the New York Philharmonic, however, the Board of Directors faced a crisis that, unlike the proclaimed "crisis" that motivated Robert McNamara to hire McKinsey & Company to reorganize the World Bank, came from external financial and critical pressures, not internal doubts about the organization's mission and organizations.

When the Board of Trustees of the New York Philharmonic hired Cresap, McCormick and Paget in January 1956, the management consulting survey followed several seasons of declining royalties from record sales, falling attendance at concerts, and, perhaps most significant for the consultants, the board's shake-up of the administration.[87] By 1956, the Philharmonic was in real trouble – the symphony's recording royalties had steadily dropped from $91,823 in the 1949–50 season to $33,300 in the 1954–5 season, even as total concert attendance declined from 252,000 to 228,000 over the same five-year period.[88] Unfortunately, the symphony's problems were not just with its management but were a product, as well, of the orchestra's disappointing performances.[89] As critic Paul Henry Lang wrote in the *Herald Tribune* in June of 1956, "it becomes more apparent with each season that our orchestra, the New York Philharmonic-Symphony, is a deteriorating artistic institution."[90] Confronted by these problems, the trustees moved to turn things around in early 1956: they installed David Keiser as the new president, agreed to participate in the development of Lincoln Center, hired Leonard Bernstein to become the symphony's guest conductor, and commissioned Cresap, McCormick and Paget to make a survey of the symphony's administration.[91]

All of the trustees' decisions proved excellent in hindsight. Howard Shanet, the historian of the Philharmonic, argues that Bernstein's directorship in combination with better management under the new President completely transformed the symphony.[92] Cresap, McCormick and Paget's survey was only one part of the many important changes that the trustees made. In this case, the consultants functioned as a double-check against changes already underway, making sure that the trustees were doing everything they could to improve the Philharmonic. Even so, the trustees acknowledged that Cresap, McCormick and Paget's suggested changes to the organization, its accounting procedures, and committee structure were "valuable recommendations," and they put most of the management consulting firm's suggestions into effect by mid-1957.[93]

A different problem confronted the Board of Governors of the Philadelphia Museum College of Art, which hired Cresap, McCormick and Paget in 1957 to help it decide if the trustees should separate the school from the central art museum.[94] The founding governors who chartered the Philadelphia Museum of Art in 1875 intended to create a textile and art school in the city, but the institution shifted its focus from education to collection in the 1920s after several wealthy donors bequeathed large art collections to the museum.[95] After new trustees, more interested in the art than in education, joined the board of the museum in the 1930s, the independent trustees of what became the Philadelphia College of Textiles broke away from the museum in frustration over the institution's changing mission. The trustees of the college who hired Cresap, McCormick and Paget to survey the school in 1957 also hoped to separate from the museum and believed that the consulting firm's study would be the first step toward their goal.

Cresap, McCormick and Paget's survey of the Philadelphia Museum College of Art was like any number of the firm's other surveys of educational institutions. For example, the consultants suggested, as they had at Johns Hopkins and Yale, that administrators create the position of Dean of Students "to coordinate related student functions."[96] What was unusual about this survey was that the trustees of the school did not push to make most of the changes that Cresap, McCormick and Paget had recommended until after they had decided to spin off the Philadelphia College of Art from the museum nearly six years later.[97] As a result, Cresap, McCormick and Paget's report became a planning document for the newly separated educational institution, not a set of immediate administrative changes to the ongoing school. With this report, Cresap, McCormick and Paget had created an administrative structure for a nonprofit organization that did not yet exist.

### Associations

In the mid-1950s, the market for management consulting surveys of nonprofits became much more competitive just as it had in the market for government surveys. Cresap, McCormick and Paget had never had a monopoly over nonprofit surveys, and the competition for these assignments increased as the other leading management consulting firms came to realize how fast the sector was expanding. In 1955, a year after it had forecasted a tenfold growth in the market for consulting services to nonprofits, Cresap, McCormick and Paget published the first of several brochures aimed exclusively at

these organizations.[98] At the same time, other management consulting firms like A. T. Kearney & Company, began working for professional associations, like the American Institute of Physics and the
American Chemical Society, helping these national nonprofit organizations to restructure the administration of their central offices.[99]
Nevertheless, Cresap, McCormick and Paget remained, for a time,
the leading choice for associations, both in volume and prestige, in
the mid-1950s – after all, the firm had restructured the New York
YWCA and the American Civil Liberties Union in 1955 before
working for the American Cancer Society in 1956.

Then, however, the firm began to face tougher competition. The
American Cancer Society, for example, hired Cresap, McCormick
and Paget based on factors other than a recommendation from a former client or one of their trustees. Instead, the board of directors
solicited three management consulting firms based in New York –
Stevenson, Jordan & Harrison; Cresap, McCormick and Paget; and
McKinsey & Company – to submit proposals for a study of the
society's New York office.[100] The trustees felt little need to justify
their decision to hire outside consultants, but consulting firms like
Cresap, McCormick and Paget increasingly needed to explain to
trustees why their firm was better for a specific assignment than other
well-known competitors. This process of competitive bidding contributed to a trend that consultants already faced in the government
and business sectors – corporations were increasingly hiring specialized consulting firms to solve discrete problems instead of hiring a
single firm to make a comprehensive general survey of their organization. Among nonprofit organizations, Cresap, McCormick and
Paget's general surveys remained the norm, but even professional
associations like the American Chemical Society were hiring consultants for specific studies in the 1950s.[101]

Cresap, McCormick and Paget's work for the American Cancer
Society looked much like its survey of the Presbyterian Church,
although the consultants found considerably more potential for cost

savings in the society. By eliminating twenty-five staff members, and adding only six additional staff to offset these losses, the consultants estimated that the association could save $100,000 a year.[102] Although the potential savings were considerable, they did not represent a large percentage of the association's expenditures – a fact that Cresap, McCormick and Paget emphasized in their report to the board of trustees.[103] It was important for the consultants to reassure the association of the cost-effectiveness of their advice. In this case, the society used the opportunity to promote its own efficiency, proudly quoting Cresap, McCormick and Paget's conclusion that the "'study did not reveal any gross overstaffing or major inefficiencies' in the operations of the National Society," in their 1956 Annual Report.[104] Thus, a management consulting study could be used for external as well as internal reason, to improve administration or to prove to outsiders that they carefully shepherded their finances – or both. The consultants at Cresap, McCormick and Paget understood the importance of boosterism, and they were always careful to praise the overall management of a nonprofit association before they proceeded to describe its specific problems.

Cresap, McCormick and Paget's enthusiasm reached its zenith in its 1954 survey of the University of Pittsburgh. In the final report, the two consultants who made the survey, Walter Vieh and Monty Montgomery, wrote that "the University of Pittsburgh has an unusual opportunity to develop as an outstanding institution of higher education."[105] Clearly, the president of the University of Pittsburgh appreciated the consultants' fervor, and their survey, because he hired consultant Walter Vieh to become Assistant Chancellor of Business Affairs in June 1956, and Vieh, in turn, hired Monty Montgomery as his assistant.[106] Vieh and Montgomery's departure followed a pattern common in the business sector – both James O. McKinsey, who left his firm in 1935 to run Marshall Fields in Chicago, and Mark Cresap, who quit his young firm in 1951 to become Assistant to the President of Westinghouse, chose to leave the partnerships they founded to manage former corporate clients.[107] Between 1955 and 1960, at least eight management consultants left Cresap, McCormick and Paget to work for their former clients.[108] Although the majority of the consultants left to work for corporate clients like Delta, Borden, and TWA, Walter Vieh and Monty Montgomery's departure for the University of Pittsburgh suggests that nonprofits, like businesses, often believed that the consultants who performed the surveys would be the best people to put the survey's suggested changes into effect.

## Hospitals

Unlike the surprising surge in demand for surveys of religious denominations after Vatican II, the upswing in demand for studies by consultants of hospitals in the late 1960s was a long-standing expectation that was finally fulfilled. In 1954, Cresap, McCormick and Paget estimated that surveys of hospitals might eventually make up 14 percent of the total market for consultants' services – more than the rest of the combined nonprofit market. As a result, the management consulting firm marketed itself as an advisor to medical institutions like Georgetown University Hospital in Washington, D.C. and the Rockefeller Institute for Medical Research in New York.[109] Cresap, McCormick and Paget, however, never succeeded in attracting many hospitals as clients. In fact, a large percentage of the hospitals for whom the firm worked, like Georgetown and the Rockefeller Institute, might better be thought of as educational institutions, so closely were their hospital and teaching functions linked. Still, assignments like Cresap, McCormick and Paget's six volume study of Beth Israel Hospital's organization and management in 1957 were tantalizing signs that large nonprofit hospitals might be a source of large and potentially lucrative contracts.[110] In the late 1960s and early 1970s, Cresap, McCormick and Paget started working for more hospitals as increased competition and greater government oversight by programs like Medicare put administrative pressures on these health care institutions.[111] Large hospitals, like Mount Sinai in New York, hired Cresap, McCormick and Paget to help them devise organizational plans better suited to the new commercial pressures than their previous professional arrangements, which focused on superior health care but largely ignored administrative costs.[112]

Cresap, McCormick and Paget's work for Mount Sinai Hospital was a straightforward organizational study. Surveys that focused exclusively on the structure of an organization became more common in the late 1960s and were a sharp contrast with the firm's early studies of office efficiency. As a Cresap, McCormick and Paget partner described the change in the *Wall Street Journal*, whereas "mostly in the past we were called on for housekeeping types of services like personnel administration and grounds functions and food service," large hospitals now called on Cresap, McCormick and Paget for studies of their administrative structure.[113] Mount Sinai needed a new organizational structure because the trustees had decided to found a medical school, an enormous undertaking that would require the board to realign administrative responsibilities between the hospital, the centralized administration, and the new faculty of the medical school.

Mount Sinai's decision to found a medical school in the late 1950s was a radical departure from the norm of university founded medical schools.[114] Historian Kenneth Ludmerer argues that two external pressures drove administrators of the nationally known research hospital to create a medical school. First, doctors at Mount Sinai believed that leading research hospitals would increasingly require access to the basic science of university-based chemists and biologists in order to stay at the vanguard of medical research.[115] Second (and perhaps more interestingly), administrators noted, with irony, that the decline of institutionalized anti-Semitism in America had brought with it more competition for the top Jewish students. This meant that Mount Sinai faced a declining pool of top researchers from which to pick without the captive graduates provided by an internal medical school.[116] The board of trustees' solution, in the late 1950s, was to plan the creation of a new medical school at Mount Sinai, an enormous institutional endeavor that, in turn, required the reorganization of the administration of the entire hospital.

The organizational structure that the trustees finally installed was the result of a series of compromises between the trustees at Mount Sinai and the consultants from Cresap, McCormick and Paget. Dr. S. David Pomrinse was the first person, in 1963, to consider what the institutional structure for the new organization would have to involve and his initial plan became the basis for subsequent discussions between the trustees and the consultants.[117] Although Cresap, McCormick and Paget agreed to Pomrinse's suggestion that the trustees create "The Mount Sinai Medical Center" to oversee both the old hospital and the new medical school, they disagreed that a single administrator could run the two institutions.[118] Cresap, McCormick and Paget's solution, pictured here, looked more like a corporation with line and staff positions and a functional, not divisionalized, organizational structure.

Pomrinse, who had first suggested a new organization for Mount Sinai, disagreed with Cresap, McCormick and Paget's proposed structure for the medical center. Instead, Pomrinse recommended that the consultants' hierarchical structure be collapsed into only two executives, one to head the hospital and one to lead the school (see Figure 5.2), because, in his words, "effective management is not created by the introduction of unnecessary echelons of executives but rather by having as lean an organization as is compatible with the discharge of the duties of the various executives."[119] In other cases where administrators opposed the Cresap, McCormick and Paget's suggested reorganization, executives often ignored the consultants' proposals and created their own solutions. For example, in 1967, the president of the United Negro College Fund, Stephen Wright, disagreed with Cresap, McCormick and Paget's organizational plan and simply set aside their proposed changes.[120] In contrast, the chairman

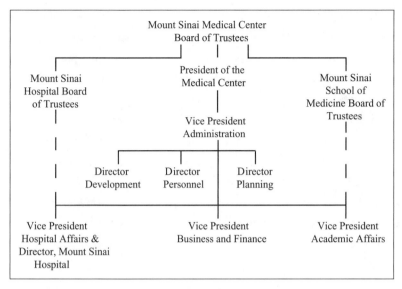

Figure 5.2. Chart of Proposed Organization for Top Management of Mount Sinai in 1967.

of the board of trustees of Mount Sinai, a Goldman Sachs partner named Gustave Levy, had Cresap, McCormick and Paget prepare a revised organizational structure that moved the vice president of Business and Finance to a staff position alongside the directors of Development, Personnel, and Planning.[121]

To help the trustees make the transition to the new organizational structure, the consultants at Cresap, McCormick and Paget created an interim plan "to meet the immediate needs of the medical center."[122] Levy, however, did not let the adhoc administration become complacent and, in May 1969, he directed Cresap, McCormick and Paget to update the long-term organizational plan.[123] Through the process of this organizational survey, Levy was able to change the structure of Mount Sinai without disturbing existing administrators or sidelining the consultants' suggested changes.

These "implementation plans" were a new addition to Cresap, McCormick and Paget's surveys in the late 1960s and helped management consultants make their abstract proposals seem workable within existing organizational structures. Consultants found that these multi-stage plans provided a blueprint for complicated managerial transitions and they used them to great advantage in the 1960s to compete with investment bankers in providing merger advice to large corporations. McKinsey & Company, for example, used detailed schedules and interim plans to help Sun Oil integrate the companies that it acquired in the late 1960s.[124] The practice carried over to the nonprofit sector, which, the consultants discovered, had similar ideas to make smooth transitions to a new organizational structure. In this and other ways, methods and concepts from the corporate sector were being used by the consultants to reshape the nonprofit sector.

## The Decline of Cresap, McCormick and Paget

The decline in the number of studies that Cresap, McCormick and Paget did for nonprofits after the mid-1960s reflected the slowing demand from academic institutions for surveys of their organizational structure, but it was also an outward sign of the internal decline of Cresap, McCormick and Paget as a vibrant consultancy. The partners, who were perhaps looking forward to retirement, tried a number of approaches to revitalize their firm. In 1960, the consultancy entered into negotiations to buy George Fry & Associates, a small but well-respected firm that, like Cresap, McCormick and Paget, had spun off from Booz Allen & Hamilton in the 1940s.[125] The proposed purchase of George Fry & Associates fell through, but, in 1963, Cresap, McCormick and Paget entered into talks to merge with A. T. Kearney & Company, another well-known consulting firm that was the Chicago branch of James O. McKinsey's original management consulting firm.[126] Again the deal fell through and, in 1970, the partners of Cresap, McCormick and Paget, now very close to retirement age, agreed to sell their firm to Citicorp, the large commercial bank headquartered in New York. Where banks had once lost the function of consulting in the 1930s, Citibank tried to buy it back in the 1970s.[127] In less than a decade, therefore, the perspective of the partners of Cresap, McCormick and Paget had shifted from market expansion to market protection to the outright sale of their firm. Although the partners in Cresap, McCormick and Paget were a particularly small circle, and thus particularly vulnerable to the temptation to sell the firm on their retirement, this pattern was common in the governance of management consulting firms as the previously elite consultancies were sold on the retirement or death of their senior partners.

When the remaining partners of Cresap, McCormick and Paget bought the consultancy back from Citicorp in 1977, the firm was a shell of its former self – the firm had lost money in five of the six years that Citicorp managed it and the consultancy had lost many of its best employees.[128] The firm never recovered from its sale to Citicorp. Even though Cresap, McCormick and Paget's eventual corporate successor, Towers Perrin, elected to keep the consulting firm's fancy Park Avenue offices, Towers Perrin eventually decided to drop the once prestigious consulting firm's name.

Interestingly, even when Cresap, McCormick and Paget was losing money in the 1970s, the Institutional Division (which handled nonprofits) remained the consulting firm's strongest practice, accounting for a third of the firm's revenues in any given year. Large nonprofit organizations continued to hire Cresap, McCormick and Paget: in the early 1970s, Dartmouth selected the firm to study the effect of coeducation at Yale and Princeton, Union Memorial Hospital in Baltimore hired the firm to restructure its administration, and the Mormons chose them to reorganize the top administration of the Church of Jesus Christ of Latter-Day Saints.[129] Although the Institutional Division continued to do well, this was not sufficient to maintain the declining organization. By the mid-1970s, with the decline of Cresap, McCormick and Paget as a firm and the rapid growth of rival consultancies like The Boston Consulting Group that offered strategic advice, only a few important nonprofits continued to hire Cresap, McCormick and Paget to survey their organizations.[130]

## Conclusion

Cresap, McCormick and Paget's most successful years working for nonprofit organizations contributed to the widespread perception that "nonprofits" constituted a distinct sector of the economy in the United States. Two factors were crucial in this transformation: political attacks on the tax-exempt status of nonprofit organizations, which culminated in the 1969 Tax Reform Act, and the apparent similarities between the organizational problems of nonprofit institutions, whether they were religious denominations, associations, or museums.[131] Scholars have already described how their defense of threatened tax benefits united American elites and the institutions that they governed during the 1960s even though these institutions previously had very little in common except for their "nonprofit" status in the American tax code. Few academics, however, have investigated how the work of management consultants resulted in a common perception among previously independent institutions that the apparently similar administrative problems identified by consultants and the largely identical solutions that consultants offered meant that they were all part of a common "third sector" of the American economy.[132] By restructuring many of the leading nonprofit organizations in the United States using corporate models, the consultants from Cresap, McCormick and Paget helped to create a universe of institutions that employed the same vocabulary and the same organizational tools in their daily management. Thus, nonprofit organizations accepted the conceptual framework of themselves as a distinct "sector," in large part, because of the work of Cresap, McCormick and Paget and other consulting firms in reorganizing the major American nonprofit organizations in the image of for-profit corporations.

If, as I conclude, the "social construction" of the nonprofit sector partly stemmed from the role of management consultants in disseminating corporate models, this concept has important implications. As the title of this chapter emphasizes, Cresap, McCormick and Paget wanted to find profit in these nonprofits. The firm's declaration that nonprofit organizations were inefficiently managed was central to the consultants' sales pitch. Such "inefficiencies," however, may not have had as much meaning as the consultants suggested. Organizational overcapacity, after all, may actually be a useful characteristic in institutions that are less concerned with economic efficiency than the overwhelming importance of their institutional mission. For example, religious organizations and universities, which emphasize collective (often "inefficient") decision making over streamlined managerial control, have had unmatched organizational longevity lasting for hundreds, if not thousands, of years. Similarly, in universities, Cresap, McCormick and Paget argued that "the variety of management problems faced by university administrators requires the skills of an educator, business executive, and public relations expert," but acknowledged that if the structures of a business were overemphasized, the university's primary mission of academic excellence would suffer.[133] Unfortunately, by adopting the organizational structures of corporations in the postwar era, nonprofit organizations implicitly accepted the consultants' ideology that for-profit business necessarily represented the superior organizational form.[134]

Unlike in business or the state, the consultants within Cresap, McCormick and Paget saw the transfer of organizational models between businesses and nonprofits moving in only one direction. In government, in contrast, while management consultants may have preached the benefits of importing corporate organizational models into the state bureaucracy, in actual practice the consultants in Booz Allen & Hamilton and Cresap, McCormick and Paget carried organizational ideas first developed in the federal government back to the corporate sector when they returned from their government assignments.[135] Although the consultants in Cresap, McCormick and Paget may have argued that "nonprofit organizations usually are more difficult to finance, organize, and operate than business or industrial organizations of comparable size," they clearly did not believe that nonprofit organizations offered any valuable lessons for either business or government organizations.[136] Although business and government were important both as sources of organizational knowledge and as markets for consultants' professional services, consultants only saw nonprofits as a source of revenues and not as a source of organizational knowledge. It is unfortunate, therefore, that management consultants from Cresap, McCormick and Paget emphasized the shortcomings of the nonprofit sector in comparison to the business sector, because this perception, which clearly contributed to the social construction of the nonprofit sector, continues to color contemporary perceptions of nonprofit organizations.[137]

Cresap, McCormick and Paget's decision to seek out assignments among nonprofit organizations had two lasting legacies: the transfer of corporate organizational models by management consultants to many of the largest nonprofit organizations and the resulting perception that nonprofit organizations were a distinct, related set of institutions comprising a third sector of the economy. The historical case studies discussed in this chapter point to the very real organizational efficiencies and financial savings that Cresap, McCormick and Paget's surveys produced in many of the leading nonprofit organizations. What this chapter can only speculate about are the potential benefits that businesses could have reaped had the consultants at Cresap, McCormick and Paget reversed this process of organizational transfer during the 1950s and 1960s and carried the concept of an institutional mission, the central governance device of nonprofits, into the largest American corporations and government agencies.[138]

# SIX

# The Gilded Age of Consulting

## A Snapshot of Consultants Circa 1960

By 1960, the three leading management consulting firms in the United States – Booz Allen & Hamilton, Cresap, McCormick and Paget, and McKinsey & Company – had reached the height of their power.[1] Not necessarily the largest consultancies, these three firms oversaw the most prestigious assignments and referred to themselves, like the American automobile oligopoly, as the "big three" of management consulting firms.[2] As the journalists at *Forbes* magazine explained in a feature article on Booz Allen & Hamilton:

> The firms that Booz Allen likes to compete with are the other members of the club that includes McKinsey; Cresap, McCormick and a few others. All of these are sufficiently comfortable with one another's approach, work and pricing that they will often recommend that a prospective client also price a job with the others.[3]

Like the "big three" automotive manufacturers, this elite "club" of consulting firms exercised significant economic influence and power.[4] As management consulting firms, like the large law, accounting, and engineering firms, became a crucial element of the institutional infrastructure that undergirded the American economy, the leading management consulting firms commanded greater respect

and authority.[5] Thus, when these leading firms expanded overseas in the early 1960s, consultants not only transferred American
managerial models but also the American institutional system that
had routinized the use of management consultants within large
organizations.[6]

In retrospect, the big three consulting firms reached the height
of their influence in the United States during the early 1960s.
Marc Galanter and Thomas Palay's analysis of the "golden age" of
American corporate law firms could equally well describe the status
of the leading consultancies during those same years:

> We locate this golden age in the period of the late 1950s and the early
> 1960s – let us call it 'circa 1960' – when big firms were prosperous, sta-
> ble, and untroubled. The form had been tested; it was well established;
> it exercised an unchallenged dominance. It was a time of stable rela-
> tions with clients, of steady but manageable growth, of comfortable
> assurance that an equally bright future lay ahead ...[7]

Although the power controlled by these elite consulting firms, like
the influence wielded by corporate law firms and accountants, would
continue to increase, the relative position of the leading management consultancies underwent dramatic economic, cultural, and
structural changes beginning in the 1970s.[8] By the mid-1970s, for
example, Cresap, McCormick and Paget had lost money for five of
the six years that followed the firm's sale to Citibank in 1970; the
consultants at Booz Allen & Hamilton had decided to buy back
their shares after their firm's stock price had plummeted in the years
following the consultancy's initial public offering in 1971; and the
directors within McKinsey & Company were trying to reassure their
fellow partners that "a decline in *profits* does not necessarily mean
a decline in *profitability*."[9] This analysis, therefore, is not of a system
in permanent equilibrium but of a moment in time – a perceived
"golden age" for these firms – that would soon disappear as greater

competition within the field of consulting and a more challenging world economy took hold.

This chapter, however, is not entitled the "Golden Age" but instead the "Gilded Age," as corrosive pressures on young consultants were hidden beneath the burnished image of the leading firms. Prior to the 1960s, management consulting firms had been so concerned with their outward appearance that any individuality was actively discouraged in favor of collective conformity.[10] Because only a privileged few – almost exclusively white males from the elite American universities – were allowed to join these professional firms, their disenchantment with the status quo was voiced only in private. Although cynicism, disillusion, and stress within professional firms has always been a concern, it is worth remembering that for the young consultants in 1960, the pressures that they dealt with during this "golden" age were no easier to bear than the burdens on young management consultants in the present day.[11]

For the elite consulting firms in the United States, however, 1960 was the peak period in which they enjoyed a dominant corporate culture and a common institutional strategy.[12] This is as apparent in the cartoons of that time as it is in the records (see Figure 6.1). To anchor the text visually, this chapter will use cartoons drawn by McKinsey associates in the early 1960s alongside illustrations commissioned by George Fry & Associates (a spin-out from Booz Allen & Hamilton) in 1958 to illustrate the largely quantitative data that follow.[13] Although the cartoons and the illustrations both exhibit their own distinctive styles – much like the wide variety of empirical data points – the visual evidence indicates a remarkable homogeneity in the culture of consulting. Whether serious or in jest, contemporary illustrations of this "Gilded Age" depicted a corporate culture that would remain central to the public's image of consultants for many years after its peak in 1960. This chapter, therefore, is a "snapshot" of the leading management consulting firms at the height of their

This Is A Consultant.

He Is A Professional.

Color His Hat Professional Grey,

  His Tie Sincere Grey,

  His Garters Confident Grey.

Clothes Maketh The Man.

Figure 6.1. *The Consultants' Coloring Book, Circa* 1962.
Reproduced with Permission of McKinsey & Company.

power using magazine articles, trade statistics, and archival sources. The picture that emerges is similar to the existing narratives describing the golden age of American accounting and law firms in the years immediately surrounding 1960. For the leading professional service firms, it was a good time.

## The Market for Consulting

In 1960, like now, small, recently incorporated practitioners, not large firms, dominated the market in the quasi-professional field of management consulting.[14] In 1962, *The Wall Street Journal* estimated that there were 2,500 separate firms and approximately 30,000 active consultants working in the United States.[15] Of the 705 consulting firms listed in the 1960 directory of the American Management Association, less than half had been around for more than a decade, and only 175 firms had more than fifteen consultants on their professional staff.[16] From this perspective, the leading management consulting firms, like the giant law firms, held the most authority and performed the important assignments, but they represented only a small percentage of the overall field.[17] In 1960, management consulting was still a quasi-profession in a field dominated by a few big names but largely populated by small firms and individual practitioners (see Table 1).

Leading the elite minority in 1960 was the giant consulting firm of Booz Allen & Hamilton with a consulting staff of 300 and billings of $12 million a year.[18] By comparison, McKinsey & Company, the second largest general management consulting firm in the United States, was half the size of Booz Allen & Hamilton with 165 consultants on staff and $6.7 million in billings, while Cresap, McCormick and Paget was half again the size of McKinsey & Company, with approximately 75 consultants and billings of approximately $2.1 million.[19] These three firms, McKinsey & Company, Cresap, McCormick and Paget, and Booz Allen & Hamilton, joined

TABLE 1: *The leading American management consulting firms in 1960*

| Consulting firm | Firm founded | Total offices | Yearly clients | Professional staff | Client billings (in millions) |
|---|---|---|---|---|---|
| Arthur D. Little, Inc.[1] | 1886 | 7 | 1,400[2] | 700[2] | $23.0[2] |
| Booz Allen & Hamilton | 1914 | 8 | 500 | 300 | $12.0 |
| McKinsey & Company | 1939 | 6 | 300[3] | 165 | $ 6.7 |
| A. T. Kearney & Company | 1926 | 1 | 275 | 110[2] | $ 3.2[2] |
| Cresap, McCormick and Paget | 1945 | 4 | 150 | 75 | $ 2.1 |

[1] Approximately one-third of ADL's work was in management consulting.
[2] As of 1961.
[3] As of 1962.
*Source of estimates:* corporate archives and contemporary articles.

by two others, A. T. Kearney & Company, then a regional firm based in Chicago, and Arthur D. Little, Inc., a Boston-based consultancy best known for its technological prowess, together employed fewer than 900 consultants (less than 3 percent of the 30,000 consultants nationally) and billed slightly more than 30 million dollars per year (roughly 5 percent of the $600 million that consultants billed nationally).[20] Although in economic terms the five firms were not an oligopoly, they were consistently described as the dominant organizations in the United States.[21]

The three leading firms all had offices in New York, Chicago, San Francisco, and Los Angeles by 1960. In particular, although their New York offices were extremely important, all three of the leading firms had strong ties to Chicago (see Figure 6.2). Booz Allen & Hamilton, of course, had been founded in Chicago in 1914 and was headquartered there until the 1970s when it moved its corporate offices to New York. McKinsey & Company started as the New York branch of James O. McKinsey's original Chicago-based consultancy, and both Richard Paget and Mark Cresap began their careers

Figure 6.2. *Consultants from George Fry & Associates at the University Club in Chicago in 1958.*
Reproduced with Permission of Franklin McMahon.

in Chicago at Booz Allen & Hamilton after they graduated from Northwestern University.[22] It was the firms' satellite offices, however, that secured the reputations of the three leading consultancies in the postwar era. The staff in the California branch offices, for example, gave McKinsey & Company, Cresap, McCormick and Paget, and Booz Allen & Hamilton an edge over single-office, regional firms like A. T. Kearney & Company in Chicago and Robert Heller & Associates in Cleveland, when negotiating with potential clients for national studies.[23] Indeed, one of A. T. Kearney's first strategic moves outside of Chicago was to purchase a small consulting firm in Los Angeles in 1961. In McKinsey & Company, by 1960, the firm's San Francisco and Los Angeles offices together brought the consultancy more than a million dollars of revenue, which represented 16 percent of the firm's overall billings.[24]

Yet, while other regions were important, New York was by far the most important market for management consulting services in 1960. For McKinsey & Company, despite the firm's six other offices stretching from L.A. to London, the New York office was responsible for 60 percent of the firm's overall billings.[25] The predominance of New York, of course, would change as consultants' international assignments became more important; and already, by 1960, the leading consultancies were "expanding their overseas operations at a breathtaking clip."[26] But perhaps the most striking correspondence among Cresap, McCormick and Paget, McKinsey & Company, and Booz Allen & Hamilton would occur in 1967 when all three elite consulting firms chose a single location, the new American Brands Building at 245 Park Avenue near Grand Central Station, for their offices in New York City.[27] Consultants from these three firms would later remember that you could stand in the lobby of the American Brands Building and guess, based on the bank of elevators that a corporate chief executive officer (CEO) entered, which Fortune 500 Company was working with which management consulting firm. Paralleling economist Harold Hotelling's famous description of ice cream vendors crowding each other on the beach, the elite consulting firms not only closely imitated each other in their range of services but also clustered together in their choice of office location.[28]

## Work and Clients

The partners at Cresap, McCormick and Paget, Booz Allen & Hamilton, and McKinsey & Company all characterized their consulting firms as generalists, able to handle a wide range of assignments and clients. As a partner at Booz Allen & Hamilton said in defense of the consulting firm's size, "You have to be large enough to provide research, training, depth and variety of personnel. . . . "[29] Booz Allen & Hamilton's scale enabled the firm to handle 500 individual clients annually. For a *Business Week* cover story, staff members piled the one thousand reports that they prepared every year around the firm's patriarch Jim Allen to emphasize the sheer volume of paper that the firm produced.[30] Booz Allen & Hamilton's annual output was visually extraordinary, but not beyond comparison – McKinsey & Company, for example, worked for approximately 300 separate clients in 1962.[31] Booz Allen & Hamilton performed one quarter of its studies for "a few steady repeat customers," but, in sharp contrast with legal and accounting firms where steady clients made up the great majority of a firm's business, 75 percent of Booz Allen & Hamilton's customers were not repeat customers.[32] Moreover, the studies that the leading management consulting firms performed were just as varied as their clients. In the three years between 1959 and 1961, McKinsey & Company's clients spanned twenty industries, with only one industry, petroleum, comprising more than one-tenth of the firm's average billings.[33] McKinsey's range of topics was equally diverse, with strategic planning representing the single largest practice at nearly one-fifth of their business, and computer systems, marketing, and organizational studies each providing roughly 15 percent of their annual revenues.[34] In 1958, Richard Cresap estimated that "three out

Figure 6.3. *Consultants at Work in the Offices of George Fry & Associates in 1958.* Reproduced with Permission of Franklin McMahon.

of every four of the larger businesses in the country have used management consultants at one time or another" suggesting that there was still room to grow, but that the market for consultants' services was increasingly mature (see Figure 6.3).

Although McKinsey & Company, Cresap, McCormick and Paget, and Booz Allen & Hamilton all performed a variety of assignments among a range of industries, they emphasized their work in specific sectors of the economy to differentiate their services. At McKinsey & Company, for example, government work averaged only 5 percent of the firm's total billings, and nonprofit assignments less than 1 percent of the consultancy's revenues.[35] In contrast, at Cresap, McCormick and Paget, nonprofit work averaged nearly one-third of the firm's billings and the consultants at Booz Allen & Hamilton performed nearly 30 percent of their assignments for government agencies.[36] All three consulting firms, however, boasted of their ability to handle assignments in all the sectors throughout the world. To outsiders, the competition among these elite management consulting firms, like the friendly rivalry between Harvard, Yale, and Princeton, emphasized the striking homogeneity among the elite firms more than any immediate differences.

### Firm Composition and Rewards

Observers still thought of management consulting as a "young profession" in 1960. In many ways, those observers were right, as all three of the leading consulting firms in 1960 were still led by one of the founding partners – although in each case, at least one of the eponymous partners had already retired or died. Although Edwin Booz had died, Jim Allen ran Booz Allen & Hamilton. Whereas Mark Cresap had left his firm to join Westinghouse, Dick Paget still managed Cresap, McCormick and Paget and Marvin Bower directed the firm that he had refounded as "McKinsey & Company" soon after James McKinsey's death in 1937.[37] Indeed, Marvin Bower, whether through retrospective justification or long-range planning, subsequently explained that he preferred having a dead partner's name on the door because new clients couldn't demand to work with James McKinsey.[38]

Most clients, however, did not work directly with a "name" partner, but met, instead, with one of the firm's many other partners.[39] By 1960, Booz Allen & Hamilton had grown to include forty-two partners while McKinsey & Company had thirteen directors (senior partners) and nineteen principals (junior partners).[40] The true growth of these firms, however, came lower in the hierarchy from the young associates who represented at least two-thirds of the consulting

Figure 6.4. *The Consultants' Coloring Book, Circa 1962.*
Reproduced with Permission of McKinsey & Company.

workforce (see Figure 6.4). At McKinsey, for example, the younger associates made up 77 percent of the firm's professional personnel (127 of 165) and in the newer offices their relative presence was even higher. By comparison, in 1958, the largest law firm in America, Shearman & Sterling, had thirty-five partners and ninety associates in its New York offices.[41] Thus, by 1960, the largest consulting firms were already larger than the largest law firms but smaller than an accounting firm like Price Waterhouse that had more than 100 partners and 500 staff accountants in 1960.[42] Furthermore, one should not forget the administrative and operational infrastructure that held the system together, for the 165 consultants within McKinsey were supported by 176 researchers, operational staff, and administrators;

similarly, the 300 consultants in Booz Allen were supported by 300 clerical staff.[43] Thus, the 42 partners at McKinsey were surrounded by nearly three hundred personnel, or a ratio of seven to one.

It is not surprising to see why partnerships were such coveted prizes, because, as the trade journal, *Television Magazine*, said of Booz Allen, "the rewards of partnership are juicy. Those in control qualify for ranking among the top fifty wage earners in America . . . six-figure salaries are common."[44] But six-figure salaries, however "juicy" the partnerships might have been, were not common in 1960 (although not unheard of either). In 1959, *Television Magazine* reported that Jim Allen, of Booz Allen & Hamilton, earned more than $200,000, making him one of the highest paid people in business; among the very largest American companies, with over $400 million in sales, the average salary for a CEO was $133,000.[45] By comparison, in 1962, the highest paid partner at A. T. Kearney in Chicago earned $110,000 with an "average" partner, of the fourteen, earning $50,000, and enjoying a billing rate of $300 per day for his services ($1,800 in current terms).[46] By comparison, an "average" CEO of a company with $25 million in annual sales would have made $50,000 a year and only the CEOs of the very largest industrial companies earned $100,000 or more annually.[47] Of course, the financial rewards of consulting did not just go to the senior partners; at A. T. Kearney & Company junior partners, called principals, earned from "the low twenties to $40,000."[48] Such a salary, in 1962, would have compared favorably with the traditional professions – the average annual salary for American college professors in 1962, for example, was $7,486, while the average salary for engineers was $12,720 and the average income for a physician in private practice was $24,300. Consulting could be very lucrative indeed for those who succeeded in landing a job within the elite American firms.[49]

If the leading management consulting firms seemed similar from the outside, by 1960, their internal cultures were no less homogeneous. Marvin Bower's decision to recruit at the Harvard Business

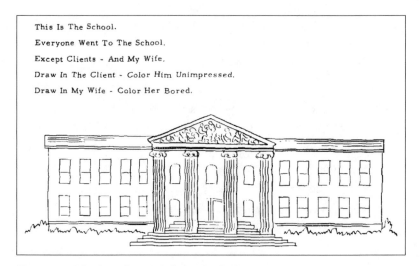

This Is The School.

Everyone Went To The School.

Except Clients - And My Wife.

Draw In The Client - Color Him Unimpressed.

Draw In My Wife - Color Her Bored.

Figure 6.5. *The Consultants' Coloring Book, Circa 1962.*
Reproduced with Permission of McKinsey & Company.

School, in the 1950s, had a lasting impact not only on McKinsey & Company but on the entire field of management consulting. By the early 1960s, the Harvard Business School had become the primary recruiting ground for new staff with heavy competition among the firms for the "Baker Scholars," the top 5 percent of the graduating class (see Figure 6.5).[50] In 1961, the average pay for starting consultants graduating from Harvard was $8,348, 12 percent more than the $7,500 starting salary for accountants from Harvard or associates at the top corporate law firms in New York.[51] Although the leading consulting firms had once drawn their staffs from a broad range of academic and socioeconomic backgrounds, that was no longer the case after the elite consultancies began recruiting at the top business schools and adopted the "up or out" system first pioneered by Cravath, Swaine & Moore in law firms. Thus, management consulting progressively moved from a low-status occupation to one dominated by the upper middle class.[52] Bower's strategic innovations, when copied by McKinsey & Company's competitors, led to the increasing homogenization of management consulting in the early 1960s. And that homogeneity

Figure 6.6. *Consultant from George Fry & Associates Listening to a Client in 1958.* Reproduced with Permission of Franklin McMahon.

would eventually create trouble for these organizations when they were forced to respond to new techniques and new social norms in the cultural and managerial upheavals of the early 1970s.

## The Men in the Gray Flannel Suits

By the 1960s, the conformity of American management consultants had become the basis for humor. This happened both within the elite consulting firms and in the media (for example in the feature film *Desk Set* starring Spencer Tracy and Katharine Hepburn).[53] Sloan Wilson may have written his famous novel, *The Man in the Gray Flannel Suit*, about an advertising executive, not a management consultant, but by the 1960s, consultants seemed just as uniformly "grey," if not more so, than advertising executives and corporate executives (see Figure 6.6).[54] Even the young consultants at McKinsey & Company, restrained by their firm's strict dress code, joked that Californians often mistook them for government agents because McKinsey and the FBI were the only two groups in Los Angeles still wearing dark suits in the 1960s.[55]

To be fair, the conservative dress and manners of the leading management consulting firms were an important means for reassuring corporate clients that consultants were serious, both in their attitude and in their work. As *Business Week* explained, in 1960, "First impressions are often telling ones. The men [in Booz Allen] wear uniformly dark suits, white shirts, and sober ties."[56] That their conservative dress resulted in greater demand for their services was not lost on the partners of the leading consultancies, for as the managing director of McKinsey & Company, Marvin Bower explained to young associates in 1959:

> The attitudes of top executives toward us as people often carry more weight in the shaping of Firm reputation than even the major recommendations we develop for them. And those attitudes – whether favorable or unfavorable – are fashioned from an accumulation of little things. Example: one top-management Englishman, asked by another how our consultants get along with his people, said, "Fine. They even wear conservative neckties."[57]

By wearing "conservative neckties," the leading consulting firms tried to minimize their visual impact as outsiders within client organizations even if their conservatism sometimes made them stand out. Nevertheless, the new associates at McKinsey & Company still grumbled about the old-fashioned hats that they had to wear at the same time that John F. Kennedy had decided to forgo a hat at his presidential inauguration in 1961 to emphasize his youthfulness (see Figure 6.7).[58]

The superficial tension between the young associates and the older partners over the dress and demeanor at the leading consulting firms reflected a deeper struggle to maintain the corporate culture that the partnerships had cultivated in the 1950s, when management consulting, in *Business Week*'s words, first hit "the big time."[59] The young consultants' reaction in the early 1960s to the strong "personality" (as corporate culture was called in the 1960s) of the leading management consulting firms emerged not through active resistance to the senior partners, but parodies by the associates of the dominant

This Is My Hat.

Consultants Wear Hats Because They Like Hats.

My Hat Makes Me Look Older.

Clients Like Me When I'm Older.

Why Don't Clients Wear Hats?

Figure 6.7. *The Consultants' Coloring Book, Circa 1962.*
Reproduced with Permission of McKinsey & Company.

corporate culture.[60] The cartoons featured in this chapter are an example. Not coincidentally, the young executives within these bureaucratic organizations, often recent graduates of elite universities like Yale, Harvard, and Stanford, were well aware of the critiques by C. Wright Mills and Sloan Wilson of the stifling conventions of corporate America.[61] When several young associates at McKinsey & Company created a hilarious self-parody of their employer's corporate culture in 1962, they arranged the cartoons to resemble a children's coloring book, and, like the *Harvard Lampoon*, poked fun at McKinsey's rigid hierarchy, the senior partners' educational and social pretensions, and the inflexible lifestyle the associates endured (see Figure 6.8).[62] Drawn only six years after the publication of *The Man in the Gray Flannel Suit*, "The Consultants' Coloring Book" vividly reflected postwar concerns about the demands for conformity

This Is Where The Principals Work.

It Is Called The Yale Club.

You Know What To Color That.

Figure 6.8. *The Consultants' Coloring Book, Circa 1962*.
Reproduced with Permission of McKinsey & Company.

within professional workplaces and the high price that this conformity exacted on the life of these young consultants. The consultants
recognized that they had chosen to live in a gilded cage.

## Conclusion

By 1960, management consultants had successfully established, institutionalized, and defended management consulting from other professional competitors. To quote Richard Paget's talk to the partners
of Booz Allen on the firm's forty-fifth anniversary in 1958:

> Today, no one in our kind of work has to explain what he does. There
> are books written about us, we are the subjects of frequent articles,
> we have been honored in numerous cartoons and stories, and serious
> groups even hold meetings to discuss how we can best be utilized.[63]

With their reputations established, consultants turned their attention from external "turf battles" to the internal management of their
firms.[64] As they shifted their focus from external to internal development, however, management consultants chose not to emphasize
differences from other rival professional groups, but the continuities
between management consulting and other leading professions like
accounting, engineering, and, especially, law.[65] In the years leading
up to 1960, management consultants not only received prestigious
assignments within the largest corporate, nonprofit, and government
organizations, but also developed lasting professional governance
structures, modeled after other professional organizations, to manage
their expanding firms. By copying the culture of other firms, consultants chose to institutionalize a highly stable system. Their strong
internal cultures were a strategic strength, but they would become a
deep liability in the years ahead.

As the leading management consulting firms expanded overseas
during the 1960s, they carried with them a deeply American corporate ethos that would remain despite the increasingly international

composition of the firms. McKinsey chose to Americanize its international staff, not internationalize its own, American, culture. That culture would be of tremendous value when Europeans were desperate to purchase American "know-how" and when the consultants needed to integrate a young staff. In the late 1970s, however, consultants' homogeneity would become a liability both because its rigidity prevented the leading firms from diversifying their largely white, male workforce and because it encouraged the elite consultancies to look inward in times of trouble, not outward. Students of strategic management are taught that the best way to identify a core competence – the quality that distinguishes you from your competitors and defines your competitive advantage – is to look for an organization's greatest apparent weakness over its long history. Why else would an organization tolerate this obvious flaw except that it provides a tremendous benefit? In 1960, just like today, there was no question of the core competence of the leading consulting firms, because their distinctive corporate culture was simultaneously their greatest asset and their most glaring Achilles heel.

# SEVEN

# The American Challenge

## Exporting the American Model

In the Autumn of 1967, Jean-Jacques Servan-Schreiber's, *Le Défi Américain*, or the "American Challenge," became an immediate sensation in France, selling more than 400,000 copies in the first few months after its release.[1] Servan-Schreiber argued that European economic problems, and particularly French ones, were not the result of poor fiscal or trade policies, but the direct result of the inability of European companies to compete with American organizations. Unless French executives adopted American-style management, they would become employees of the American conglomerates that were expanding into Europe.[2] Although the public furor over Servan-Schreiber's work cooled down as the 1968 student strikes in Paris heated up, his message resonated with corporate executives who, during the previous decade, had tried to reshape their companies using what they perceived as superior American organizational forms.

Although many historians have written about the resulting "Americanization" of business in Europe in the 1960s and early 1970s, most accounts have focused on the fascination that European managers and politicians showed for American management. In contrast, this chapter will look not at the demand for American "knowhow," but at its supply. The American management consulting firms that set up offices in Europe during the late 1950s and 1960s sold organizational know-how to French, German, Italian, British, Swiss, and Dutch executives. Servan-Schreiber himself highlighted that American management consulting firms were integral to the transmission of corporate organizational models, pointing out that hand in hand with the growth of American industrial subsidiaries in Europe, "the three American consultant firms with European branches (Booz Allen & Hamilton, Arthur D. Little, and McKinsey and Co.) have *doubled* their staffs *every year* for the past five years."[3] The hiring of American management consultants represented an immediate and practical solution to Servan-Schreiber's "American Challenge."

He was right. American management consulting firms served as the primary institutional conduits for the transfer of American organizational models to Europe in the 1960s and early 1970s.[4] Many European managers sought out American models, and the leading U.S. consulting firms convinced many others of the advantages of American managerial techniques. Historian Matthias Kipping has argued that American consulting firms were not generally effective in restructuring European corporations because of the vast cultural differences between European and American businesses.[5] In contrast, like my Oxford colleague Richard Whittington, I would argue that many academics have been too quick to dismiss the lasting influence, both structural and cultural, of consultants in widely disseminating the American corporate model in Europe during the 1960s.[6] The standard bearer among consultancies was McKinsey & Company, which Europeans considered the most important American firm both for the firm's well-known introduction of the divisional corporate model to Europe and for its high profile assignments for the state.[7] As a journalist from *The Times* in London explained, "Ask anyone to name a management consultant and chances are, if he is British, that the answer will be 'McKinsey.'"[8] Through an analysis of the firm's expansion into Europe, the clients that it served, and the strategic response from McKinsey's competitors, this chapter will demonstrate the remarkable influence that American management consultants had in disseminating to Europe the decentralized organizational model, new techniques of control, and ultimately the *zeitgeist* of American business culture.

## A Century of Americanization: From Taylorism to the Marshall Plan

The transfer of American business models to Europe, of course, had been going on since the turn of the century. The U.S. consulting firms that opened offices in Europe in the late 1950s and early 1960s represented the third wave of American business knowhow to sweep through Europe in less than fifty years.[9] In the first wave, during the 1920s and 1930s, a fascination with American-style Taylorism and Fordism developed in Western Europe and even made a considerable impact on the Soviet Union as a result of Lenin's interest in the productivity gains possible under scientific management.[10] During the second wave immediately following the Second World War, the U.S. government, under the auspices of the Marshall Plan, sent organizational "experts" to Europe to advise corporate executives on how to rebuild their war-torn economies in the image of American business.[11] When American management consultants set up branch offices in Europe in the late 1950s and early 1960s, they were following well-worn paths for the transfer of American organizational models.

Earlier in the century, the European fascination with Taylorism took off just as the craze for scientific management began to die down in the United States. As Mary Nolan has observed in *Visions of Modernity*, after the First World War, leaders in Weimar Germany seized on scientific management as the best means to achieve a "rationalized" economy. German commentators favored a Fordist mix of accumulation, Taylorism, and increased consumption over pure worker efficiency.[12] French supporters of Taylor created two competing organizations for the promotion of scientific management, the Comité de l'Organisation Française and the Commission Général de l'Organisation Scientific du Travail in 1926, at a time when American followers of Taylor were opening offices in Paris to advise French companies on applying Taylorist models to their organizations.[13] As the American popularity of scientific management declined, American Taylorists like the French-born Charles Bedaux turned to Europe to expand their market: by 1937, 225 British, 144 French, 49 Italian, and 39 Dutch companies had employed International Bedaux to "rationalize" their businesses.[14] Eventually, colleagues of these Taylorist consultants would found the British and French management consultancies that became the "local" competitors to American firms like McKinsey in the early 1960s.[15] European Taylorists, like religious missionaries, spread the word overseas.

The Second World War interrupted the transfer of American managerial know-how, but the postwar reconstruction of European industry greatly accelerated this process. In 1948, under the auspices of the Marshall Plan, the United States began sending engineers and executives to Europe as advisors under the Technical Assistance Plan.[16] Although the Technical Assistance Plan focused on the transfer of engineering skills and technology, the United States also spent a percentage of the £13.5 billion earmarked for European aid on management training, executive seminars, and American technical consultants.[17] Some of the smaller American consulting firms, like Stevenson, Jordan & Harrison and Mead, Carney & Company, opened offices in London by the early 1950s, but the leading American management consulting firms did not expand to Europe until a decade later.[18] The U.S. government favored hiring federal employees and American corporate executives over independent consultants for its productivity missions to Europe. With American knowhow being dispensed for free and European businesses unable, or at least unwilling, to pay high fees for the services of U.S. consultancies, European corporations would wait until the early 1960s before succumbing to the siren song of the American consultants.

### A Brief History of McKinsey & Company

McKinsey & Company grew quickly in the 1940s, partly because of its location among the headquarters of the largest American corporations and partly because of the firm's emphasis on working exclusively for chief executives. McKinsey & Company's growth was remarkable even if an allowance is made for the postwar demand for management consultants to help retool American production. By 1951, McKinsey & Company was making $633,000 in profits, had offices in New York, San Francisco, Chicago, Los Angeles, and Washington, D.C., and employed 88 consultants on its staff.[19] By the time McKinsey & Company expanded into Europe in the late 1950s, it was in a dominant competitive position in its home market.

Firms like McKinsey & Company largely replaced Taylorist consultancies in America during the 1930s, even though Taylorists continued to dominate the market for organizational advice in Europe through the 1950s. In Britain, four Taylorist firms (PA Consulting, Urwick Orr, P.E., and A.I.C.), all offshoots of Charles Bedaux's original British firm, controlled three-fourth of the £4 million consulting market by 1956, while in France, the leading Taylorist firms organized a trade association, the Association Français des Conseils en Organisation Scientifique, in the late 1940s to promote the benefits of scientific management.[20] In contrast, although a few American Taylorist firms, like Harrington Emerson's, managed to stay in business during the postwar era, in the United States, as the second chapter described, the leading management consulting firms were neither founded by Taylorists nor promoted scientific management techniques. As Michael Shanks explained the difference to British readers in 1967,

> Management consultancy in Britain has a long and distinguished history, but British management consultants have never acquired the status and prestige of their American counterparts. They have tended historically to solve problems of factory-floor organisation rather than the higher-level problems of business strategy and company organisation and structure.[21]

The distinction between the two approaches would become all the more striking when American firms began competing with European consultancies because of the strong demand among European clients for the board-level advice of the American firms.[22]

The work that McKinsey & Company performed in the 1940s and 1950s included helping corporate boards calculate executive compensation, conducting marketing surveys, and installing budgetary control systems, but the most prestigious and visible assignments for McKinsey & Company involved the restructuring of corporations, most often using the "decentralized" or "multidivisional" model. By 1962, when the business historian, Alfred Chandler, published the history of decentralization in the United States, he could be certain that the multidivisional structure had become the dominant organizational form among American industrial companies in large part through its dissemination by management consulting firms.[23] European corporations, however, without the influence of American consultants, had not yet undergone the same transformation.[24]

## Turning toward Europe

Like the transfer of American organizational models to Europe, direct investment by American companies in European factories, raw goods, and distribution networks predates the postwar expansion of U.S. firms. Already, by 1914, the value of American direct overseas investment totaled $2.65 billion, or 7 percent of the U.S. gross national product.[25] From the end of the First World War to the American stock market crash in 1929, American corporations more than doubled their investments in European manufacturing and distribution from $375 to $770 million.[26] In contrast, from 1930 through 1945, during the prolonged Great Depression and the Second World War, American executives kept their European factories and affiliates, but did little to try to expand them. This strategy of neglect continued in the immediate postwar era when European currency controls, socialist governments, and restrictions on foreign trade scared off American investments in European subsidiaries. A booming American economy also kept executives' attention away from Europe. As a result, American corporate investment in Europe remained stagnant during the first decade after the Second World War, even as U.S. public investment through the Marshall Plan soared.[27]

Beginning in 1956, however, American companies began to reinvest in their European subsidiaries in order to guarantee access to the continent before the European Common Market put up trade barriers in 1958. As American commercial interest in Europe grew in the late 1950s, the leading American management consulting firms followed their clients into this "new" market.[28] Ironically, European firms responded to their U.S. competitors by hiring these same American management consulting firms to learn how their competitors were organized. In 1960, *The New York Times* described this booming European market for American knowhow,

> Besides being asked to aid United States companies seeking to stake out new markets abroad, [an unnamed management consultant] explained, the consultants are also in heavy demand among foreign concerns eager to resist their invaders.[29]

Although the leading consulting firms initially expected to serve European divisions of American companies, more than three-fourths of the assignments they accepted in Europe were from European-based firms.[30] As an official from KLM explained their decision in 1962 to bring in consultants from the United States, "McKinsey had already completed a similar project for American Airlines and had experience with the airline industry that European consultants couldn't match."[31] Using fire to fight fire, Europeans hired American management consultants to meet the "American Challenge."

As early as 1953, the directors of McKinsey & Company had begun considering whether to open an office in London or Paris to serve American subsidiaries in Europe and "European companies for projects to be carried on in the U.S."[32] Even though the managing director of McKinsey & Company, Marvin Bower, initially decided against establishing "a 'beachhead' in Europe," by 1958, he had reversed his position as European companies began to demand McKinsey's services.[33] Although both Booz Allen & Hamilton and McKinsey & Company had planned to work primarily for American subsidiaries, the consultants soon abandoned that initial strategy as European demand rose. Although the planning committee at McKinsey & Company recommended in 1956 that the firm "emphasize assistance to domestic companies in expanding their international businesses" over securing assignments from foreign companies, McKinsey & Company readily agreed to a proposed study of Shell Oil's Venezuela operations because of the "prestige of the client."[34]

Of course, as they had hoped, prestigious overseas assignments soon led to other equally "prestigious" jobs and, in 1954, IBM hired McKinsey & Company to reorganize its World Trade division.[35] This study eventually carried McKinsey consultants to France, Germany, Switzerland, Britain, and the Netherlands. Moreover, the conversations that the McKinsey managing director, Marvin Bower, had with Shell and Monsanto executives while in Europe for the IBM World Trade study convinced him to open an office in Europe. As Bower concluded:

The Monsanto discussion confirms what we have previously understood, i.e., that our approach differs fundamentally from the approach
of English and continental management consulting firms. Since our
experience indicates that our approach is applicable, the fact that it is
*different* gives us a quality of uniqueness in the international field that
may be even greater than in the domestic field.[36]

In 1957, the chairman of Royal Dutch Shell Oil, the largest company in the world headquartered outside the United States, asked
McKinsey & Company to install a multidivisional organization in
the company's dual London/Hague headquarters.[37] Faced with this
large, long-term assignment in Britain, the directors of McKinsey &
Company decided to use the study as a "bridge" to an office in London
by 1959.[38]

By comparison, Booz Allen & Hamilton's expansion outside the
United States mirrored McKinsey & Company's incremental net-
working in Europe. In the early 1950s, when government officials
in the Philippines (1953), Egypt (1953), and Iran (1956) offered
the consultants at Booz Allen lucrative overseas assignments, the
Chicago-based firm quickly shed any apprehensions about international expansion and ventured outside the United States.[39] Paralleling the process through which McKinsey's work in Argentina led
to the divisionalization of Shell's European headquarters in 1957,
Booz Allen & Hamilton's assignment for the Iranian Oil Company
brought the consultancy to the attention of ENI (Ente Nazionale
Idrocarburi), the nationalized Italian petroleum producer, in 1956.[40]
The reorganization of ENI would last more than two years, as the
consultants evaluated ENI's organizational design, cost structure,
and operations as part of the company's emphasis on introducing
modern management methods.[41] Like McKinsey's work within Shell
Oil, the consultants from Booz Allen decentralized ENI: the oil company's "...headquarters functions were regrouped and plans were
made to delegate authority."[42] During those same two years (1956–7),

the consultants at Booz Allen would also take on assignments in Italy for two steel companies, Italsider and Carnigliano, the motorcycle manufacturer Ducati, and the tractor manufacturer, Otto Melaro. Although Booz Allen & Hamilton did not focus exclusively on European business – in 1956–7, for example, it also worked for the Bank of Cuba, a Syrian investment bank, and a Peruvian copper-mining company – by the early 1960s, the consultancy was serving clients in Italy, Switzerland, Germany, Britain, Luxembourg, the Netherlands, and Sweden. Although Booz Allen & Hamilton initially entered the European market primarily through Italy, not Britain (like McKinsey), or Switzerland (like Arthur D. Little), the result was the same.[43] Each of the large American consulting firms rapidly created professional networks throughout Western Europe in the 1960s.[44]

McKinsey & Company's London office was quick to attract other large corporate clients. Within only three months of opening the office in 1959, McKinsey had eight consultants there and an extraordinarily high "utilization level" of 92 percent.[45] By 1962, they had worked for several British subsidiaries of major North American firms, including Heinz, Massey Ferguson, and Hoover.[46] Their British clients included Dunlop Rubber and ICI, one of the world's largest chemical companies.[47] By 1966, the London office, with a consulting staff of thirty-seven, had become the second largest office in McKinsey & Company, just ahead of Chicago's thirty-one consultants, and behind New York's staff of ninty-six. Following such rapid acceptance in Britain, McKinsey's directors opened a second European office in Geneva in 1961, followed only three years later by offices in Paris, Amsterdam, and Düsseldorf. By the end of the decade, half of McKinsey & Company's total revenues would come from outside the United States.[48]

While McKinsey's continental offices did not attract clients as quickly as the London operation, they still grew very rapidly, serving a "who's who" list of the largest companies in Europe. McKinsey's

TABLE 1: *Profitability of continental offices of McKinsey & Company*

| Year | Profit | Staff | Per Person |
|------|--------|-------|------------|
| 1962 | $59,100 | 5 | $11,820 |
| 1963 | $115,100 | 9 | $12,789 |
| 1964 | $127,900 | 12 | $10,658 |
| 1965 | $219,400 | 18 | $12,189 |
| 1966 | $456,800 | 26 | $17,569 |
| 1967 | $753,500 | 42 | $17,940 |
| 1968 | $1,370,200 | 62 | $22,100 |
| 1969 | $2,324,400 | 91 | $25,524 |

Source: McKinsey & Company Archives

early clients in Switzerland included Nestlé, Sandoz, and Union Bank; in the Netherlands, KLM, United Fruit, and the Ministry of Education; in France, they worked for Pechiney, Rhône-Poulenc, and Air France; while in Germany, McKinsey's clients included Volkswagen, Deutsche Bank, and BASF.[49] With so many clients, and a limited number of trained European consultants, McKinsey's continental offices were profitable from their start.[50] On average, profits grew an astonishing 69 percent per year from 1962 to 1969 (see Table 1).[51] In part, these profits were a result of the tremendous growth in the number of management consultants that McKinsey & Company hired in Europe during the 1960s.[52] But even if one discounts the rapid increase in staff numbers and subtracts the significant startup costs for these new offices, the profits per consultant in McKinsey's European offices grew, on average, at the impressive rate of 12 percent per year between 1962 and 1969. McKinsey and Company charged more than most observers believed the market could bear, and yet their client list kept growing.[53] As a London *Times* journalist reported in 1969, "McKinsey has been turning away work [even though] the American companies charge, and get, up to 50 percent more than their British competitors."[54] It was no wonder that contemporary European observers were astonished by the power and profits emanating from McKinsey & Company, a source of the "American Challenge" and, apparently, its best solution.[55]

## Conduits for Decentralization

Although internal memos from McKinsey & Company in the late 1950s and early 1960s make it clear that the partners in the consulting firm did not set out to "sell" decentralization to their European clients, the final result would not have been very different if that had been their initial competitive strategy.[56] In Britain, the firm decentralized 22 of the largest 100 companies, and in Germany, McKinsey "alone was involved in, and largely shaped, over a dozen divisionalizations of major German firms."[57] As one German academic summarized the trend, "the main driving force in Germany, as elsewhere, has been provided by the American management consultants McKinsey."[58] In a very direct and central way, U.S. firms, especially McKinsey & Company, were responsible for transferring the dominant organizational model in business to Europe during the 1960s.

The contrast between the widespread adoption of the multidivisional form within the European Union during the 1960s and 1970s and its absence in Spain is particularly instructive. In 1965, a leading Spanish bank contacted the consultants in McKinsey, anxious to hire them to reorganize the industrial companies under the bank's control. McKinsey's directors, however, decided not to take the assignment and not to use the study as a bridge to open an office in Spain (despite interest from the younger consultants) because Marvin Bower argued that Spain's position outside the European Common Market and the risk of operating under a dictatorship mitigated the potential gains from establishing yet another European office.[59] As sociologist Mauro Guillén has written in *Models of Management*, McKinsey's decision not to open an office in Spain until 1977 had important structural consequences. Because McKinsey and the other leading American consulting firms did not set up offices in

Spain during the 1960s and early 1970s, not a single large Spanish company adopted the decentralized organizational form before the 1980s.[60] Unlike Britain, Germany, France, or Italy, where American consultants rapidly transferred the new organizational technologies, the business models disseminated by local consultants in Spanish companies during the 1960s and 1970s lagged behind their Europeans counterparts.[61]

At the other extreme, in Britain, where McKinsey had its greatest impact, 72 of the 100 largest businesses adopted the multidivisional structure by 1970; 32 under the guidance of management consultants.[62] Of course, many firms like Unilever had already decentralized their production into regional divisions in the 1950s, so when growth strained their organizations, their executive boards felt comfortable hiring McKinsey & Company to further divisionalize their operations.[63] In other cases, however, the reason behind the decision to bring in American consultants was not simply economic but also political. At Royal Dutch Shell, for example, there was an intensely pragmatic reason why John Loudon, a Dutch managing director at Shell, preferred an American consultancy over the European competitors: "I couldn't have a Dutch [consultant] because the British wouldn't like it, and I couldn't have a Britisher because the Dutch wouldn't like it."[64] The very nature of Shell's dual-national heritage pushed Loudon to hire presumably "neutral" outsiders from the United States.

At Royal Dutch Shell, prior to McKinsey's reorganization, the joint Anglo-Dutch directors managed the company through regional divisions supported by functional departments located in London (marketing, finance, and distribution) and The Hague (exploration, manufacturing, and research).[65] In the late 1950s, however, this structure became increasingly unwieldy when Shell began diversifying into petro-chemical production (see Figure 7.1).[66] The U.S. petroleum industry had gone through the same experience in the postwar era and their executives had felt, according to historian

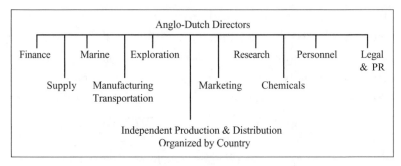

Figure 7.1. *Organizational Structure of Royal Dutch Shell in 1957.*

Alfred Chandler, a "powerful pressure for decentralization."[67] When John Loudon assumed the chairmanship of the managing directors at Royal Dutch Shell in 1957, he immediately brought in McKinsey to study the organization of the company's headquarters.[68]

McKinsey & Company's study, which took nine months ("the usual gestation period," quipped one commentator), recommended creating a new division, Shell Chemicals, which the parent company would run separately from its oil operations.[69] The consultants from McKinsey & Company advised the seven joint directors of Royal Dutch Shell to spend more of their time thinking about corporate strategy and less about operational details.[70] Even so, by the 1970s, the original emphasis on functional departments had reemerged as the headquarters staff became stronger at the expense of the regional directors. Indeed, Shell's chemical division remained divided by function (marketing, manufacturing, finance, etc.) unlike most chemical companies, which were fully "organized in self-contained product divisions by the 1970s (see Figure 7.2)."[71] Four years after Shell's reorganization by McKinsey, with the managerial staff reduced by 25 percent, the Company's Chairman, John Loudon, "called for a review of the post-McKinsey changes – 'not to start a further revolution but to see if, by sound evolution, further improvements can be made on the base already won.' "[72] At Royal Dutch Shell, ICI, and other large British companies, McKinsey's consultants helped boost profits and reduce administrative

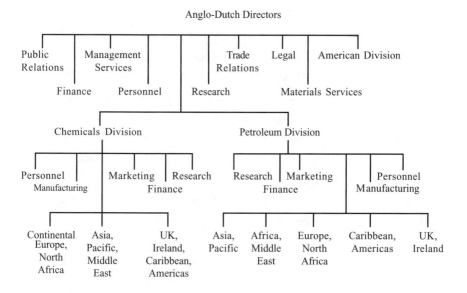

Figure 7.2. Organizational Structure of Royal Dutch Shell After McKinsey & Company Recommendations.

overhead.[73] They became an important instrument in a long-term shift in corporate structures.

On the continent, as in Britain, McKinsey had to modify American organizational models so that they would work in nationalized companies, government organizations, or unusual hybrid corporate structures. For example, McKinsey's consultants soon found that the legal and organizational constraints on German companies made it impossible to use the basic multidivisional model with its emphasis on a single executive board.[74] Unlike businesses in other countries, German companies had (and still have) two boards of directors: the *Aufsichtsrat*, which represents the stockholders' interests and often includes union representatives, and the *Vorstand*, which is the executive management board.[75] Ironically, German companies may have chosen to hire outside management consultants because of this split board. The consultants from McKinsey & Company understood how to redistribute the responsibilities of the *Vorstand* within a decentralized organization, a lesson "which the

Vorstand would have been unlikely to develop internally."[76] Even though historian Alfred Chandler may have been flattered that, "one European manager even reported that he advised his colleagues to save the $100,000 fee McKinsey charged by reading...*Strategy and Structure*," in retrospect, it is clear that the management consultants who disseminated the multidivisional model throughout Europe added value by adapting the American model to fit the specific needs of European corporations, not simply by selling executives a useful book on the subject.[77]

Similarly, in France, the consultants from McKinsey learned to adapt their techniques for use in the French public sector, which controlled nearly half of the country's gross national product.[78] In 1968, for example, Rhône-Poulenc, France's largest private corporation, hired McKinsey & Company to reorganize its struggling synthetic fiber division. Yet, as John Macomber, who ran McKinsey's Paris office remembered, executives in Rhône-Poulenc were dealing with questions that went beyond this business unit to the core of the company's strategic position: "Are we a chemical company, are we a pharmaceutical company, a fine chemical company, and by the way, what's our relationship with the government?"[79] Yet, even if the consultants did tailor their models to fit the particularities of each corporation, the French executives who came to McKinsey for advice were buying what *Le Monde* would later term "Prêt à Penser" – not off-the-rack fashion, but off-the-rack ideas. Despite the many cultural and political differences in Europe, the consultants from McKinsey & Company invariably suggested installing the decentralized organizational structure in Dutch, French, German, and Swiss companies.[80]

In 1967, McKinsey & Company reorganized the Swiss chemical and pharmaceutical giant Geigy along multidivisional lines.[81] The Basel newspaper, *National Zeitung*, reported that Samuel Koechlin, the chairman of Geigy, believed that this new organization would increase productivity, identify clear spheres of responsibility, help train future executives, and strengthen the company's research and development capacity.[82] Indeed, in subsequent correspondence with the German chemical company, Henkel, executives in Geigy, "characterized its reorganization as 'the most important and beneficial decision since the founding of the company.' "[83] In Geigy, McKinsey & Company created the classic decentralized structure by dividing the organization into groups based on the types of customers for its various products. There were five business groups: dyestuffs, chemicals, pharmaceuticals, agricultural chemicals, and consumer products (for all brand-named goods).[84] With the addition of functional departments (research, production, finance, legal, personnel, and advertising) supporting the product divisions and regional responsibilities, Geigy's structure looked identical to those adopted by other leading chemical manufacturers including DuPont, Monsanto, ICI, Rhône-Poulenc, and BASF. This similarity was no accident because McKinsey consultants had reorganized all of these international chemical manufacturers during the 1960s.

## Being "McKinseyed"

In the 1960s in Europe, McKinsey & Company enjoyed the most unusual of corporate accolades: it became a verb. Just as "to Xerox" became synonymous with copying a document, "to Fedex" meant to send a package for overnight delivery in America, and "to Hoover" meant to vacuum in Britain, "to McKinsey" came to mean the complete restructuring of a corporation.[85] As the London *Sunday Times* explained:

> **McKinsey**: n. & v.t. **1**. To shake up, reorganize, declare redundant, abolish committee rule. Mainly applied to large industrial companies but also to any organisation with management problems. See: British Broadcasting Corporation, the General Post Office and Sussex University. **2**. n. An international firm of American management consultants.[86]

The term was not limited to Britain because after McKinsey reorganized Geigy, *National Zeitung* described how the company had been, in their words, "McKinseyed."[87] Or, as the editors of the London *Times* reminisced years later, "There was even talk of the word *McKinsey* entering the Oxford English Dictionary as a transitive verb."[88] McKinsey & Company had become the recognized brand name in management consulting.

More than in any other country in Europe, Britain was "McKinseyed." Starting in the mid-1960s, the consultants at McKinsey made a lasting impact on British organizations and culture because many of the businesses that McKinsey restructured, including Cadbury, Cunard, and Rolls Royce, were at the center of British life and pride.[89] Especially galling to public critics of the process was the fact that this *American* consulting firm was reorganizing state institutions as quintessentially *British* as British Rail, the British Broadcasting Corporation (BBC), and, in 1968, the 250-year-old Bank of England![90] Although the members of Parliament had mistakenly worried that every public sector assignment was going to American-owned firms (in fact only two consulting assignments out of sixty went to American firms over the two and a half years prior to November 1967), McKinsey's assignment for the Bank of England made it seem that there was an active invasion in progress.[91] In the midst of the uproar over the bank assignment, the London correspondent of *Science* magazine commented: "and then there is McKinsey, projecting an image which suggests that, if God decides to redo creation, He will call in McKinsey."[92] To those who might not understand the clamor, *The Economist* explained that:

> To many of the staunch British Public, let alone City men [financiers], there is something faintly improper about the thought of any consultants, and particularly foreign ones, poking their noses into the Old Lady's business [the Bank of England is often referred to as the "Old Lady of Threadneedle Street"].[93]

Whether in the many cartoons, innumerable magazine profiles, or even mock interviews like the one devised by *The Financial Times* on Santa Claus' visit with McKinsey "to see how he could improve productivity," the American consultancy, along with its elite clients, found itself with a flood of publicity in the late 1960s in Great Britain.[94]

What is striking in hindsight, however, is not simply the ensuing uproar, but that the governors of the Bank of England had anticipated just how controversial their decision would be and yet still elected to hire McKinsey & Company over rival British consultancies. Whether they were right or wrong, the Bank of England's enquiries soon revealed that the British establishment believed McKinsey was superior to either its British or American competitors. As James Selwyn, an advisor to the Bank explained in late July 1968, more than two months before the Board of Governors ultimately decided to hire McKinsey & Company:

> The first problem is whether we should consider American consultants, or whether we should rule them out on the grounds that we 'ought to buy British'. The best known American consultants are McKinsey and they are probably the only ones we would need to consider.... Whatever the Bank does will be headline news. There have recently been three parliamentary questions about the employment of American consultants in Government Departments and nationalized industries.... So unless we feel that there is an outstandingly strong case for having McKinsey, I would be inclined to choose a British firm, but this is not an easy decision.[95]

Thus, before the Bank of England had made any enquiries, it had already decided against hiring an American consulting firm because officials believed that they would invite unnecessary controversy. The same day that James Selwyn advised against hiring an American firm, however, the deputy governor of the Bank, Sir Maurice Parsons, spoke with the heads of both Dunlop Tyres and Midland Bank, both of whom "enthusiastically" recommended hiring McKinsey.[96] Little more than a week later, the chief accountant in the Bank of England concluded that McKinsey & Company was "on an objective judgment, the best in the field."[97] As the head of the Bank of England, Sir Leslie O'Brien, concluded, "Everything I hear suggests that McKinseys [sic] have no equal."[98] Following these ringing endorsements, Leslie O'Brien, as governor of the Bank, quickly secured approval from the various committees and began seeking ways to minimize the political fallout, noting that officials at the Treasury:

> ...agree that McKinseys [sic] are the best and have nothing to say on the possible repercussions if we announce that we are employing them. Allen [Sir Allen Douglas, Permanent Secretary of the Treasury] agreed that a combination of McKinsey for top management and a British firm for routine office processes might have some presentational advantages.[99]

On the 15th of August, the governors of the Bank formally agreed to offer McKinsey the assignment.[100] In return for total fees of £142,900, the partners at McKinsey & Company had accepted their most publicly visible study and the Bank of England had committed itself to a public relations nightmare.[101]

At the end of October, the press leak that the Bank of England had long feared finally happened.[102] Anthony Thomas, a reporter from *The Times* telephoned Bank officials to tell them that he was preparing a story about McKinsey & Company's discussions with the Bank of England.[103] The Bank immediately responded to this "leak" by issuing a press release that was reported in the major newspapers throughout Britain.[104] By the next day, the British press, British consulting associations, and British politicians were all calling for an explanation for the Bank's decision to hire an American firm with jingoistic headlines like, "McKinsey plum chokes Britain's own consultants."[105] It wasn't until Sir Leslie O'Brien, the governor of the

Figure 7.3. *Punch Cartoon from September 1969.*
Reproduced with permission of Punch Ltd.

Bank, finally agreed to meet with both the chairman of the Management Consultants' Association and the president of the Institute of Management Consultants, that the Bank managed to soothe their ruffled feathers, and even then officials remained on the defensive about their decision.[106]

The irony was that the public uproar over McKinsey's work in the BBC, National Health Service, and Bank of England, only served to solidify the widespread perception that the "elite" management consulting firm embodied the cutting edge of superior American organizational knowhow.[107] Whether or not McKinsey really had access to superior American knowhow, there seemed to be no institution immune from the consultants' attention (see Figure 7.3). After British management consultants complained that these lucrative assignments should not have gone to an American firm, the *Manchester Guardian* commented: "British management consultants, up in arms yesterday about the allocation of yet another bumper public contract to Americans: If you really want to know what the trouble is, why not call in McKinsey?"[108] Whether restructuring corporations, government institutions, or nonprofit organizations, American management consulting firms were a genuine "American Challenge" to the European management consulting firms trying to compete with McKinsey & Company's almost mythical stature.

This publicity helped the firm garner assignments in the short run, but ultimately caused problems for McKinsey. Since it became synonymous with the installation of the decentralized model, as Marvin Bower noted, McKinsey "became known, exclusively to many, as reorganizers."[109] That reputation served McKinsey well when the decentralized model was new and uncommon in Europe, but by the early 1970s, the market was saturated. McKinsey had, quite literally, decentralized most of the large companies in Europe. As Allen Stewart, from McKinsey's Paris office, subsequently admitted:

> What happened in France is that in 5 or 6 years [1965–1971] we had gone through what London went through in about 12 years [1959–1971]. And that initial phase of restructuring came to an end. Also that favorable climate of the early days of the Paris office – respect for all things American – also diminished. There was probably a feeling in the marketplace that these McKinsey people have been just about everywhere and what have they achieved?[110]

The subsequent decline in business was not limited to McKinsey & Company, but McKinsey felt it most acutely because the firm had exhausted the market for their organizational studies.[111] Although McKinsey denied in the *Financial Times* that it was "feeling the economic squeeze more than the major U.K. consulting firms," as the head of the London office later remembered, "Somewhere about 1970 the phone stopped ringing."[112]

### From *"Défi"* to Defeat and Back Again

As corporate demand for American consultants dried up in Western Europe during the early 1970s, competition for the remaining consulting assignments intensified.[113] Given McKinsey's dwindling revenues, the firm could no longer casually turn down marginal European clients.[114] At the same time, the decline in corporate demand accelerated a long-term shift in the range of studies that management consulting firms performed. As their reputation grew during the 1960s, American consultants had shifted from working for the subsidiaries of giant multinationals (IBM, Shell, and Hoover), to decentralizing European corporations (ICI, Rhône-Poulenc, and Geigy) in the mid-1960s, and then to reorganizing large government departments (British Rail, BBC, and the Bank of England) in the late 1960s. By the early 1970s, paralleling developments in the United States during the 1950s and 1960s, European governments had become a significant customer of the American consultancies.[115] The importance of state assignments increased still further as corporate customers cut back on their use of consultants during the extended recession following the energy crisis in the 1970s.

In the early 1970s, British officials began to employ American consulting firms not simply to reorganize the administration of government departments, but to evaluate "objectively" the economic performance of industrial sectors.[116] Between 1970 and 1975, for example, McKinsey & Company surveyed the economic viability of the British automobile industry, Booz Allen & Hamilton studied the commercial prospects of the British shipbuilding industry, and The Boston Consulting Group (BCG) evaluated the international market for the British motorcycle industry.[117] Not surprisingly, the Ministers in the Department of Trade and Industry decided to employ consultants to analyze state-owned enterprises just when bipartisan support in Parliament for nationalization vanished as deficits surged.[118] Each successive consulting study of a national industry, therefore, served as an implicit referendum on whether particular British industries should be supported by the state.[119] British cabinet ministers, faced with limited means to fund their growing portfolio of troubled companies, learned how to shift the blame for closing troubled factories from themselves to the consultants.[120] American consultants soon began to wonder whether these public assignments, despite the depressed market for consulting, were really worth the inevitable notoriety.

The American consulting firms naturally differed on their estimates of the value of high profile assignments in the British public sector. Even if McKinsey gained more than it lost from its reorganization of the Bank of England (in 1972, McKinsey would bid to reorganize the World Bank in part based on the firm's international experience at the Bank of England and Royal Dutch Shell), the firm became wary of public sector assignments following charges of unethical behavior while working for the city of New York in 1970.[121] For several weeks, the consultants from McKinsey & Company were dragged over the coals on the front pages of the *New York Times* as political opponents of New York's Mayor John Lindsay charged him with "intellectual patronage" of the elite consulting firm.[122] As a result, the directors in McKinsey began to ask themselves not simply whether their actions were ethical, but "whether our actions will be *perceived* as being professional."[123] In comparison, for a rising consultancy like The Boston Consulting Group, the immediate benefit in accepting a high profile assignment in Britain, where the firm was still relatively unknown, was too appealing to forgo even if it opened the firm to potential criticism. The consultants from BCG expected that they could avoid much of the potential controversy in their study of the British motorcycle industry as the British government did not ask them to provide a conclusive opinion but instead to offer a range of potential strategic options.[124] As it turned out, the BCG consultants underestimated the potential risks because their study of the British motorcycle industry eventually became the most famous and controversial case in the history of management consulting when prominent academics later criticized its emphasis on what they said was a linear view of business strategy.[125] Yet even if one accepts the academic criticism of BCG's report, the BCG study also foreshadowed the crucial trends that would come to dominate management consulting over the next decade.[126]

The Boston Consulting Group's report on the British motorcycle industry combined three distinct elements that would become increasingly influential among consultants during the 1970s and early 1980s: a focus on competitive strategy and not just administrative structure; the use of explicit theoretical models (including the experience curve that showed that industrial companies became more efficient simply by entering infant industries early); and, perhaps most important, a detailed analysis of the apparently superior Japanese system that had overtaken the American model.[127] As historian Robert Locke has argued, European preoccupation with the American corporate model only disappeared when the Japanese "economic miracle" was touted during the early 1980s: "for Europeans *le défi américain* had turned into the *le défi japonais*."[128]

By the mid-1970s, the energy crisis and the extended recession of the early 1970s had made the United States business system appear less of an economic "challenge" than a system that was itself "challenged." In response, the consultants from The Boston Consulting Group and McKinsey & Company began promoting organizational models imported from Japan to their American and European clients who were struggling against the apparently superior management methods of Asian manufacturers. In particular, the consultants from The Boston Consulting Group had the advantage over McKinsey & Company as demand for the multidivisional organizational model waned because BCG had become the first mover in both the new specialty of "strategy consulting" and, equally important, had established its first overseas office in Tokyo in 1966, five years before McKinsey & Company opened their first office in Japan. McKinsey's response, to fund research on Japanese business models, strategic management, and corporate culture, however, would revitalize the firm in the 1980s both in Europe and in the United States. The 1982 publication of the international bestseller, *In Search of Excellence*, by two consultants from McKinsey, signaled the firm's ability to recast itself in the market as a popularizer of new management models on a par with BCG.[129]

## Conclusion

When Rhône-Poulenc, France's largest private corporation, hired McKinsey & Company to reorganize its struggling synthetic fiber division in 1968, the American magazine *Business Week* noted that Rhône-Poulenc's choice "underlines the irony of the French government's complaints that America is dominating French business."[130] Perhaps McKinsey's work for Rhône-Poulenc was not so much ironic as symbolic – symbolic of the rapid European adoption of American managerial techniques. Whether reorganizing industrial companies like Degussa in Germany, nonprofit organizations like the Royal Automobile Club of the Netherlands, or government departments like the National Health Service in Britain, McKinsey & Company served as the institutional conduit for the rapid transfer of American organizational knowhow in the 1960s and early 1970s.[131] Once European bureaucratic organizations no longer needed to install the multidivisional model, McKinsey set out to shift its emphasis to strategic planning, profitability studies, and merger advice.[132]

Management theorists are positivists by nature and most of them have treated corporate organizational models as part of an ascending hierarchy, much like new scientific paradigms.[133] I would argue that this progressive view has had as much to do with the claims of the purveyors of these models as the results from their practical use. The benefits that management consultants predicted from decentralization often failed to materialize, and cynical observers have long noted that owners sometimes used management consulting firms simply to "dress up" a company before its sale to another large corporation.[134] Whether American management consultants were ultimately effective in helping European organizations become more competitive is a question that will probably never be resolved. What is clear, however, is that a handful of American management consulting firms, including, most prominently, McKinsey & Company, were largely responsible for the widespread dissemination of American organizational models in Europe during the 1960s in response to problems arising in European institutions and to fears about the "American Challenge."

EIGHT

# Selling Corporate Culture

## Codifying and Commodifying Professionalism

Management theorists spent much of the 1980s and 1990s analyzing "corporate culture," the unique culture of a company or, more generally, the culture of white-collar work, with considerable success.[1] Their scholarship on corporate culture, in turn, spilled over into other academic disciplines with historians tracing the paternalism of big business, economists analyzing how shared values foster economic efficiency, and cultural critics attacking the hegemonic influence of American capitalism.[2] But research on corporate cultures was not purely academic, for it was chiefly management consultants from McKinsey & Company, alongside academic theorists sponsored by McKinsey, who first popularized the concept of "corporate cultures." Although "softer" managerial concerns about the impact of social factors on organizational efficiency predate Elton Mayo's studies at Western Electric in the 1930s, the particular phrase "corporate culture" gained momentum through a trio of influential management books published in the early 1980s that the consultants from McKinsey & Company underwrote.[3] The best-known of these books, Thomas Peters and Robert Waterman's *In Search of Excellence*, written when both men were partners at McKinsey, eventually sold over five million copies.[4] As a journalist from the *New York Times* wrote in 1983:

> As these two books indicate [*In Search of Excellence* and *Corporate Cultures*], nowhere has the notion of corporate culture been more enthusiastically embraced than at McKinsey. In fact, a cynical interpretation of the latest management vogue is that it nicely positions McKinsey itself for the 1980s.[5]

Thus, the concept of corporate culture, frequently used by academics to dissect the vagaries of corporate life, was itself a corporate product – devised, marketed, and popularized by management consultants from McKinsey.[6]

McKinsey & Company's commodification of corporate culture was not accidental. The managing partners at McKinsey & Company created "corporate culture" as a strategic response to the declining demand for the consulting firm's central "product" – the organizational study.[7] As Michael Porter, an expert in corporate strategy at the Harvard Business School, described McKinsey & Company's dilemma in 1979:

> ...partly as a result of BCG's [The Boston Consulting Group's] success, managers are very interested in concepts. BCG has had something specific to say to people, rather than having a client betting on its competence. McKinsey has reacted to that, by setting up a bunch of task forces within the firm to try and pull together their practice and codify what they've learned.[8]

McKinsey's strategic decision to codify and commodify its professional practice resulted in the publication of *In Search of Excellence*.[9] Peters and Waterman's work, in combination with McKinsey's sponsored scholarship of Anthony Athos and Richard Pascale's research on the culture of Japanese management, and Terrence Deal and Allan Kennedy's work on "the rites and rituals of corporate life," would constitute the theoretical and empirical underpinnings of the academic study of "corporate culture."[10] Moreover, because the researchers at McKinsey, and in the two business schools associated with the firm's project (Harvard and Stanford), felt comfortable analyzing the culture at McKinsey, the consulting firm itself served as the implicit model for corporate culture. In a telling introduction to *Corporate Cultures*, Deal and Kennedy quoted the former Managing Director of McKinsey & Company, Marvin Bower, when they were defining the concept of corporate culture.[11] Yet the authors felt no need to explain who Bower was, nor why he might be an authority on corporate culture. Deal and Kennedy, however, were right. Marvin Bower had long understood the impact of corporate culture, because, as he later wrote, "I recommend that every company codify its culture rather than just letting it grow through the inevitable self-molding process."[12] This self-conscious "codification" of McKinsey's professional practice provided both the basis for academic research on corporate culture, and, as the directors of the consulting firm intended, the underlying logic for the consultancy's revamped practice during the 1980s and 1990s.[13]

McKinsey & Company's "corporate culture" had its historical roots in the consulting firm's governance structure.[14] The drive to institutionalize and expand their firm led the partners at McKinsey & Company and the other leading consulting firms to devise an amalgam of professional practices first codified in the 1940s and eventually commodified during the 1980s.[15] This chapter will trace the development of these managerial practices, their lasting importance in the leading management consulting firms, and, briefly, their impact on a wide variety of organizations through the dissemination of "corporate culture." It is because of McKinsey & Company's prominence, the strong archival evidence for the firm's development, and the subsequent commodification of culture in its own professional practices, that McKinsey & Company is the central focus of this chapter. McKinsey was not, however, the only consulting firm to foster a strong corporate culture. As this chapter will demonstrate, the other elite management consulting firms during the postwar era – Booz Allen & Hamilton, A. T. Kearney & Company, Arthur D. Little, Inc., and Cresap, McCormick and Paget – also devised similar governance structures to manage their expanding firms. Ultimately, the organization and culture of the leading management consulting firms would exert a powerful influence on large-scale bureaucratic institutions as executives began increasingly to remodel their organizations after knowledge-based, team-led consultancies.[16] The consultants from McKinsey & Company had always promised to remake their corporate clients in the image of other successful organizations, but by the 1990s, former McKinsey partners like Tom Peters were busy convincing executives to restructure their organizations after McKinsey & Company.[17] This chapter traces the consultants' struggles as they created, codified, and finally commodified, their influential form of "corporate culture."

## Seeking Professional Status

Prior to the 1930s, the most prestigious firms offering management consulting services operated in several different professional fields.[18] Consultants tended to define themselves as bankers, cost accountants, or management engineers, based on the nature of their assignments, not their place of work, and so the leading firms offering consulting services did not see themselves as part of a unified professional field and rarely competed directly with one another for individual jobs.[19] In the late 1930s, however, as a result of New Deal banking legislation, the partners at Booz Allen & Hamilton, McKinsey & Company, Stevenson, Jordan & Harrison, George Armstrong & Company, and Robert Heller & Associates began to see themselves united within the same professional field of "management engineering" or, later, "management consulting" and competed with each other for routine assignments.[20]

Once management consulting firms gained jurisdictional control of the field in the 1930s, consultants turned their attention to securing professional status for the nascent discipline. As the jurisdictional conflict with other professions declined, "the prizes won by medicine and law (or by their elites)" inspired management consultants to emulate the success of the older, more prestigious professions.[21] No longer scrambling to define their work, consultants now fought to make their work respectable. As a result, consultants displayed, according to Richard Paget, "an almost narcissistic concern with [their] appearance as professionals" during the 1930s and 1940s.[22] Once unified, management consultants saw their reputation not only as a barrier against potential rivals from the other bureaucratic professions, but also as a means to establish cultural authority that would, in turn, generate more assignments and higher fees for their firms.[23]

Although Marvin Bower of McKinsey & Company noticed a rise in the general standing of management engineers in the late 1930s, professional status did not automatically accompany the surge in demand for management consulting surveys.[24] Federal banking legislation had defined the jurisdiction of management consulting, but consultants' cultivation of cultural authority through professionalization was a slow process.[25] Engineers associated with scientific management and the rebelling cost accountants had each tried to professionalize during the 1910s and 1920s only to fail in their bids for professional status and power.[26] The professionalization of management engineering represented a second effort for cost accountants and the advocates of scientific management to professionalize. This legacy of failed ambitions explains, in part, why consultants thought professionalization so important and, conversely, why consultants did not achieve immediate success. Despite the leadership of highly-respected accountants like Charles Stevenson, Harvard-trained lawyers like Marvin Bower, and politically-connected engineers like George Armstrong, outsiders continued to view consultants as a dubious amalgam of professional factions or, worse yet, disreputable hucksters.

Unfortunately for those who wanted to improve consulting's reputation, the field was rife with aggressive salesmen and self-declared experts including two of the best known consultants of the 1930s and 1940s, George S. May and Charles E. Bedaux.[27] Bedaux in the 1930s and May in the 1940s and 1950s would each create the largest consultancies in the world, earning more individually from their consulting firms than any of their rivals. Each of them would also test the ethical boundaries of the field. Bedaux, an engineer who trained himself by studying "Taylor, Emerson, and other scientific management writers," eventually rose to become "the leading practitioner of scientific management on either side of the Atlantic."[28] In the late 1930s, from the château that he owned in France, Charles Bedaux wined and dined the international elite, including the Duke and Duchess of Windsor, while he installed his wage system in hundreds of organizations in the United States and Europe.[29] Charles Bedaux's notoriety would, however, turn to ignominy when, at the end of World War II, facing trial as a Nazi collaborator, Bedaux committed suicide in a Florida jail cell.[30] In 1945, in the newsreels and in *The New Yorker*, Bedaux served as an exemplar of all that was wrong with consultants.[31] By the 1950s, however, George S. May had taken Bedaux's place as the scapegrace of disreputable practices in consulting.[32]

Unlike Bedaux, who began his career as a pimp in France, George S. May entered business as a door-to-door Bible salesman in Illinois. In the 1920s, May trained as a consultant at L.V. Estes, a Taylorist consulting firm, before founding his own consultancy in 1925. May was a relentless marketer and by the 1950s his consulting firm was spending $1 million annually on direct solicitations, sending out 8,500 to 20,000 pieces of mail each day from the firm's headquarters in Chicago to nearly 700,000 prospective clients.[33] George S. May explicitly contrasted his sales approach to consulting with the professionalism of the elite consultancies, because, as the firm's survey manual for its employees explained:

> you are there [in the client's office] for one purpose and only one, to sell the client an engineering program to start Monday morning. That is the commodity you are sent out to sell. Just like the Buick salesman is sent out to sell Buick cars.[34]

May's marketing methods, including sponsoring the "World's Championship of Golf," led journalist Hal Higdon to dub May a "brazenly resourceful self-publicist," but Higdon acknowledged that earlier exposés, like one in *Fortune* magazine in 1954, emphasizing May's lack of ethics, did little to slow the firm's growth.[35] By specializing in counseling small businesses – laundries, building contractors, auto dealers, and trucking companies – George S. May & Co. fashioned a niche market of clients not already served by the elite consulting firms.[36] Although May was under constant investigation by the Better Business Bureau, and even cited for contempt by the Kefauver Commission of the U.S. Senate because he would not answer questions about his relationship with Chicago gangsters, he was a success in business. "As sole proprietor of a business that grossed close to $200 million in his lifetime, May probably reaped riches unequaled by anyone else in management consulting."[37] May's success, like that of Bedaux before him, reminded outsiders that management consultants did not have to take a professional approach to build phenomenally successful consultancies.[38]

Clearly the leaders who aspired to professional status had to improve the public image of their field. One way for management consultants to rid the field of shady promoters like Charles Bedaux and George S. May would have been state regulated licensing.[39] Although government enforced certification was an effective way to achieve professional status, the partners at the leading management consulting firms consistently opposed certification.[40] From its start, the Association of Consulting Management Engineers

(ACME), which was open only to firms, not to individual members, sought self-regulation and opposed any form of state enforced licensing.[41] As Marvin Bower would later emphasize, consultants created ACME in order "to keep the scoundrels out *without* legal controls...the management consulting associations have been trying to *avoid* legislation instead of trying to *shape* it."[42] Ultimately, engineers would be licensed by the state, accountants certified by the CPA examination, and lawyers regulated by the bar examination, but management consultants actively campaigned to avoid government oversight. As a result, like investment banking and advertising, professional prestige within management consulting accrued not to individual consultants, but to the prestigious firms that enforced high standards.[43]

Besides state enforced licensing, management consultants lacked other qualifications that the older professions had adopted. Management consultants did not have the specialized journals, formalized university training, centralized body of abstract knowledge, or social mission of the classical professions.[44] The absence of professional credentials led Joel Dean, a professor at Chicago and a former McKinsey consultant, to observe, in 1938, that management consultants were not technically professionals: "they do not possess standards of admission and performance comparable to those of recognized professions, such as Medicine and Law."[45] Although ACME committees occasionally tried to make management consulting conform to "the basic characteristics of a profession," the partners at the leading consulting firms rejected any proposals that would have increased the professional standing of individuals at the expense of the power held by their firms.[46] Years later, in the late 1960s, when journalist Hal Higdon described management consulting as a "profession," he was challenged by a vice-president at Chase Manhattan Bank: "'May I gently chide you for stating that management consulting is a profession. I do not think it is but I would be interested if you can furnish me proof.'"[47] Without the codified qualifications of the older professions like law, medicine, or the ministry, Higdon could not offer "proof" of management consulting's professional status.

Consultants quickly decided, however, that objective standards of professionalism were not as important as recasting the public perception of consulting as a professional activity. Instead of focusing on the intrinsic professional standing of management consulting, the individual consultants, their firms, and the professional association emphasized the metaphorical similarity between consulting and the established professions. Borrowing from academics their emphasis on professionalization as a process – one element of the broader transformation of society through modernization – management consultants echoed sociologists like Talcott Parsons by emphasizing consulting's ongoing journey toward the professional ideal.[48] Consultants dismissed concerns about whether management consulting would ever achieve full professional status, stressing instead their own professional bearing and ethical standards. For, as the partners at McKinsey & Company explained to newly hired staff members, behaving like a professional would serve just as well as becoming one.[49]

To reinforce their professional comportment and overcome their lack of explicit professional credentials, management consultants employed the language and metaphors of professionalism to gain cultural authority.[50] As sociologist Andrew Abbott points out in *The System of Professions*, although professional metaphors are a relatively "weak means of jurisdictional extension," professional metaphors are a particularly strong method of promoting public respect.[51] Once management consultants had, after the New Deal banking legislation, secured their territorial claims, consultants deployed metaphors and imitation of the prestigious, older professions to extend their cultural authority. By emphasizing the association between management consulting and better established professionals, consultants sought the authority and rewards of the more respected professions.

Not all professions, consultants soon decided, served equally well as analogues to their field. As a result, management consultants carefully chose their professional metaphors for compatibility with corporate authority. Consultants were initially tempted to compare themselves with medicine, one of the oldest and most successful professions.[52] Management consultants, according to *Fortune* magazine's 1944 article on the "Doctors of Management," "constantly describe their activities in medical analogies."[53] The comparison appeared ideal. Medicine offered, it seemed, a valuable association since medical care was not only rooted in science, but the public perceived doctors as both ethical and discrete.[54] As Thomas Watson, Jr. explained to a vice-president at IBM, consultants were "like your doctor, you have to tell them everything."[55] But, the analogy between medicine and consulting contained a potentially damaging subtext, that the consultant as physician should only serve the truly ill.[56] The description "business doctor," which was popular in the 1930s, "instantly raised," according to Marvin Bower, "the image of 'sick' companies – an anathema to the managers of successful companies."[57] In contrast, the partners at McKinsey & Company tried to emphasize that healthy organizations often employed consultants because, as Bower explained to *Fortune* magazine in 1954, "those who use us the most, need us the least."[58] Management consultants sought not just to promote professional metaphors, but to shift those metaphors away from medicine toward the more "bureaucratic" professions.[59]

Other successful professions, like accounting and engineering, were easier referents for management consulting since many consultants had their initial training in accounting or engineering. During the 1930s, for example, the leading "management engineering" firms performed "management audits" for their corporate clients.[60] The comparison with engineering and accounting, however, posed a problem for consulting, not because of pejorative associations, but because management consulting had only recently distinguished itself from the engineering and accounting professions.[61] With leading engineering firms like Ford, Bacon & Davis and well-known accounting firms like Arthur Andersen already acting as consultants,

202 • The World's Newest Profession

drawing the analogy between consulting and the established professions of engineering and accounting seemed less valuable as the metaphorical association blurred rather than emphasized the distinctions between these recently separated professional fields.

Management consultants ultimately decided that the most powerful professional comparison was to corporate law. As McKinsey & Company's brochure from 1940 explained, "we serve business concerns on management problems in much the same way that the larger law firms serve them on legal problems."[62] More than the other professions, corporate law offered a powerful professional metaphor, for lawyers were highly trained, well paid, and discreet, and corporations had already acknowledged lawyers' value. Executives expected to grant lawyers, far more than other professionals, access to the corporate boardroom.[63] Hoping to piggyback on this professional authority, consultants worked metaphorically to adopt the scientism of engineering, the precision of accounting, but, most importantly, the influence and access of corporate lawyers.[64]

The metaphorical comparison between consulting and the prestigious, established professions worked as consultants had hoped. For example, when Edwin Nourse, the vice president of the Brookings Institution, wrote in 1945 to Walter Carpenter, the President of DuPont, to ask his opinion of "professional management of corporate business," Carpenter replied that management consulting firms, not corporate executives, might be "more properly referred to as 'professional management' because they seem . . . more akin to other professional organizations; such as, legal firms."[65] Carpenter's view that management consultants were like other leading professions was tangible proof of how well metaphors worked to redeem management consulting's tainted reputation. On the other hand, Nourse's reply that "efficiency engineers" lacked the credentials of true professionals suggests why consultants were never able to achieve universal acceptance as professionals purely through metaphor.[66]

Management consultants ultimately failed to professionalize because their use of strong professional metaphors could not fully

compensate for consultants' weak professional credentials.[67] Repeatedly, the leading management consulting firms were unwilling to
make the sacrifices that were necessary to achieve full professionalization. For example, when ACME created the Institute for Management Consulting (IMC) in the late 1960s to certify consultants,
the leading consulting firms chose not to require that their staff
obtain the "Certified Management Consultant" (CMC) designation,
because the certification of independent consultants would have
weakened a management consulting firm's implicit certification of its
own staff.[68] The consultants at McKinsey, Booz, BCG, and Andersen
were unwilling to acknowledge that individual practitioners were all
of equal professional standing – an inherent attribute of the professions – with the staff at their own elite firms.[69] Without mandatory
state certification, and in the absence of the full support of the leading professional association, the CMC designation never became a
significant factor. Professionalism, ultimately, became a characteristic of individual firms, not management consulting as a field. Instead
of individual consultants rallying behind the collective strategy of
professionalization, the partners of some of the most prestigious management consulting firms selectively employed the form of professionalism to strengthen their firms' practices.

### Competitive Advantage through Professional Practice

At a few management consulting firms, especially McKinsey & Company and A. T. Kearney & Company, partners employed professionalism not just as a way to burnish their public image but as the
embodiment of their firm's competitive strategy.[70] They made professional language a crucial element of their "corporate" strategy
because professional rhetoric reinforced the partners' ideology.[71] By
wielding professional language, consultants were able in the 1940s
and 1950s to differentiate their firm from the other increasingly similar consultancies.[72] At McKinsey & Company, for example, the partners believed that the professional approach distinguished them from

other firms because "most of the firms in the field give only lip service; they don't really build it into their practice."[73] As Marvin Bower explained to several new consultants:

> If a man today were to take one day away from his current engagement and spend that one day learning the professional approach he would be doing himself and the firm a much greater service than he would be to produce seventy-five, a hundred, or a hundred and fifty dollars a day of income for McKinsey & Company in 1945.[74]

Once McKinsey & Company's partners began to proclaim that their firm's competitive advantage flowed from the consultancy's professional ideology, professionalism stopped being a "narcissistic concern," in Richard Paget's words, and became a pragmatic manifestation of long-term planning.[75]

The degree to which the leading management consulting firms adopted the ideology of professionalism did not, however, correlate perfectly with their success.[76] Professionalism was one of many effective strategies; these included Arthur D. Little's emphasis on scientific prowess and Robert Heller & Associates' reliance on political contacts. These various strategies allowed the firms to position themselves in the fluid arena of consulting. Consultants' long-term emphasis on professionalism, scientific knowledge, or political acumen differentiated firms that were otherwise increasingly similar.[77] Booz Allen & Hamilton, for example, was one of the most prosperous consulting firms, but the firm's partners were more likely to describe themselves as part of an "enterprise" or an "industry" in order to emphasize their broad range of services rather than promote themselves as professionals.[78] As James Allen told *Business Week* in 1960, "'I think we were pioneers in making a business out of this business.'"[79] In contrast, as Marvin Bower explained in 1945, McKinsey & Company was trying to: "stamp out...the use of the term 'business' as characterizing McKinsey and Company. We do not have a business; we have a professional practice."[80] To emphasize the firm's distinctiveness, McKinsey & Company's training emphasized professional language, professional metaphors, and professional comportment as central elements in the firm's initial socialization of its new consultants.[81]

To create a professional atmosphere, McKinsey & Company explicitly "indoctrinated" the firm's staff in the consultancy's professional ethos. As Marvin Bower explained to the new members of the San Francisco office in 1945:

> We have an indoctrination program...to give [new employees] not only a background in the technical aspects of our work but also to give them what is more important, an understanding of the professional approach, an understanding of the McKinsey approach to management consulting work.[82]

For those staff members who did not understand why professionalism was so important, Bower explained that professionalization was not an "altruistic" decision: "our income will be greatly augmented by the professional approach, because that is the thing that builds stature and reputation."[83] Marvin Bower's blend of utilitarian practicality with professional ideology would prove a potent combination. Journalists, former partners, and management theorists would all eventually agree with Bower that McKinsey's ideology of professionalism was the consultancy's " 'secret' strength in attracting, serving, and maintaining relations with clients."[84] The firm's professional ethos would become an even more palpable advantage in the early 1950s after Marvin Bower reshaped McKinsey & Company to resemble the partnership system first developed at the large corporate law firms.

In the early 1950s, the comparison between management consulting and the legal profession moved, at McKinsey & Company, beyond rhetoric. By imitating the leading corporate law firms, Marvin Bower institutionalized the process of recruitment, selection, and promotion of new consultants, simultaneously narrowing the gap between corporate lawyers and management consultants. Prior to the 1950s, the process of finding consultants and subsequently promoting staff had always been difficult because there was no uniform route for recruitment or advancement.[85] James McKinsey, like Arthur Andersen at Northwestern University, sometimes recruited new staff from his students at the University of Chicago Business School, but after McKinsey's death in 1937, finding new staff became a more difficult process.[86] In the 1940s, like most consulting firms, McKinsey & Company acquired its staff in an ad hoc fashion from "industry, trade, and finance."[87] Marvin Bower, in contrast, sought to institutionalize McKinsey & Company's hiring by adopting the same system employed at the large corporate law firms.[88]

Marvin Bower looked to the structure developed by Paul Cravath at the elite New York law firm of Cravath, Swaine, and Moore at the turn of the century.[89] The "Cravath system," as Cravath's partner Robert Swaine dubbed it, differed from the older system of legal apprenticeship because Paul Cravath selected only a few top graduates from the elite law schools and then trained these young lawyers on a fixed salary with the understanding that only a few of them would progress to partnership.[90] Those lawyers who did not become partners would eventually have to leave Cravath, Swaine, and Moore.[91] This "up-or-out" system transformed corporate law firms because, in Wayne Hobson's words,

> the Cravath system, once institutionalized, churned out anonymous organization men, steadfastly loyal to the firm that had hired them fresh out of law school, moving only if the firm informed them that it could not advance them to partnership.[92]

Bower had first encountered the "up-or-out" system when he was hired by the law firm of Jones Day in the 1930s. His first hand experience with the system inclined him to propose in 1944 that McKinsey & Company "explore" the professional practices of the "leading law and accounting firms." Initially the consulting firm did not adopt this practice, but then in 1952, after Bower had become the Managing Partner, he pushed the idea again. Bower circulated specific excerpts from Robert Swaine's history of Cravath, with the suggestion that McKinsey "consider applying" some of Cravath's principles.[93] One year later, in 1953, the partners at McKinsey & Company "agreed to start recruiting directly from graduate business schools."[94] Then, in 1954, McKinsey & Company formally adopted an "up-or-out" policy.[95] McKinsey's structure had, according to historian Alfred Chandler's famous dictum, followed the firm's professional strategy – and ideology.[96] Form followed function here. When translated into professional practices, McKinsey & Company's professional ideology gave the consulting firm an advantage not only by appealing to important corporate clients, but also by improving the consultancy's recruitment and retention of top caliber staff.[97]

The MBA candidates at the top business schools, particularly the Harvard Business School, found Marvin Bower's conception of a "professional" career very attractive. In carefully crafted recruiting materials aimed at MBA candidates, Bower and his partners stressed McKinsey & Company's unique "personality" and the similarity between the graduate training at the Harvard Business School in the case method and the real-world skills necessary to solve corporate problems.[98] If students did not find this intellectual and professional challenge appealing then they could always look to the material rewards that Bower promised. He was quite explicit about the potential financial rewards, explaining that, "on a current income basis the successful consultant will be among the top earners in his class."[99] Bower's message came through loud and clear. Young MBAs, just out of Harvard, responded to Marvin Bower's potent combination of a high starting salary and an organization committed to professional values. As one Harvard MBA recruited by McKinsey & Company in the late 1950s explained years later, "McKinsey was probably a firm with revenues of $3 million and a handful of partners, but it was professional."[100] By 1967, of the 358 consultants at McKinsey

& Company, more than one-third of them, 121 in total, held a Harvard MBA.[101] By imitating the recruiting practices of the large corporate law firms, Marvin Bower had institutionalized the link to the Harvard Business School. There was a steady flow of young MBAs from the Harvard Business School to McKinsey & Company.

One unanticipated outcome of McKinsey's adoption of the "up-or-out" system was that many of the consultants that the firm euphemistically "separated" remained remarkably loyal to McKinsey & Company after their departure.[102] These "alumni," as they were called within McKinsey, like the unsuccessful associates at the elite law firm of Cravath, Swaine, and Moore, were highly sought after by other consultancies and by client companies filling staff positions.[103] Former McKinsey & Company consultants often went on to assume important positions outside the consulting firm and, as a result, the partners at McKinsey & Company tried "to maintain good personal relationships with those who have left the firm, simply for goodwill purposes."[104] In their subsequent careers, former associates and partners remained surprisingly devoted to the "Firm." As they moved up the corporate ladder, they passed along information to their former colleagues and often hired their former colleagues at McKinsey & Company. In 1959, McKinsey formalized this relationship by gathering the addresses of their "alumni" in order to forward the results of the partnership elections, send out an annual "Christmas letter," and eventually organize luncheons.[105] For many of these young associates, their years spent as a consultant added to their status regardless of whether they were ultimately promoted to partnership.[106] Thus McKinsey & Company's adoption of the professional model institutionalized the difficult process of hiring and firing and also created a network of former employees who served as ambassadors for McKinsey within other organizations that might otherwise have been wary of employing consultants.[107]

Management consultants' emphasis on professional norms ultimately became integral to the long-term success of firms like

McKinsey & Company, not simply because professionalization led consultants to adopt innovative administrative measures, but because the dominant professional ideology discouraged the senior partners from selling their firms. At McKinsey & Company, Marvin Bower's emphasis on professional governance – widely dispersed ownership among the partners joined with an ethos of stewardship for the next generation of partners – ultimately favored the long-run dominance of McKinsey over commercially-oriented rivals, in part because McKinsey & Company simply outlasted its competitors. Those founders of rival consulting firms who were less concerned with professionalism often sold their proprietorships when they retired and this cycle – consisting of the growth of a consultancy during the founder's lifetime and its dispersal upon the founder's retirement or death – recurred dozens of times during the 1940s and 1950s. Thus, the founders of Griffenhagen & Associates, George Fry & Associates, and Barrington Associates, all of whom had built prominent firms during the 1940s and 1950s, sold their firms in the late 1950s and 1960s.[108] In contrast, the top partners at the more "professionally" oriented consultancies like McKinsey & Company and A. T. Kearney & Company chose not to sell their firms to outsiders partly because the founding partners had initially decided to divide their firm's ownership among their younger partners, but largely because their internal ethos of stewardship discouraged retiring partners from selling the firm.[109]

The ideology of professionalization, then, helps us to understand an ostensible paradox in the evolution of the "market structure" of management consulting: although professionalization did not necessarily result in greater profitability, professional firms came to dominate the field of consulting.[110] The partners of the professionalized consultancies balanced their explicit desire to maximize organizational revenues with an implicit understanding that professionalism dictated that they serve as the stewards for the next generation of partners. "Professional" firms were not necessarily the most successful consultancies at any given moment during the evolution of manage-ment consulting, but over time they came to dominate the field.[111] The longevity of the professional consultancies gave those firms an edge on their rivals over the long-term, because reputation, exist-ing social contacts, and continual client referrals contributed to a firm's success.[112] As a result of this evolutionary process, the profes-sional firm ultimately became the dominant organizational form in the field of management consulting.

The managing partners in a select group of consultancies, most notably McKinsey & Company, employed professional metaphors, and later professional structures, to institutionalize their practices and add to their strength during the 1940s and 1950s. As the staff members within the large consultancies adopted the rhetoric and reality of professionalization, consulting firms became increas-ingly similar, not just in the assignments that they performed for their clients, but also in their internal cultures. This long-term pro-cess of institutional evolution, like the process of natural selec-tion in biology, led to an increasingly homogeneous population of consultancies.[113] Consulting's homogenization was analogous to the broader homogenization of American culture in the late 1950s and early 1960s. The increasing similarity of the leading consultancies and the prosperity of consulting as a field turned the elite firms into a symbol of good business practice in the American Century. But beneath that surface image there was a portent of the troubles they would encounter in the 1970s.[114]

### Commodifying Corporate Culture

In the 1970s, two very different firms, Arthur Andersen & Company and The Boston Consulting Group (BCG), surpassed Booz Allen & Hamilton and McKinsey & Company to become, respectively, the largest and the most profitable consulting firms in the world.[115] The partners at Andersen and BCG achieved their success by build-ing consulting practices quite different from the organizational and production advice offered by the traditional consulting firms.[116] Arthur Andersen & Company specialized in the installation and integration of computer systems – operational advice that generally did not require oversight by senior executives.[117] In contrast, The Boston Consulting Group offered clients strategic counsel on the acquisition of corporate divisions and the creation of new product lines – executive decisions that placed BCG consultants in contact with senior executives.[118] From an external perspective, then, Andersen's explosive growth came at the expense of operational specialists, "small industrial engineering firms" at the low end of the consulting market, while The Boston Consulting Group battled the elite consultancies for the high end of the market – a pincer attack upon the market for consulting services.[119] Ultimately, Andersen and BCG's success would wreak havoc within McKinsey & Company, Booz Allen & Hamilton, and Cresap, McCormick and Paget, as the three elite consultancies scrambled to reposition themselves in an increasingly competitive market.[120] As a former BCG consultant described this sea change: "McKinsey got blind-sided. They didn't see this coming."[121]

Ironically, however, Arthur Andersen and The Boston Consulting Group modeled themselves on their older competitors even as the elite consulting firms tried to emulate the success of their new rivals. By the early 1970s, through a mix of inherited professional values and self-conscious imitation, both Arthur Andersen & Company and The Boston Consulting Group had created professional governance structures strikingly similar to those already in place at the older management consulting firms.[122] Arthur Andersen & Company and The Boston Consulting Group had broken the ruling triumvirate of elite consultancies, but the institutionalized, professional model of consulting remained intact.

Although McKinsey & Company's professional model remained popular, corporate executives were increasingly disenchanted with McKinsey's "professional" services.[123] By the late 1960s, as the previous chapter described, the consultants at McKinsey had played a prominent role in the reorganization, specifically the decentralization, of many of the largest corporate, nonprofit, and government organizations in the United States and Europe.[124] Then, during the recessionary years of the early 1970s, corporate demand for McKinsey & Company's services suddenly declined; the bottom fell out of the firm's market. As a McKinsey partner in Düsseldorf characterized the problem: "our base – organization studies – became thinner and the new products on which we were working were not yet available. Organization was no longer the main concern of our clients."[125] McKinsey was suffering, and both the staff and the revenues of The Boston Consulting Group expanded twice as fast as those of McKinsey & Company, while the McKinsey senior partners struggled to increase the firm's revenues.[126] But these problems could not be willed away. Marvin Bower had guided McKinsey & Company for seventeen years between 1950 and 1967, but, between 1968 and 1978, four different managing directors headed the consultancy, two of whom were forced to resign abruptly after they lost the support of their fellow partners.[127]

In the late 1970s, the partners at McKinsey responded to almost a decade of turmoil by reexamining the consultancy's past successes – the firm's professional growth and culture – through a series of firm histories, that were used to plan for the future.[128] Equally important were initiatives undertaken by the younger partners to analyze what rival consulting firms were doing and to propose new "products" that the McKinsey consultants could offer.[129] As journalist Sandra Salmans explained in the *New York Times*:

> In the 1960's, decentralization was the vogue in management. In the 1970's, corporate strategy became the buzzword. Now, corporate culture is the magic phrase that management consultants are breathing into the ears of American executives.[130]

Although the consultants from McKinsey had scrambled to catch up with The Boston Consulting Group's innovative strategy practice,

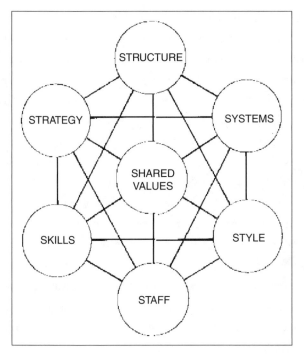

Figure 8.1. McKinsey's 7-S© framework. Reproduced with permission of McKinsey & Company.

McKinsey's own internal studies agreed with industry analysts like James Kennedy of *Consultants News* that The Boston Consulting Group had "taken the initiative away from McKinsey."[131] So, instead of protesting that the early versions of BCG's "matrix strategy analysis and the product portfolio...were developed by McKinsey," or that BCG's frameworks were "a poor mirror of the real world," the consultants from McKinsey & Company created and promoted their own simplified, copyrighted models.[132] The McKinsey 7-S© framework was the most influential product from this initiative (See Figure 8.1).[133] Popularized by Tom Peters and Bob Waterman's *In Search of Excellence*, the 7-S© model for analyzing corporate strategy would catapult McKinsey & Company back into the top ranks of the "innovative" strategy consultancies during the 1980s.

Peters and Waterman created the 7-S© framework to provide a strategic model that executives could easily remember and use. As the two consultants explained, "putting the stamp of McKinsey, long known for its hard-nosed approach to management problem solving, behind the new model added immense value" – and that value accrued to McKinsey & Company as much as to the managers who employed Peters and Waterman's framework.[134] Peters and Waterman stressed that the innovative element of their framework was not the outside ring of the "happy atom," but its inner core of "shared values (i.e. culture)."[135] Eventually, the clunky "7th S," would evolve from its initial incarnation and become "Shared Values," but it was their phrase "corporate culture" that finally caught on.[136] Tom Peters and Bob Waterman changed the practice of management not by studying "excellent" companies – indeed, consultants from Stevenson, Jordan & Harrison had done exactly the same thing more than twenty-five years earlier – but, instead, through their popularization of the concept of "corporate culture."[137]

## Conclusion

Having weathered the difficulties of the 1970s, McKinsey & Company reemerged during the 1980s as the preeminent management consulting firm in the world. The firm of Booz Allen & Hamilton would also prosper in the 1980s, although Cresap, McCormick and Paget would not survive the turmoil of first being bought by Citibank and then repurchased by the firm's principals six years later.[138] The partners in The Boston Consulting Group and Andersen Consulting would also thrive during the 1980s as the expansion of multinational corporations fueled a double-digit expansion of the major consultancies.[139] The basis of consultants' renewed success, however, would also become the source of their future difficulties as the transfer of management models accelerated and industrial companies tried to transform themselves into management consulting firms.

The lessons from the success of Arthur Andersen & Company, The Boston Consulting Group, and McKinsey & Company in the 1980s were not lost on the succeeding generation of consultants. They worried with good cause that they might fail to identify the next great managerial fad even as they continued to sell executives on the benefits of "corporate culture."[140] As the head of services for Arthur Andersen's UK office explained in 1992: "Andersen's greatest challenge is constant commoditization of its products and services. Our success depends on our ability to stay ahead of the commoditization envelope."[141] The ceaseless process of codification and commodification became a double-edged sword that threatened not only the business executives who were subjected to an accelerating barrage of new management models, but also endangered the livelihood of the very management consultants who first codified and then commodified that successive model of management.[142] That growing danger, particularly for Arthur Andersen and McKinsey, would ultimately erupt in the corporate governance crisis that brought down a company that was particularly acclaimed for adopting McKinsey's corporate culture: Enron.[143]

# NINE

# Watchdogs, Lapdogs, or Retrievers?

## Liability and the Rebirth of the Management Audit

No event made management consulting more visible than the collapse of Enron in 2001. Unlike the other corporate failures after the
"New Economy" stock market crashed in 2000, Enron's bankruptcy
was followed by breathless descriptions of late-night shredding of
documents by Arthur Andersen employees. The story captivated the
public in a way that no other corporate bankruptcy had.[1] As Arthur
Andersen's international partnership broke apart in 2002 under the
threat of criminal indictment in the United States, public officials
in America explicitly linked Andersen's malfeasance to the inherent conflict of interest between the firm's $27 million in manage-
ment consulting fees for Enron and the $25 million that Andersen
earned from Enron for its audit work.[2] In 2002, for example, *The Wall
Street Journal* highlighted the fact that more than 85 percent of the
Dow Jones Industrial companies, "paid their auditors more for consulting, tax, and other services than for the company's audit."[3] It was
no coincidence, therefore, that Congress wrote into the Sarbanes-
Oxley Corporate Reform Act (which followed the collapse of Arthur
Andersen), language that specifically barred accounting firms from
offering consulting within any company in which they were simultaneously performing an audit.[4] Following the public outcry and

regulatory changes, the large accounting firms divested themselves of their consulting divisions, effectively ending the ascendancy of the multidisciplinary professional service firms.[5]

The Enron crisis highlighted the potential conflicts of interest facing the giant accounting firms and also the absence of supervision by the associated business professionals – investment bankers, corporate lawyers, and strategy consultants – who had all profited from Enron's success.[6] In particular, the business press had a field day with the fact that Jeffrey Skilling, the architect of Enron's complex financial structure, had spent a decade as a consultant at McKinsey before he joined Enron in 1990.[7] As *The Wall Street Journal* reported, "indeed the celebrated consulting firm was a major force at Enron [and] in exchange for its strategic advice to Enron, McKinsey received millions of dollars in consulting fees."[8] Even McKinsey's corporate research appeared tainted when journalists at *The Economist* and *The New Yorker* pointed out that two bestselling management books, each of which had lavishly praised Skilling's innovations within Enron, were written by fellow consultants at McKinsey.[9]

Worst of all for McKinsey was the circumstantial evidence that Richard Foster (the McKinsey partner who coauthored *Creative Destruction*) attended an Enron board meeting where Andrew Fastow (Enron's CFO who eventually pleaded guilty to corporate fraud) outlined the external private partnerships that would later bankrupt Enron.[10] As journalists from *The Wall Street Journal* rhetorically asked, "At a time when Enron's collapse is churning up thorny ethical and legal problems for its accountants, lawyers, and executives, the question arises: How accountable should McKinsey, its strategy advisor, be?"[11] John Coffee (the Adolf Berle Professor of Law at Columbia University) did not sugar coat his opinion of the professionals' culpability for the failure of Enron's corporate governance: "it's about the gatekeepers, stupid."[12] Where auditors, consultants, lawyers, and investment bankers had once served as true gatekeepers of corporate legitimacy, the apparent lack of independence among modern professionals emerged as the central explanation for the crisis in American corporate governance.[13]

In retrospect, the regulatory response that followed the American excesses of the 1990s and the collapse of the technology boom in 2000 mirrored the New Deal legislation of the 1930s that followed the stock market boom and bust of the 1920s.[14] So clear were the parallels that regulators and public commentators not only noted the similarity but also made explicit reference to the 1930s, revisiting the original logic of the Securities and Exchange Commission (S.E.C.) and Banking Acts as they were framing the Sarbanes-Oxley Act in 2002.[15] Yet, in the rush to explain the "recurrent crisis" in corporate governance (to borrow Paul MacAvoy and Ira Millstein's description), more attention was lavished on Andersen's inability to oversee Enron's financial statements than was spent on McKinsey's crucial role in corporate governance. This was the case despite the fact that both professional firms acted as important reputational intermediaries for Enron.[16] We need to look more closely at the means by which the elite consulting firms and the leading accounting firms that created management consulting divisions became so important in the governance of corporations from the 1980s onwards. That will help us to understand why, ironically, current boards of directors have become even more reliant on the advice of consultants after the passage of the Sarbanes-Oxley Act. Far from being an isolated case, the failure of lawyers, accountants, consultants, and investment bankers to intervene when Enron executives broke the law was the result of important legal and regulatory changes during the 1980s and 1990s, changes that fundamentally altered the way that boards of directors governed American corporations.

In order to explain the evolution of management consulting during the 1980s and 1990s, we must in effect return to the regulatory environment of the 1930s. There are macroeconomic parallels between the two periods and a concomitant need for corporate legitimacy, brought on by regulatory pressures, that encouraged the initial use and the subsequent revival of the "management audit" in the 1990s. The worldwide scandals in corporate governance, culminating in the failures of Enron, WorldCom, and Parmalat, were a consequence of two decades of surging demand for accounting and consulting services by directors and officers attempting to offset corporate liability for potential managerial malfeasance.[17] In the 1930s, the fear of increasing legal liability during the Great Depression drove investment firms to hire management consultants to perform "management audits." During the 1990s, similar fears drove corporate executives to employ consultants to perform modern "management audits" as a form of defensive due diligence.[18] Thus, the changing use of consultants at the end of the twentieth century and its lasting institutional consequences can be traced to juridical and regulatory changes with roots that extend more than half a century earlier into the depths of the Great Depression.

## The Regulatory Origins of the Management Audit

When Marvin Bower, who re-founded McKinsey & Company in 1939, was a student at the Harvard Business School (from 1929 to 1931), he wrote two little-known articles for the *Harvard Business Review*, publications that anticipated his subsequent career at McKinsey. In his first article, Bower considered how businessmen could institutionalize the emerging market for "plans for reorganizing, consolidating, and refinancing companies." He wrote this before he was even aware that specialized professional firms, then called "management engineers," already existed to solve these managerial problems.[19] It was Bower's second article in 1931, however, on the potential dangers in joining a board of directors that may have been even more prescient, as external reports for corporate boards would become a crucial line of business for consultants during the 1930s.[20] Indeed, Marvin Bower's concern for the potential liability of board membership would have found a warm welcome with James

McKinsey, who had written, only two years earlier, about the potential dangers faced by corporate boards.[21] Bower and McKinsey, both of whom were trained as lawyers, independently agreed that although executives on corporate boards had been treated well by the courts in the past, "a director at the present time especially should know how to govern himself so as to avoid personal liability."[22] Even before the advent of the New Deal regulation of the 1930s, lawyers had begun to worry about the potential liability that corporate directors faced.

Whatever the merits of Marvin Bower and James McKinsey's articles, they would soon be overshadowed by the publication of Adolf Berle and Gardiner Means's *The Modern Corporation and Private Property* in 1932.[23] As economist George Stigler has written, Berle and Means's book – to this day a canonical text in corporate law – was received "warmly, and often extravagantly," by contemporary reviewers for the authors' analysis of the separation of ownership and control in the large, modern corporation.[24] Berle and Means, both Harvard-trained colleagues at the Columbia Law School, argued that the historic trustee relationship between shareholders and corporate boards had been corrupted by the divorce of ownership from administrative control.[25] In the two years that followed the publication of Berle and Means's book, the American legislature, under the tutelage of James Landis from the Harvard Law School, fused Berle and Means's academic language with the populist critiques of Louis Brandeis, Thorstein Veblen, and William Ripley in the construction of the Securities Act of 1933, the Glass-Steagall Banking Act of 1933, and the Securities Exchange Act of 1934.[26] The American Congress, fearing for the governance of unchecked corporate boards and the power of unrestrained monopolies, found academic justification in Berle and Means's analysis of the modern corporation.[27] The academic critiques in the 1920s and 1930s of the institutional evolution of American corporate governance provided the philosophical underpinnings to the new regulatory system for financial markets under President Roosevelt's New Deal.[28]

Worried that the separation of ownership and control promoted an inherent conflict of interest, Congress stiffened the legal liability that corporate board members faced for negligent acts. The legislators were worried that board members would not be constrained by financial losses because they no longer had a substantial equity interest in the corporation.[29] As we saw in the first chapter, the directors and officers of American corporations responded to the new regulatory requirements of the New Deal legislation by hiring accountants, investment bankers, and consultants to certify that the board's actions were both legal and prudent.[30] Management consultants, in particular, produced "bankers' surveys" or, by another name, "management audits," that paralleled the "financial audits" produced by the accountants and the "valuation reports" produced by investment bankers. The "management audit," like a financial audit, did not bring new methods into the firm or seek to change the way that a firm was run, but rather served as independent, external confirmation of management's judgment.[31] Corporate boards quickly concluded, with a not-so-gentle push from the Securities and Exchange Commission (S.E.C.), that their first line of defense against increased legal liability would be to pay, "experts such as accountants, engineers, and appraisers whose professions give authority to their statements" to certify their actions according to William Douglas (who succeeded James Landis as Chairman of the S.E.C.).[32] During the 1930s, boards of directors shrewdly marshaled the legitimacy of professional opinion, in part through the use of management consultants, to reduce their potential liability in the face of increased regulation.

In the early 1940s corporate boards began to employ an even more straightforward device to offset their potential liability from shareholder lawsuits: liability insurance. Before the 1940s, it was not clear if it was legal for corporations to promise to indemnify board members if they were involved in litigation. Indeed, in one high profile case, the New York State Supreme Court ruled in 1939 that it was explicitly *illegal* for public corporations to reimburse board members for their legal costs connected with their official duties even when the individuals were subsequently proven innocent.[33] Both academics and businessmen, however, began to complain that "stockholders cannot expect to obtain high-caliber directors under such conditions."[34] Administrators in the S.E.C. supported their position by withdrawing the agency's opposition to reimbursing corporate officers for litigation expenses, and state legislatures, including that of New York, quickly amended their general corporate statutes to permit reimbursement for legal fees.[35] The immediate result, following the new legislation, was a flood of corporations purchasing indemnity insurance for their officers. As an article in the *Harvard Business Review* explained:

> In 1938, stockholders had not heard of agreements for general indemnification of directors and officers for expenses incurred by them in connection with litigation to which they might become subject by virtue of their corporate positions. The few proposals made in 1939 and 1940 were shown in 1941 to have been merely the precursors of a fad that a host of corporations would scramble to adopt.[36]

This so-called fad for the provision of directors' indemnity insurance, or "directors and officers (D&O) liability insurance" as it would come to be known, soon became a de facto corporate policy for the protection of executives in large corporations.[37] With the introduction of insurance policies to bear the potential risks of litigation, the use of professionals, like consultants, as a hedge against legal liability faded away except where federal and state laws explicitly mandated their use. Management consultants returned to selling advice, not due diligence, as their primary product, until the next crisis in American corporate governance.

### The Return of Arthur Andersen to Consulting, 1940–1985

When the partners in Arthur Andersen decided in the 1930s to follow the path of least resistance and jettison their management engineering practice in favor of audit work, they never expected that their accounting firm would reenter the market for management consulting.[38] After all, by the mid- 1930s, more than 90 percent of all corporations listed on the New York Stock Exchange hired external accountants to audit their accounts, far more than ever hired by a management engineering firm to perform a consulting study.[39] Management engineering was a lucrative niche market for small firms like Stevenson, Jordan & Harrison, James O. McKinsey & Company, and Edwin G. Booz Surveys, but for an already large, professional firm like Arthur Andersen, the choice between accounting and consulting was clear – in the 1930s audits were both profitable and dependable. The U.S. Congress had followed Berle and Means's suggestion in *The Modern Corporation and Private Property* that public companies be required to file audited accounts and thus created a stable, regulated market for the leading accounting firms.[40] Under the new legislation, public accountants examined the financial statements and then offered their firm's opinion as to whether they were fair and whether they reflected generally accepted accounting practices. This was in contrast to the older system in which accountants first examined the books and then prepared the financial statements, which were certified by the same accounting firm. As a result of this new system, the public accountants, during the 1930s and the 1940s, like the management engineers, became involved less in the direct transmission of new professional practices than in publicly certifying the legitimacy of prior corporate decisions. By the 1950s, the leading accounting firms, including the fast growing Arthur Andersen & Company, came to embody and legitimate the American system of corporate governance.

Not surprisingly, accounting firms and consulting firms followed similar paths in their development during the 1950s and 1960s. The leading accounting firms had already expanded overseas; indeed, many of the leading firms were partnerships between Scottish and American firms that dated back to the early twentieth century.[41] Like James McKinsey, Arthur Andersen & Company pioneered a system of professional training that would result in a powerful collective culture within the firm.[42]

The most important development during the 1950s, however, took the accountants down a new institutional path. This happened when Arthur Andersen decided to build a professional practice around the use of computer systems for accounting. As the previous chapters described, in the 1950s a few young Andersen accountants became fascinated by the potential impact of electronic computers on accounting systems. Encouraged by the senior partners to move ahead, they created a distinctive practice area around the installation of information technology.[43] The revenues from computer consulting, however, were initially limited, because computers were not yet widely used within corporations. As a result, the practice area was subsidized for many years by the more profitable audit and tax practices within the rest of Andersen.[44] Although the profits from "Administrative Services" (none of the large accounting firms referred to their management consulting work as "consulting" until the 1980s) trailed the returns from traditional auditing until the early 1970s, by the late 1970s, following the rapid growth of the use of information technology in corporations, management consulting contributed more than one-fifth of Arthur Andersen's revenue.[45] Coupled with a brief surge in litigation against accountants in the late 1960s and early 1970s, information technology consulting revenues grew rapidly even as auditing revenues began to decline.[46]

Ominously for Andersen, two distinct cultures developed in the firm during the late 1970s. Their common culture broke down as a result of the partners' pragmatic decision in the 1960s not to train the accountants and the consultants jointly. The subsequent surge in consulting profits, of course, made the allocation of income all the more divisive. In 1979, after the S.E.C. raised questions about whether the two groups could truly offer independent advice, the managing partner of Arthur Andersen suggested splitting the accountants and the consultants into two independent firms.[47] By this point, however, the revenues from consulting were beginning to prop up the incomes for the audit partners who, of course, could not see the logic of spinning off a profitable enterprise.[48] Although the Andersen partners would reject the proposed breakup and their accounting and consulting practices would remain united within single partnership for another twenty years, the interests of the two sides continued to diverge.

Thus, by the mid-1980s, within the large accounting firms, there were two festering problems, both of which were particularly magnified within Arthur Andersen: the potential danger of class action lawsuits that would result in significant judgments; and the increasing tension between the information technology consultants and the auditors.[49] In 1985, for example, Arthur Andersen's consulting practice was more profitable per partner than its traditional accounting and tax business.[50] By that time, Arthur Andersen was the largest consulting firm in the world, with more than $450 million in revenues (nearly 30 percent of the firm's $1.6 billion in total revenues). The partnership was under increasing pressure from regulators, the courts, and the dissenting partners, and even before the liability crisis of the mid-1980s, Andersen and the other giant accounting and consulting firms were facing rising professional liability insurance rates and internal dissension.[51] They were then hit by their clients' corporate litigation crisis, the first shot in a struggle that would ultimately bring these professional service firms down.[52]

## The Liability Crisis of the mid-1980s

Once institutionalized in the early 1940s, the subject of D&O liability insurance faded from public view as it was, at best, a necessary evil. There was little theoretical or even management interest in the issue. In the late 1960s, when there was a flurry of shareholder lawsuits, the *Columbia Law Review* explained that "directors' and officers' liability insurance, though available for more than two decades, has only in recent years attracted the attention of corporate management."[53] This wave of concern passed. Inflammatory advertisements by insurance companies in *The Wall Street Journal* threatened that bitter shareholders "might just sue every company director reading this newspaper," but the warnings aroused little long-term interest.[54] As the percentage of American public corporations holding directors' and officers' liability insurance rose, an increasing number of insurance companies began offering D&O coverage.[55] For the most part, the dull topic of directors' and officers' liability insurance was relegated to insurance brokers, corporate counsel, and academic footnotes, except for the occasional alarmist article, during the four decades between the mid-1940s and the mid-1980s.[56] With few corporate lawsuits and even fewer guilty verdicts against directors and officers, there seemed to be little reason to worry about corporate liability.

Corporate executives were initially right not to be concerned about their exposure to corporate liability, because they were generally well protected from litigation by the "business judgment rule." As Marvin Bower explained to the readers of the *Harvard Business Review* in 1931, "fortunately, the law has so developed that the honest and careful director can usually avoid personal liability without keeping counsel constantly by his side."[57] In essence, the business judgment rule that evolved in American common law presumed, as the courts interpreted the concept, that "in making a business decision the directors of a corporation acted on an informed basis, in good faith, and in the honest belief that the action taken was in the best interest of the company."[58] Thus, dissident stockholders challenging executives' actions could not base their claim on the economic outcome but instead had to challenge the legal presumption that the board of directors had acted in good faith and to the best of their abilities in reaching a decision.[59] For most of the twentieth century, the business judgment rule turned on the process of corporate decision making, therefore board members could only be held liable for mistakes if shareholders could prove that the board had demonstrated gross negligence. In 1985, however, the issue of directors' and officers' liability insurance would become a national crisis after a board of directors was found negligent in a prominent legal decision that led to a full-blown crisis in corporate governance.[60]

In 1985, the Delaware Supreme Court ruled that the board of directors of the Trans Union Corporation had failed to exercise "informed business judgment" in approving the acquisition of the company in 1980 by Jay Pritzker, the billionaire whose family built the Hyatt Hotel chain.[61] In particular, in the precedent-setting *Smith v. Van Gorkom* case, the Delaware Supreme Court overruled the lower Chancery Court determining that, despite an emergency two-hour meeting by the board of directors, and despite the fact that Pritzker's offer price was significantly above the stock market price, the board members were "grossly negligent" in approving the sale of the company.[62] As Bayless Manning, former dean of the Stanford Law School, described the resulting turmoil, the court's decision in the Van Gorkom case had "exploded a bomb."[63] Stunned corporate lawyers, searching for a way to insulate their clients against potential liability, seized upon the court's criticism of the Trans Union board for not seeking outside advice (Manning jokingly referred to this decision as the "Investment Bankers' Relief Act of 1985") even though the justices claimed that external studies were *not* essential "to support an informed business judgment."[64] Jonathan Macey and Geoffrey Miller explained in the *Yale Law Journal*, that as a practical matter the Van Gorkom decision virtually guaranteed the increased "use of investment bankers and lawyers in corporate decision making."[65]

It was not only investment bankers and lawyers, however, who benefited, because one of the key pieces of evidence used by the dissenting justice to show that the Trans Union board had exercised "informed business judgment" was the fact that less than two months earlier, "the board had reviewed and discussed an outside study of the company done by The Boston Consulting Group."[66] As lawyers from

Wachtell Lipton, echoing comments from other leading law firms, would announce to a staff reporter from *The Wall Street Journal*, "this decision underscores once again the critical need for the retention of independent experts."[67] In short, by toughening the standard interpretation of the business judgment rule in 1985, the Delaware court had resuscitated the dormant logic of the "management audit" that had once been the central product of the leading management consulting firms during the 1930s.

The Van Gorkom decision quickly led to a national crisis in corporate liability insurance. Emboldened by the judgment, American corporate lawyers launched a barrage of class action lawsuits against public companies with the result that between 1984 and 1987, the number of lawsuits against directors and officers rose by a factor of five and the associated monetary judgments rose by 750 percent.[68] The editors of *The Wall Street Journal* explained the subsequent chain of events in an editorial criticizing the new legal standard:

> The problem began with the Delaware Supreme Court rule last year in *Smith vs. Van Gorkom* ... The 10 directors were held liable for $23.5 million, only $10 million of which was covered by insurance. The rest would have come out of their pockets if the Pritzkers hadn't picked up the tab. Premiums skyrocketed when insurers realized that directors could be held personally liable even when their corporation is sold at a huge profit.[69]

The problem, however, was not simply that insurance companies increased their premiums but that for some corporations there was no available supply at any price.[70] As the *New York Times* reported, despite significantly reduced coverage and premiums rates that rose as much as tenfold, "... in certain industries – such as steel, petroleum, and electronics – there may be a problem simply finding an insurer."[71] Even though corporations had no choice but to pay the higher rates for directors' and officers' liability insurance, many of the large insurance companies withdrew from the market for D&O

insurance, cancelled long-standing policies, and forced large corporations to self-insure.[72]

With corporations unable to offer boards of directors adequate liability coverage to cover the increase in shareholder lawsuits, outside directors began to defect.[73] In September 1985, for example, the
chairman of the board and six external directors resigned from the
eleven-member board of Continental Steel when the corporation
ceased to carry D&O liability insurance because, in the words of
the corporate spokesman, "the cost of providing the coverage wasn't
'economically viable.'"[74] To the rich and powerful executives who
remained on the boards of the largest American companies, their
financial exposure to unlimited personal liability was simply unac-
ceptable and the directors and officers of the giant corporations were
willing to pay a great deal for some – even any – form of personal
protection.[75] So, corporate boards once again embraced the "management audit" of the 1930s to protect themselves from possible liability.

Corporations dealt with the D&O liability crisis by pursuing three
parallel lines of defense: purchasing what little insurance they could,
pushing the legislature for tort reform, and employing external professional counsel.[76] Executives bought as much insurance as they
could at the newly inflated rates. Contemporary accounts make clear,
however, that what D&O insurance was available was simply not
enough to cover the potential liability that boards faced. As a leading insurance broker from Alexander & Alexander explained in
1986: "'where it used to be possible to get $200 million of cover-
age for a client, it would now be an outstanding feat to put together
$35 million.'"[77] Meanwhile, companies began to agitate for new leg-
islation and revised corporate statutes to limit their exposure. In
Delaware, for example, the state legislature quickly passed a new
law that allowed shareholders to vote to "exempt outside directors
from liability [in order to] reduce director liability and thus the cost
of premiums."[78] Eventually, the clamor for tort reform that began

in the aftermath of the Van Gorkom decision would result in the U.S. Congress passing the Private Securities Reform Act of 1995 and the Securities Litigation Uniform Standards Act of 1998 in order to reduce the number of class action lawsuits by corporate shareholders.[79] Nevertheless, directors and officers solicited external opinions on their important corporate decisions because, as the Van Gorkom decision had made clear, the courts did not consider a two-month-old study from The Boston Consulting Group to be relevant. With increased liability came the natural instinct to offset potential losses by purchasing insurance to guard against shareholder lawsuits, by agitating to lower the legal threshold, and by increasing corporate legitimacy through outside affirmation of specific internal decisions.[80]

In the face of the liability crisis, corporate boards hired management consultants to defend themselves against potential claims that corporate officers had failed to act with due diligence in their oversight of company policy.[81] As a result, from the late 1980s onward, consultants increasingly found themselves selling legitimacy, not simply knowledge transfer. Critics of the consulting profession, who are prone to ridicule management consultants for "borrowing a client's watch in order to tell them the time," saw the evolution of consultants' assignments from transferring knowledge to legitimating corporate decisions as further proof that management consultants were really charlatans. Even historically-minded critics of consulting, however, failed to acknowledge that the widespread use of consultants to provide "management audits" was a revival of the older form of consulting that paralleled the traditional financial audit performed by accountants.[82] The "Strategic Audit," what Gordon Donaldson, in the *Harvard Business Review*, called a "new tool," for corporate boards to lessen their liability, was in fact a very old idea rediscovered by executives and academics when the need arose once again.[83] The need was a product of the judicial system, not of the consultants – happy as they were with the results.

Where management consultants had previously proposed a suggested course of action to be ratified by independent board members, the tables were turned during the 1990s, when consultants, in practice, became the independent outsiders who endorsed the "internal" board's previous decisions. Management consulting advice, of course, had always been used as a political tool to legitimate executive decisions, but, beginning in the late 1980s, consultants' role in conferring legitimacy began to be more openly employed as a legal hedge against corporate liability.[84] In particular, two influential cases in American corporate law involving Fortune 500 corporations illustrate how corporate boards came to depend on management consultants to prove that the directors had exercised good judgment in their decisions. In the first case, the Delaware Chancery Court (subsequently upheld on appeal) ruled in *QVC v. Paramount* (1993) that the board of directors of QVC had been negligent in approving a merger with Paramount. The court based its decision, in part, on evidence that the QVC Board of Directors had relied upon a Booz Allen report that was only a preliminary "first cut" and not an exhaustive analysis of the benefits that would come from the proposed merger.[85] In the second case, the Superior Court of North Carolina ruled in *First Union v. Suntrust Banks* (2001) that the board of directors of Wachovia Bank had conclusively demonstrated good judgment in pursuing a merger with First Union. The court based its decision on evidence that the Wachovia Bank board of directors had followed the corporate strategy outlined in a McKinsey report that included the consultants' analysis of a possible merger with First Union.[86] Thus, both cases made it clear that a board of directors needed to commission a management consulting study – preferably exhaustive – of any significant strategic decision. When the board of directors relied only on their own judgment or an outdated or incomplete report – as in Trans Union's reliance on an old BCG report in 1985 or QVC's use of a preliminary study by Booz Allen in 1993 – the directors could well be found negligent.[87] It is no wonder that during the 1990s, American corporations like AT&T hired management consultants with abandon, because consulting reports came with the added bonus that they also represented a form of insurance against shareholder lawsuits.[88]

## The Push to Reduce Professional Liability, 1986–1995

As corporations came to depend on management consultants and other professionals – accountants, lawyers, and investment bankers – to provide a shield against class action lawsuits, professional firms were increasingly named in court cases as co-defendants with their clients.[89] For a shareholder lawsuit to succeed, the shareholders needed to prove that both the corporate officers and the independent management consultants had exercised faulty judgment.[90] If, however, the shareholders were somehow able to prove gross negligence, or criminal intent, the judgments could far exceed the normal limits of professional liability insurance.[91] In general, however, professional expertise functioned as promised and most lawyers counseled disgruntled shareholders who brought suits against corporate boards to settle the case quickly if a leading consulting firm had backed up the board's decision. Those cases that did go to court were generally dismissed.[92] As a result, insurance underwriters offered the leading strategy consulting firms far better terms for professional liability insurance than other professional service firms as strategy consultants were the least likely to be found guilty in a shareholder lawsuit.[93] Conversely, with consulting studies from McKinsey, Bain, BCG, or Booz Allen serving to bolster the business judgment rule, executives understood that the exhorbitant fees they paid were as much a premium for corporate liability insurance as a direct payment for consulting advice. Other professionals, however, were not as lucky as the strategy consultants.

As the work performed by lawyers, accountants, and investment bankers increasingly became a shield for class action lawsuits, the leading professional firms' own potential liability began to mount. As the professionals within the very large firms soon learned, providing corporate liability insurance was both a highly profitable and a highly risky business.[94] For the major accounting, law, and information technology consulting firms, the demand for them to insure corporate reputation came with associated costs. As their revenues rose with this new line of business, so did their own professional liability.[95] As a result of this dramatically increased risk, in the early 1990s, the price of liability insurance for professional firms, including accountants and lawyers, sky-rocketed.[96] The internal archives of Coopers & Lybrand, one of the "Big Six" accounting firms, show that by 1990 the firm's cumulative court judgments, settlement costs, and legal defense fees, cost the partners 4 percent of the firm's annual revenues.[97] That 4 percent, however, would have seemed almost reasonable only four years later when, in 1993, the partners in Coopers & Lybrand were spending more than twice that, or 8 percent of the firm's revenues, on litigation. Even more remarkable was the fact that the partners in Coopers & Lybrand were doing well in comparison to their competitors, who were spending between 12 and 20 percent of their total professional revenues on litigation judgments, settlements, and defense by the mid-1990s.[98] Corporate directors and officers had successfully transferred a portion of their potential liability to the professional firms, but the professional firms had not yet found a way, short of increased liability insurance for themselves, to transfer their potential liability to another party.[99]

The only reasonable strategic response open to the large accounting firms, short of abandoning their near monopoly over corporate audits, was to push for legislative reform. In 1992, the Big Six accounting firms (Arthur Andersen & Co., Coopers & Lybrand, Deloitte & Touche, Ernst & Young, KPMG Peat Marwick, and Price Waterhouse) issued a joint statement promoting legislative action to deal with the "liability crisis."[100] Eugene Freedman, the Chairman of Coopers & Lybrand, promised his firm's staff that, "the Big

Six firms have launched an aggressive and coordinated program to achieve substantive liability reforms at both the federal and state levels."[101] The accounting firms urged their professional staff to send individual letters on "personal stationery" to their local senators and congressional representatives (as well as a copy to the accounting firm's political consultants) in order to push for liability reform.[102] Like the directors of corporate boards, public accountants believed that the best way for them to achieve a lasting solution to their liability problems would be legislative changes, or from their perspective, reforms.

In particular, the large firms targeted two areas for legal relief: the longstanding problem that professionals were subject to "joint and several liability" and the S.E.C. Rule 10b-5 that held professionals liable for "aiding and abetting."[103] The leading accounting firms targeted the legal doctrine of "joint and several liability" because under a well-established legal precedent, professional firms were potentially responsible for the entire judgment alongside a corporation, in a class action lawsuit, no matter the severity of their offense, if they were both found guilty by the courts.[104] Professional firms were also uncomfortable with Section 10(b) of the Securities and Exchange Act of 1934 and Rule 10b-5 of the Securities and Exchange Commission that had always been interpreted by the courts to hold accountants, lawyers, and consultants liable for civil action for "aiding and abetting" fraud.[105] The managing partners of the Big Six accounting firms warned legislators that without significant legal changes the leading audit firms would have to practice risk reduction "by avoiding what are considered high-risk audit clients."[106] The accounting firms were arguing, in effect, that the state should protect the implicit right of every large company to be audited by one of the six accounting firms that monopolized this market.

In retrospect, risk reduction would have required Arthur Andersen & Company to abandon auditing Enron because Andersen's internal risk assessment department classified Enron among the accounting firm's fifty clients who deserved a "maximum risk" rating.[107] Unfortunately for everyone connected with both Arthur Andersen and Enron, the U.S. Congress bowed to the pressure of corporate boards, professional firms, and presumably the lure of substantial monetary contributions to their election campaigns.[108] Between 1988 and 1996, according to figures collected by the accountant Robin Roberts, the U.S. public accounting profession donated more than $17 million to political campaigns, with their donations peaking during the 1994–6 period when Congress was drafting and debating liability legislation.[109] Relief came first from the Supreme Court and then from Congress. In 1994, an increasingly conservative Supreme Court (a legacy of Presidents Reagan and Bush, Sr.) overturned all previous judicial precedents by ruling that professionals were not liable for "aiding and abetting" under S.E.C. Rule 10b-5. A year later, Congress (overriding President Clinton's veto) passed the Private Securities Reform Act of 1995, which abolished "joint and several liability" in favor of proportional liability for professional firms.[110] In short order, the accounting firms had achieved both of the changes for which they had been lobbying. The American courts and legislature had granted the leading professional firms the means to escape the professional liability that had been transferred to them by corporate boards since the mid-1980s.[111] With this remarkable turn of events, the decade-long liability crisis had, most professionals presumed, finally come to an end.

### The Backlash against the Integration of Auditing and Consulting

Struggling during the late 1980s and early 1990s to keep their audit practices profitable, the partners in these giant professional firms had meanwhile pioneered a new business model that allowed them to subsidize loss-leading corporate audits through more profitable information technology consulting assignments.[112] Although Arthur Andersen had been a pioneer in the development of a consulting practice, the other large accounting firms soon followed Andersen's lead, either through rapid internal expansion of their consulting divisions or by acquiring existing consulting firms, or both. In 1984, for example, Touche Ross (one of the Big Eight accounting firms) acquired Braxton (one of the ten largest management consulting firms in the United States at the time) and in 1985, both Price Waterhouse and Coopers & Lybrand purchased consultancies.[113] As a result of this rapid expansion, by 1992, the revenue from non-audit work ($6.2 billion) within the Big Six accounting firms had surpassed the fees from corporate audits ($5.3 billion).[114]

In their drive to expand into consulting, however, the partners of the giant accounting firms unwittingly caused more problems than they solved. Their consulting assignments created the appearance of a conflict of interest that endangered the accounting profession's entrenched support among government regulators. As the "Big Six" accounting firms (soon to be the "Big Five" after the merger of Price Waterhouse and Coopers & Lybrand in 1997) pushed to expand their consulting divisions, the accountants, consultants, and regulators found themselves increasingly at odds.[115] Those management consultants affiliated with the large accounting firms could readily see that they were subsidizing the work of the auditors (even if the auditors generated the initial contacts) and, as a result, consultants complained that their pay didn't reflect the profits that they brought into the firms.[116] In contrast, although the accountants did not want to kill the goose that laid the golden eggs, the partners recognized that their intense competition for consulting contracts had led to cross-subsidies that promoted cutthroat price competition for corporate audits.[117] In the late 1990s, this issue came to a head when Arthur Levitt, the Chairman of the S.E.C., decided that the leading auditors were no longer truly independent from their corporate clients because the large accounting firms had become so reliant on consulting revenues.[118] Unable to broker a deal with the managing partners of the leading accounting firms, Levitt publicly petitioned Congress to separate accounting and consulting.[119]

Although academic opinion remains divided on whether the relative scale of consulting revenues swayed auditor's opinions, both regulators and public officials grew increasingly suspicious of the potential risks from the integration of the two functions.[120] As the former head of Deloitte & Touche, Michael Cook, argued with Arthur Levitt at the S.E.C., "'...maybe this is more a perception problem than a real problem, and maybe you helped create the perception,' Cook said. 'But the fact is, the perception is the deciding factor.'"[121] By the late 1990s, following Arthur Levitt's crusade, the general public began to believe that the consulting work of accounting firms interfered with accountants' ability to offer independent audits. Thus, in contrast to the self-reinforcing "iron triangles" of common interest that political scientists once imagined decided public policy, the hostile triangle of accountants, consultants, and regulators incessantly attacked and undermined each other in the public eye.[122]

The tension between auditors and consultants had been rising within Andersen since 1989 when the partners in Arthur Andersen had agreed to split the accounting and consulting divisions into two distinct legal entities (Arthur Andersen and Andersen Consulting – which would ultimately rename itself "Accenture").[123] Still, the two entities were never fully separated because the auditors remained dependent on the extra income. Unable to satisfy the rising demands of their consulting partners, by the late 1990s these "multidisciplinary professional service firms" (for what else could one call a firm like Arthur Andersen that employed thousands of practicing lawyers and consultants in addition to traditional accountants?) vacillated between adding further professional services and jettisoning those divisions completely. The giant accounting firm, KPMG, for example, briefly created an investment banking affiliate in 1995 and then, only five years later, decided to sell its entire consulting division.[124] Although the accountants' liability had significantly declined following the passage of the Private Securities Reform Act of 1995, political pressure on accountants to exit consulting was continuing to mount. By the late 1990s, following more than a decade of double-digit increases in revenues from consulting, the large accounting firms began to suspect that the officials from the SEC would not allow them to continue to serve both as accountants and consultants.[125]

Under pressure from the SEC, with internal pressure from their partners who were consultants, and facing a potential windfall of billions of dollars if they chose to sell their consulting practices, the accounting partners in the Big Five began to separate themselves from consulting.[126] In retrospect, the scale of this transfer is remarkable because, by 1998, the Big Five employed more than 65,000 consultants and billed more than $12 billion annually.[127] By 2002, each of these five consulting firms had new names and new owners: Andersen Consulting had become Accenture; Ernst & Young Consulting was bought by Cap Gemini (the European computer services consulting firm), Pricewaterhouse Coopers Consulting was sold to IBM, Deloitte Consulting completed a management buyout and reverted to its legacy name "Braxton" (the strategy consulting firm that had been purchased by Touche Ross in 1984); and finally KPMG Consulting became a publicly traded company and renamed itself BearingPoint.[128] Of course, this brief overview skips past the fact that in the short interval between 1998 and 2002, one of the largest companies in America, Enron, went bankrupt, dragging down Arthur Andersen, their corporate auditors, and the resulting public fiasco rapidly turned into the worst crisis in corporate governance since the 1930s.[129] Worst of all was the fact that far from a strange anomaly, the Enron/Andersen debacle was clearly a consequence of the professional liability crisis that hearkened back to the mid-1980s.

## The Liabilities of Enron and Arthur Andersen

Rebecca Smith and John Emshwiller, the *Wall Street Journal* reporters who wrote the series of articles that ultimately brought down both

Enron and Arthur Andersen, would later be compared with Bob Woodward and Carl Bernstein, the reporters at *The Washington Post* who exposed the Watergate scandal.[130] Like Woodward and Bernstein's dogged investigation, Smith and Emshwiller's digging produced an international financial scandal – a story that they pieced together from scattered, fragmentary clues.[131] The parallels between Enron and Watergate, however, went beyond the actual process of newspaper reporting to the underlying explanation for the public's outrage. As a journalist with *The Financial Times* pointed out, like Watergate, people were far less interested in the primary illegal act (the intricate accounting gimmickry that led to the bankruptcy of Enron) than the clumsy attempt to cover up the crime after the fact (Arthur Andersen's shredding of audit files, for example).[132] Had the collapse of Enron not been followed by the investigation, indict-ment, and collapse of Arthur Andersen, Enron might have slipped out of the public consciousness and into the nebulous company of Worldcom, Tyco, Global Crossing, and the dozens of dotcoms that failed at the turn of the twenty-first century.[133]

Enron's failure was a complicated financial and accounting mess that took months to untangle and years to settle in the courts, but it is clear that Enron executives manipulated their financial statements in order to avoid disclosing the full extent of their fiscal liabilities.[134] Through a series of off-balance-sheet partnerships improperly con-trolled by Enron insiders, executives maintained the illusion that the company was generating enormous profits without holding either significant assets or liabilities.[135] Thus, Enron's profits looked partic-ularly impressive to Wall Street analysts as the company's "return on assets" was much higher than a traditional energy pipeline operation; Enron resembled, at least on paper, a trading company more akin to an investment bank like Goldman Sachs than a traditional utility.[136] The problem, of course, was that Enron's appearance was a fiction that was eventually exposed when the company's falling stock price triggered a series of required payments to the hidden partnerships that, in turn, revealed the significant off-balance-sheet liabilities.[137] As the extent of these outside liabilities became publicly known, the stock price of Enron further declined, triggering still more payments to hidden partnerships that drove down the price even further in a vicious spiral.

As a result of these disclosures, in early December 2001, Enron, once the seventh largest company in America, declared bankruptcy in what was then the largest corporate failure in history. In less than a year, Enron's stock price had declined from $75 to $0.72, or more than 99 percent, in the process wiping out more than $50 billion in total shareholder equity. When Enron filed for Chapter 11 bankruptcy protection, the corporation owed its three main commercial banks, J. P. Morgan, Citibank, and Bank of New York, roughly $7.5 billion in unsecured loans and still had unpaid obligations to its corporate auditors, Arthur Andersen, of nearly two million dollars.[138]

Enron was such an enormous bankruptcy, and involved such extensive internal fraud, that government regulators immediately began to ask why Arthur Andersen, the company's auditors, had not noticed the company's fiscal irregularities. Yet, even as the Department of Justice subpoenaed Arthur Andersen's audit records, Joe Berardino, Andersen's managing partner and CEO, went on the offensive and wrote an aggressive editorial in *The Wall Street Journal* arguing that Enron's failure demonstrated that the current accounting rules in the United States were hopelessly antiquated because the system "was created in the 1930s for the industrial age."[139] Less than a month later, however, Berardino would regret this aggressive counterattack when it emerged that Andersen's audit team in Houston (along with their counterparts in Portland, Oregon, and London) had shredded photocopies and deleted computer files related to the Enron audit.[140] With Andersen's professional reputation in tatters, corporate clients like Colgate Palmolive, Lands' End, and Delta Airlines announced that they would move their corporate audits to another accounting firm.[141] Unable to stop the outflow of important clients, to prevent their partners (and even entire practices) from defecting to their competitors, or to mollify angry federal regulators, Andersen quickly disintegrated.[142] In June 2002, a Houston jury voted to convict Arthur Andersen of obstruction of justice. Not long after the legal verdict, the remaining partners in Arthur Andersen, which once had more than 4,500 partners and 80,000 employees, came to an agreement with the regulators at the S.E.C. to close the accounting firm's hallmark mahogany doors for good.[143]

As a result of the public outcry against the Enron/Andersen crisis, Congress took up the question of financial regulation at the end of 2001 with a determination not seen since the corporate governance scandals of the 1930s. In particular, from the beginning of 2002, running parallel to the criminal prosecution of Arthur Andersen and Enron, both the U.S. Senate and the House of Representatives held official hearings on the regulation of the accounting profession and the need for reform of corporate governance. This culminated in the passage of the Sarbanes-Oxley Act of 2002 "to protect investors by improving the accuracy and reliability of corporate disclosures."[144] Although the subsequent legislation was first drafted in the mid-1990s during the Congressional debates over liability reform, the details had been further refined by staff within the S.E.C. during the late 1990s under the direction of Arthur Levitt.[145] Described repeatedly by analysts as "the most significant piece of U.S. business legislation since the post-Depression 1930s," the Sarbanes-Oxley Act revisited the original New Deal legislation, strengthening and updating "accountability by public companies in the areas of financial reporting, disclosure, audits, conflicts of interest, and governance."[146] In particular, the Sarbanes-Oxley Act forbade accounting firms from offering management consulting services to any corporate client with whom they also served as an auditor.[147] After Sarbanes-Oxley, as a practical matter, no large accounting firm based in the United States could simultaneously provide management consulting services to the same corporate client.

The flip-side of the Sarbanes-Oxley Act, however, was that the legislation significantly increased the legal obligation of corporate directors to monitor internal management decisions.[148] Interestingly, then, just as the failure of the associationalist movement spearheaded by cost accountants during the late 1920s had led to more explicit corporate oversight by management engineers during the 1930s, the transfer of legal liability from corporate boards that began in the 1980s, and eventually climaxed in the corporate governance crisis of the early 2000s, persuaded American regulators to compel corporations to employ additional outsiders to perform routine management audits. The failure of consultants, along with the other professional gatekeepers, to regulate corporate behavior, in turn induced federal regulators to require board members to enlist even more frequently the services of the same consultants. Soon after the passage of the new legislation, one of the best-known scholars of corporate strategy in the world, Cynthia Montgomery from the Harvard Business School, argued that given the legal requirements under Sarbanes-Oxley, corporations should follow best practices in corporate governance and automatically provide independent funding to board members so that they could employ external consultants at their discretion.[149] Thus, having failed to prevent the corporate governance crisis, management consultants were nevertheless once again touted as the best solution to rising corporate liability.

## Conclusion

Even George Armstrong, the management consultant who earnestly declared in his autobiography that "those who forget the past have no future," would not have failed to see the irony.[150] Jeffrey Skilling, the CEO of Enron, the seventh largest company in America (and a former McKinsey Partner), who had transformed an old fashioned gas pipeline company into a new economy service firm, exaggerated when he told *Business Week* in February 2001 that, "'I've never not been successful in business or work, *ever*.' "[151] Although Skilling graduated as a Baker Scholar (in the top 5 percent of his MBA class) from the Harvard Business School, he had flunked Harvard's required business history course.[152] So the spectacular collapse of Enron was the second time that Skilling had failed to grasp the real lessons of business history. What George Armstrong might have seen (had he lived to be 117), but Jeffrey Skilling never understood, was that Enron, Andersen, and McKinsey, the penultimate icons of American *laissez-faire* capitalism, all owed their historical success to regulation.

In the same issue of *Business Week* in which Jeffrey Skilling declared his virtual infallibility, he explained what the executives in Enron had learned from the failure of a recent spin-off company:

> It reinforced the realization that it's very hard to earn a compensatory rate of return on a traditional asset investment. . . . In today's world, you have to bring intellectual content to the product, or you will not earn a fair rate of return.[153]

In other words, Skilling was focused on further exploiting "economies of knowledge" in the energy trading market, when he should have been asking the more fundamental question of how the deregulation of energy markets had made his innovative business model in Enron a possibility and what future events might reverse that transformation.[154] Corporate executives in traditional industrial businesses with valuable assets, like gas pipelines or telephone lines, learned long ago that not only are human assets valuable (the "symbolic analysts," lauded by the former Secretary of Labor, Robert Reich), but equally important are the mutable regulatory systems that favor first movers.[155] The senior executives in what was once the largest corporation in America, AT&T, were not bested by the superior technology of their competitors at MCI (AT&T's Bell Labs invented almost all of MCI's technology) but by MCI's innovative use of corporate lawyers to overturn nearly a century of regulatory precedents in long distance telephone service.[156] Entrepreneurs within McKinsey, Andersen, and Enron all seized the opportunity when regulators created new markets in the 1930s, the 1950s, and the 1990s, to dominate an emerging professional jurisdiction.[157]

If McKinsey, Andersen, and Enron all shared the good fortune to be first movers in management consulting, computer consulting, and energy trading, all three firms ran the risk common to professional firms that their knowledge was a wasting asset and that their professional reputation was only one disaster away from permanently destroying their legitimacy. Unfortunately for both Enron and Arthur Andersen, this culture of risk ultimately became an institutional calculation based not on the political risk of jurisdictional change but on the systemic transfer of legal liability. The executives at Enron counted on the auditors from Andersen and the consultants from McKinsey to extinguish their legal risk, while Andersen had come to believe that guilty judgments and legal fines were simply a cost of doing business. Both were wrong. They should have known what George Armstrong always knew: that management consulting, like all professional services, was as much a product of regulatory politics as a permanent feature of the knowledge economy. As such, the continued success of management consulting was particularly vulnerable to political change and the economies of knowledge upon which Andersen and Enron both depended.

# The World's Newest Profession?

At the end of the twentieth century, academic and journalistic coverage of consulting took off as the leading management consulting
firms exploded in size and prominence. After *Business Week's* cover
proclaimed that there was an ongoing "Craze for Consultants," journalists published a popular exposé on management gurus, *The Witch
Doctors*, and a tell-all book on the large consulting firms, *Dangerous
Company*.[1] Simultaneously academics, emboldened by the "critical
management studies" movement in business schools, began to analyze the broad theoretical and institutional implications of the rapid
growth in management consulting.[2] This swell of interest in management consulting stood in stark contrast to the isolated, intermittent
studies that had preceded it. Ever since the modern form of management consulting had first emerged in the 1930s, the academic analysis of consulting had not only been sporadic, but also disconnected
from the preceding scholarship. In the 1990s, however, management
consulting became the focus of an active group of scholars across
a variety of academic disciplines.[3] Management consulting finally
had a serious academic following even if consultants still viewed the
field's development as a recent phenomenon.[4]

This new scholarship on consulting took a different tack from the older, spasmodic analysis. In the 1950s, when Richard Paget, of Cresap McCormick and Paget, addressed the management consultants at Booz Allen & Hamilton on the anniversary of the firm's founding and Homer Hagedorn, a doctoral student in history at Harvard, wrote his thesis on the historical evolution of consulting, they each analyzed the extent to which consultants had achieved professional status.[5] By the 1990s, however, neither academic scholars nor journalists worried about the professional credentials of consultants but instead presumed that they responded to market forces like any other occupational group.[6] If much of the public debate over Arthur Andersen's role in Enron took as its premise the lamentable breakdown in professional standards among accountants, the same was not true of the criticism of consultants because the general public did not start with the presumption that management consulting was a "true" profession.[7] Moreover, given the negative coverage of many of the leading professional firms during the Congressional hearings, few people gave any thought to reviving the archaic notion of professional values.[8]

The public perception that professionalism was an outmoded goal, however, came just as consultants had reached a turning point in their longstanding campaign to professionalize.[9] Even using the outmoded checklist by which sociologists once defined the "classical" professions, management consultants had made considerable progress toward professionalization during the 1990s.[10] In particular, where consulting had once lacked a clear educational path, specialized publications, and a codified body of knowledge, the increasing numbers of MBAs entering consulting, the contribution of consultants to scholarly journals, and the new interest in studying professional service firms among academics, carried consultants further down the path toward professionalization.[11] And even though the critics of management consulting and multidisciplinary firms might have been surprised to realize that they too bolstered this ongoing process of professionalization, the growing corpus of

academic knowledge, demands for state licensing, and explicit discussions of ethical lapses actually strengthened the objective case
that consulting might finally emerge as a full profession.[12] Even the
renaissance of the management audit in the 1990s, in contrast to
consultants' longstanding role as knowledge brokers, suggested that
management consultants controlled a distinct professional service
and not simply a marketable skill.[13] What still remained to be proven
was whether consultants really had a commitment to a higher moral
purpose and were not simply paying lip service to a code of professional ethics.[14]

We have all grown cynical of old-fashioned virtues. As the political theorist Alan Ryan likes to tell the story, during a faculty meeting
at Princeton, a colleague responded to one of Ryan's flippant comments by remonstrating him that, "we don't appreciate your constant
sarcasm." An American friend quickly spoke up on Ryan's behalf:
"Alan is British – he was being ironic – I'm the one who is always
sarcastic."[15] Whether one is American or British, sarcastic or ironic,
contemporary discussions of ethics, morality, and professional values seem destined to provoke ridicule from postmodern scholars and
scandal-weary readers who insist that we need to move past this
anachronistic view of the professions. As sociologist Andrew Abbott
argued more than twenty years ago, for professionals, ethics function as a means for existing elites to achieve higher status in their
careers and within the wider society.[16] From my perspective, however, I could care less whether these ethical standards are heartfelt or
simply a cynical means to a calculated end so long as they eventually
become the cultural norm in consulting.[17] From a pragmatic perspective, the recent scandals in corporate governance, the relative institutional stability of the leading consulting firms, and the renewed
emphasis on personal accountability all suggest that a focus on professional values, and the "old-fashioned" goal of full professional status, might just succeed at this historical moment.[18] All cynicism
aside, management consulting could still become the world's newest
profession.

The skeptics around me, however, might well ask why consultants would want to adopt the full trappings of a profession. As we saw in earlier chapters, consultants succeeded in large part by assuming the outward appearance of a profession – including the rhetorical language, the career rewards, and the dignified style of client interaction – even as they avoided the most confining elements of professional status like state regulation, individual accreditation, and, most remarkably, professional liability. For if, as the McKinsey partners learned during the 1940s, behaving like a professional works just as well as actually becoming one, why bother to take the additional step and become a full profession?[19] The answer, I would argue, is that however confining it is to take on the responsibilities of adulthood, management consulting eventually needs to grow up.

From the 1930s on, American management consultants sought first to institutionalize and then to enlarge the nascent professional field unintentionally created by antitrust legislation. First in business, and then in government and nonprofit organizations, management consultants institutionalized the flow of organizational knowledge even as they encouraged the increased use of their services by reshaping their major clients in their own image. Faced with variable demand and a narrow range of products, consultancies expanded their services and broadened their appeal, differentiating themselves from one another even as they diversified their professional practices. This strategy worked. By the late 1950s, executives no longer hesitated to call on the services of consultants, often creating the standing budgets for consultants' services that we saw emerge in Lukens, the federal government, and a range of nonprofit institutions. No longer an "extraordinary expense" on corporate income statements, by 1960, Booz Allen already received one-fourth of its annual billings from repeat clients and the firm's proportion of continuing assignments would only increase over time.[20] At the same time, the leading domestic American consulting firms expanded overseas. By 1970, half of McKinsey's total revenues would come from outside the

United States making the consulting firm far less dependent on the American economy than before.[21] Although market forces and legislative changes occasionally disrupted the consulting firms' strategic plans and management consulting remained strongly tied to the national political economy, overall demand for consultants' services became remarkably stable by the 1950s.

The internal evolution of the leading management consulting firms followed a similar path of institutionalization. During the first fifty years, from the consultancies' shaky beginnings in the 1930s to the widespread adoption of the professional partnership model by the 1960s, consultants stabilized the internal organization of their firms just as they had the external demand for their services.[22] Beginning with consultants' self-conscious mimicry of the established professions, to the resale of their internal culture to businesses, nonprofits, and state institutions in the 1980s, consultants first codified and then commodified their professional culture. Although the ultimate cost of the installation of the culture of consulting within organizations like Enron remains unclear, there is no question that by the 1980s management consultants had achieved the same level of institutional stability within their professional firms that they had also realized in the external market for their professional services. Even if management consultants had not yet attained full professional status within society, they had achieved both internal stability in their firms and durable institutional demand for their services.

Yet even when consultants succeeded in their work and corporate clients relied on their professional services, the ethics of individual consultants remained suspect. An infamous example, from Tom Watson's autobiography, of Booz Allen & Hamilton's work for IBM illustrates why organizations continued to employ the leading management consulting firms even when corporate executives doubted the probity of the individual consultants.[23] In 1956, when Booz Allen first installed the multidivisional form in IBM, the senior partner on the assignment was John Burns, a Harvard Ph.D., whom

Tom Watson, Jr., knew "casually" (according to Watson's ghost-written memoir).[24] John Burns had previously worked as a consultant for RCA, which at the time also manufactured computers, so Burns explained to Watson that he would first have to get RCA's permission before accepting an assignment with IBM.[25] At this point the story becomes really interesting. After taking on the job, the Booz Allen consultants asked one of the IBM executives for some particularly sensitive pricing information, and the vice president, in turn, responded by asking Tom Watson if he was required to give this information to the consultants. As Watson later explained, the executive's fear was that if the information became public, their competitors could target those IBM products where the pricing margins were highest. Although Tom Watson told the executive that "like your doctor, you have to tell them everything," Watson also conceded that if the vice president felt particularly uneasy, he was authorized to withhold this crucial information from the Booz Allen consultants.[26] Less than three months after the completion of that consulting assignment, John Burns telephoned Tom Watson to tell him that David Sarnoff, the longstanding head of RCA, had offered Burns the presidency of the company. Despite Watson's objections that "we had entrusted him with detailed knowledge of our organization and methods and plans," Burns accepted the presidency of RCA.[27] For years afterwards, the standing joke around IBM was that if you allowed a consultant inside the company, your competitors would know your secrets within six months.[28] Yet whatever Tom Watson thought of John Burns' ethics as a management consultant, Watson would later confide in a partner from McKinsey that his firm's work, in 1954, reorganizing IBM's World Trade division in Paris, "contributed substantially to IBM's success in taking over the European computer market."[29] Thus, the executives within IBM had concluded that their practical need for consulting advice outweighed the potential cost that their competitors might learn trade secrets. Even so, it is clear that Tom Watson remained angry at John

Burns for more than thirty years.[30] This example suggests that even if the studies that consulting firms performed for their clients were so valuable that consultants were able to overcome the lingering doubts about their ethical standards, there remained a hidden cost. How often did Tom Watson, or any other chief executive, consider employing a management consulting firm only to decide that the potential danger of an ethical lapse exceeded the potential gains from the consultants' economies of knowledge?

By the end of the twentieth century, no credible observer could honestly claim that management consulting still constituted a young professional field. While the market for consultants had expanded at a double-digit pace during the 1990s, those pounds (and dollars) were being added to a mature frame, not an adolescent skeleton.[31] As the recent growth of new consulting practices to address the Sarbanes-Oxley Act demonstrates, the corporate governance crisis of the twenty-first century and the concomitant slowdown in consulting at the end of the 1990s did not substantially alter the overall development of management consulting.

In an odd way it is regrettable that the consulting crisis did not last a while longer. Management consultants had dreamed, for so many years, of the opportunity to achieve full professional status, yet when the opportunity finally came to reshape their professional field at the end of the twentieth century, consultants shrank from their definitive organizational challenge.[32] No one appeared from the long shadow that Marvin Bower still cast over management consulting to force the leading firms to accept their responsibility as a true profession.[33] The world's newest profession would have to wait for the next century.

# Notes

INTRODUCTION: MAKING A CAREER OF CONSULTING

1. John Rolfe and Peter Troob, *Monkey Business: Swinging Through the Wall Street Jungle* (New York: Warner Business Books, 2001), 13–14; Henry Mintzberg, *Managers not MBAs* (Harlow, Essex: FT Prentice Hall, 2004), 85–6.
2. Peter Drucker, "The Post-Capitalist Executive," in Peter Drucker, *On the Profession of Management* (Boston: Harvard Business School Press, 1998), 175–88.
3. A similar process, half a century earlier, took place when the leading engineers and their employers had redirected the curriculum within the leading technical universities like MIT to suit their professional needs. See David F. Noble, *America by Design: Science, Technology, and the Rise of Corporate Capitalism* (Oxford: Oxford University Press, 1977), xxv.
4. Louis Brandeis, *Business – A Profession* (Boston: Small, Maynard & Company, 1914); Richard Edwards, *Contested Terrain: The Transformation of the Workplace in the Twentieth Century* (New York: Basic Books, 1979), 182.
5. Nicholas Lemann, "The Kids in the Conference Room: How McKinsey & Company became the Next Big Step," *The New Yorker* (18 & 25 October 1999), 216.
6. Lemann, "The Kids in the Conference Room," 216.
7. Mariam Naficy, *The Fast Track* (New York: Broadway Books, 1997), 1–5.
8. Lemann, "The Kids in the Conference Room," 211.
9. James Waldroop and Timothy Butler, "Is Management Consulting the Right Career – For You?" in Jason Dehni (ed.), *The Harvard Business School Guide*

*to Careers in Management Consulting* (Boston: Harvard Business School Press, 1999), 2.

10. Geoffrey Colvin, "CEO Super Bowl," *Fortune*, Vol. 140, No. 3 (2 August 1999), 238.

11. Colvin, "CEO Super Bowl," 239.

12. Colvin, "CEO Super Bowl," 239. Of course, executive pay is generally correlated with the market capitalization of the companies that they manage.

13. "Consultants Take Over," *Accountancy* (6 August 1997), 24.

14. Matthias Kipping and Celeste Amorim, "Consultancies as Management Schools," in Rolv Petter Amdam, Ragnhild Kvålshaugen, and Eirinn Larsen (eds.), *Inside the Business Schools. The Content of European Business Education*, (Oslo: Copenhagen Business School Press, 2003), 133–54.

15. Richard M. Paget, "Management Consulting Careers," *Career Guide*, Vol. 2, No. 2 (February 1962), 1.

16. Marvin Bower and D. Ronald Daniel, "General Management Consulting," *Career Guide*, Vol. 2, No. 2 (February 1962), 5.

17. Richard Paget was then the senior partner of his eponymous firm, Cresap, McCormick and Paget, Marvin Bower was the managing director of McKinsey & Company, while D. Ronald Daniel would go on to be Managing Director of McKinsey between 1976 and 1988, Leonard Spacek was the long-standing Managing Partner of Arthur Andersen & Co., and Bruce Henderson would resign that same year from his current position as Vice President of Arthur D. Little to found The Boston Consulting Group. In short, the HBS *Career Guide* represented a cross section of the managing partners of the most important consulting firms in the 1960s and beyond.

## 1. ECONOMIES OF KNOWLEDGE: A THEORY
## OF MANAGEMENT CONSULTING

1. "Advisers on Advisers," *Business Week* (9 April 1930), 42.

2. Joel Dean, "The Place of Management Counsel in Business," *The Harvard Business Review*, 16 (1938), 451; "Doctors of Management," *Fortune* (July 1944), 144–5; Jack R. Ryan, "Consultant Field Shows Big Growth," *The New York Times* (27 December 1953); Peter B. Bart, "Exports of Know-How Booming: Demand Soaring for Services of U.S. Consultants," *The New York Times* (13 January 1960), 27; Hal Higdon, *The Business Healers*, (New York: Random House, 1969), 20–1. Ralph Nader, "Introduction," in Daniel Guttman and Barry Willner, *The Shadow Government* (New York: Pantheon Books, 1976), ix–xiv; "Bad News Can be Good News for Management Consultants," *Money* (June 1980), 92; Geoffrey Rowan, "Explosive Growth Shapes Consulting Industry Today," *The Boston Herald* (6 July 1986); John A. Byrne, "The Craze for Consultants," *Business Week* (July 25, 1994), 60; Joseph B. White,

"Consulting Firms Break Revenue Records, *The Wall Street Journal* (3 March 1997).

3. "What Management Consultants Can Do," *Business Week* (23 January 1965), 88; Bureau of Labor Statistics, *Occupational Outlook Handbook: 1998–1999 Edition* (Washington, DC: U.S. Government Printing Office, 1998), 48, 66.

4. Peter F. Drucker, "Why Management Consultants," in Melvin Zimet and Ronald G. Greenwood (eds.), *The Evolving Science of Management* (New York: American Management Associations, 1979), 475–8. For the consultants' own answer, see Boston Safe and Deposit Company, "The Bulletin," No. 72 (15 August 1963), 4; Miller, Franklin, Basset & Company, *The First Quarter Century* (New York: Miller, Franklin, Basset & Company, 1927); McKinsey & Company, *Supplementing Successful Management* (New York: McKinsey & Company, 1940); George Fry & Associates, *Resource to Dynamic Management* (Chicago: George Fry & Associates, 1958).

5. Miller, Franklin, Basset & Company, *The Industrial and Production Engineering Service of Miller, Franklin, Basset & Company* (New York: 1920); "The Consultants Face a Competition Crisis," *Business Week* (Nov. 17, 1973), 72; Jonathan D. Glater, "Hurt by Slump, a Consulting Giant Looks Inward," *The New York Times* (30 June 2002), Sect. 3, 4.

6. John Whitmore of Cresap, McCormick and Paget quoted in Higdon, *The Business Healers*, 304. Doug Henwood, editor of the *Left Business Observer*, describes consultants' constant preoccupation with "accelerating change" as the "fetishizing of the second derivative."

7. During the same period, profits at McKinsey's competitor, A. T. Kearney & Co., grew 32% per annum. McKinsey & Company, "Comparison of Earnings," McKinsey & Company corporate records, New York City. On the early history of McKinsey & Company see Marvin Bower, *Perspective on McKinsey* (New York: McKinsey & Company, 1979); John G. Neukom, *McKinsey Memoirs: A Personal Perspective* (New York: Privately Printed, 1975), and James O'Shea and Charles Madigan, *Dangerous Company: The Consulting Powerhouses and the Businesses They Save and Ruin* (New York: Times Books, 1997).

8. Ronald H. Coase, "The Nature of the Firm," *Economica*, Vol. 4 (1937), 386–405. Coase, however, never posed his question directly in that form. For that particular restatement of Coase's query, see Louis Putterman and Randall S. Kroszner, "The Economic Nature of the Firm: A New Introduction," in Louis Putterman and Randall S. Kroszner (ed.), *The Economic Nature of the Firm: A Reader* (New York: Cambridge University Press, 1996), 9.

9. G. B. Richardson, "The Organization of Industry," *Economic Journal*, Vol. 82 (1972), 883. When the Swedish Academy chose Coase for the 1991 Nobel Prize, they used Richardson's vivid description of the classical view as the foil for Coase's elegant reinterpretation, see Lars Werin, "The Bank of Sweden Prize in Economic Sciences in Memory of Alfred Nobel," in Torsten Persson (ed.),

*Nobel Lectures in the Economic Sciences, 1991–1995* (Singapore: World Scientific, 1997), 3–5.

10. For consultant Staffan Canback's thoughtful analysis of the centrality of transaction cost economics to understanding management consulting, see Staffan Canback, "The Logic of Management Consulting," *Journal of Management Consulting*, Vol. 10, No. 2 (1998), 3–11. In contrast, for a critique of Coase's framework based on the very success of consultancies, see Michael Dietrich, *Transaction Cost Economics and Beyond: Towards a New Economics of the Firm* (London: Routledge, 1994), 18. As these diametrically opposing views suggest, and as Oliver Williamson has admitted, the application of the transaction cost framework to management is a very complex task. Oliver E. Williamson, "Corporate Governance," *Yale Law Journal*, Vol. 93 (1984), 1216.

11. Oliver E. Williamson, *The Economic Institutions of Capitalism* (New York: Free Press, 1985), xi–xiv.

12. Coase, "The Nature of the Firm," 400–1; James William Culliton, *Make or Buy: A Consideration of the Problems Fundamental to a Decision Whether to Manufacture or Buy Materials, Accessory Equipment, Fabricating Parts, and Supplies* (Boston: Harvard Business School, Bureau of Business Research, 1942), 1–2; A. R. Oxenfeldt and M. W. Watkins, *Make or Buy: Factors Affecting Executive Decisions* (New York: McGraw Hill, 1956), 10; Gordon Walker and David Weber, "A Transaction Cost Approach to Make-or-Buy Decisions," *Administrative Science Quarterly*, Vol. 29 (September 1984), 373–91.

13. Kenneth J. Arrow, "The Economic Implications of Learning by Doing," *The Review of Economic Studies*, Vol. 29, No. 3 (June 1962), 155; James R. Markusen, "Trade in Producer Services and in Other Specialized Intermediate Inputs," *The American Economic Review*, Vol. 79, No. 1 (March 1989), 85; Luis A. Rivera-Batiz and Paul M. Romer, "Economic Integration and Endogenous Growth," *The Quarterly Journal of Economics*, Vol. 106, No. 2 (May 1991): 551–2.

14. Oliver E. Williamson, "The Economics of Organization: The Transaction Cost Approach," *American Journal of Sociology*, Vol. 87, No. 3 (1981), 548–77.

15. Indeed, this Coasian logic applies to almost all bureaucratic professionals. Ronald Gilson, for example, has described corporate lawyers as glorified "transaction cost engineers" because they reduce the risks and the costs associated with corporate deal-making. Ronald Gilson, "Value Creation by Business Lawyers: Legal Skills and Asset Pricing," *Yale Law Journal*, Vol. 94 (1984), 253–5.

16. Francis Bacon, *The Essays or Counsels, Civil and Moral, of Sir Francis Bacon, Lord Verulam, Viscount St. Albans* (Mount Vernon, NY: The Peter Pauper Press, 1963), 82.

17. Herbert Goldhamer, *The Advisor* (New York: Elsevier, 1978), 7–27. The citations from Bacon, Hobbes, and Machiavelli also follow Goldhamer's discussion.

18. Thomas Hobbes, *Leviathan* (Cambridge: Cambridge University Press, 1996), 177; Niccolò Machiavelli, *The Prince and the Discourses* (New York: The Modern Library, 1950), 513–16.

19. Bacon, *The Essays or Counsels*, 82.

20. Thomas Haskell, *The Authority of Experts: Studies in History and Theory* (Bloomington: University of Indiana Press, 1984).

21. On the growth of the "prominstrative" state, see Brian Balogh, *Chain Reaction: Expert Debate and Public Participation in American Commercial Nuclear Power, 1945–1975* (New York: Cambridge University Press, 1991), 12–16. See also, Samuel P. Hays, *Beauty, Health, and Permanence: Environmental Politics in the United States, 1955–1985* (New York: Cambridge University Press, 1988); Susan Strange, *The Retreat of the State: The Diffusion of Power in the World Economy* (Cambridge: Cambridge University Press, 1996), 135–46.

22. Charles Derber, William A. Schwartz, and Yale Magrass, *Power in the Highest Degree: Professionals and the Rise of the New Mandarin Order* (New York: Oxford University Press, 1990), 3–8.

23. Adam Smith, *The Wealth of Nations* (Harmondsworth: Penguin Books, 1979), 110–21; William Lazonick, *Business Organization and the Myth of the Market Economy* (New York: Cambridge University Press, 1991), 2.

24. These calls for generalists may be an outward manifestation of internal power struggles within the professions. Indeed, sociologist Magali Sarfatti Larson has argued that "overspecialization" is a product of the power relations within the professions since overspecialization ties professionals to firms, limiting their individual autonomy. Magali Sarfatti Larson, *The Rise of Professionalism: A Sociological Analysis* (Berkeley: University of California Press, 1977), 204–5.

25. Joseph L. Badaracco, Jr., "The Boundaries of the Firm," in Amitai Etzioni and Paul R. Lawrence (ed.), *Socio-Economics: Toward a New Synthesis* (Armonk, NY: M. E. Sharpe, 1991), 295.

26. Jaola Weingarten, "And Now – The Captive Consultant," *Dun's Review*, Vol. 88 (November 1966), 57–8; Robert J. Gale, "Internal Management Consulting in Modern Business," *Financial Executive*, Vol. 38 (March 1970), 16–19; Richard Martin, "Many Companies Decide Management Consulting Can Be Done by Insiders, *The Wall Street Journal*, 2 May 1973, 1; "The Benefits of Doing Your Own Consulting," *Business Week* (16 May 1977), 62, Robert E. Kelley, "Should You Have an Internal Consultant?" *Harvard Business Review* Vol. 57, (November-December, 1979), 110–20.

27. Elizabeth M. Fowler, "Tackling Company Problems," *The New York Times* (9 February 1983), D17.

28. E. J. Kahn, Jr., *The Problem Solvers: A History of Arthur D. Little, Inc.* (Boston: Little, Brown, 1986); David Neal Keller, *Stone & Webster, 1889–1989, A Century of Integrity and Service* (New York: Stone & Webster, 1989); Jim Bowman,

*Booz Allen & Hamilton: Seventy Years of Client Service, 1914–1984* (Chicago: Booz, Allen & Hamilton, 1984); Arthur Andersen & Co., *The First Sixty Years, 1913–1973* (Chicago: Arthur Andersen & Co., 1974).

29. Here I should make clear that economists, following philosophers, have rightly pointed out the distinction between information – a raw, unrefined commodity that can be easily codified – and knowledge – processed information that is generally tacit. This discussion, however, will largely run roughshod over the important epistemological distinction between knowledge and information, since corporate executives seldom require unprocessed data streams. In other words, consultants sell knowledge, not information. For a more formal discussion, see Fred I. Dretske, *Knowledge and the Flow of Information* (Montgomery, VT: Bradford Books, 1981).

30. For a journalist's corroboration of this broad pattern, see Linda Corman, "The Uneasy Relationship," *Banking Strategies* (November/December 1998), 86.

31. Andrew B. Hargadon, "Firms as Knowledge Brokers: Lessons in Pursuing Continuous Innovation," *California Management Review*, Vol. 40, No. 3 (1998), 209–27; Andrew B. Hargadon and Robert I. Sutton, "Technology Brokering and Innovation in a Product Development Firm, *Administrative Science Quarterly*, Vol. 42 (1997), 716–49. See also, Smith, *The Idea Brokers*.

32. Joel Dean, "The Place of Management Counsel in Business," *The Harvard Business Review*, Vol. 16 (1938); Richard F. Amon, et al., *Management Consulting* (Boston: Management Consulting Report Associates, 1958).

33. Walter N. Thayer to John Hay Whitney, 30 September 1958, page 5, file: "Whitney, John Hay, 1958," box 35, subject file series, WHITCOM series, Walter N. Thayer Papers, Hoover Presidential Library, West Branch, Iowa. For a detailed account of McKinsey & Company's work at the *Herald Tribune*, see Christopher D. McKenna, "Two Strikes and You're Out: The Demise of the New York Herald Tribune," *The Historian*, Vol., 63, No. 2 (Winter 2001), 287–308.

34. At this point my argument teeters dangerously close to critics of Coase, and transaction cost economics in general, that the very concept of transaction costs is itself tautological. To his critics' charge that the logic of transaction cost analysis is inherently circular, Ronald Coase has wittily replied that a tautology is "the criticism people make of a proposition that is clearly right." See Ronald Coase, "The Nature of the Firm: Origin, Meaning, Influence," *Journal of Law, Economics, and Organization*, Vol. 4 (1988), 18; Oliver E. Williamson, "Hierarchies, Markets and Power in the Economy," *Industrial and Corporate Change*, Vol. 4, No. 1 (1995), 33–4. See also Sumantra Goshal and Peter Moran, "Bad for Practice: A Critique of the Transaction Cost Theory," *Academy of Management Review*, Vol. 21, No. 1 (1996), 13–47.

35. Martin Fransman, "Information, Knowledge, Vision and Theories of the Firm," *Industrial and Corporate Change*, Vol. 3, No. 3 (1993), 734.

36. Oliver E. Williamson, "The Logic of Economic Organization," in Oliver E. Williamson and Sidney G. Winter (eds.), *The Nature of the Firm: Origins, Evolution, and Development* (New York: Oxford University Press, 1991), 90.

37. Oliver E. Williamson, "The Modern Corporation: Origins, Evolution, and Attributes," *Journal of Economic Literature*, Vol. 19 (December 1981), 1537.

38. Coase, "The Nature of the Firm," 400.

39. J. M. Clark, "Overhead Costs in Modern Industry," *The Journal of Political Economy*, Vol. 31, No. 5 (October 1923), 21–2.

40. James Brian Quinn, Thomas L. Doorley, and Penny C. Paquette, "Beyond Products: Services Based Strategy," reprinted in Cynthia A. Montgomery and Michael E. Porter (eds.), *Strategy: Seeking and Securing Competitive Advantage* (Boston: Harvard Business School Press, 1991), 310; Carla S. O'Dell and C. Jackson Grayson, Jr., *If Only We Knew What We Know: The Transfer of Internal Knowledge and Best Practice* (New York: Free Press, 1998).

41. Drucker, "Why Management Consultants?" 475. For Herbert Simon's formulation, "why are not all the actors independent contractors?" see Herbert A. Simon, "Organizations and Markets," *The Journal of Economic Perspectives*, Vol. 5, No. 2 (Spring 1991), 25.

42. For a variety of views on why firms are different, see Jeffrey R. Williams, "Strategy and the Search for Rents: The Evolution of Diversity among Firms;" Richard R. Nelson, "Why Do Firms Differ and How Does It Matter?" and Glenn R. Carroll, "A Sociological View on Why Firms Differ," all reprinted in Richard P. Rumelt, Dan E. Schendel, and David J. Teece (eds.), *Fundamental Issues in Strategy: A Research Agenda* (Boston: Harvard Business School Press), 229–96. For consultants in particular, see D. B. Nees and L. E. Greiner, "Seeing Behind the Look-Alike Management Consultants," *Organizational Dynamics*, Vol. 13 (Winter, 1985), 68–79.

43. On the rise of the "knowledge economy" more generally, see Max Boisot, *Knowledge Assets: Securing Competitive Advantage in the Information Economy* (New York: Oxford University Press, 1998); Michael H. Zack, *Knowledge and Strategy* (Boston: Butterworth-Heinemann, 1999); Richard C. Huseman, and Jon P. Goodman, *Leading with Knowledge: The Nature of Competition in the 21st Century* (Thousand Oaks, CA: Sage Publications, 1999); and James G. March, *The Pursuit of Organizational Intelligence* (Malden, MA: Blackwell, 1999).

44. Edwin J. Perkins, *Wall Street to Main Street: Charles Merrill and Middle-Class Investors* (New York: Cambridge University Press, 1999); "Seagram's Recipe: A Dash of Advice," *Business Week* (30 January 1965), 126–8. The records of Seagram's work with its retailers – consulting studies by experts in retail marketing within Seagram's who were available for the use of retailers – are deposited in the archives at the Hagley Museum and Library in Wilmington, Delaware.

45. Tom Peters, *Liberation Management: Necessary Disorganization for the Nanosecond Nineties* (New York: Alfred A. Knopf, 1992), 133; Morten T.

Hansen and Thomas H. Davenport, "Knowledge Management at Andersen Consulting," (HBS Case #499032), (Boston: Harvard Business School Publishing, 1999), Miklos Sarvary, "Knowledge Management and Competition in the Consulting Industry," *California Management Review*, Vol. 41, No. 2 (Winter 1999), 100; Morten T. Hansen, Nitin Nohria, and Thomas Tierney, "What's Your Strategy for Managing Knowledge?" *Harvard Business Review* (March, 1999). For a broader analysis of the adoption of managerial fashions, see Eric Abrahamson, "Managerial Fads and Fashions: The Diffusion and Rejection of Innovations," *Academy of Management Review*, Vol. 16, No. 3 (1991), 586–612. For the specific example of consultants, see Jos Benders, Robert-Jan van den Berg, and Mark van Bijsterveld, "Hitch-Hiking on a Hype: Dutch Consultants Engineering Re-Engineering," *Journal of Organizational Change Management*, Vol. 11, No. 3 (1998), 201–15.

46. "IBM as Consultant: A Transformation History," *Chain Store Age* (1 September 1995), 2C.

47. Of course, this battle is far from over, but the recent decision by lawyers to permit mergers with consulting firms and the continuing expansion of consulting firms into realms like business education, publishing, and even venture capital suggests that consultants are on the offensive, not the defensive. See James O'Shea and Charles Madigan, *Dangerous Company: The Consulting Powerhouses and the Businesses They Save and Ruin* (New York: Times Books, 1997); John Micklethwait and Adrian Wooldridge, *The Witch Doctors: Making Sense of the Management Gurus* (New York: Times Books, 1996).

48. Richard N. Farmer, *New Directions in Management Information Transfer* (Ruschlikon-Zurich: Gottlieb Duttweiler Institute for Economic and Social Studies, 1968), 18–20; Peter F. Drucker, *Post-Capitalist Society*, (New York: Harper Business, 1993), 20; James B. Quinn, *Intelligent Enterprise: A Knowledge and Service Based Paradigm for Industry* (New York: The Free Press, 1992), 3–5.

49. Joseph L. Badaracco, Jr., *The Knowledge Link: How Firms Compete through Strategic Alliances* (Harvard Business School Press, 1991); Ikujio Nonaka and Hirotaka Takeuchi, *The Knowledge Creating Company: How Japanese Companies Create the Dynamics of Innovation* (New York: Oxford University Press, 1995), 3–7; Louis Galambos, *Competition and Cooperation: The Emergence of the National Trade Association* (Baltimore: The Johns Hopkins University Press, 1966), 3–6; James A. Smith, *The Idea Brokers: Think Tanks and the Rise of the New Policy Elite* (New York: The Free Press, 1991), 8–11; David F. Noble, *America By Design: Science, Technology, and the Rise of Corporate Capitalism* (New York: Oxford University Press, 1977), 312–20; Robert A. Kagen and Robert E. Rosen, "On the Social Significance of Large Law Firm Practice," Vol. 37, *Stanford Law Review* (1985), 407.

50. Theodore J. Kreps, "The Political Economy of International Cartels," *The American Economic Review*, Vol. 35, No. 2 (May 1945), 299. On Coase's lifelong

interest in the integration of economics and regulation, see Ronald H. Coase, "The Institutional Structure of Production," Nobel Lecture, 9 December 1991, reprinted in Torsten Persson (ed.), *Nobel Lectures in the Economic Sciences*, 17–18; Williamson, *The Economic Institutions of Capitalism*, 68–102.

51. Robert Z. Lawrence, "Japan's Different Trade Regime: An Analysis with Particular Reference to *Keiretsu*," *Journal of Economic Perspectives*, Vol. 7, No. 3 (Summer 1993), 11–15; Masahiko Aoki, "Towards an Economic Model of the Japanese Firm," *Journal of Economic Literature*, Vol. 28 (1990), 1–27; Keiichiro Nakagawa, "Business Management in Japan – A Comparative Historical Study," *Industrial and Corporate Change*, Vol. 2, No. 1 (1993), 25–43; Steven B. Webb, "Tariffs, Cartels, Technology, and Growth in the German Steel Industry, 1879–1914," *The Journal of Economic History*, Vol. 40, No. 2 (June 1980), 309–30; Lothar Gall, Gerald B. Feldman, Harold James, Carl-Ludwig Holtfrerich, and Hans E. Büschgen, *The Deutsche Bank, 1870–1995* (London, Weidenfled & Nicolson, 1995), 582–98. For an opposing interpretation see Caroline Fohlin, "The Rise of Interlocking Directorates in Imperial Germany," *Economic History Review*, Vol. 52, No. 2 (1999), 307–33. Although American officials initially tried to dismantle the tight institutional linkages that encouraged oligopolistic behavior in Germany and Japan during their postwar reconstruction of both countries, in each instance local government officials soon reversed these institutional changes. See Hans A. Adler, "The Post-War Reorganization of the German Banking System," *The Quarterly Journal of Economics*, Vol. 63, No. 3 (August 1949), 331; Masahiko Aoki, "Aspects of the Japanese Firm," in Masahiko Aoki (ed.), *The Economic Analysis of the Japanese Firm* (Amsterdam: North Holland, 1984), 12. See also Marie-Laure Djelic, *Exporting the American Model: The Postwar Transformation of European Business* (Oxford: Oxford University Press, 1998).

52. Richard Hofstadter, "What Happened to the Antitrust Movement? Notes on the Evolution of an American Creed," in *The Business Establishment* Earl F. Cheit (ed.), (New York, 1964), 114–36; Louis Galambos with Barbara Barrow Spence, *The Public Image of Big Business in America, 1880–1940: A Quantitative Study in Social Change* (Baltimore: The Johns Hopkins University, 1975), 119–20; Robert H. Wiebe, *The Search for Order, 1877–1920* (New York: Hill and Wang, 1967), 52–3.

53. The academic literature on professionalization is vast, but several important theoretical works include, Talcott Parsons, "Professional Groups and Social Structure," in *Professionalization*, Howard M. Vollmer and Donald L. Mills (eds.), (Englewood Cliffs, New Jersey: Prentice Hall, Inc., 1966), 55–7; Magali Sarfatti Larson, *The Rise of Professionalism: A Sociological Analysis* (Philadelphia: Temple University Press, 1973); Eliot Freidson, *Professional Powers: A Study of the Institutionalization of Formal Knowledge* (Chicago: University of Chicago Press, 1986). For contextualizing the professional competition within the field

of consulting, however, the best theoretical model is Andrew Abbott, *The System of Professions: An Essay on the Division of Expert Labor* (Chicago: University of Chicago Press, 1988).

54. Arthur Andersen, "The Accountant, the Industrial Engineer, and the Banker," *Administration* (1 August 1921): reprinted in Arthur Andersen, *Behind the Figures: Addresses and Articles by Arthur Andersen, 1913–1941* (Chicago: Arthur Andersen & Company, 1970), 23–8. On the use of consultants to "advise the investment bankers as to the industrial and commercial soundness, past and prospective, of any enterprise that is to be underwritten," see Thorstein Veblen, *The Engineers and the Price System* (New York: Augustus Kelley, 1965 [originally 1921]), 65.

55. Quotation from Armstrong, *An Engineer in Wall Street*, 68–9; Thomas K. McCraw, *Prophets of Regulation* (Cambridge: Harvard University Press, 1984), 170–7; Jay W. Blum, "The Federal Securities Act, 1933–1936," *The Journal of Political Economy*, Vol. 46, No. 1 (February 1938), 52–96. Economist Milton Freedman remembered that the Securities Act "was regarded as so drastic that people were afraid to register securities for fear of any liabilities that could be imposed," see Milton V. Freedman, "The Securities and Exchange Commission," in *The Making of the New Deal: The Insiders Speak* (Cambridge: Harvard University Press, 1983), 142. See also, "Comment: Secondary Liability under Section 12(2) of the Securities Act of 1933," *Northwestern University Law Review*, Vol. 78 (1983), 832–45.

56. Robert Mednick and Gary John Previts, "The Scope of CPA Services: A View of the Future from the Perspective of a Century of Progress," *Journal of Accountancy* (May 1987), 224–6; J. K. Lasser and J. A. Gerardi, "The Relation of Accountants to the Federal Securities Act," *National Association of Cost Accountants Bulletin*, Vol. 17, No. 22 (15 July 1936), 1293–7.

57. Arthur Andersen, "Industrial and Financial Investigations," *N.A.C.A. Bulletin*, Vol. 5, No. 15 (1 April 1924): reprinted in Andersen, *Behind the Figures*, 29–40; Joseph S. Glickauf, "Reflections on a Quarter Century in Administrative Services," in *Footsteps Toward Professionalism: The Development of an Administrative Services Practice over the Past Twenty-Five Years* (Chicago: Arthur Andersen & Company, 1971), 173–4. Most accounting firms gladly traded their "management engineering" practice for the growth that they experienced as a result of the S.E.C.'s mandated reporting schedules, see Paul J. Miranti, Jr., *Accountancy Comes of Age: The Development of an American Profession, 1886–1940* (Chapel Hill: University of North Carolina Press, 1990); Paul J. Miranti, Jr., "Associationalism, Statism, and Professional Regulation: Public Accountants and the Reform of Financial Markets, 1896–1940," *Business History Review*, Vol. 60 (1986), 443.

58. Between 1930 and 1940, the number of management consulting firms grew, on average, 15% a year from an estimated 100 firms in 1930 to 400 firms by 1940,

see Association of Consulting Management Engineers, Inc. (ACME), *Numerical Data on the Present Dimensions, Growth, and other Trends in Management Consulting in the United States* (New York: ACME, 1964), Table 2.

59. Joel Dean, "The Place of Management Counsel in Business," *The Harvard Business Review*, Vol. 16 (1938), 451.

60. Abbott, *The System of Professions*, 1. For a similar discussion of the emergence of the French consulting profession as a distinct jurisdictional field (*"espace"*), see Odile Henry, "Le Conseil, Un Espace Professionnel Autonome?" *Enterprises et Histoire*, No. 7 (December 1994), 37–58.

61. George S. Armstrong, *An Engineer in Wall Street* (New York: Privately Printed, 1962). George Armstrong also served as the President of the Association of Consulting Management Engineers (ACME), from 1941 to 1942, and, after World War II, worked for several large companies in Europe.

62. Armstrong, *An Engineer in Wall Street*.

63. Jim Bowman, *Booz Allen & Hamilton: Seventy Years of Client Service, 1914–1984* (Chicago, Booz, Allen & Hamilton, 1984), 7, vi.

64. John G. Neukom, *McKinsey Memoirs: A Personal Perspective* (New York, privately printed, 1975), 11.

65. Bower, *Perspective on McKinsey*, 17.

66. Years later, Marvin Bower, the attorney-turned-consultant who refounded McKinsey & Company in the late 1930s, wrote, with institutional amnesia, that the history of consulting demonstrated that "the management consulting associations have been trying to *avoid* legislation instead of trying to *shape* it," see Marvin Bower, "Comments," *Journal of Management Consulting*, Vol. 3, No. 1 (1986), 36, emphasis in original.

67. Homer Hagedorn, who wrote a dissertation on the career of Harry Hopf, the consultant who founded H. A. Hopf & Co., was the first historian to contextualize the use of consultants as conduits for organizational knowledge, see Homer Hagedorn, "The Management Consultant as Transmitter of Business Techniques," *Explorations in Entrepreneurial History* (February, 1955), 164–73.

68. On the turn-of-the-century fears of the "Money Trust," see Louis D. Brandeis, *Other People's Money and How the Bankers Use It* (New York: Frederick A. Stokes Company, 1914); Vincent P. Carosso, "The Wall Street Money Trust from Pujo through Medina," *Business History Review*, Vol. 47 (Winter 1973), 421–8; U.S. Congress, House Committee on Banking and Currency, *Money Trust Investigation* (Washington: Government Printing Office, 1913), 1472–9, 1568–71. For a reinterpretation of the "Money Trust" as losing control of their previous hold over banking, see Gabriel Kolko, *The Triumph of Conservatism: A Reinterpretation of American History, 1900–1916* (New York: The Free Press, 1963), 139–46; Ellis W. Hawley, *The New Deal and the Problem of Monopoly: A Study in Economic Ambivalence* (Princeton: Princeton University Press, 1966), 304–6.

69. Mark J. Roe, "A Political Theory of American Corporate Finance," *Columbia Law Review*, Vol. 91, No. 10 (1991), 32–45; J. Bradford De Long, "Did J. P. Morgan's Men Add Value? An Economist's Perspective on Financial Capitalism," in *Inside the Business Enterprise*, Peter Temin (ed.), (Chicago: University of Chicago Press, 1991), 205–36. The comparison with the case of universal banking in Germany is immediately apparent. On the influence of leading banks like Deutsche Bank on German corporate boards, see Jürgen Kocka, "The Rise of the Modern Industrial Enterprise in Germany," in *Managerial Hierarchies: Comparative Perspectives on the Rise of the Modern Industrial Enterprise*, Alfred D. Chandler, Jr. and Herman Daems (eds.), (Cambridge: Harvard University Press, 1980), 90–2. For a specific case study of the impact of German bankers acting much like modern management consultants within an industrial company, see Gerald D. Feldman, "Thunder from Arosa: Karl Kimmich and the Reconstruction of the Stollwerk Company, 1930–1932," *Business and Economic History*, Vol. 26, No. 2 (Winter 1997), 686–95.

70. Brandeis, *Other People's Money and How the Bankers Use It*, 72–8. Of course, such collusive power did not need to be coordinated at the board level by bankers, but could also be handled entirely within a bank if all of the companies shared the same bank lending officer. For an account of how John E. Rovensky, a vice president at National City Bank, oversaw the "canned milk monopoly" between 1921 and 1931, see Donald L. Kemmerer, *The Life of John E. Rovensky, Banker and Industrialist* (Champaign: Stipes Publishing Co., 1977), 129–36.

71. Economist David Teece has described the general need to share knowledge within industries and the specific difficulties in doing so in the United States given stringent American antitrust laws, see David J. Teece, "Information Sharing, Innovation and Antitrust," in *Collusion through Information Sharing? New Trends in Competition Policy*, Horst Albach, Jim Y. Jin, and Christoph Schenk (eds.), (Berlin: Ed. Sigma, 1996), 51–68; Thomas M. Jorde and David J. Teece, "Innovation and Cooperation: Implications for Competition and Antitrust," *Journal of Economic Perspectives*, Vol. 4, No. 3 (Summer 1990), 75–96. On the role of trade associations, and their promotion in the 1910s and 1920s of "open-price groups," see Galambos, *Competition and Cooperation*, 74–85. For the example of the famous "Gary Dinners" where the head of U.S. Steel openly invited journalists and Justice Department officials to see that their agreements were not illegal price fixing, but rather "gentlemen's agreements," see Kolko, *The Triumph of Conservatism*, 33–9.

72. Neil Fligstein, *The Transformation of Corporate Control* (Cambridge: Harvard University Press, 1990): 2. On the need for cooperation among businesses, see Mark Granovetter, "Coase Revisited: Business Groups in the Modern Economy," *Industrial and Corporate Change*, Vol. 4, No. 1 (1995), 93–5.

73. Thomas J. Watson, Jr. and Peter Petre, *Father, Son & Co.: My Life at IBM and Beyond* (New York: Bantam Books, 1990), 268–70.

74. Arthur Andersen & Co., *The First Sixty Years*, 13–14.

75. Arthur M. Lewis, "The Accountants are Changing the Rules," *Fortune* (15 January 1965).

76. Despite Arthur Andersen's current position as the largest management consulting firm in the world, in the 1956 study completed by students at the Harvard Business School, Arthur Andersen & Company was not included in a list of the 42 leading management consulting firms. See Amon et al., *Management Consulting*, 14. By 1962, however, Leonard Spacek, the managing partner at Arthur Andersen & Company, was explicitly recruiting Harvard Business School students into consulting careers at Andersen. *Career Guide: A Harvard Business School Student Publication*, Vol. 2, No. 2 (February 1962).

77. Robert Heller, *The Fate of IBM* (London: Little, Brown and Company, 1994), 24.

78. F. C. "Buck" Rodgers with Robert L. Shook, *The IBM Way: Insights into the World's Most Successful Marketing Organization* (New York: Harper and Row, 1986), 128–9.

79. Robert Sobel, *IBM: Colossus in Transition*, 76.

80. Regis McKenna, *Who's Afraid of Big Blue? How Companies are Challenging IBM – and Winning* (Reading, MA: Addison-Wesley Publishing Co., 1989), 155. Historian Robert Sobel points out that in 1939, IBM profits were greater than its four largest competitors' combined. Sobel, *IBM: Colossus in Transition*, 87.

81. Watson and Petre, *Father, Son & Co.*, 268.

82. *United States v. International Business Machines Corporation*, Civil Action No. 72-344, United States District Court for the Southern District of New York, 25 January 1956.

83. Richard Thomas DeLamarter, *Big Blue: IBM's Use and Abuse of Power* (New York: Dodd, Mead & Company, 1986), 23, 339–41.

84. Mark Stevens, *The Big Six* (New York: Touchstone, 1991), 112–13.

85. DeLamarter, *Big Blue*, xiv.

86. "IBM Will Put Emphasis on Service," *Star Tribune* (20 October 1992), 3D; Glenn Rifkin, "IBM Searches for Blue Skies in Consulting," *The New York Times* (9 October 1994), sec. 5, 5.

87. "IBM as Consultant: A Transformation History," *Chain Store Age* (1 September 1995), 2C; Laura B. Smith, "Sound Advice? Compaq Computer Corp., Other Vendors Offer Consulting Services," *PC Week Executive* (15 January 1996), E1. By 1997, one-fourth of all of IBM's revenues came from consulting services, see IBM's *1997 Annual Report*.

88. George J. Benston, *The Separation of Commercial and Investment Banking: The Glass-Steagall Act Revisited and Reconsidered* (New York: Oxford University Press, 1990). Until the late 1990s, Regulation Y, enforced by the Federal Reserve Board, allowed bank holding companies to offer management consulting services only to other depository institutions (generally banks).

89. Deutsche Bank, for example, purchased the largest domestic consulting firm in Germany, Roland Berger & Co., as part of its broader expansion into investment banking services, see Haig Simonian, "Banking as Three-Pronged Attack," *Financial Times* (8 Sept. 1989), Sec. 1, 27; On Deutsche Bank's subsequent divestiture of Roland Berger & Co., see Graham Bowley, "News Digest: Roland Berger in Shake-Up," *Financial Times* (22 July 1998), 16.

90. For a similar perspective on how consultants' lack of historical insight has hurt their attempts to achieve professional status, see David Grayson Allen, "Bound by their Past or in Transition? An Analysis of U.S. Management Consulting Associations," *Journal of Management Consulting*, Vol. 3, No. 1 (1986), 27–35.

91. Armstrong, *An Engineer in Wall Street*.

92. Paul L. Joskow, "Asset Specificity and the Structure of Vertical Relationships: Empirical Evidence," in Oliver E. Williamson and Sidney G. Winter, *The Nature of the Firm: Origins, Evolution, and Development* (New York: Oxford University Press, 1991), 118.

93. Hawley, *The New Deal and the Problem of Monopoly*, 3–16.

94. F. E. Emery and E. L. Trist, "The Causal Textures of Organizational Environments," *Human Relations*, Vol. 18 (1965), 21–32; Alexander James Field, "Do Legal Systems Matter?" *Explorations in Economic History*, Vol. 28 (1991), 1–35.

## 2. ACCOUNTING FOR A NEW PROFESSION: CONSULTANTS' STRUGGLE FOR JURISDICTIONAL POWER

1. "Doctors of Management," *Fortune* (1944), 142.

2. Hal Higdon, *The Business Healers* (New York: Random House, 1969), 113; Thomas G. Cody, *Management Consulting: A Game without Chips* (Fitzwilliam, New Hampshire, Consultants News, 1986), 24. For a European restatement, see the Organization for European Economic Cooperation, *Some Aspects of Consultant Engineering in the United States* (Paris, European Productivity Agency, 1958), 283. For a more nuanced argument that places the Taylorists as the first of three "waves" in the evolution of management consulting, see Matthias Kipping, "Trapped in their Wave: The Evolution of Management Consultancies," in Timothy Clark and Robin Fincham (eds.), *Critical Consulting: New Perspectives on the Management Advice Industry* (Oxford: Blackwell, 2002), 30–2.

3. The problem may be, as literary theorist Michel Foucault has argued, that genealogies stand in opposition to the straightforward search for historical "origins." See Michel Foucault, "Nietzsche, Genealogy, History," in Paul Rabinow (ed.), *The Foucault Reader* (New York: Pantheon Books, 1984), 77.

4. In 1937, for example, only three of the seventeen member firms in the Association of Consulting Management Engineers (ACME) had Taylorist

roots – Wallace Clark & Company, Hopf, Kent, Willard & Co., and Miller, Franklin & Co., Inc. The remainder, including George S. Armstrong & Co.; Booz, Fry, Allen & Hamilton; Ford, Bacon & Davis; Griffenhagen & Associates, Robert Heller & Associates, McKinsey, Wellington & Co., and Stevenson, Jordan & Harrison had roots in banking, psychology, accounting, or engineering but not scientific management. See, Association of Consulting Management Engineers, Inc., "The Profession of Management and the Function of the Consulting Management Engineer," (New York: ACME, 1937), 29, contained in file 29, Box 4, Emerson Papers, Industrial and Labor Relations Archive, Cornell University, Ithaca, New York.

5. "Doctors of Management," *Fortune*, 144–6. The same was also true of Charles Bedaux, who by the 1930s had forsaken the American market for Europe assignments.

6. Andrew Abbott, *The System of Professions: An Essay on the Division of Expert Labor* (Chicago: University of Chicago Press, 1988), 230, 371.

7. H. Thomas Johnson and Robert S. Kaplan, *Relevance Lost: The Rise and Fall of Management* Accounting (Boston: Harvard Business School Press, 1987), 14.

8. William Lazonick, "Controlling the Market for Corporate Control," *Industrial and Corporate Change*, Vol. 1, No. 3 (1992), 445–88.

9. Mark Roe, *Strong Managers, Weak Owners: The Political Roots of American Corporate Finance* (Princeton: Princeton University Press, 1994); Neil Fligstein, *The Transformation of Corporate Control* (Cambridge: Harvard University Press, 1990). In particular, both authors use classic academic accounts of the evolution of American corporate governance – respectively, Adolf A. Berle and Gardner C. Means's, *The Modern Corporation and Private Property* (New York: McMillan Company, 1932) and Alfred D. Chandler, Jr.'s, *Strategy and Structure: Chapters in the History of the American Industrial Enterprise* (Cambridge: The MIT Press, 1962) – to reject the dominant argument of rational, economic efficiency as the central explanation for the emergence of the American system.

10. Ellis W. Hawley, "Herbert Hoover, the Commerce Secretariat, and the Vision of an 'Associative State,' 1921–1929," *Journal of American History*, Vol. 61, No. 1 (June 1974).

11. Jonathan P. Charkham, *Keeping Good Company: A Study of Corporate Governance in Five Countries* (Oxford: Clarendon Press, 1994); Kenneth J. Lipartito and Paul J. Miranti, "Professions and Organizations in Twentieth Century America," *Social Science Quarterly*, Vol. 79, No. 2 (June 1998), 301–20.

12. Louis Galambos, "The American Economy and the Reorganization of the Sources of Knowledge," in A. Oleson and J. Voss (eds.), *The Organization of Knowledge in Modern America, 1860–1920* (Baltimore: The Johns Hopkins University, 1979), 273.

13. Colin Gordon, *New Deals: Business, Labor, and Politics in America, 1920–1935* (New York: Cambridge University Press, 1994), 35; Ellis W. Hawley, *The New*

*Deal and the Problem of Monopoly* (Princeton: Princeton University Press, 1966), 166–8; George S. Armstrong, *An Engineer in Wall Street*, (New York, George S. Armstrong & Co., 1962).

14. David F. Noble, *America by Design: Science, Technology and the Rise of Corporate Capitalism* (Cambridge: The M.I.T. Press, 1977), 124.

15. Andre Millard, *Edison and the Business of Innovation* (Baltimore: The Johns Hopkins University Press, 1990), 43–4; William J. Baldwin, "Contracted Research and the Case for Big Business," *The Journal of Political Economy*, Vol. 70, No. 3 (1962), 294–8.

16. Thomas P. Hughes, *American Genesis: A Century of Invention and Technological Enthusiasm* (New York: Penguin Books, 1989), 162–3; Carroll Pursell, *The Machine in America: A Social History of Technology* (Baltimore: The Johns Hopkins University Press, 1995), 222–3; Ron Chernow, *Titan: The Life of John D. Rockefeller, Sr.* (New York: Random House, 1998), 286–7; Leonard S. Reich, "Industrial Research and the Pursuit of Corporate Security: The Early Years at Bell Labs," *Business History Review*, Vol. 54 (1980), 504–29.

17. Alan Trachtenberg, *The Incorporation of America: Culture and Society in the Gilded Age* (New York: Hill and Wang, 1982), 64; John W. Servos, "The Industrial Relations of Science: Chemical Engineering at M.I.T., 1900–1939," *Isis*, Vol. 71 (1980), 531–49; Elizabeth Brayer, *George Eastman: A Biography* (Baltimore: The Johns Hopkins University Press), 340–5; Alfred D. Chandler and Stephen Salsbury, *Pierre S. du Pont and the Making of the Modern Corporation* (New York: Harper and Row, 1971), 17–22.

18. David A. Hounshell, "The Evolution of Industrial Research in the United States," in Richard S. Rosenbloom and William J. Spencer (eds.), *Engines of Innovation: U.S. Industrial Research at the End of an Era* (Boston: Harvard Business School Press, 1996), 40–1.

19. Thomas R. Navin and Marian V. Sears, "The Rise of a Market for Industrial Securities, 1887–1902," *Business History Review*, Vol. 29 (June 1955), 124–5; Vincent P. Carosso, *Investment Banking in America: A History* (Cambridge: Harvard University Press, 1970), 44; David Neal Keller, *Stone & Webster, 1889–1989: A Century of Integrity and Service* (New York: Stone & Webster, Inc., 1989), 16; Charles C. Wittelsey, *For Human Needs: The Story of Ford, Bacon & Davis* (New York: Ford, Bacon & Davis, 1967).

20. E. J. Kahn, Jr., *The Problem Solvers: A History of Arthur D. Little, Inc.* (Boston: Little, Brown and Company, 1986), 28; Keller, *Stone & Webster*, 30.

21. Kahn, *The Problem Solvers*, 63.

22. Noble, *America by Design*, 124.

23. Kahn, *The Problem Solvers*, 28.

24. Isaiah Berlin, *The Hedgehog and the Fox: An Essay on Tolstoy's View of History* (New York: Simon and Schuster, 1953). Consider, for example, that Arthur D.

Little, Inc., as late as 1961, refused to take on a job "if it had ever worked for a competitor on a similar task." "Brains for Hire," *Time* (7 July 1961), 66.

25. Alfred D. Chandler, *The Visible Hand: The Managerial Revolution in American Business* (Cambridge: Harvard University Press, 1977), 468; Alfred P. Sloan, Jr., *My Years with General Motors* (New York: Doubleday, 1969), 249.

26. Kahn, *The Problem Solvers*, 43.

27. Norman S. Buchanan, "The Origin and Development of the Public Utility Holding Company," *The Journal of Political Economy*, Vol. 44, No. 1 (1936), 31–53.

28. Keller, *Stone & Webster*, 21–3.

29. Cited in Thomas P. Hughes, *Networks of Power: Electrification in Western Society, 1880–1930* (Baltimore: The Johns Hopkins University Press, 1983), 387.

30. "Stone & Webster, *Fortune*, Vol. 2 (Nov. 1930), 94.

31. Keller, *Stone & Webster*, 24.

32. Hughes, *Networks of Power*, 388; Buchanan, "The Origin and Development of the Public Utility Holding Company," 37.

33. Vincent P. Carosso, *More than a Century of Investment Banking: The Kidder, Peabody & Co. Story* (New York: McGraw Hill & Co., 1979), 72–4.

34. Hughes, *Networks of Power*, 390.

35. Kahn, *The Problem Solvers*, 49–52.

36. "Royal Little," *Who's Who in America*, 1960; "Stone & Webster, *Fortune*, 96.

37. Carosso, *More than a Century of Investment Banking*, 73–4; "His Engineers will Meet Atomic Power," *Business Week*, (19 June 1954), 114; Royal Little, *How to Lose $100,000,000 . . . and Other Valuable Advice* (Boston: Little, Brown & Company, 1979); Neil Fligstein, "The Interorganizational Power Struggle: The Rise of Finance Personnel to Top Leadership in Large Corporations, 1919–1979," *American Sociological Review*, Vol. 52, No. 1 (Feb. 1987), 50.

38. Kurt Salmon Associates, founded in 1935, remains one of the oldest and most respected niche consulting firms in America. Based in Atlanta, the consultancy has at various times expanded beyond the textile industry, but the core capability of the firm has always been its expertise in textile production and marketing. Isadore Barmash, "Consultant to Seventh Avenue: Kurt Salmon," *The New York Times*, 5 March 1972, F7.

39. "Stone & Webster Scope is Broad," *Wall Street Journal* (19 Feb. 1930), 8; "The Men Who Guide the Atomic Industry," *Business Week* (19 Nov. 1955), 123–8; David E. Nye, *Electrifying America: Social Meanings of a New Technology* (Cambridge: The M.I.T. Press, 1990), 170–6; Thomas P. Hughes, *American Genesis: A Century of Invention and Technological Enthusiasm, 1870–1970* (New York: Penguin Books, 1989), 390–1.

40. As Alfred Chandler has written, "[integrated industrial enterprises] use[d] the specialized research companies, such as Arthur D. Little and Stone & Webster in the United States, for testing, setting standards, and other more routine, less

proprietary activities." Alfred D. Chandler, Jr., *Scale and Scope: The Dynamics of Industrial Capitalism* (Cambridge, Massachusetts, Harvard University Press, 1990), 33.

41. James Allen (ed.), *Democracy and Finance: The Addresses and Public Statements of William O. Douglass as Member and Chairman of the Securities and Exchange Commission*, (New Haven: Yale University Press, 1940), 175–80.

42. Although almost nonexistent by the 1940s, the "efficiency engineer" would become a classic foil within corporate settings in popular culture. See, for example, the classic Spencer Tracy and Katherine Hepburn film *Desk Set*, dir. Walter Lang (1957), released by Twentieth Century Fox.

43. Frederick Winslow Taylor, *The Principles of Scientific Management* (New York: W. W. Norton & Company, 1967 [Orig. Pub. 1911]), 48.

44. Robert Kanigel, *The One Best Way: Frederick Winslow Taylor and the Enigma of Efficiency* (New York: Viking Books, 1997), 107–9.

45. Hugh G. J. Aitken, *Scientific Management in Action: Taylorism at Watertown Arsenal, 1908–1915* (Princeton, Princeton University Press, 1965), 14; Kanigel, *The One Best Way*, 429–36.

46. H. L. Gantt, *Work, Wages, and Profits: Their Influence on the Cost of Living* (New York, The Engineering Magazine, 1910); Frank B. Gilbreth, *Motion Study: A Method for Increasing the Efficiency of the Workman* (New York, Van Nostrand, 1911); Harrington Emerson, *The Twelve Principles of Efficiency* (New York, The Engineering Magazine, 1912).

47. Taylor, *The Principles of Scientific Management*; Mauro F. Guillén, *Models of Management, Work, Authority, and Organization in a Comparative Perspective* (Chicago, University of Chicago Press, 1994), 40–2; JoAnne Yates, *Control Through Communication: The Rise of System in American Management* (Baltimore: The Johns Hopkins University Press, 1989), 15.

48. Kanigel, *The One Best Way*, 170–1.

49. Aitken, *Scientific Management in Action*, 32–3.

50. Richard Edwards, *Contested Terrain: The Transformation of the Workplace in the Twentieth Century* (New York, Basic Books, 1979), 116–17.

51. Henry Ford, "Mass Production," *Encyclopedia Britannica*, Vol. 30 (New York, The Encyclopædia Britannica, Inc., 1926), 821–3.

52. Edwards, *Contested Terrain*, 98.

53. For a French psychologist's historical perspective on Taylor's continuing symbolism, see Bernard Doray, *From Taylorism to Fordism: A Rational Madness* (London: Free Association Books, 1988).

54. Harry Braverman, *Labor and Monopoly Capital: The Degradation of Work in the Twentieth Century* (New York: Monthly Review Press, 1976); Daniel Nelson, *Managers and Workers: The Origins of the New Factory System in the United States* (Madison: University of Wisconsin Press, 1975).

55. Although not Taylor's invention, as Robert Kanigel has pointed out, the phrase first used by Brandeis and later repeated in an influential article in *System* magazine, became widely associated with Taylorism. Kanigel, *The One Best Way*, 629.

56. Daniel Nelson, "Scientific Management in Retrospect," in Daniel Nelson (ed.), *A Mental Revolution: Scientific Management since Taylor* (Columbus: Ohio State University Press, 1992), 5.

57. If Taylor resisted breaking down his system into its constituent elements, he was nonetheless aware of the taxonomy. As Taylor testified, "Scientific management was 'not any efficiency device...It is not a new system of figuring costs; it is not a new system of paying men...it is not motion study...' In fact, it was not any of the devices which the average man calls to mind when scientific management is spoken of.'" Nelson, "Scientific Management in Retrospect," 5.

58. Milton Nadworthy, "Frederick Taylor and Frank Gilbreth: Competition in Scientific Management," *Business History Review*, Vol. 31, No. 2 (1957), 23–34.

59. Aitken, *Scientific Management in Action*, 3–11.

60. *Modern Times*, dir. Charles Chaplin (1936), released by United Artists.

61. Nelson, "Scientific Management in Retrospect," 11.

62. Milton J. Nadworny, "Frederick Taylor and Frank Gilbreth: Competition in Scientific Management," *The Business History Review*, Vol. 31, No. 1 (Spring, 1957), 23–34.

63. Frank Gilbreth, Jr. and Ernestine Gilbreth Carey, *Cheaper by the Dozen* (New York: Thomas Y. Cromwell & Co., 1948). Indeed, given Frank Gilbreth's decision not to institutionalize his practice, Lillian's success in continuing his business after Frank's early death was all the more remarkable. See, Brian Price, "Frank and Lillian Gilbreth and the Manufacture and Marketing of Motion Study, 1908–1924," *Business and Economic History*, Vol. 18 (1989), 88–98; Lancaster, Jane, *Making Time: Lillian Moller Gilbreth, a Life Beyond "Cheaper by the Dozen"* (Boston: Northeastern University Press, 2004).

64. For the evolution of French consultants, see Odile Henry, "Le Conseil, Un Espace Professionnel Autonome?" *Enterprises et Histoire*, No. 7 (December 1994): 37–58, while the development of British consultancies is covered in Patricia Tisdall, *Agents of Change: The Development and Practice of Management Consultancy* (London, 1982), 20–39; for a more general survey of the American influence on the development of European consulting firms, see Matthias Kipping, "American Management Consulting Companies in Western Europe, 1920 to 1990: Products, Reputation, and Relationships," *Business History Review*, Vol. 73 (Summer 1999), 193.

65. Harrington Emerson to W. B. Edgecombe, 28 April 1925, Harrington Emerson Papers, Box 1, File 18, Historical Collections and Labor Archives, Pattee Library, The Pennsylvania State University, State College, Pennsylvania.

66. James P. Quigel, Jr., *The Business of Selling Efficiency: Harrington Emerson and the Emerson Efficiency Engineers, 1900–1930* (Ph.D. Dissertation, Pennsylvania State University, 1992).

67. Harrington Emerson to Dillon, Read & Co., 8 January 1926, Harrington Emerson Papers, Box 1, File 16, Penn State Archive.

68. Edwin T. Layton, Jr., *The Revolt of the Engineers: Social Responsibility and the American engineering Profession* (Baltimore: The Johns Hopkins University Press, 1986 [originally published, 1971]), 144–6.

69. Frank Gilbreth offered his alternative "one best way" in Frank B. Gilbreth, "The Training Required for Engineers, discussion" *Engineering Education*, Vol. 9 (February 1919), 238–9.

70. Sharon Hartman Strom, *Beyond the Typewriter: Gender, Class, and the Origins of Modern American Office Work, 1900–1940* (Urbana: University of Illinois Press, 1992), 24.

71. T. W. Eustis, "The Engineer and Cost Accountant – Their Joint Problems," *N.A.C.A. Bulletin*, Vol. 10, No. 9 (1929), 581.

72. S. Paul Garner, *The Evolution of Cost Accounting to 1925* (University, Alabama: University of Alabama Press, 1954), 346.

73. For an overview of this debate, see Gary J. Previtts and B. D. Merino, *A History of Accounting in the United States: A Historical Interpretation of the Cultural Significance of Accounting* (New York, 1979), 181–4, and Johnson and Kaplan, *Relevance Lost*, 129–35.

74. A. Hamilton Church, "On the Inclusion of Interest in Manufacturing Costs," *Journal of Accountancy*, Vol. 15 (1913): 236–40.

75. For a detailed discussion on why accountants at the Harvard Business School agreed with the cost accountants, see Thomas Henry Sanders, *Problems in Industrial Accounting* (Chicago: A. W. Shaw Company, 1925), 286–95.

76. J. P. Jopin, "Interest Does Not Enter Into the Cost of Production," Journal of Accountancy, Vol. 15 (1913): 334–5.

77. American Association of University Instructors, *Papers and Proceedings of the Third Annual Meeting*, Vol. 3 (1919), 38–9, cited in Gerald Berk, "Discursive Cartels: Uniform Cost Accounting Among American Manufacturers Before the New Deal," *Business and Economic History*, Vol. 26, No. 1 (1997), 234.

78. "Interest in Relation to Cost," *American Institute of Accountants' Yearbook* (1918), 110, cited in Sanders, *Problems in Industrial Accounting*, 292.

79. Hawley, "Herber Hoover, the Commerce Secretariat, and the Vision of an 'Associative State,' 1921–1928," 116–40; Gerald Berk, "Communities of Competitors: Open Price Associations and the American State, 1911–1929," *Social Science History*, Vol. 20, No. 3 (1996), 375–400.

80. Guy Alchon, *The Invisible Hand of Planning: Capitalism, Social Science, and the State in the 1920s* (Princeton: Princeton University Press, 1985), 71–2; Robert F. Himmelberg, *The Origins of the National Recovery Administration: Business,*

*Government, and the Trade Association Issue, 1921–1933* (New York: Fordham University Press, 1976).

81. Quoted in John M. Jordan, *Machine-Age Ideology: Social Engineering & American Liberalism, 1911–1939* (Chapel Hill: University of North Carolina Press, 1994), 121.

82. Ellis W. Hawley, "Three Facets of Hooverian Associationalism: Lumber, Aviation, and Movies, 1921–1930," in Thomas K. McCraw (ed.), *Regulation in Perspective: Historical Essays* (Cambridge: Harvard University Press, 1981), 95–8.

83. Louis Galambos, *Competition and Cooperation: The Emergence of a National Trade Association* (Baltimore, The Johns Hopkins University Press, 1966), 45–6.

84. American Association of University Instructors, *Papers and Proceedings of the Third Annual Meeting*, Vol. 3 (1919), 38–38, cited in Gerald Berk, "Discursive Cartels: Uniford Cost Accounting Among American Manufacturers Before the New Deal," *Business and Economic History*, Vol. 26, No. 1 (1997), 234.

85. Charles R. Stevenson, "The Future of Trade Association Cost Work," *N.A.C.A. Yearbook* (1923), 297–301; See also, Thomas W. Howard, "The Value to Industry of Association Work in Cost Accounting," *N.A.C.A. Bulletin*, Vol. 12, No. 5 (1930), 381–8.

86. Arthur Andersen, "The Accountant, the Industrial Engineer, and the Banker," *Administration* (August 1921), reprinted in *Behind the Figures: Addresses and Articles by Arthur Andersen, 1913–1941* (Chicago: Arthur Andersen & Co., 1970): 23–8.

87. For individual industries, see R. H. Rositzke, "Standard Costs as Applied to Dress Manufacture," *N.A.C.A. Bulletin*, Vol. 13, No. 18 (1932), 1239–59; Rodolph H. Redmond, "Setting Standards for Plating and Jappanning Costs in a Job-Order Industry," *N.A.C.A. Bulletin*, Vol. 15, No. 13 (1934), 809–29; Charles C. James, "The Application of Standard Cost Accounting to Railroad Administration," *N.A.C.A. Bulletin*, Vol. 18, No. 1 (1936), 1–8; H. C. Moorman, "A Unified Method of Cost Keeping and Production Control for a Small Plant, *N.A.C.A. Bulletin*, Vol. 13, No. 19 (1932), 1317–30. In contrast, for a broader perspective on management problems, see Earl P. Stevenson, "The Research Laboratory and Its Relation to Cost Reduction," *N.A.C.A. Bulletin*, Vol. 10, No. 19 (1929), 1265–74 and Carle M. Bigelow, "Market Analysis and Sales Control," *N.A.C.A. Bulletin*, Vol. 13, No. 10 (1932), 659–80.

88. Richard P. Adelstein, "The Nation as an Economic Unit:" Keynes, Roosevelt, and the Managerial Ideal," *The Journal of American History*, Vol. 78, No. 1 (1991), 160–87; Theda Skocpol and Kenneth Finegold, "State Capacity and Economic Intervention in the Early New Deal," *Political Science Quarterly*, Vol. 97, No. 2 (1992): 262–8.

89. Ronald Edsforth, *The New Deal: America's Response to the Great Depression* (Oxford, Blackwell Publishers, 1999).

90. Hawley, *The New Deal and the Problem of Monopoly*, 53–71.
91. A. P. Haake, "The National Industrial Recovery Act from the Standpoint of the Trade Associations and Code Authorities," *N.A.C.A. Yearbook* (1934), 15–30; Eric A. Camman, "Selling-Below-Cost Provisions in Industrial Codes: An Analysis of 152 Codes," *N.A.C.A. Bulletin*, Vol. 15, No. 10 (1934), 623–49.
92. Thomas Ferguson, "From Normalcy to New Deal: Industrial Structure, Party Competition, and American Public Policy in the Great Depression," *International Organization*, Vol. 38, No. 1 (1984), 85–6.
93. John G. Neukom, *McKinsey Memoirs: A Personal Perspective* (New York, Privately Printed, 1975), 11; Jim Bowman, *Booz, Allen & Hamilton: Seventy Years of Client Service* (Chicago: Booz, Allen & Hamilton, 1984), 13–20.
94. Thomas W. Lamont Papers, Box 133, File 6, Historical Collections, Baker Library, Harvard Business School.
95. Cited in N. S. B. Gras, and Henrietta M. Larson, *Casebook in American Business History* (New York: F. S. Crofts & Company, 1939), 619.
96. Ford, Bacon & Davis, *United States Steel Company: Final Study Summarizing the Survey* (New York, 1938). The drop in revenues following the conclusion of the U.S. Steel study in 1938, in combination with the death of James O. McKinsey in 1937, led to the 1939 separation of McKinsey and Company in New York from the older Chicago office which became A. T. Kearney & Co. Both firms remain among the oldest and most influential management consulting firms in the world.
97. Paul A. Tiffany, *The Decline of American Steel: How Management, Labor, and Government Went Wrong* (New York, Oxford University Press, 1988), 15–17.
98. James Don Edwards, *History of Public Accounting in the United States* (East Lansing: Michigan State University Business Studies, 1960), 161–3; Harold van B. Cleveland and Thomas F. Huertas, *Citibank, 1812–1970* (Cambridge: Harvard University Press, 1985), 197–198.
99. For evidence of Peat, Marwick, Mitchell & Co.'s involvement in cost accounting and the NRA codes, see Eric A. Camman, "Selling-Below-Cost Provisions in Industrial Codes: An Analysis of 152 Codes," *N.A.C.A. Bulletin*, Vol. 15, No. 10 (1934), 623–49.
100. Joseph S. Glickauf, *Footsteps Toward Professionalism: Addresses and Articles by Joseph S. Glickauf* (Chicago: Arthur Andersen & Co., 1971), v–vi.
101. For a collection of Arthur E. Andersen's influential writings, see Arthur Andersen & Company, *Behind the Figures: Addresses and Articles by Arthur Andersen, 1913–1941* (Chicago: Arthur Andersen & Company, 1970).
102. Arthur Andersen & Company, *The First Sixty Years, 1913–1973* (Chicago: Arthur Andersen & Co., 1973), 15.
103. Arthur Andersen & Company, *The First Sixty Years*, 13–14.

104. Association of Consulting Management Engineers, "ACME's Growth," Folder: "History of ACME," Corporate Archives, Association of Management Consulting Firms, New York City.

105. Abbott, *The System of Professionals*, 91–8.

106. Leonard Spacek, "The Growth of Arthur Andersen & Co., 1928–1973," Oral Interview, Center for Professional Education, Arthur Andersen & Co., St. Charles, Illinois, 26 October 1983, deposited at Northwestern University, 51.

107. James O. McKinsey, "James O. McKinsey & Company: Program for New York Office, 2 May 1935, Page 4, Corporate Archives, McKinsey & Company, New York; Microfiche of Reports, A. T. Kearney Corporate Archives, Chicago (A. T. Kearney & Co. was the original Chicago office of James O. McKinsey & Company before the split in 1939); Arthur Andersen & Co., *The First Sixty Years*, 14.

108. James O. McKinsey, "James O. McKinsey & Company: Program for New York Office, 2 May 1935, Page 4, Corporate Archives, McKinsey & Company, New York.

109. Walter Dill Scott, who was President of Northwestern University north of Chicago, had institutionalized the management of his consulting firm within the first year of its operations in 1919. The problem, however, as Scott soon learned was that the market for the Scott Company's services was simply not large enough. See Papers of Walter Dill Scott, University Archives, Northwestern University, Evanston, Illinois. On the particular problems of managing professional firms, see David H. Maister, *Managing the Professional Service Firm* (New York: Free Press, 1993).

110. William B. Wolf, *Management and Consulting: An Introduction to James O. McKinsey* (Ithaca: Cornell University Press, 1978), 42.

111. Neukom, *McKinsey Memoirs*, 11.

112. Neukom, *McKinsey Memoirs*, 12.

113. Numerous specific examples in the corporate archives of A. T. Kearney & Company in Chicago bear out this general pattern. See for example, James O. McKinsey & Company's series of assignments Armstrong Cork and Phoenix Hosiery in the early 1930s that followed the consultancy's initial general survey.

114. Lloyd Wendt and Herman Kogan, *Give the Lady What She Wants! The Story of Marshall Field & Company* (Chicago: Rand McNally & Company, 1952), 320–7; Wolf, *Management and Consulting*, 10–11.

3. HOW HAVE CONSULTANTS MATTERED? THE CASE OF LUKENS STEEL

1. Lukens's long history of independence ended in December 1997 when it agreed to be acquired by Bethlehem Steel for $650 million. Douglas Harbrecht, "Looking for a Lift, Bethlehem Bags Lukens," *Business Week* (15 December 1997).

2. Although I am not looking at public relations firms, the fact that Lukens executives hired Hill & Knowlton in 1949, and brought them back again in 1952, to help them institutionalize their public relations department is further evidence that Lukens consistently hired the best-known corporate advisors for professional counsel. File 23, box 23, Lukens Steel Collection.

3. The Lukens Steel Collection, Acquisition 50, Hagley Museum and Library, Wilmington, Delaware, will be the source of all archival materials cited unless otherwise noted.

4. Historian Thomas Misa has described how this pattern of product differentiation was the rational response of small and medium sized producers in a market plagued by price wars. Thomas J. Misa, *A Nation of Steel: The Making of Modern America, 1865–1925* (Baltimore, The Johns Hopkins University Press, 1995).

5. Bethlehem Steel filed for Chapter 11 bankruptcy protection in 2001 and was, in turn, purchased by the International Steel Group in 2003.

6. Paternalistic managers at Lukens emphasized this continuity in their workforce. The company newsletter, devised by Hill and Knowlton to increase worker support, celebrated examples of brothers who worked alongside each other and sons who followed their fathers into the steel mills. See *Lukens Life*, Pamphlet Collection, Hagley Museum and Library.

7. The lack of change at Lukens in the 19th century frustrated historian Julian Skaggs's attempts to trace the influence of managerial and technical innovation at Lukens. As Skaggs concluded:

> Lukens, which had always been a small manufacturer of steel plate, was unable to exercise any control over the market. They were also largely reactive in their technical changes (and probably their administrative structure)....Nor was there ever any significant problem with labor in terms of wages, strikes, or a proper supply of skills or manpower. Finally, there was no shortage of capital when needed.

> Julian C. Skaggs, "Lukens, 1850–1870: A Case Study in the Mid-Nineteenth Century American Iron Industry," (Ph.D. Diss., University of Delaware, 1975), 165, 178.

8. The domination of the U.S. steel industry by the largest firms, which was firmly in place by the beginning of this century, steadily increased through the 1950s, before electric mini-mills and foreign competition began to threaten the steel oligopoly in the 1970s. "In 1901, the top [twelve] producers controlled more than half of the total steel capacity, by 1950 they produced 82.7%." Gertrude G. Schroeder, *The Growth of Major Steel Companies, 1900–1950* (Baltimore, 1953), 16–17. For his discussion of the distinct advantages of flexible production in textile manufacturing in the Philadelphia region see Phillip Scranton, *Figured Tapestry: Production, Markets, and Power in Philadelphia Textiles, 1885–1941* (New York, 1989).

9. Mark Reutter, *Sparrows Point: Making Steel – The Rise and Ruin of Industrial Might* (New York, 1988), 384.

10. While Lukens profits as a percentage of sales (ROS) were 25% lower on average than Republic's between 1940 and 1959 (3.9% versus 5.2%), Lukens's rate of return on equity (ROE) was 20% higher over the same 20 years (12.2% versus 10.1%). This still understates Lukens's success since its retained earnings (or "book value") increased, on average, 9.5% annually while the book value at Republic Steel grew at a more modest 4.6% annually over the same two decades. Thus, not only were Lukens profits consistently higher but comparisons of respective returns on equity are based on a much faster growing capital base at Lukens Steel. Ratios derived from the Annual Reports of Lukens Steel and Republic Steel from 1940 to 1959.

11. "Translators," as Hugh Aitken described them, are those individuals who transfer a critical piece of information from one network to another. I believe that consultants institutionalized the "translation" of organizational knowledge between businesses. See Hugh G. J. Aitken, *The Continuous Wave: Technology and American Radio, 1900–1932* (Princeton, 1985), 16–22.

12. Sociologists refer to this transfer of organizational models as "mimetic institutional isomorphism." See Paul J. DiMaggio and Walter J. Powell, "The Iron Cage Revisited: Institutional Isomorphism and Collective Rationality in Organizational Fields," *American Sociological Review*, 48 (April 1983): 147–60.

13. Alfred D. Chandler, Jr., *The Visible Hand: The Managerial Revolution in American Business* (Cambridge, Mass., 1977). The role of management consultants as conduits of organizational ideas was first proposed in Homer Hagedorn, "The Management Consultant as Transmitter of Business Techniques," *Explorations in Entrepreneurial History* (February, 1955): 164–73.

14. Frederick Winslow Taylor, *The Principles of Scientific Management* (1911; reprint New York, 1967).

15. For the classic discussion of labor's role in steel production at the turn of the century see David Brody, *Steelworkers in America: The Nonunion Era* (Cambridge, 1960).

16. Suffern & Son, "Report on Distribution of Cost of Power," 16 May 1912, file: "Suffern & Son, Accountants, 1911–1914," box 1999, Lukens Steel.

17. Suffern & Son to Lukens Iron & Steel Company, 28 May 1912, Ibid.

18. Ibid.

19. Charles L. Huston to Messrs. Suffern & Son, 2 June 1912, Ibid.

20. Suffern & Son to Charles L. Huston, 4 September 1912 and 24 November 1912, Ibid.

21. Lukens Iron and Steel Company to Messrs, Suffern & Son, 2 December 1913, Ibid.

22. Daniel Nelson, "Scientific Management in Retrospect," in *A Mental Revolution: Scientific Management Since Taylor* (ed.), Daniel Nelson (Columbus, Ohio State University Press, 1992), 12.

23. David J. Goldberg, "Richard A. Feiss, Mary Barnett Gilson, and Scientific Management at Joseph & Feiss, 1909–1925," in *A Mental Revolution*, 43; Hugh G. J. Aitken, *Scientific Management in Action: Taylorism at Watertown Arsenal, 1908–1915* (Princeton, 1960), 5; John C. Rumm, "Scientific Management and Industrial Engineering at DuPont," in *A Mental Revolution*, 176–80.

24. Judith A. Merkle, *Management and Ideology: The Legacy of the International Scientific Management Movement* (Berkeley, 1980), 2; The Emerson Company to A. F. Huston, Pres., Lukens [sic] Iron & Steel Co., 4 January 1915, file 15, box 1991, Lukens Steel.

25. At DuPont, the Efficiency Division, which operated from 1911 to 1915, was not only largely unsuccessful in finding ways to apply Scientific Management to the production of explosives but it was subsequently blamed for speeding up the production of dynamite that in turn caused an explosion in 1914 killing several workers. Rumm, "Scientific Management and Industrial Engineering at DuPont," 76–8. Cf. Donald R. Stabile, "The DuPont Experiments in Scientific Management: Efficiency and Safety, 1911–1919," *Business History Review*, 61 (Autumn 1987): 365–86.

26. For Huston's doubts about the wisdom of hiring a Taylorist firm see Charles L. Huston to P. M. Sharpless, 20 November 1919, file 14, box 1998, Lukens Steel. For the letters of reference see Charles L. Huston to Messrs. S. Morgan Smith Co. [reference letter for Miller, Franklin, Basset & Company], 13 November 1919, Ibid. and W. W. Galbreath, President, Youngstown Pressed Steel, to Charles L. Huston [reference letter for L. V. Estes, Inc.], 3 December 1919, file 27, box 1991, Lukens Steel.

27. Charles L. Huston to Messrs. C. E. Knoeppel & Co., Inc., 21 June 1920 and Charles L. Huston to Messrs. C. E. Knoeppel & Co., Inc., 29 October 1920, both in file 13, box 1994, Lukens Steel. Frederick R. Shanley, Business Manager, L. V. Estes, Incorporated to Charles L. Huston, 26 November 1919, file 27, box 1991, Lukens Steel.

28. S. B. Schlaudecker to Mr. C. L. Huston, 17 and 25 November 1920, Ibid.

29. Charles L. Huston to S. B. Schlaudecker, 29 November 1920, Ibid.

30. Matthias Kipping and Thomas Armbruster, "The Burdens of Otherness: Limits of Consultancy Interventions in Historical Case Studies," in Matthias Kipping and Lars Engwall, *Management Consulting: Emergence and Dynamics of a Knowledge Industry* (Oxford, Oxford University Press, 2002), 203–21.

31. Charles L. Huston to S. B. Schlaudecker, 29 November 1920, Ibid.

32. Taylor, *The Principles of Scientific Management*, 135.

33. Charles L. Huston to S. B. Schlaudecker, 29 November 1920, file 27, box 1991, Lukens Steel.

34. S. B. Schlaudecker to Mr. C. L. Huston, 22 December 1920, Ibid.

35. S. B. Schlaudecker to Mr. Huston, 27 December 1920 quoting "Mr. Spackman's letter" of 15 December 1920, Ibid.

36. Charles L. Huston to L. V. Estes, Inc., 24 March 1921 and L. V. Estes to Mr. C. L. Huston, 30 March 1921, Ibid.

37. Charles L. Huston to L. V. Estes, 7 June 1921, Ibid.

38. In April, 1921, Kelly, Cooke & Company wrote to Charles Huston asking if Lukens was in the market for "an investigation of your cost and production departments in order to put them on a more efficient basis." In the middle of his disagreement with L. V. Estes, Inc. over their charges, Huston replied, inquiring if Kelly, Cooke, and Company used, "any of the methods used by Emerson Co., Fred Gant, or H. L. Taylor [sic], or any of the other leading Industrial Engineers, who have worked out thoroughly revised systems for control in manufacturing operations and management of employees." A week later, Huston wrote to Kelly, Cooke & Company to tell them that he was not interested. See William F. Kelly to Mr. Charles L. Huston, 18 April 1921 and Charles L. Huston to Messrs. Kelly, Cooke and Company, 20 April and 28 April 1921, all in file 13, box 1994, Lukens Steel.

39. Charles L. Huston to Messrs. Miller, Franklin, Basset Co. [sic], 21 March 1923, file 31, box 1995, Lukens Steel.

40. Baker to Charles L. Huston, 7 September 1922, file 13, box 1997, Lukens Steel. Walter N. Polakov to Charles L. Huston, 26 August 1922, Ibid.

41. Thomas P. Hughes, American Genesis: A Century of Invention and Technological Enthusiasm 1870–1970 (New York, 1989), 257. Hughes draws the story of Polakov from Merkle's, Management and Ideology.

42. For the history of British management consultancies see Patricia Tisdall, Agents of Change: The Development and Practice of Management Consultancy (London, 1982), 20–39. On the history and professionalization of management consulting in France see Odile Henry, Un Savoir en Pratique: Les Professionnels de L'Expertise et du Conseil, (Ph.D. Diss., Ecole des Hautes Etudes en Sciences Sociales, Paris, 1993), 235–48.

43. For a different interpretation of Bedaux's work that emphasizes their employment as proxies for the political tensions among the executives in Lukens, see Matthias Kipping, "Consultancy and Conflicts: Bedaux at Lukens Steel and the Anglo Iranian Oil Company," Entreprises et Histoire, Vol. 25 (2000), 9–25.

44. Steven Kreis, "The Diffusion of Scientific Management: The Bedaux Company in America and Britain, 1926–1945," in A Mental Revolution, 168.

45. Rumm, "Scientific Management and Industrial Engineering at Du Pont," 184; Kreis, "The Diffusion of Scientific Management," 168. For a detailed contemporary description of the Bedaux system see William F. Watson, The Worker and Wage Incentives: The Bedaux and Other Systems (London, The Hogarth Press, 1934), 27–32.

46. Kreis, "The Diffusion of Scientific Management," 157.

47. Robert W. Wolcott to Charles L. Huston, 30 August 1930, file 12, box 1993, Lukens Steel.

48. "Engineer's Report, #72," 7 December 1931, Ibid.

49. "Engineer's Report, #92," 19 September 1932, Ibid.

50. National Industrial Conference Board, *Systems of Wage Payment* (New York, 1930), 109.

51. Ibid., 59.

52. Charles L. Huston to R. W. Wolcott and the Board of Directors, 11 January 1938, file: "Corporate Records – Committee Reports," box 2159, Lukens Steel.

53. Still, questions persisted about the Bedaux system's effectiveness. In 1938, Charles L. Huston wondered whether Lukens should conduct a systematic review of the Bedaux system at Lukens to, "show whether the bonus money paid to workers has been and is of benefit to Lukens, and whether its cost has been and is more than its benefit." Charles L. Huston to Robert W. Wolcott, 11 January 1938, Ibid.

54. On the general trend of rising administrative personnel in relation to production workers see Reinhard Bendix, *Work and Authority in Industry: Ideologies of Management in the Course of Industrialization* (New York, John Wiley & Sons, 1956): 212–21.

55. The strong historical links between the needs of merchant banks and the services of management engineering firms are described in Christopher D. McKenna, "The Origins of Modern Management Consulting," *Business and Economic History*, 24 (Fall 1995): 51–8.

56. Although the contemporary term was "management engineering," in the late 1940s, under pressure from engineers in New York who complained that management "engineers" frequently lacked professional training in engineering and lacked an engineers license, leading firms like McKinsey & Company increasingly adopted the term "management consultant" to describe themselves. Thus, the descriptions "management engineering" or "management consulting" can be used interchangeably without historical imprecision.

57. Association of Consulting Management Engineers, Inc. (ACME), *Numerical Data on the Present Dimensions, Growth, and other Trends in Management Consulting in the United States* (New York, 1964), Table 2.

58. Columbia University economist Joel Dean noted the rapid growth of management engineering in: "The Place of Management Counsel in Business," *The Harvard Business Review*, 16 (1938). For an industry perspective available to executives at Lukens see "Management Engineers Help Renew Borrower's Earnings," *Bankers Monthly* (March 1941) reprinted by George S. May Company in file 14, box 2019, Lukens Steel.

59. U.S. Steel, *Annual Report*, 1938.

60. Marvin Bower, *Perspective on McKinsey* (New York, 1979), 19.

61. McKinsey & Co. to Kuhn, Loeb and Company, *Proposed Consolidation of Republic Steel Corporation, Corrigan, McKinney Steel Company and Otis Steel Company*, 22 May 1934, iii, Microfiche, A. T. Kearney & Co. Corporate Archives.

62. Ford, Bacon & Davis, "Report: Lukens Steel Company, As of 11 June 1927," files 28–30, box 1991, Lukens Steel.

63. Charles L. Huston to W. Findlay Downs, Pres., 16 March 1933, Lukens Steel, file 24, box 2016, Lukens Steel.

64. Robert W. Wolcott to Mr. Stewart Huston, 1 December 1937, file 2, box 1977, Lukens Steel.

65. Charles L. Huston to R. W. Wolcott and the Board of Directors, 11 January 1938, file: "Corporate Records – Committee Reports," box 2159, Lukens Steel.

66. File 12, box 2190, Lukens Steel. Of course the same recessionary downturn hit the large steelmakers like U.S. Steel just as severely. See 1938 annual report for U.S. Steel previously cited.

67. W. Findlay Downs to Charles L. Huston, 20 December 1937, file 1, box 1991, Lukens Steel.

68. Robert W. Wolcott to Mr. Stewart Huston, 1 December 1937, file 2, box 1977, Lukens Steel.

69. "Report for Manufacturing Committee," prepared by Stewart Huston [c. Jan 1938], file: "Corporate Records – Committee Reports," box 2159, Lukens Steel.

70. Day & Zimmerman to Robert W. Wolcott, Report #3182, 6 July 1937, file 1, box 1991, Lukens Steel.

71. Charles L. Huston to Robert W. Wolcott, 16 July 1936, Ibid.

72. "Report for Manufacturing Committee," prepared by Stewart Huston [c. Jan 1938], file: "Corporate Records – Committee Reports," box 2159, Lukens Steel.

73. Charles L. Huston to R. W. Wolcott and the Board of Directors, 11 January 1938, Ibid.

74. Stevenson, Jordan & Harrison, Management Engineers, "Principles and Practices" [c. 1934], Business Pamphlet Collection, New York Public Library, 1.; Ford, Bacon & Davis, Inc., Engineers, "Location of Airport: Philadelphia, PA. District," 7 December 1928, Pamphlet Collection, Hagley Museum and Library.

75. Chandler, *The Visible Hand*, 468. For further evidence of this transformation, see Arthur D. Little, Inc.'s letterhead from 1918, which describes them as "Chemists Engineers Managers." H. J. Skinner, Vice President, Arthur D. Little, Inc., to Charles L. Huston, Vice President and Works Manager, May 17, 1918, file 17, box 1994, Lukens Steel.

76. E. J. Kahn, Jr., *The Problem Solvers: A History of Arthur D. Little, Inc.* (New York, 1986), 215.

77. Many other emerging professions also borrowed terminology or titles from older, established professions to increase their own authority and status. For the specific case of intelligence testing and a discussion of this rhetorical strategy, see JoAnne Brown, *The Definition of a Profession: The Authority of Metaphor in the History of Intelligence Testing, 1890–1930* (Princeton, 1992).

78. The letterhead at McKinsey changed between 3 January 1931 and 22 October 1933. James O. McKinsey and Company to the Union Carbide Company, 3 January 1931; James O. McKinsey and Company to the Carrier Corporation, 22 October 1933, both in Microfiche, A. T. Kearney & Co. Corporate Archives.

79. Harry Arthur Hopf, "The Present Status, Responsibilities and Future of the Management Engineer," 6, address delivered at the 19th National Convention of the Society of Industrial Engineers, Chicago, 29 June 1933, Business Pamphlet Collection, New York Public Library.

80. Stevenson, Jordan & Harrison, Management Engineers, "Principles and Practices" [c. 1934], 16, Business Pamphlet Collection, New York Public Library.

81. William B. Wolf, *Management and Consulting: An Introduction to James O. McKinsey* (Ithaca, 1978), 48. Edwin Booz, the founder of Booz Allen & Hamilton, also specialized in general surveys. In 1924, Booz changed the description on his office door from "Business Engineering Service" to "Business Surveys." Jim Bowman, *Booz Allen & Hamilton: Seventy Years of Client Service, 1914–1984* (Chicago, 1984), 7.

82. Heller's reputation was so well established that the Commission on the Organization of the Executive Branch of Government ("The First Hoover Commission") hired Robert Heller & Associates in 1947 to reorganize the U.S. Post Office because committee members agreed that Robert Heller & Associates was the "best talent in America." Statement by George Mead, Conference Minutes, 15 December 1947, 10, National Archives, RG 264, Hoover Commission I, Records of the Secretaries Office, NC 115, box 27.

83. Robert W. Wolcott to the Board of Directors, Lukens Steel Company, 28 October 1946, file 3, box 1977, Lukens Steel.

84. Robert Heller & Associates, Incorporated to R. W. Wolcott, President, 26 January 1946, 5–6, file 21, box 1992, Lukens Steel.

85. "Status of Recommendations to Date by Robert Heller and Associates, Inc.," 28 October 1946, 3, file 3, box 1977, Lukens Steel.

86. Although Robert Heller & Associates detailed how the market research department should function, Lukens was unable to make it work properly. In March, 1943, Wolcott hired Coverdale & Colpitts, a management consulting firm, to study their product line and suggest new markets for them after the war ended. Interestingly, among the many board members present when Wolcott reported commissioning the survey, it was W. Findley Downs, the President of Day & Zimmerman, who alone asked why Lukens could not have performed the study internally instead of hiring outside consultants. Management Committee Meeting, 8 March 1943, file 1, box 2154, Lukens Steel. See also Coverdale & Colpitts, *Record of the Professional Experience of Coverdale & Colpitts* (New York, 1956), 21, Pamphlet Collection, Hagley Museum and Library.

87. "Status of Recommendations to date by Robert Heller and Associates, Inc.," 28 October 1946, 16, file 3, box 1977, Lukens Steel.

88. On the origins of the decentralized corporation see Alfred D. Chandler, Jr., *Strategy and Structure: Chapters in the History of the American Industrial Enterprise* (Cambridge, Mass., 1962).

89. On Cresap's decentralization of Westinghouse, see *Fortune* (December 1952), 184. On the reorganization of I.B.M. by Booz Allen see Thomas J. Watson, Jr. and Peter Petre, *Father, Son & Co.: My Life at IBM and Beyond* (New York, 1990), 284–95.

90. Robert W. Wolcott to Mr. Stewart Huston, 1 December 1937, file 2, box 1977, Lukens Steel.

91. This is based on an estimated 10,000 practicing management consultants in 1950. Association of Consulting Management Engineers, Inc. (ACME), *Numerical Data on the Present Dimensions, Growth, and other Trends in Management Consulting in the United States* (New York, 1964), Table 4. See also "Consultants Numbers Grow," *Management Review* (March, 1954).

92. In the 1950s at McKinsey & Co. the general survey fell out of everyday use although an outline of it appeared in McKinsey & Co.'s training manual as late as 1962. Wolf, *Management and Consulting*, 52.

93. "Consulting and Other Outside Services, Fiscal Year 1958," Lukens Steel, box 2015, file: "Consulting and Outside Service Expense, 1954–1958," box 2015, Lukens Steel. Management at Lukens Steel," 5 February 1954, "Controller's Office, 1953–1954," box 2015, Lukens Steel.

94. Scovell, Wellington & Company, "Audit of the University of Chicago, 1958," title page, Box 147, Folder 1, President's Papers, 1952–1960, Department of Special Collections, The University of Chicago.

95. Cresap, McCormick and Paget, "Survey of Markets for Heads and Job Stampings," 28 June 1956, box 2040, Lukens Steel.

96. File: "Consulting and Outside Service Expense, 1954–1958," box 2015, Lukens Steel.

97. For the example of George S. May Company, a management engineering firm that "bombarded," in Stewart Huston's words, executives at Lukens with advertising materials in the 1930s see Stewart Huston to Charles L. Huston, Jr., Director of Personnel, 21 February 1940, and the accompanying fliers, all in file 14, box 2019, Lukens Steel. The ACME code of ethics is reproduced in Management Consulting Report Associates, *Management Consulting* (Concord, Mass., 1958), 81–3.

98. After he retired from the Lukens presidency in 1948, Robert Wolcott served as Chairman of the Task Force on Military Procurement of the Second Hoover Commission. See the *Final Report to Congress, Second Hoover Commission,* (Washington, D.C., 1955), 9. Cresap, McCormick and Paget promoted itself through constant references to its work for the First Hoover Commission, even though half a dozen other consulting firms also worked for the Hoover Commission. See Cresap, McCormick and Paget, *A Summary of The Hoover Report*

(New York, Cresap, McCormick and Paget, 1950), Pamphlet Collection, Hagley Museum and Library.

99. In 1957, the *Harvard Business Review* reported that 24% of the 70,000 executives in America read the *Harvard Business Review*. This may explain why, during the 1950s, consultants from McKinsey & Co. contributed at least six articles, staff at Booz Allen & Hamilton contributed three articles, and consultants from Arthur D. Little, Inc. contributed another five articles to the *Harvard Business Review*. For *Harvard Business Review* readership figures see Edward C. Bursk, "New Dimensions in Top Executive Reading," *Harvard Business Review*, 35 (September-October 1957): 96.

100. Although Arthur Andersen & Company would become the largest management consulting firm in the world by the 1990s, in a 1956 study done by students at the Harvard Business School, Arthur Andersen & Co. was not included in a list of the 42 leading management consulting firms. Management Consulting Report Associates, *Management Consulting*, 14.

101. Arthur Andersen & Co., *A Vision of Grandeur* (Chicago, 1988), 95–6.

102. Roddy F. Osborn, "GE and UNIVAC: Harnessing the High-Speed Computer," *Harvard Business Review*, 32 (July–August 1954), 106.

103. Osborn, "GE and UNIVAC," 107. Other well known clients from the 1950s included Carrier Corp. and Bank of America. Arthur Andersen & Co., *A Vision of Grandeur*, 99.

104. Norman Dixon to Members of Management Committee, 11 September 1956, file: "Controllers Office, 1956–1957," box 2015, Lukens Steel.

105. Arthur Andersen & Co. to Robert W. Bowman, Controller, 28 November 1956, Ibid.

106. L. I. Mandich, Chairman, Management Committee to Board of Directors, 4 August 1965, 4, file 19, box 2152, Lukens Steel.

107. Booz Allen & Hamilton, Inc. to Charles L. Huston, Jr., President, 20 June 1966, "Lukens' Business Information System, Phase II," 6, file 30, box 2012, Lukens Steel. Very few of the initial estimates were accurate, indeed Booz Allen & Hamilton had estimated its own fees for the project between $120,000 and $150,000 yet Booz Allen & Hamilton's bills exceeded the upper estimate by another $35,000 within a year's time. File: "Board Minutes, Feb.-May 1966," box 2152, Lukens Steel.

108. Ibid., 3.

109. "Board of Director's Tour," file 5, box 2153, Lukens Steel.

110. Booz Allen & Hamilton, Inc. to Charles L. Huston, Jr., President, 20 June 1966, "Lukens' Business Information System, Phase II," 5, file 30, box 2012, Lukens Steel.

111. Ibid., 4.

112. For a short discussion of how The Boston Consulting Group advised its corporate clients and a description of the "Growth Share Matrix," see Davis Dyer

and David B. Sicilia, *The Labors of a Modern Hercules: The Evolution of a Chemical Company* (Boston, 1990), 362–3. See also John A. Seeger, "Reversing the Images of BCG's Growth/Share Matrix," *Strategic Management Journal*, Vol. 5, No. 1 (1984): 93–7.

113. So similar was McKinsey & Co.'s work and culture to investment banking that the directors of McKinsey and Co. seriously considered a merger with the elite Wall Street firm of Donaldson, Lufkin & Jenrette. They were stopped only by an impassioned plea by the retired managing director, Marvin Bower, who had worked for thirty years to keep McKinsey & Co. independent. Bower, *Perspective on McKinsey*, 288–9.

114. The reports for Sun Oil prepared by McKinsey & Co. between 1965 and 1969 are deposited in Archives and Manuscripts at the Hagley Museum and Library, Acquisition 1317, Series 1e, box 339.

115. Christopher Baer, "Company History," 5, Finders Aid, Lukens Steel.

116. Although the records of Cresap, McCormick and Paget's first study of the "Markets for Heads and Job Stampings" survive (see note 93), the records of their subsequent study have not survived in Lukens's corporate archives deposited at the Hagley Museum and Library. The reports that Cresap, McCormick and Paget prepared, however, do survive in the archives of Towers Perrin, the corporate successor to Cresap, McCormick and Paget, in Valhalla, New York. See Cresap, McCormick and Paget, "Lukens Steel Company: A Plan for Growth by Corporate Acquisition, Phase I," November 1968, 3–4, microfilm, Towers Perrin Corporate Archives.

117. Exhibit IV-1, Ibid.

118. Cresap, McCormick and Paget, "Lukens Steel Company: Memorandum Supplementary to Report of January, 1969," 8, microfilm, Towers Perrin Corporate Archives.

119. Cresap, McCormick and Paget, "Lukens Steel Company: Supplementary Information on the Industrial Fastener Market," June 1969, 5, microfilm, Towers Perrin Corporate Archives.

120. Cresap, McCormick and Paget, "Lukens Steel Company: A Survey of Four Companies," May, 1970, Section III, 1–2, microfilm, Towers Perrin Corporate Archives.

121. Lisa J. Chadderdon, "Teaching Note: The General Mills Board and Strategic Planning and Lukens, Inc.: The Melters Committee (A) & (B)," Harvard Business School Publishing, No. 5–796–082 (27 June 1996).

122. "Lukens Plans More Non-Steel Acquisitions, Wilson Says," *Iron Age* (7 June 1985): 14; "Lukens Steel Seeks Change in its Name to Lukens Inc.," *The Wall Street Journal* (16 March 1982), 38.

123. Roberta C. Yafie, "R. W. Van Sant: Stepping Up to the Plate," *Journal of Business Strategy*, 16 (September–October 1995), 42–4; Andy Zipser, "Strong as Steel, Getting Stronger," *Barron's*, 73 (28 June 1993), 34–5. For the classic

argument against corporate diversification, see C. K. Prahalad and Gary Hamel, "The Core Competence of the Corporation," *Harvard Business Review*, Vol. 68, No. 3 (May–June 1990), 79–91.

124. Lukens, Inc., "Third Quarter Earnings," 17 October 1995.

125. Eileen C. Shapiro, *Fad Surfing in the Boardroom: Managing in the Age of Easy Answers* (Reading, Massachusetts, Addison Wesley, 1995).

126. "Accenture Ltd.: Revenue, Profit Up in Quarter, Fueled by Growth in All Sectors," *The Wall Street Journal*. (8 July 2005), 1; Spencer E. Ante, "Accenture's New High-Wire Act, *Business Week* (15 November 2004), 92.

127. John Huey, "How McKinsey Does It," *Fortune* (1 November 1993), 59.

128. Baker, Manager of Production to Charles L. Huston, 7 September 1922, file 13, box 1997, Lukens Steel.

129. W. Findlay Downs, Management Committee Meeting, 8 March 1943, file 1, box 2154, Lukens Steel.

130. Baker, Manager of Production to Charles L. Huston, 7 September 1922, file 13, box 1997, Lukens Steel.

131. This estimate is based on the following calculation: if total management consulting fees averaged $80,000 per year over the thirty years from 1940 to 1969 (a very high estimate), during which time Lukens earned $4.1 million on average per year after taxes, then consulting firm fees represented 1.5% of Lukens's average profits, assuming an average corporate income tax rate of 20%. See the *Annual Reports* for Lukens Steel, 1940–1969.

### 4. CREATING THE CONTRACTOR STATE: CONSULTANTS IN THE AMERICAN FEDERAL GOVERNMENT

1. Brian Balogh, *Chain Reaction: Expert Debate and Public Participation in American Commercial Nuclear Power, 1945–1975* (New York: Cambridge University Press, 1991), 21.

2. Ibid., 26.

3. Statistics derived from George Thomas Kurian, *Datapedia of the United States, 1790–2000* (Lanham, Maryland: Bernan Press, 1992), 440.

4. Paul C. Light, *The True Size of Government* (Washington, D.C.: Brookings Institution Press, 1999), 99–101.

5. Daniel Guttman and Barry Willner, *The Shadow Government: The Government's Multi-Billion-Dollar Giveaway of its Decision Making Powers to Private Management Consultants* (New York: Pantheon Books, 1976).

6. R. A. W. Rhodes, "The Hollowing Out of the State: The Changing Nature of the Public Service in Britain," *Political Quarterly*, Vol. 65 (1994), 138–42.

7. Francis E. Rourke and Paul R. Schulman, "Adhocracy in Policy Development," *The Social Science Journal*, Vol. 26, No. 2 (1989), 131–42.

8. Light, *The True Size of Government*, 48–52.

9. George Fry, a partner with Edwin Booz since 1934 (when the firm was called "Edwin G. Booz and Fry Surveys"), eventually left to found his own management consulting firm in 1942, which became George Fry & Associates by 1946. George Fry's consulting firm would continue to operate in Chicago until Fry sold the firm in 1967. In 1958, George Fry hired an illustrator to create drawings of the firm at work. Those illustrations appear in chapter six of this book and also in Robert Corby Nelson, "The Business Beat: Report from Chicago," *The Christian Science Monitor*, 19 February 1960, 10; 24 February 1960, 10; and 8 March 1960, 15. For the precise details of the partnership arrangements, see Jim Bowman, *Booz Allen & Hamilton: Seventy Years of Client Service, 1914–1984* (New York, Booz Allen & Hamilton, 1984), 24–7.

10. Guttman and Willner, *The Shadow Government*.

11. Balogh, *Chain Reaction*, 22.

12. "Wide Reorganizing of Congress Urged," *The New York Times*, January 17, 1945, 1.

13. John Nuveen to John Foster Dulles, December 29, 1952, Dwight D. Eisenhower Presidential Library, Abilene, Kansas, Central Files, Official File 103-A, "Commission on the Organization of the Executive Branch of Government, 1952–1954 (1)."

14. Marvin Bower, *Perspective on McKinsey*, (New York: McKinsey & Company, 1979), 59.

15. Department of Defense Management Committee, Minutes, 27 July 1949, National Archives, RG 330, "Office, Secretary of Defense," entry 208B, box 1.

16. Bowman, *Booz Allen & Hamilton*, 21–2.

17. Booz, Fry, Allen & Hamilton, "Preliminary Report on Organization and Administration of the Office of Naval Operations," 5 November 1942, RG 80, Records of the Secretary of the Navy, Box 119. In 1942, George Fry, upset that Edwin Booz was neglecting his corporate customers while working for the government, resigned and founded his own management consulting firm, Fry, Lawson, & Company.

18. Bowman, *Booz Allen & Hamilton*, 24.

19. Hewes, *From Root to McNamara*, 194.

20. Rear Admiral C. W. Fisher, "Questions Likely to Arise Regarding Industrial Survey Division," 24 June 1944, National Archives, RG 80, "Records of Sec. of Navy, James Forrestall, 1940–47," series: "General Correspondence, 1944–47," box 120.

21. "Form Management Engineering Firm," *New York Herald Tribune*, February 5, 1946.

22. Ibid.

23. Ewing W. Reilley, McKinsey & Company, "Recruiting, Training, Developing, and Supporting the O & M Staff," 1 February 1949, National Archives,

RG 330, entry 208B, box 102, file 1, "Organization and Management Papers – Industrial and General."

24. Richard Paget to Eugene S. Duffield, "Reorganization of Navy Yards and the Establishment of Naval Bases," 7 November 1945, National Archives, RG 80, "Records of Sec. of Navy, James Forrestall, 1940–47," series: "General Correspondence, 1944–47," box 119.

25. Indeed each shipyard would have its own "Management Planning and Review Division," staffed with internal consultants to "provide expert assistance to the Commanding Officer." Ibid., 16.

26. Navy Department, "Special Meeting on Review of the Organization & Administration of Navy Yards & U.S. Naval Drydocks," 27 July 1945, 18, National Archives, RG 80, "Records of the Secretary of the Navy, James Forestall, 1940–47, General Correspondence, 1944–47," box 119.

27. The boundary problem that was posed by the need for internal control by the military during the war does not lend itself to transaction cost analysis. For a similar critique of transaction costs in business see, Sumantra Ghoshal, and Peter Moran, "Bad for Practice: A Critique of the Transaction Cost Theory," *Academy of Management Review*, Vol. 21, No. 1 (1996), 13–47.

28. Statistics derived from U.S. Department of Commerce, Bureau of the Census, *Historical Statistics of the United States: Colonial Times to 1970* (White Plains, New York: Kraus International Publications, 1976), 1102, 1141.

29. William E. Pemberton, "The Struggle for the New Deal: Truman and the Hoover Commission," *Presidential Studies Quarterly*, Vol. 16, No. 3 (1986), 516.

30. Herbert Hoover, "Manuscript for the Encyclopedia Britannica Book of the Year," February 2, 1949, 1–2, Herbert Hoover Presidential Library, West Branch, Iowa, First Hoover Commission, Box 33, "EAS-EWI."

31. John D. Millett, *Government and Public Administration* (New York, McGraw-Hill, 1959), 128–9.

32. Peri E. Arnold, *Making the Managerial Presidency: Comprehensive Reorganization Planning* (Princeton: Princeton University Press, 1986), 133.

33. "Fifth Meeting of the President's Advisory Committee on Management Improvement," 59, Harry S. Truman Presidential Library, RG 220, President's Advisory Committee on Management, Box 2, General Records, 1949–1953, "Fifth Meeting – April 17–18, 1950."

34. "Exhibit No. 2," Herbert Hoover Presidential Library, First Hoover Report, Box 31, "Concluding Report – Correspondence."

35. John D. Millett, *Government and Public Administration* (New York: McGraw-Hill, 1959), pp. 123–4.

36. The President's Committee on Administrative Management, *Administrative Management in the Government of the United States* (Washington, D.C., Government Printing Office, 1937), 3.

37. Herbert Emmerich, *Federal Organization and Administrative Management* (University, Alabama: The University of Alabama Press, 1971), 86–7; Steven Skowronek, *The Politics Presidents Make: Leadership from John Adams to George Bush* (Cambridge, MA: Belknap Press, 1993), 318–19.

38. Ellis W. Hawley, "Herbert Hoover, the Commerce Secretariat, and the Vision of an 'Associative State,' 1921–1929," *Journal of American History*, Vol. 61, No. 1 (June 1974), 121.

39. For example, the Personnel Policy Task Force included current and retired executives from Montgomery Ward, Prudential Life Insurance, Bloomingdale's, Westinghouse, Pure Oil, and Penn Mutual Insurance. *The Hoover Commission Report: On Organization of the Executive Branch of the Government* (New York: McGraw-Hill, 1950), 509–10.

40. James E. Webb, "Use of an Advisory Committee in Preparing Reorganization Plans for Presentation to the Congress in Early 1947," August 12, 1946, Harry S. Truman Presidential Library, Papers of James E. Webb, Bureau of the Budget, Box 19, "Reorganization."

41. Association of Consulting Management Engineers, Inc. (ACME), *Numerical Data on the Present Dimensions, Growth, and other Trends in Management Consulting in the United States* (New York: Association of Consulting Management Engineers, Inc., 1964), Table 2.

42. As Herbert Hoover put it: "there are only one or two of them in the country whose life practice is exactly this." "Commission on Organization of the Executive Branch of the Government," December 15, 1947, 11, National Archives, RG 264, Hoover Commission I, Records of the Secretaries Office, NC 115, Box 11. Hereafter, "Commission Minutes."

43. Ibid., 14.

44. Ibid., 8.

45. Ibid., 10.

46. Ibid., 8–10.

47. "Announcing the Formation of a Partnership," *Chicago Daily Tribune*, February 5, 1946, 23.

48. The 1948 monthly bulletin from the Association of Consulting Management Engineers (ACME) reported that the twenty-four clients served by Cresap, McCormick and Paget in 1947 gave the firm such "highly favorable endorsements" that the ACME's membership committee voted unanimously to admit the young firm. Association of Consulting Management Engineers, Inc., "A.C.M.E. Bulletin," April–May, 1948, 1. ACME Archives, New York, New York.

49. Commission Minutes, December 15, 1947, 38.

50. Memo from T. D. Morris, Cresap, McCormick and Paget, January 26, 1948, National Archives, RG 264, Hoover Commission I, Records of the Task Force

on Personnel Management, Records Relating to the Administration of the Task Force, 1948–1949, Box 1, NC 115, Entry 66, Folder 11, "Plan of Study."

51. Frank Gervasi, *Big Government: The Meaning and Purpose of the Hoover Commission Report* (New York: McGraw Hill, 1949), 191–3.

52. William Pemberton, *Bureaucratic Politics: Executive Reorganization during the Truman Administration* (Columbia, University of Missouri Press, 1979), 168. The consultants from Robert Heller & Associates recommended that what little political patronage remained be eliminated so that no one below the Postmaster General would be a political appointee. The Commission on Organization of the Executive Branch of Government, *Task Force Report on the Post Office [Appendix I]* (Washington, D.C.: Government Printing Office, 1949), 44. Hereafter, Hoover Commission, *Task Force Report on the Post Office*.

53. Ibid., 12.

54. Ibid., 1.

55. Cartoon, "This is the Forest Primeval," *Morning Union*, Manchester, New Hampshire, May 13, 1950, 4.

56. Hoover Commission, *Task Force Report on the Post Office*, 1.

57. Ibid., 36.

58. Ibid., 36.

59. Ibid., 40.

60. Alfred D. Chandler, *Strategy and Structure: Chapters in the History of the American Industrial Enterprise* (Cambridge, MIT Press, 1962), 2.

61. Hewes, *From Root to McNamara*, 72–4; *Fortune* (December 1952), 184; Microfilm, Cresap Archives, Chandler, *Strategy and Structure*, 325.

62. Hoover Commission, *Task Force Report on the Post Office*, 39.

63. Ibid., 40.

64. Minutes, President's Advisory Committee on Management Improvement, April 17–18, 1950, 86, Truman Presidential Library, RG 220, President's Advisory Committee on Management, Box 3, General Records, 1949–1953, "Fifth Meeting – April 17–18, 1950."

65. U.S. Senate, *Action on Hoover Commission Reports: Report of the Committee of Expenditures in the Executive Departments* (Washington, Government Printing Office, 1950), 57.

66. The Hoover Commission, *Personnel Management: A Report to Congress by the Commission on the Organization of the Executive Branch of the Government*, February, 1949 (Washington, Government Printing Office, 1949), 45–6.

67. Memo from T. D. Morris, Cresap, McCormick and Paget, January 26, 1948, National Archives, RG 264, Hoover Commission I, Records of the Task Force on Personnel Management, Records Relating to the Administration of the Task Forces, 1948–1949, Box 1, NC 115, Entry 66, Folder 11, "Plan of Study."

68. Commission Minutes, December 15, 1947, 22.

69. Margaret C. Rung, *Administrators and the Administrative State: Personnel Management and the Struggle for Control of the Federal Civil Service, 1933–1962* (Ph.D. Dissertation, Johns Hopkins University, 1993).

70. The Commission on Organization of the Executive Branch of Government, *Task Force Report on the Federal Personnel [Appendix A]* (Washington, D.C., Government Printing Office, 1949), 7.

71. Ibid.

72. Memo from T. D. Morris, Cresap, McCormick and Paget, January 26, 1948, National Archives, RG 264, Hoover Commission I, Records of the Task Force on Personnel Management, Records Relating to the Administration of the Task Forces, 1948–1949, Box 1, NC 115, Entry 66, Folder 11, "Plan of Study."

73. Cresap, McCormick and Paget, "Draft Version of Plan of Study of the Commission on Organization of the Executive Branch," March 18, 1948, Microfilm, Cresap Archives.

74. Memo from T. D. Morris, Cresap, McCormick and Paget, January 26, 1948, National Archives, RG 264, Hoover Commission I, Records of the Task Force on Personnel Management, Records Relating to the Administration of the Task Forces, 1948–1949, Box 1, NC 115, Entry 66, Folder 11, "Plan of Study."

75. Cresap, McCormick and Paget, "Personnel Procurement Policies and Practices – Preliminary Report," April 23, 1948, Microfilm, Cresap Archives.

76. The Hoover Commission, *The Hoover Commission Report*, 132.

77. U.S. Senate, *Action on Hoover Commission Reports: Report of the Committee of Expenditures in the Executive Departments* (Washington, Government Printing Office, 1950), 32.

78. Ibid., 41.

79. Harry S. Truman, August 3, 1953, Harry S. Truman Presidential Library, Independence, Missouri, Papers of Harry S. Truman, Post Presidential Files, "Memoirs" File, Box 644, "Memoirs – Domestic Policy – Reorganization of the Government.

80. Dean Acheson, *Present at the Creation: My Years in the State Department* (New York: W. W. Norton Company, 1969), 243.

81. National Archives, RG 264, Hoover Commission II, Box 46A, NC 116, "Fiscal Records, Allotment Ledger;" Sidney A. Mitchell to Bernice Miller, April 6, 1948, Hoover Presidential Library, First Hoover Commission, Box 25, "Post Office, Correspondence – Robert Heller."

82. Commission Minutes, December 15, 1947, 10.

83. Robert Heller to Herbert Hoover, August 11, 1948, Hoover Presidential Library, First Hoover Commission, Box 25, "Post Office, Correspondence – Robert Heller."

84. Louis A. Johnson to Herbert Hoover, July 29, 1949, Hoover Presidential Library, First Hoover Commission, Box 34, "Louis A. Johnson, 1949," President's Office to Robert Heller, August 17, 1948, Hoover Presidential Library,

First Hoover Commission, Box 25, "Post Office, Correspondence – Robert Heller."

85. Cresap, McCormick and Paget, "A Personal Management Engineering Service," May, 1949, Cresap Archives.

86. Cresap, McCormick and Paget to Hon. Matthew J. Connelly, September 25, 1950, Truman Library, Papers of Harry S. Truman, Official File, 285 E (1950–1953), Box 920. Cresap, McCormick and Paget, A Summary of The Hoover Report (New York, Cresap, McCormick and Paget, 1950), Pamphlet Collection, Hagley Museum and Library.

87. Cresap, McCormick and Paget company brochure, 1950, Cresap Archives; Hoover Commission, The Task Force Report on the Federal Personnel, 45.

88. Hoover Commission, Final Report to Congress, Second Hoover Commission, (Washington, D.C.: U.S. Government Printing Office, 1955), 9; Cresap, McCormick and Paget, "Survey of Markets for Heads and Job Stampings," June 28, 1956, Lukens Steel Collection, Box 2040, Archives and Manuscripts, Hagley Museum and Library, Wilmington, Delaware.

89. "Progress in Improving Federal Administration: A Report to the President by the President's Advisory Committee on Management Improvement," September 7, 1950, 56–8, Truman Presidential Library, Papers of Frank Pace, Jr., Correspondence, Box 11, "President's Advisory Committee on Management Improvement."

90. McKinsey & Co., Restaffing the Executive Branch of the Federal Government at the Policy Level, October 15, 1952 and McKinsey & Co., Organizing the White House Office: A Preliminary Report, December 15, 1952, both in the Dwight D. Eisenhower Library, Office of the Special Assistant for Personnel Management, Box 58.

91. Rourke and Schulman, "Adhocracy in Policy Development," 135.

92. Hewes, From Root to McNamera, 222–4; Cresap, McCormick and Paget, "Survey of the Department of the Army," 15 April 1949, microfilm, Cresap Archives.

93. Cresap, McCormick and Paget, "Survey of the Civil Aeronautics Administration," 7 June 1954; Cresap, McCormick and Paget, "Department of Health, Education, and Welfare: Plan of Organization, Management Staff Activities," 11 October 1954, both in Cresap Archives; McKinsey & Co., "The Peaceful Uses of Atomic Energy: An Analysis of AEC's Role," in Joint Committee on Atomic Energy, Background Material for the Report of the Panel on the Impact of the Peaceful Uses of Atomic Energy (Washington, DC: Government Printing Office, 1956), 675–749.

94. J. L. Kelehan to K. E. Fields, "Meeting with McKinney Panel on December 5, 1955," 6 December 1955, National Archives, RG 326, "Records of the Atomic Energy Commission," "Office of the Secretary, General Correspondence, 1951–1958," box 71, file: "Organization and Management 7, McKinney Panel."

95. T. Keith Glennan, "Memorandum to NASA Senior Staff," 29 September 1958, NASA History Office, Record 3464, file: "Program Organization."

96. Department of Defense Management Committee, Minutes, 27 July 1949, 2–3, National Archives, RG 330, "Office, Secretary of Defense," entry 208B, box 1.

97. Ibid., 3.

98. Department of Defense Management Committee, Minutes, 2 August 1949, 54–67, National Archives, RG 330, "Office, Secretary of Defense," entry 208B, box 1.

99. Ibid., 66–73.

100. General Accounting Office, Brochure, Eisenhower Presidential Library.

101. A. T. Kearney & Co., Partners' Minutes, 10 March 1956, A. T. Kearney & Co., Chicago; Bower, Perspective on McKinsey, 70.

102. Balogh, Chain Reaction, 317.

103. On the history of the space race see Walter A. McDougall, . . . The Heavens and the Earth: A Political History of the Space Age (New York: Basic Books, 1985). For a very different account of NASA emphasizing its consumerist mission, see Michael L. Smith, "Selling the Moon: The U.S. Manned Space Program and the Triumph of Commodity Scientism," in Richard Wightman Fox and T. J. Jackson Lears (eds.), The Culture of Consumption: Critical Essays in American History, 1880–1980 (New York: Pantheon Books, 1983), 177–209.

104. Roger D. Launius, "Introduction," in J. D. Huntley (ed.), The Birth of NASA: The Diary of T. Keith Glennan (Washington, DC: National Aeronautics and Space Administration, 1993), xxii.

105. Huntley (ed.), The Birth of NASA, 4.

106. The initial survey cost $33,000, a figure that McKinsey & Company assured Keith Glennan was comparable with "the rates regularly charged other public and private clients." McKinsey & Company to Dr. T. Keith Glennan, 26 September 1958, 3; T. Keith Glennan to McKinsey & Company, Inc., Contract NASW-1, 10 October 1958, 1–3, both in NASA History Office, box: "Administrative History," file: "Organizational Developments – 1958: McKinsey Report, NASW-1."

107. McKinsey & Company, "Organizing Headquarters Functions: National Aeronautics and Space Administration," 31 December 1958, NASA History Office, Record 3419, "McKinsey Reports," Huntley (ed.), The Birth of NASA, 8.

108. Robert L. Rosholt, An Administrative History of NASA, 1958–1963 (Washington, DC: National Aeronautics and Space Administration, 1995), 55.

109. Ibid., 51; McKinsey & Company, "Organizing Headquarters Functions," section 2, 18.

110. Rosholt, An Administrative History of NASA, 55–6; Robert Rosholt, Interview with John Corson, 26 April 1963, NASA History Office, Record 2716, file: "Biography NASA, Miscellaneous Co." John D. Young, one of the McKinsey consultants who worked at NASA from 1959 to 1961, joined NASA in 1961

as the head of the agency's Management Analysis Division. See for example, John D. Young to James E. Webb, 21 July 1961, NASA History Office, box 15: "Administrative History," file: "Organizational Developments, 1961" In contrast, Gil Clee, a director of McKinsey, offered Keith Glennan a position at McKinsey & Company in October 1960. The next day, John Corson had Glennan over for dinner with James Webb, (who would be Glennan's successor at NASA), Elmer Staats (the deputy director of the Bureau of the Budget), Bob Calkins (the head of the Brookings Institution), and Larry Henderson (a vice-president at the Rand Corporation). Huntley (ed.), *The Birth of NASA*, 250–1.

111. Huntley (ed.), *The Birth of NASA*, 5. Sylvia K. Kraemer, "Organizing for Exploration," in John D. Logsdon (ed.), *Exploring the Unknown: Select Documents in the History of the U.S. Civil Space Program, Volume 1: Organizing for Exploration* (Washington, DC: National Aeronautics and Space Administration, 1995), 614.

112. Huntley (ed.), *The Birth of NASA*, 5. On NASA's organizational culture see Howard E. McCurdy, *Inside NASA: High Technology and Organizational Change in the U.S. Space Program* (Baltimore: The Johns Hopkins University Press, 1993).

113. Rosholt, *An Administrative History of NASA*, 176.

114. John J. Corson to T. Keith Glennan, 15 December 1959, NASA History Office, Record 3418, file: "McKinsey & Company."

115. John J. Corson to T. Keith Glennan, 26 January 1960, NASA History Office, box 11, "Administrative History," file: "Organizational Developments – 1960, Work of Klimpton Committee."

116. McDougall, . . . *The Heavens and the Earth*, 376–7.

117. John J. Corson to T. Keith Glennan, 26 January 1960, NASA History Office, box 11, "Administrative History," file: "Organizational Developments – 1960, Work of Klimpton Committee."

118. McCurdy, *Inside NASA*, 34–50.

119. NASA Negotiated Contract, NASW-144, 26 February 1960, NASA History Office, box 33, "Administrative History," file: "Procurement/Contracting, 1960: McKinsey Report."; McKinsey & Company, "An Evaluation of NASA's Contracting Policies, Organization and Performance," October 1960, section 1, page 2, NASA History Office, Record 3419, "McKinsey Reports."

120. For NASA's adoption of PERT see News Release 62–148, 27 June 1962, "NASA and DOD Adopt Guide on PERT Cost System Design," in NASA History Office, "Administrative History," file: "PERT." PERT itself was a product of a collaboration between Booz Allen & Hamilton and the Navy for the Polaris missile program and one of the most famous instances of the commercial installation of operations research. On the role of Booz Allen & Hamilton consultants in the development of PERT, see Booz Allen & Hamilton International,

*The Management Implications of PERT* (New York: Booz Allen & Hamilton, Inc., 1962), 4.

121. McKinsey & Company, "An Evaluation of NASA's Contracting Policies, Organization and Performance," October 1960, section 2, page 9, NASA History Office, Record 3419, "McKinsey Reports."

122. Ibid., section 2, page 8.

123. Ralph J. Cordiner, "Competitive Enterprise in Space," 4 May 1960, page 4, cited in Ibid., section 2, page 8.

124. McKinsey & Company, "An Evaluation of NASA's Contracting Policies, Organization and Performance," section 1, page 8. Glennan circulated the final report to NASA's department supervisors for comment. Their various opinions are retained in the NASA History Office, record 3419, "McKinsey Reports."

125. Ibid., section 2, page 11.

126. This conclusion would be echoed less than a month later when the Kimpton Committee, an ad hoc, advisory committee headed by Lawrence Kimpton of MIT and supported by McKinsey staff members, repeated the admonition that NASA do internally "only enough work to equip its staff to give leadership to outside scientists and to contract out, effectively, all other research, development, and production." Advisory Committee on Organization, "National Aeronautics and Space Administration – Its Organization and Management," October 12, 1960, 9, NASA History Office, Record 3419, "McKinsey Reports."

127. Balogh, for example, describes NASA as a continuing symbol of the "extremes of the prominimistrative struggle" in his book, *Chain Reaction*. Balogh, *Chain Reaction*, 317. Light, *The True Size of Government*, 165.

128. McDougall, *. . . The Heavens and the Earth*, 362.

129. Figures from Sylvia K. Kraemer, "Organizing for Exploration," in Logsdon (ed.), *Exploring the Unknown*, 613.

130. Advisory Committee on Organization, "National Aeronautics and Space Administration – Its Organization and Management," 8.

131. Statistics derived from U.S. Department of Commerce, Bureau of the Census, *Historical Statistics of the United States* and Bureau of the Budget, "Report to the President on Government Contracting for Research and Deveopment," 30 April 1962, reprinted in Logsdon (ed.), *Exploring the Unknown*, 652.

132. Report to the President on Government Contracting for Research and Development, S. Doc. 94 (Washington, D.C.: Government Printing Office, 1962) quoted in Paul C. Light, "Testimony Before the U.S. Subcommittee on Oversight of Government Management, The Federal Workforce, and the District of Columbia" (24 July 2003), 1.

133. Bower, *Perspective on McKinsey*, 73.

134. Ibid., 73–7.

135. Booz Allen & Hamilton, "Dismantling Railroad Freight Cars: A Study of Improved Methods with Application to Other Demolition Problems" (Rockville, Maryland: U.S. Bureau of Solid Waste Management, 1969); Booz

Allen Applied Research, Inc., "Trading Opportunities for U.S. flag bulk carriers, for Competitive Merchant Ship Project, U.S. Department of Commerce, Maritime Administration" (Bethesda, Maryland: U.S. Maritime Administration, 1969); Arthur D. Little, Inc., "Center City Transportation Project – Consumer Analysis Guideline" (Washington, DC: Urban Mass Transportation Administration, 1970).

136. Booz Allen & Hamilton, "The Purchase of Social Service: A Study of the Experience of Three States in the Purchase of Service by Contract under the Provisions of the 1967 Amendments to the Social Security Act" (Washington, DC: Department of Health, Education and Welfare); Arthur D. Little, Inc., "Transportation and the Environment: A Synthesis for Action, The Impact of the National Environmental Policy Act of 1969 on the Department of Transportation" (Washington, DC: Department of Transportation, 1971).

137. See for example, Arthur D. Little, Inc., "Economic Analysis of Proposed Effluent Guidelines: The Rubber Processing Industry" (Washington, DC: Environmental Protection Agency, 1974); Harbidge House, Inc., "A Review of National Railroad Issues" (Washington, DC: United States Congress, Office of Technology Assessment, 1975); Booz Allen & Hamilton, Inc., "Energy Use in the Food System" (Washington, DC: Federal Energy Administration, 1976).

138. Daniel Guttman and Barry Willner, *The Shadow Government: The Government's Multi-Billion-Dollar Giveaway of its Decision Making Powers to Private Management Consultants* (New York: Pantheon Books, 1976).

139. Donald Kettl, *Sharing Power: Public Governance and Private Markets* (Washington, D.C.: Brookings Institution Press, 1993); R. A. W. Rhodes, "The Hollowing Out of the State: The Changing Nature of the Public Service in Britain," *Political Quarterly*, Vol. 65, 1994, 138–49; Herman Bakvis, "Political-Bureaucratic Relations and the Role of Management Consulting Firms," conference paper delivered at Ben Gurion University of the Negev, Beersheva, Israel, 16–18 February 1997.

140. Balogh, *Chain Reaction*, 19–20.

141. The push to reduce the number of federal civil servants would continue through the presidencies of both William J. Clinton and George W. Bush. See William J. Clinton, "1994 State of the Union Address," and "1996 State of the Union Address," and Richard W. Stevenson, "Government May Make Private Nearly Half of Its Civilian Jobs," *The New York Times* (15 November 2002), 1.


5. FINDING PROFIT IN NONPROFITS: THE INFLUENCE OF CONSULTANTS
ON THE THIRD SECTOR

1. Peter Dobkin Hall, *Inventing the Nonprofit Sector and Other Essays on Philanthropy, Voluntarism, and Non-profit Organizations* (Baltimore, 1992), 244.

2. House Committee to Investigate Tax-Exempt Foundations and Comparable Organizations, *Tax-Exempt Foundations: Hearings on H.R. 561*, 82nd Cong., 2nd sess., 19 November 1952, 55–64; Cresap, McCormick and Paget, "Professional Counsel for the Management of Nonprofit Organizations" (New York, 1955), scrapbooks, corporate archives, Towers Perrin, Inc., Valhalla, New York. [henceforth, Cresap Archives].

3. The original client reports were microfilmed and retained in the files of Cresap, McCormick and Paget but when available, I will cite reports and manuscripts available in public archives.

4. Statistics derived from tables in Eli Ginzberg, Dale L. Hiestand, and Beatrice G. Reubens, *The Pluralistic Economy* (New York, 1965), 115.

5. This phenomenal expansion was more than three times the growth rate of the other two sectors. Cresap, McCormick and Paget, "Survey of the Market for Professional Consulting Services," October 1954, Appendices A & B, Exhibits III-13, III-18, III-21, III-23, Cresap Archives.

6. While nonprofit organizations are legally incorporated, most Americans perceive a difference between these 501(c)(3) nonprofit organizations and the typical for-profit "business" or "corporation" which is not bound by the nondistribution constraint. Thus, when I refer to these "businesses" or "corporations," I am following this popular distinction, even if modern nonprofits and for-profits share many legal and administrative characteristics.

7. Michael O'Neill, *The Third America: The Emergence of the Nonprofit Sector in the United States* (San Francisco, 1989), 177. Talcott Parsons's structural-functionalism continues to influence important elements of business history through Parsons's influence on Alfred D. Chandler, Jr. See Thomas K. McCraw, *The Essential Alfred Chandler: Essays Toward a Historical Theory of Big Business* (Boston, 1988), 6.

8. Paul J. DiMaggio and Walter J. Powell, "The Iron Cage Revisited: Institutional Isomorphism and Collective Rationality in Organizational Fields," in Powell and DiMaggio (eds.), *The New Institutionalism in Organizational Analysis* (Chicago, 1991), 70.

9. Cresap, McCormick and Paget, "Professional Counsel for the Management of Nonprofit Organizations."

10. Christopher D. McKenna, "The Origins of Modern Management Consulting," *Business and Economic History*, 24 (Fall 1995), 51–8.

11. James O. McKinsey & Company, "University Clinics, University of Chicago: Survey of Management and Financial Operations," 17 August 1932, File 1, Box 126, Papers of Harold Swift, Department of Special Collections, University of Chicago; Jim Bowman, *Booz Allen & Hamilton: Seventy Years of Client Service, 1914–1984* (Chicago, 1984), 18.

12. "Form Management Engineering Firm," *New York Herald Tribune*, 5 February 1946.

13. Cresap, McCormick and Paget, "Cresap, McCormick and Paget: Policy, Organization, Services, Clients," 1947, Cresap Archives.
14. "Consultants Invade Non-Profit Field," *The New York Times*, 21 July 1968.
15. Merle Curti and Roderick Nash, *Philanthropy in the Shaping of American Higher Education* (New Brunswick, 1965), 238.
16. Cresap, McCormick and Paget, "Development of the Institutional Division," 29 May 1954, Cresap Archives.
17. C. Wright Mills, *The Power Elite* (New York, 1956), 63.
18. Cresap, McCormick and Paget, "Professional Management Counsel to Colleges and Universities." Two examples of Cresap, McCormick and Paget's international work with universities include: "University of Liberia: Campus Development and Master Plan," and "Free University of Brussels: Study of Organization," both from 1969 in the Cresap Archives.
19. Charles D. Dickey to Henry C. Kittredge, 7 October 1948, St. Paul's School Archives, Concord, New Hampshire; Henry C. Kittredge, "The Rector's Letter," *Alumni Horae* (Autumn 1918), 79, St. Paul's School Archives.
20. Cresap, McCormick and Paget, "Survey of the Business Administration of St. Paul's School, Concord, New Hampshire," 13 December 1948, I-1, I-5, Cresap Archives.
21. Cresap, McCormick and Paget, "Survey of St. Paul's School," I-3, Cresap Archives.
22. Ibid., I-6.
23. Reeve Schley to Henry C. Kittredge, 2 December 1948, St. Paul's School Archives.
24. Henry C. Kittredge to Charles D. Dickey, 23 December 1948, St. Paul's School Archives.
25. Henry C. Kittredge, "The Rector's Letter," *Alumni Horae* (Spring 1949), 3, St. Paul's School Archives.
26. Ibid., 4.
27. Cresap, McCormick and Paget, "Survey of the Nonacademic Activities of Yale University," 23 October 1950, File 684, Box 75, YRG 2-A-16, Manuscripts and Archives, Yale University [henceforth, Yale Archives].
28. Christopher D. McKenna, "The Origins of Modern Management Consulting," *Business and Economic History*, 24 (Fall 1995), 51–8.
29. Henry C. Kittredge, "The Rector's Letter," *Alumni Horae* (Autumn 1948), 80, St. Paul's School Archives; Cresap, McCormick and Paget, "Survey of St. Paul's School," I-8.
30. Everett Case, President of Colgate University, to D. Luke Hopkins, 23 April 1951; Howard Bruce to John R. Sherwood, 6 April 1951, File 241, Box 3, Series 1, Office of the President, RG 02.001, Ferdinand Hamburger, Jr. Archives, The Johns Hopkins University [henceforth, Johns Hopkins

Archives]; Cresap, McCormick and Paget, "Study of the Business Management and Related Functions of Colgate University," 15 July 1949, Cresap Archives.

31. Interview with Charles Dollard, February 17, 1967, p. 254, Oral History Research Office, Columbia University.

32. Ibid.

33. Charles Dollard, President of the Carnegie Corporation, to Detlev Bronk, President of The Johns Hopkins University, 14 March 1951, File: "Correspondence (cont.) 4/2/51," Box 47, "Minutes and Supporting Papers, Series 2, Records of the Board of Trustees, RG 01.001, Johns Hopkins Archives.

34. Howard Bruce to John R. Sherwood, 6 April 1951, File 242, Series 1, Office of the President, RG 02.001, Johns Hopkins Archives.

35. Cresap, McCormick and Paget, "The Johns Hopkins University: Survey of the Activities of the Homewood Campus," 7 March 1952, Box 1, RG 16.020, Johns Hopkins Archives.

36. Carlisle Barton to the Board of Trustees, 18 July 1952, 10, File: "Cresap, McCormick & Paget (1951–1953)," Box 10, Sub-Series 3, Series 1, Office of the Provost, RG 03.001, Johns Hopkins Archives.

37. Carlisle Barton to the Board of Trustees, 18 July 1952, 2–3; President Detlev Bronk to Carlisle Barton, 29 September 1952, 1; Harold E. Ingle, "Reply of the Director of the Johns Hopkins Press to the Report Submitted by Cresap, McCormick & Paget Relative to the Operations of the Press," April 1952, XI; Homer Halvorson, "Cresap, McCormick & Paget Report on the Libraries," 1 October 1952, 4, all four documents located in File: "Cresap, McCormick & Paget (1951–1953)," Box 10, Sub-Series 3, Series 1, Office of the Provost, RG 03.001, Johns Hopkins Archives.

38. P. Stewart Macaulay, Provost, to Dr. T. E. Blackwell, Vice Chancellor of Washington University, 26 January 1953, 1, File: "Cresap, McCormick & Paget (1951–1953)," Box 10, Sub-Series 3, Series 1, Office of the Provost, RG 03.001, Johns Hopkins Archives.

39. Ibid., 2.

40. Cresap, McCormick and Paget, "Survey Organization," File: "Cresap, McCormick and Paget (1951–1953)," Box 10, Sub-Series 3, Series 1, Office of the Provost, RG 03.001, Johns Hopkins Archives. John Batchelor, by this point, was an old hand at general management surveys, having been a vice president at George S. Armstrong & Company for four years before joining Cresap, McCormick and Paget in 1949. See "John Batchelor, Engineer, Dies: Electronics Expert who was also in Management Concern," *The New York Times*, 29 December 1967, 27.

41. "You might expect to derive some benefit" in President Reed's words. See Lowell J. Reed, President of Johns Hopkins, to Harold W. Dodds, President of Princeton, 7 January 1955, File 953, Box 242, Series 1, Office of the President, RG 02.001, Johns Hopkins Archives; A. Whitney Griswold, President of Yale,

to J. E. Wallace Sterling, President of Stanford, 15 January 1957, File 685, Box 76, YRG 2-A-16, Yale Archives.

42. Ernest Dale, *The Great Organizers* (New York: McGraw-Hill, 1960), 9; quoted in Mary Soo and Cathryn Carson, "Managing the Research University: Clark Kerr and the University of California," *Minerva* (forthcoming).

43. P. Stewart Macaulay, Provost, to Dr. T. E. Blackwell, Vice Chancellor of Washington University, 26 January 1953, 1, File: "Cresap, McCormick and Paget (1951–1953)," Box 10, Sub-Series 3, Series 1, Office of the Provost, RG 03.001, Johns Hopkins Archives.

44. Everett Case, President of Colgate University, to D. Luke Hopkins, 23 April 1951, File 241, Box 3, Series 1, Office of the President, RG 02.001, Johns Hopkins Archives.

45. Cresap, McCormick and Paget, "Survey of the Activities of the Homewood Campus," III-4; Cresap, McCormick and Paget, "Survey of the Nonacademic Activities of Yale University," III-4.

46. Cresap, McCormick and Paget, "Survey of the Activities of the Homewood Campus," Exhibit II-A; Cresap, McCormick and Paget, "Survey of the Nonacademic Activities of Yale University," II-6.

47. Interview with Harold Dodds, 1968, p. 50, Oral History Research Office, Columbia University.

48. Norman Sidney Buck, Master of Branford College, to A. Whitney Griswold, 2 November 1957, File 685, Box 76, YRG 2-A-16, Yale Archives.

49. L. Wrigley, "Divisional Autonomy and Diversification," (Ph.D. Dissertation, Harvard Business School, 1970), 50.

50. Alfred D. Chandler, Jr., *Strategy and Structure: Chapters in the History of the American Industrial Enterprise* (Cambridge, 1962).

51. Peter F. Drucker, *The Concept of the Corporation* (New York, 1964 [reprint of 1946 edition]).

52. Chandler, *Strategy and Structure*, 381–2. On the other hand, as Chandler described, "a manager once advised a colleague that he could save the $100,000 fee that McKinsey & Company was charging corporations to oversee their reorganization by reading a copy of Chandler's Strategy and Structure which could be purchased for $2.95." Chandler, Comparative Business History, in D. C. Coleman and Peter Mathias (eds.), *Enterprise and History* (Cambridge: Cambridge University Press, 1984), 16, quoted in Richard R. John, "Elaborations, Revisions, Dissents: Alfred D. Chandler, Jr.'s, "The Visible Hand" after Twenty Years," *The Business History Review*, Vol. 71, No. 2. (Summer, 1997), 151–200.

53. On IBM's decentralization, see Watson and Petre, *Father, Son & Co.*, 284–95. On Cresap's work for Westinghouse, see *Fortune* (December 1952), 184. On the reorganizations of Chrysler and Ford, see Robert B. Reich and John

D. Donahue, *New Deals: The Chrysler Revival and The American Dream*, (New York, 1985), 17.

54. DiMaggio and Powell, "The Iron Cage Revisited," 70. On the same page, DiMaggio and Powell describe how more recently, ". . . with the advice of a major consulting firm, a large metropolitan public television station switched from a functional design to a multidivisional structure."

55. Cresap, McCormick and Paget, "University of California: Preliminary Outline Report, The Decentralization Program, May 1960," 2, Cresap Archives.

56. The University of California, *Report of the President for the Academic Year, 1958–1959*, (Berkeley, 1959), 5. See also Mary Soo and Cathryn Carson, "Managing the Research University: Clark Kerr and the University of California," *Minerva* (forthcoming).

57. The University of California, *Report of the President for the Academic Year, 1958–1959*, (Berkeley, 1959), 3.

58. Ibid., Appendix, 1; 8.

59. Cresap, McCormick and Paget, "Survey of the Nonacademic Activities of Yale University," Exhibit III-B, "Proposed Plan of Organization"; Cresap, McCormick and Paget, "Survey of the Activities of the Homewood Campus," Exhibit III-B, "Proposed Administrative Organization." The multidivisional structure installed by McKinsey & Company at Shell Oil in 1959 is described in Anthony Sampson, *Anatomy of Britain Today* (New York, 1965), 486.

60. University of California, "Report of the President," 5.

61. Cresap, McCormick and Paget, "Cornell University, Report on Top Administrative Organization" (1962), "Columbia University: A Proposal on Restructuring the University" (1969), "University of Toronto: Study of Organization and Financial Report" (1964), "University of Washington: Business and Financial Administration" (1966), all in the Cresap Archives.

62. Norman Sidney Buck to A. Whitney Griswold, 2 November 1957, File 685, Box 76, YRG 2-A-16, Yale Archives.

63. For a brief discussion of the growth of The Boston Consulting Group and its popularization of strategy consulting, see Davis Dyer and David B. Sicilia, *The Labors of a Modern Hercules: The Evolution of a Chemical Company* (Boston, 1990), 362–3. The one exception that proves the rule is Cresap, McCormick and Paget's 1965 study of Boston University, "The Long-Range Development of the University," in the Cresap Archives.

64. The Northern (Presbyterian Church of the USA) and the Southern (Presbyterian Church of the U.S.) branches of the Presbyterian Church (Church of Scotland for British readers) split over the divisive issue of slavery in 1856 and did not reunify until 1983. All references in this book are to the Northern Presbyterian Church unless otherwise indicated.

65. Mills, *The Power Elite*, 106, 127.

66. Richard W. Reifsnyder, "The Reorganizational Impulse in American Protestantism: The Presbyterian Church (U.S.A.) as a Case Study, 1788–1983" (Ph.D. Dissertation, Princeton Theological Seminary, 1984).

67. Louis B. Weeks, "The Incorporation of the Presbyterians," in Milton J. Coalter, John M. Mulder, and Louis B. Weeks (eds.), *The Organizational Revolution: Presbyterians and American Denominationalism* (Louisville, 1992), 41.

68. Reifsnyder, "The Reorganizational Impulse," 311.

69. Reifsnyder, "The Reorganizational Impulse," 25–33.

70. Richard W. Reifsnyder, "Managing the Mission: Church Restructuring in the Twentieth Century," in Coalter, Mulder, and Weeks (eds.), *The Organizational Revolution*, 62.

71. Cresap, McCormick and Paget, "Survey of Business Methods: The Presbyterian Church in the United States of America," 13 March 1952, 3, Cresap Archives.

72. Eugene Carson Blake, "Confidential Memorandum on the Department of Ministerial Relations," 7 June 1952, File 8, Box 3, Eugene Carson Blake Papers, RG 95, Presbyterian Church (U.S.A.), Department of History and Records Management Services, Philadelphia [henceforth, Presbyterian Archives].

73. Eugene Carson Blake, Stated Clerk, to Roger H. Johnson, Secretary of Finance, 26 January 1953, File 8, Box 3, Eugene Carson Blake Papers, RG 95, Presbyterian Archives.

74. "Report to the Policy Committee by the Executive Officers on a Study of the Survey of Business Methods of the Boards with Recommendations," 2 February 1954, 1, File 5, Box 2, RG 117, Office of the General Secretary, Board of National Missions, Presbyterian Archives.

75. Ibid., 1–6.

76. James Laurie, "Report of the Advisory Committee on the Office of the General Assembly, 20 October 1952; Eugene Carson Blake to George W. Renneisen, 24 July 1952; Roger H. Johnson to Eugene Carson Blake, 25 July 1952; Eugene Carson Blake to Samuel C. Slaymaker, 17 September 1952, all in File 8, Box 3, Eugene Carson Blake Papers, RG 95, Presbyterian Archives.

77. Reifsnyder, "Managing the Mission," 65.

78. Cresap, McCormick and Paget, "Professional Counsel for the Management of Nonprofit Organizations," 1; Cresap, McCormick and Paget, "Survey of the Market," Appendices B, Exhibit III-23, Cresap Archives.

79. Ibid., 46; Robert F. Harvanek, "Results of the Chicago Province Planning Program: 1968–1969," *Province Planning Program* (Oak Park, Illinois, 1969), 12, on deposit in the Loyola University Library in Chicago; "Consultants Invade Non-Profit Field," *The New York Times*, 21 July 1968.

80. Cresap, McCormick and Paget, "Mennonite Board of Education: A Study of the Future Role of the Board of Education," April 1967, Cresap Archives.

81. Cresap, McCormick and Paget, "School Sisters of Notre Dame: Planning for the Future of the Wilton Province," June 1970, Cresap Archives.

82. Beverly Koch, "Sacred Heart and the 20th Century," *San Francisco Chronicle*, 8 April 1969, 15.

83. Cresap, McCormick and Paget, "The Church of Jesus Christ of Latter-Day Saints: A Study of the Presiding Bishopric's Office, Phase I: The Health Services Corporation," August 1974, III-9 to III-10, Cresap Archives.

84. Howard Taubman, "The First Moves: Changes in Philharmonic Management May Precede New Policy Next Year," *The New York Times*, 25 September 1956, 129.

85. Cresap, McCormick and Paget, "Office of the General Assembly, Presbyterian Church in the U.S.A.: Survey of Business Methods (Preliminary Report)," 17 October 1951, 2, File 8, Box 3, Eugene Carson Blake Papers, RG 95, Presbyterian Archives.

86. Thomas J. Watson, Jr. and Peter Petre, *Father, Son & Co.: My Life at IBM and Beyond*, (New York, 1990), 286; Louis Galambos and David Milobsky, "Organizing and Reorganizing the World Bank, 1946–1972: A Comparative Perspective," *Business History Review*, 69 (Summer 1995), 156–90.

87. Cresap, McCormick and Paget, "The Philharmonic-Symphony Society of New York: Management Survey," 14 June 1956, File 8, Box: Finance and Personnel, New York Philharmonic Archives, Lincoln Center, New York (henceforth, Philharmonic Archives).

88. Floyd G. Blair, Chairman of the Board, to Maitland A. Edey, 25 April 1955, File 26, Box 005–01, Philharmonic Archives; Howard Shanet, *Philharmonic: A History of New York's Orchestra* (New York, 1975), 320.

89. Howard Taubman, "The First Moves: Changes in Philharmonic Management May Precede New Policy Next Year," *The New York Times*, 23 September 1956, 129.

90. Shanet, *Philharmonic*, 324.

91. David M. Keiser, "The Philharmonic-Symphony Society of New York, Confidential Annual Report 1955–1956, 18 September 1956, 7, File 40, Box 006–03, Philharmonic Archives.

92. Shanet, *Philharmonic*, 333–4.

93. Keiser, "Confidential Annual Report, 1955–1956," 7, Philharmonic Archives; Comptroller to Floyd G. Blair, 9 August 1957, File 26, Box 005–01, Philharmonic Archives.

94. Cresap, McCormick and Paget, "Philadelphia Museum School of Art: Survey of Organization and Management," 21 October 1957, Cresap Archives.

95. R. Sturgis Ingersoll, "Comments by R.S.I. on the Advisability and Practicability of the Creation of a New Corporation to Take Over the Functions of the Philadelphia Museum College of Art, 16 November 1959, 1–2, File: "Separation of School and Museum – Committee Reports, 1962–1963," Series 3, Subgroup: ING, Record Group: The Corporation Records, Philadelphia Museum of Art Archives.

96. Cresap, McCormick and Paget, "Survey of Organization and Management," XI-2, Cresap Archives.

97. Julius Zieget, "Special Meeting," 15 July 1963, File: "Separation of School and Museum – Committee Reports, 1962–1963, Series 3, Subgroup: ING, The Corporation Records, Philadelphia Museum of Art Archives.

98. Cresap, McCormick and Paget, "Professional Counsel for the Management of Nonprofit Organizations."

99. A. T. Kearney & Company, "American Institute of Physics: Survey of Internal Operations," 1 June 1956, and "American Chemical Society: Office of the Executive Secretary – Review of Organization and Sales Structure," 6 March 1956, both in microfiched copies in the corporate records of A. T. Kearney & Company in Chicago [henceforth, Kearney Archives].

100. American Cancer Society, "Minutes of Meeting of Executive Committee of the Board of Directors," 26 January 1956, p. 36, Archives of the American Cancer Society, Atlanta [henceforth, American Cancer Society Archives].

101. A. T. Kearney & Company, American Chemical Society engagement record, Kearney Archives.

102. Cresap, McCormick and Paget, "American Cancer Society: Survey of Organization and Management of the National Office," 9 November 1956, IX-1, American Cancer Society Archives.

103. Ibid., 1.

104. American Cancer Society, *Annual Report,* 1956, 17, American Cancer Society Archives.

105. Cresap, McCormick and Paget, "Survey of Administrative Management, 5 January 1954, I-1, Cresap Archives.

106. Cresap, McCormick and Paget, "The Inkling," 9 June 1956, 14 July 1956, Cresap Archives.

107. William B. Wolf, *Management and Consulting: An Introduction to James O. McKinsey* (Ithaca, 1978); "Westinghouse: Geared for Expansion," *Business Week,* 27 October 1951, 114. This was the second time that Vieh had quit a management consulting firm to work for one of its clients – like James McKinsey, Vieh resigned his partnership in James O. McKinsey & Co. in the 1930s to become the Chief Financial Officer at Marshall Field and Company in Chicago. "Chancellor Appoints Business Assistant," *The Pitt News,* 4 April 1956, 2, Clippings File, University Archives, Hillman Library, University of Pittsburgh.

108. Cresap, McCormick and Paget, "The Inkling," 1955–1960, Cresap Archives.

109. Cresap, McCormick and Paget, "Professional Counsel for the Management of Nonprofit Organizations," 1955.

110. Cresap, McCormick and Paget, "Beth Israel Hospital: A Study of Organization and Management," 1957, Cresap Archives.

111. Paul Starr, *The Social Transformation of American Medicine* (Basic Books, 1982), 381–8.

112. Charles Perrow, "Goals and Power Structures: A Historical Case Study," in Eliot Friedson (ed.), *The Hospital in Modern Society* (New York, 1963), 112–46.

113. "Management Consultants Work for More Schools, Hospitals, Government Agencies," *Wall Street Journal*, 16 May 1968, 1.

114. Barbara J. Niss and Nathan G. Kase, "An Overview of the History of the Mount Sinai School of Medicine of the City University of New York, 1963–1988," *The Mount Sinai Journal of Medicine*, 56, 5 (October 1989), 357.

115. Kenneth M. Ludmerer, "The Origins of Mount Sinai School of Medicine," *Journal of the History of Medicine*, 45 (July 1990), 484–6.

116. Ibid., 476–8.

117. S. David Pomrinse, "Suggested Relationships between the Mount Sinai Hospital and the Medical School," 19 February 1963, File 10, Box 2, Mount Sinai School of Medicine, Early Papers, Archives of The Mount Sinai Medical Center, New York [henceforth, Mount Sinai Archives].

118. Cresap, McCormick and Paget, "Mount Sinai Medical Center: Proposed Organization for Administration and Management," Exhibit II-A, File 8, Box 2, Mount Sinai Archives.

119. S. David Pomrinse, "Critique of the Cresap, McCormick & Paget Report," 28 April 1967, 5, File 10, Box 2, Mount Sinai School of Medicine, Early Papers, Mount Sinai Archives.

120. Cresap, McCormick and Paget, "United Negro College Fund, Inc.: A Study of Objectives, Organization, and Operation," 28 September 1967, Cresap Archives.

121. Cresap, McCormick and Paget to the Implementation Committee, "Long-Range and Interim Organization for Top Management," 16 June 1967, 4, File 12, Box 2, Mount Sinai School of Medicine, Early Papers, Mount Sinai Archives.

122. Ibid., 2.

123. Gustave L. Levy to the Board of Trustees, 9 May 1969, File 11, Box 2, Mount Sinai School of Medicine, Early Papers, Mount Sinai Archives.

124. The reports for Sun Oil prepared by McKinsey & Co. between 1965 and 1969 are deposited in Box 339, Series 1e, Acquisition 1317, Archives and Manuscripts, Hagley Museum and Library, Wilmington, Delaware.

125. Bowman, "Booz Allen & Hamilton," 26–7. In 1961, a year later, Cresap, McCormick and Paget purchased a small Los Angeles-based consultancy, Benjamin Borchardt, and made both Borchardt and the president of the firm, Fred Fisher, partners in Cresap, McCormick and Paget. See "Consulting Concerns Merge, *The New York Times*, 3 December 1961, F11.

126. Cresap, McCormick and Paget, "Negotiations on Merger with A. T. Kearney & Company," Cresap Archives.

127. The Federal Reserve stepped in soon after Citibank announced the purchase to contest the sale. Unable to find a codified law spelling out the prohibition

against the ownership of a consulting firm, they let the deal stand but only with the understanding that no other commercial bank was allowed to purchase a consulting firm and that Citibank would seek to sell off the firm as soon as it was financially possible.

128. George Petitpas, Managing Director, Cresap, McCormick and Paget to James D. Farley, Executive Vice President, Citicorp, 2 February 1977, Cresap Archives.

129. Cresap, McCormick & Paget, "Dartmouth College: An Analysis of the Impact of Coeducation at Princeton and Yale Universities," November 1971; "Union Memorial: Evaluation of the Administrative Structure," February 1972; "Church of Jesus Christ of Latter Day Saints (Mormons): A Study of the Presiding Bishopric's Office," June 1974, Cresap Archives.

130. For example, Leo Kornfeld, the head of the education practice within the Institutional Division, was clearly trying to drum up business by the early 1970s by writing articles in leading newspapers about the potential to reorganize universities. See Leo L. Kornfeld, "The Campus as a Management Problem," *The Wall Street Journal*, 9 December 1970, 16.

131. Peter Dobkin Hall, "A Historical Overview of the Private Nonprofit Sector," in Walter W. Powell (ed.), *The Nonprofit Sector: A Research Handbook* (New Haven: 1987), 20.

132. Walter W. Powell and Rebecca Friedkin, "Organizational Change in Nonprofit Organizations," in Powell (ed.), *The Nonprofit Sector*, 181.

133. Cresap, McCormick and Paget, "Development of the Institutional Division," 29 May 1954, Cresap Archives.

134. For a contemporary critique of the prevalence of the corporate model in universities, see Masao Miyoshi, "Ivory Tower in Escrow," *Boundary 2*, Vol. 27, No. 1 (Spring 2000), 7–50.

135. Donald J. Smalter, "The Influence of Department of Defense Practices on Corporate Planning," *Management Technology*, Vol. 4, No. 2 (1964), 115–38.

136. Cresap, McCormick and Paget, "Professional Counsel for the Management of Nonprofit Organizations."

137. Paul J. DiMaggio and Helmut K. Anheier, "The Sociology of Nonprofit Organizations and Sectors," *Annual Review of Sociology*, Vol. 16 (1990), 137–59.

138. Janet A. Weiss and Sandy Kristin Piderit, "The Value of Mission Statements in Public Agencies," *Journal of Public Administration Research and Theory*, Vol. 9, No. 2 (1999), 193–223.

## 6. THE GILDED AGE OF CONSULTING: A SNAPSHOT OF CONSULTANTS CIRCA 1960

1. For example, consider this description from *Business Week* in 1961: "Management consulting can be a noble profession. Among its outstanding practitioners

are such nationally recognized firms as Booz Allen & Hamilton; McKinsey & Co.; Cresap, McCormick & Paget." See, "Coast Management Consultants Pledge Ethical Behavior," *Business Week* (18 November 1961). In 1953, the *New York Times* declared that "Leaders in management consulting as such include Booz Allen & Hamilton, with headquarters in Chicago; McKinsey & Co., and Cresap, McCormick & Paget; both New York." Jack R. Ryan, "Consultant Field Shows Big Growth," *New York Times* (27 December 1953).

2. Interview, James C. Worthy, former partner at Cresap, McCormick and Paget, 12 August 1997. On Worthy's partnership at Cresap, McCormick and Paget see "J. C. Worthy Elected Partner," *New York Times* (16 January 1962): Sect. 2, 50. Perhaps a better analogy than the Detroit carmakers might be the "Big Eight" accounting firms (most recently dubbed the "Big Four" after Arthur Andersen & Co. shut down). The standing of the large management consulting firms derived from a mixture of elements including size, publicity, profitability, age of the firm, types of assignments and clients, and a host of other factors. For example, some technical consulting firms were larger than these three, but not necessarily more profitable per consultant, while many smaller consulting firms that might have been highly profitable did not garner the attention, hence the prestige, of the larger, general management consultancies.

3. "The Instant Executives," *Forbes* (15 November 1967), 41. For example, in 1965, when a consultant from McKinsey & Company contacted Philip Shay, the President of the Association of Management Consultants (ACME) to ask his opinion of which management consulting firms were best for "overall strategy in the retail field," Shay recommended Cresap, McCormick & Paget, Booz Allen & Hamilton, and A. T. Kearney & Company. Mr. Montgomery, "Consulting Firms in the Retail Field," 18 February 1965, Corporate Archives, McKinsey & Company.

4. The institutional sociologist Robert Nelson argues that the legal elite have exerted considerable influence, "not by bringing about an allocation of society's scarce resources that differs from that willed by clients, but precisely because they maintain and make legitimate the current system for the allocation of rights and benefits." Robert L. Nelson, "Ideology, Practice, and Professional Autonomy: Social Values and Client Relationships in the Large Law Firm," *Stanford Law Review*, Vol. 37 (1985), 545.

5. For evidence of consulting's increasingly favorable image, see the generally laudatory coverage by the *New York Times* of client work performed by Booz Allen & Hamilton (9 October 1960, p. 5); (6 March 1961, p. 13); and (14 March 1962, p. 51); McKinsey & Company (27 May 1959, p. 27); (20 March 1959, 18); and (7 November 1960, p. 35); and Cresap, McCormick and Paget (4 October 1963, 49).

6. Christopher McKenna, Marie-Laure Djelic, and Antti Ainamo "Message and Medium: The Role of Consulting Firms in Globalization and its Local

Interpretation," in Marie-Laure Djelic and Sigrid Quack (eds.), *Globalization and Institutions: Redefining the Rules of the Economic Game* (Edward Elgar, 2003), 83–107.

7. Marc Galanter and Thomas Palay, *Tournament of Lawyers: The Transformation of the Big Law Firm* (Chicago: The University of Chicago, 1991), 20. On the "golden age" of accounting firms in the same era, see David Grayson Allen and Kathleen McDermott's chapter, "A Golden Age, 1946–1961," in *Accounting for Success: A History of Price Waterhouse in America, 1890–1990* (Boston, Harvard Business School Press, 1993), 87–119.

8. James W. Taylor, President of Booz Allen & Hamilton, "Changing Structure of the Profession," *Management Consulting in the 1970's* (New York: Proceedings of the North American Conference of Management Consultants, 1972), 20–8.

9. George Petitpas, Managing Director, Cresap, McCormick and Paget to James D. Farley, Executive Vice President, Citicorp, 2 February 1977, Cresap Archives. McKinsey & Company, "Competitor Analysis Project," Montsoult, France, 18–20 March 1981, 5, 7; McKinsey & Company, "Economics of the Firm: Meeting of New Partners, New York Office," 21 August 1972, n.p., [italics in original] both in Corporate Archives, McKinsey & Company.

10. Richard M. Paget, "New Parameters of Professionalism in Management Consulting," *Management Consulting in the 1970s: Proceedings of the North American Conference of Management Consultants*, (New York: Institute of Management Consultants, 1972), 16.

11. Wilmar B. Schaufeli, Christina Maslach, and Tadeusz Marek (eds.), *Professional Burnout: Recent Developments in Theory and Research* (London Taylor and Francis, 1993); Christina Maslach and Michael P. Leiter, *The Truth About Burnout: How Organizations Cause Personal Stress and What to Do About It* (San Francisco: Jossey-Bass, 1997).

12. Peter Temin, "Is it Kosher to Talk about Culture?" *The Journal of Economic History*, Vol. 57, No. 2 (June 1997), 267–87.

13. The illustrations commissioned by George Fry & Associates were first reproduced in a promotional booklet issued in 1958 by the firm and later featured in a series of articles in the *Christian Science Monitor* in 1960 profiling George Fry & Associates' work. See Robert Corby Nelson, "The Business Beat: Report from Chicago," *The Christian Science Monitor*, 19 February 1960, 10; 24 February 1960, 10; and 8 March 1960, 15. Although not analyzed in this chapter, in 1969, journalist Hal Higdon would describe Booz Allen and McKinsey as the two leading management consulting firms followed by three other "generalist" firms: A. T. Kearney & Company; Cresap, McCormick & Paget, and Fry Consultants (the successor to George Fry & Associates). Hal Higdon, *The Business Healers* (New York: Random House, 1969), 22–3.

14. According to the American Bureau of Labor Statistics, 30% of all "Management Analysts," substantially more than similar occupations, were self

employed in 2003. On the ease with which individual practitioners could enter and exit consulting in the 1960s, see Wilbert E. Moore, *The Conduct of the Corporation* (New York: Vintage Books, 1962), 243–4.

15. Norman C. Miller, Jr., "Management Consulting Firms Miss Mark, Executives Say," *Wall Street Journal* (6 February 1962), 2. Because analysts have always found it difficult to gather reliable statistics on management consulting, estimates of the total number of consultants and firms are generally imprecise. By comparison, the Association of Management Consultants (ACME) estimated in 1964 that there were 2,000 individual management consulting firms in the United States in 1960. The truth is probably somewhere in between the two figures. In 1958, students at the Harvard Business School reported that "although there are several widely divergent estimates of the number of management consulting firms, the best estimate is between 2,000 and 2,500 firms. Richard F. Amon, et al., *Management Consulting* (Boston: Management Consulting Report Associates, 1958), 3. To further muddy the waters, however, Amon and his colleagues estimated that there were "probably 50,000 persons employed in management consulting." Ibid.

16. "Management Experts Thrive on Own Advice," *Business Week* (23 April 1960), 110. By comparison, in the late 1950s there were only 38 law firms in the United States with more than 50 lawyers and less than a dozen law firms that had more than 100 lawyers. Galanter and Palay, *Tournament of Lawyers*, 46.

17. For a defense of the importance of small businesses and individual practitioners in the modern economy, see Mansel G. Blackford, *A History of Small Business in America* (New York: Twayne Publishers, 1991).

18. "Management Experts Thrive on Own Advice," *Business Week* (23 April 1960), 110. To convert from 1960 dollar amounts to their approximate 2005 equivalents, simply multiply these figures by a factor of 6 to find the nominal value of 1960 dollars in 2005.

19. Fiscal year totals, Corporate Archives, McKinsey & Company; estimates for Cresap, McCormick and Paget derived from Walter Guzardi, "Consultants: The Men Who Came to Dinner," *Fortune* (February 1965), 138–41; Hal Higdon, *The Business Healers*, 309–13. For a contemporary comparison, in 2003, McKinsey had roughly 6,000 consultants and $3 billion in revenues while Booz Allen & Hamilton also employed roughly 6,000 consultants and enjoyed $2.2 billion in billings.

20. Percentages calculated from "Consultants Business is 600 Million a Year," *The New York Times*, 2 September 1962, 96. In 1958, Richard Paget estimated that general management consulting firms (excluding individuals and firms offering only a specialized service) generated $150 million per year in revenues.

21. Institutional reputation, of course, is a moving target that is very difficult to measure. In the late 1940s, for example, Robert Heller & Associates had held a reputation far greater than McKinsey & Company while Cresap, McCormick

and Paget's work for leading nonprofit and government institutions might well have placed the firm above Booz Allen & Hamilton in stature. The rapid expansion of McKinsey & Company and Booz Allen & Hamilton overseas in the late 1950s, however, gave both firms international exposure even as Robert Heller's position dropped. By contrast, A. T. Kearney & Company, which in 1960 was a regional firm in Chicago but with little national or international exposure, gained stature in the 1960s even as Cresap, McCormick and Paget lost its cachet because the firm failed to expand overseas. For an earlier benchmark, see *Fortune* magazine's profile of the leadership of eleven leading management consulting firms in 1944, a list that included Edwin Booz, Charles Stevenson, Wallace Clark, George Trundle, Robert Heller, D. J. Walsh, Jr., Harry Hopf, Guy Crockett, E. O. Griffenhagen, George Elliott, and John Nickerson. "Doctors of Management," *Fortune* (July 1944), 144–6.

22. Northwestern University was also James Allen's undergraduate institution. Both Jim Allen and Richard Paget would eventually donate significant sums to their *alma mater*. Booz Allen & Hamilton, "James Lee Allen: Remembering a Great Man," memorial pamphlet, 1992, 10–11.

23. As early as 1944, McKinsey & Company underwrote a Stanford Business School survey of the potential demand for California branch offices of the Eastern consulting firms, see Wilfrid B. Shantz, *The Need and Demand for High-Grade Management Consulting Service in California* (Palo Alto, CA: Business Research Series No. 2, Stanford University Graduate School of Business, 1944), 1–15. The partners at A. T. Kearney & Company soon recognized the competitive disadvantage of not having an office in California. In contrast, Tom Kearney, who controlled A. T. Kearney & Company until his death in 1962, consistently quashed any suggestions of expanding beyond Chicago. Several times, however, his partners explored buying another management consulting firm in order to establish a toehold outside Chicago. One possible acquisition, of Benjamin Borchardt and Associates in Los Angeles, was discussed at length in 1959, when Tom Kearney became ill, but the partners did not go beyond preliminary discussions. Two years later, Cresap, McCormick and Paget purchased Benjamin Borchardt and Associates. By October 1963, the partners at A. T. Kearney & Company were again considering possible acquisition candidates in California. See A. T. Kearney & Company, "Minutes of Partners Meeting," 23 January 1959, 27 February 1959, 3 April 1959, 15 May 1959, 14 August 1959, and 4 October 1963, n.p., Corporate Archives, A. T. Kearney & Company. On Cresap, McCormick and Paget's acquisition of Benjamin Borchardt and Associates, see "Consulting Concerns Merge," *New York Times*, 3 December 1961, F11.

24. McKinsey & Company, "Analysis of Firm Practice by Industry," 1966, Corporate Archives, McKinsey & Company.

25. Corporate Archives, McKinsey & Company. McKinsey & Company was indeed diversifying away from its previous dependence on the New York

office – by 1965, the New York office's share of total firm revenue had fallen to 41%. McKinsey & Company, "Analysis of Firm Practice by Industry, F/Y 1959–1965 Incl.," 1966, pp. 1–2, Corporate Archives, McKinsey & Company.

26. Peter B. Bart, "Exports of Know-How Booming," *New York Times*, (13 January 1960), 27.

27. Glenn Fowler, "Business Expansion Fuels Office Boom," *The New York Times*, 7 April 1968, R1, R4. For a description of Cresap, McCormick and Paget's modern offices in 245 Park Avenue, see "'Office of the Year' Honorable Mention: Consultant's Headquarters – Conservative, Imaginative," *Administrative Management*, 1968. This was the second time that the management consulting firm had won this award. For a description of the firm's earlier, more conservative offices at 342 Madison Avenue, see "Office of the Year Honorable Mention: The Offices of Cresap, McCormick and Paget," *Office Management and Equipment* (December 1950), 50–2.

28. Harold Hotelling, "Stability in Competition," *The Economic Journal*, Vol. 39, No. 153 (March 1929), 41–57; Curtis Eaton and Richard Lipsey, "Comparison Shopping and the Clustering of Homogeneous Firms," *Journal of Regional Science*, Vol. 19, No. 4 (November 1979), 421–35.

29. "The Instant Executives," Forbes (15 November 1967), 38.

30. "Management Experts Thrive on Own Advice," *Business Week* (23 April 1960), cover.

31. Marvin Bower, "Firm Information," 26 March 1963, p. 5, Corporate Archives, McKinsey & Company (figure annualized from 368 clients served over the 15 months ending in March of 1963). By comparison, Bower told *Fortune* magazine in 1954 that McKinsey & Company served 200 clients a year. Stryker, "The Ambitious Consultants," 83.

32. "Booz Allen & Hamilton," *Television Magazine* (January 1959), 50; Galanter and Palay, *Tournament of Lawyers*, 33; Allen and McDermott, *Accounting for Success*, 143.

33. The petroleum industry, at 18%, was twice the level of the nearest industrial group, aerospace and electronics. Calculations based on McKinsey's 1959 to 1961 billings. McKinsey & Company, "Analysis of Firm Practice by Industry, F/Y 1959–1965 Incl.," 1966, 1, Corporate Archives, McKinsey & Company.

34. McKinsey & Company, "Analysis of Firm Practice by Industry, F/Y 1959–1965 Incl.," 1966, p. 1, Corporate Archives, McKinsey & Company.

35. McKinsey & Company, "Analysis of Firm Practice by Industry, F/Y 1959–1965 Incl.," 1966, 1, Corporate Archives, McKinsey & Company.

36. Bowen, *Booz Allen & Hamilton*, 94.

37. On the other hand, prospective clients would not have been able to meet with all of the partners whose names were on the door. James McKinsey, Edwin Booz, and Carl Hamilton were all dead by 1960 and Mark Cresap, who was president of Westinghouse in 1960, would die suddenly three years later. See

"Mark Cresap, of Westinghouse: His Career a Rocket Rise to the Top," *New York Herald Tribune* (9 August 1963).

38. "The Real McKinsey," *The Economist* (1 February 2003), 61.

39. In contrast, in 1968, one of the partners at McKinsey & Company, who was a personal friend of Willard McCormick of Cresap, McCormick and Paget, reported a recent conversation between the two of them. In reaction to McCormick's admission that he and Dick Paget were the "enormous income producers" for the firm, the McKinsey partner voiced his suspicion that Dick Paget and Willard McCormick "massaged" every initial client meeting, acting as the ambassadors to the firm for most clients – something still possible at a consultancy of Cresap, McCormick and Paget's size. Indeed, despite the presence of 25 partners, the McKinsey consultant suspected that Paget and McCormick continued to "regard the firm as their proprietorship." H. L. Thomas, Jr., "Notes on Cresap, McCormick & Paget," 19 February 1968, pp. 1–2, Corporate Archives, McKinsey & Company.

40. McKinsey & Company, "20 Year Fiscal Review," 1979, Corporate Archives, McKinsey & Company.

41. Galanter and Palay, *Tournament of Lawyers*, 22.

42. Allen and McDermott, *Accounting for Success*, 152.

43. "Booz Allen & Hamilton," *Television Magazine* (January 1959), 48.

44. "Booz Allen & Hamilton," *Television Magazine* (January 1959), 49.

45. "Booz Allen & Hamilton," *Television Magazine* (January 1959), 49; Arch Patton, "Trends in Executive Compensation," *Harvard Business Review* (September–October 1960), 146.

46. Marvin Bower, "A. T. Kearney & Company," 30 March 1962, 1–2, Corporate Archives, McKinsey & Company; A. T. Kearney & Company, "Minutes of Partners Meeting," 10 November 1961, n.p., Corporate Archives, A. T. Kearney & Company.

47. Arch Patton, "Upturn in Executive Compensation," *Harvard Business Review*, Vol. 38, No. 5 (September/October 1960), 146; Arch Patton, "Executive Compensation in 1960," *Harvard Business Review*, Vol. 39, No. 5 (September/October 1961), 152.

48. Marvin Bower, "A. T. Kearney & Company," 30 March 1962, p. 1, Corporate Archives, McKinsey & Company; A. T. Kearney & Company. The strength of the firm, of course, had a tremendous impact on salary levels. By comparison, in 1968, the 25 partners at Cresap, McCormick and Paget earned from $40,000 to $80,000 with only a very few partners earning $100,000. H. L. Thomas, "Notes on Cresap, McCormick & Paget," 19 February 1968, Corporate Archives, McKinsey & Company.

49. U.S. Department of Commerce, "Series D: 913–926: Earnings in Selected Occupations, 1865–1970," *Historical Statistics of the United States: Colonial Times to 1970* (Washington, DC: U.S. Government Printing Office, 1975), 175.

50. For example, the annual HBS Career Guide for 1962 devoted an entire issue to careers in management consulting with articles written not only by Marvin Bower, but also by Richard Paget of Cresap, McCormick and Paget, Bruce Henderson, then still a vice president of Arthur D. Little, Inc., and Leonard Spacek, the managing partner at Arthur Andersen. The articles were accompanied by full page advertisements by the elite consulting firms. *Career Guide: A Harvard Business School Student Publication*, Vol. 2, No. 2 (February 1962).

51. Ibid, 8; Galanter and Palay, *Tournament of Lawyers*, 24. The average starting salary at McKinsey & Company in 1961 was $11,100. Marvin Bower to Directors and Principals, "Comments on Fiscal 1963 Profits," 12 August 1963, Schedule 1, Corporate Archives, McKinsey & Company.

52. While earlier production-oriented consultants tended to come from more modest backgrounds, achieving success through their functional expertise, by the late 1950s, elite educational training, a hallmark of the upper middle class, became the overwhelming means of entry into consulting. On the similar evolution in France, see Luc Boltanski, *The Making of a Class: Cadres in French Society* (New York: Cambridge University Press, 1987).

53. *Desk Set*, dir. Walter Lang (1957), released by Twentieth Century Fox.

54. Sloan Wilson, *The Man in the Gray Flannel Suit* (New York: Simon and Schuster, 1955). On the relative "squareness" of advertising executives in this era see Thomas Frank, *The Conquest of Cool* (Chicago: The University of Chicago Press, 1997), 25–50.

55. The jokes about the dark suits at McKinsey would lead others to quip that they dressed liked morticians.

56. "Management Experts Thrive on Own Advice," *Business Week* (23 April 1960).

57. Marvin Bower, "Impact of Newer Associates on Firm Reputation," 18 November 1959, p. 3, Corporate Archives, McKinsey & Company.

58. Richard Reeves, *President Kennedy: Profile of Power* (New York: Touchstone Books, 1994); John Hellmann, *The Kennedy Obsession: The American Myth of JFK* (New York: Columbia University Press, 1997).

59. To later generations (particularly given the rapid decline of men's hats other than baseball caps, *Business Week*'s measure of consulting's success seems incredibly archaic – in 1955, *Business Week* reported that consulting firms generated more than twice the total revenues of typewriter manufacturers and four times those of manufacturers of "men's fur felt hats." "Talbott Case Floodlights Growth of Management Consulting," *Business Week* (6 August 1955), 158.

60. My position stands in opposition to cultural theorists like John Fiske who see grumbling, parodies, and complaints as distinctly active forms of institutional resistance. For example, on television viewing as a means of cultural resistance see John Fiske, *Understanding Popular Culture* (Boston: Unwin Hyman, 1989), 151–8.

61. C. Wright Mills, *The Power Elite* (New York: Oxford University Press, 1956); On the prevalence of Stanford graduates in the profession see Martin Ruef, "At the Interstices of Organizations: The Expansion of the Management Consulting Profession, 1933–1997," in Kerstin Sahlin-Andersson and Lars Engwall (eds.), *The Expansion of Management Knowledge* (Stanford: Stanford University Press, 2002): 74–95.

62. "The Consultants Coloring Book," (Mimeo, circa 1962), McKinsey & Company Archives.

63. Richard Paget, "Management Consulting as a Profession: A Talk Before the Forty-Fifth Anniversary Meeting of Booz, Allen and Hamilton, Chicago, Illinois, November 15, 1958," Corporate Archives, Association of Management Consulting Firms, New York.

64. Yves Dezalay, "'Turf Battles' or 'Class Struggles': The Internationalization of the Market for Expertise in the 'Professional Society,'" *Accounting, Organizations and Society*, Vol. 20, No. 5 (1995), 331–44.

65. Andrew Abbott emphasizes that while professional metaphors are a strong means to promote public respect, they are a relatively "weak means of jurisdictional extension." Andrew Abbott, *The System of Professions: An Essay on the Division of Expert Labor* (Chicago: University of Chicago Press, 1988), 99–100.

### 7. THE AMERICAN CHALLENGE: EXPORTING THE AMERICAN MODEL

1. J. J. Servan-Schreiber, *The American Challenge* (New York: Athenaeum, 1968) [citations throughout this chapter are to the English translation, which was released in America one year after the book's publication in France]. Richard F. Kuisel, *Seducing the French: The Dilemma of Americanization* (Berkeley: University of California Press, 1993), 154.

2. Harry V. Hodson, "The Great American Invasion," *The Times*, 6 November 1967, 20.

3. Servan-Schreiber, 8, [parentheses and emphasis in original].

4. On the influence of consultants in Britain, see Derek F. Channon, *The Strategy and Structure of British Enterprise* (Boston: Harvard Business School, 1973), 239; for consultants' impact in France and Germany, see Gareth Dyas and Heinz T. Thanheiser, *The Emerging European Enterprise: Strategy and Structure in French and German Industry* (London: Macmillan, 1976), 120, 247.

5. Matthias Kipping, "The U.S. Influence on the Evolution of Management Consultancies in Britain, France, and Germany Since 1945," *Business and Economic History*, Vol. 25, No. 1 (Fall 1996), 112.

6. Richard Whittington and Michael Mayer, *The European Corporation-Strategy, Structure, and Social Science* (Oxford: Oxford University Press, 2000), 220–3.

7. "Consultants on Mount Olympus," *The Times*, 18 November 1968, 23. Out-siders also perceived an air of mystery surrounding McKinsey's work; an aura that prompted the German publication *Capital* to publish a feature on the firm in March 1971 entitled, "The Jesuits of the German Economy," describing the management consulting firm as "German industry's number one secret-holder."

8. "In This Concluding Article, Joe Roeber Analyzes the Attitudes of Top Management to their Consultants," *The Times*, 7 July 1969, 24. As Roger Morrison, who ran the London office from 1973 to 1983, later explained, "McKinsey became a household word." Elizabeth Haas Edersheim, *McKinsey's Marvin Bower: Vision, Leadership, and the Creation of Management Consulting*, (New York: John Wiley & Sons, Inc., 2004), 102.

9. These "waves" of management methods are distinct from and do not over-lap with Matthias Kipping's "three waves of management consulting" that he describes in Matthias Kipping, "Trapped in their Wave: The Evolution of Management Consultancies," in Timothy Clark and Robin Fincham, *Critical Consulting: New Perspectives on the Management Advice Industry* (Oxford: Blackwell Publishers, 2001), 28–49.

10. Thomas Hughes, *American Genesis: A Century of Invention and Technolog-ical Enthusiasm 1870–1970* (New York: Viking Books, 1989), 250–78. See also Judith A. Merkle, *Management and Ideology: The Legacy of the Interna-tional Scientific Management Movement* (Berkeley: University of California Press, 1980). Even the Italian theorist, Antonio Gramsci, considered the impact of Taylorism at length in his section entitled "Americanism and Fordism," in his prison notebooks from the late 1920s and early 1930s. Antonio Gramsci, *Selec-tions from the Prison Notebooks* (New York: International Publishers, 1971), 279–318.

11. Marie-Laure Djelic, *Exporting the American Model: The Post-War Transformation of European Business* (Oxford: Oxford University Press, 1998).

12. Mary Nolan, *Visions of Modernity: American Business and the Modernization of Germany* (New York: Oxford University Press, 1994); Charles Maier, "Between Taylorism and Technocracy: European Ideologies and the Vision of Industrial Productivity in the 1920s," *Journal of Contemporary History*, Vol. 5, No. 2 (1970), 27–61.

13. Odile Henry, "Le Conseil, Un Espace Professionnel Autonome?" *Enterprises et Histoire*, No. 7 (December 1994), 37–58.

14. Steven Kreis, "The Diffusion of Scientific Management: The Bedaux Com-pany in America and Britain, 1926–1945," in Daniel Nelson (ed.), *A Mental Revolution: Scientific Management Since Taylor* (Columbus: Ohio State Univer-sity Press, 1992), 168.

15. Matthias Kipping, "Consultancies, Institutions, and the Diffusion of Taylorism in Britain, Germany, and France, 1920s to 1950s," *Business History*, Vol. 39, No. 4 (1997), 67–83.

16. For extended description, see Michael J. Hogan, *The Marshall Plan: America, Britain, and the Reconstruction of Western Europe, 1947–1952* (New York: Cambridge University Press, 1987); Jacqueline McGlade, *The Illusion of Consensus: American Business, Cold War Aid, and the Reconstruction of Western Europe, 1948–1958* (Ph.D. Dissertation, George Washington University, 1995).

17. Nick Tiratsoo and Jim Tomlinson, "Exporting the "Gospel of Productivity": United States Technical Assistance and British Industry 1945–1960," *The Business History Review*, Vol. 71, No. 1 (Spring, 1997), 49; Kim McQuaid, *Uneasy Partners: Big Business in American Politics, 1945–1990* (Baltimore, The Johns Hopkins University Press, 1994), 47.

18. Cresap, McCormick and Paget, "Survey of the Market for Professional Management Consulting Services," October 1954, Exhibit III-3, "Location of ACME Member Offices and Affiliates by City and by Firm," 4, Microfilm, Cresap, McCormick and Paget corporate archives, Valhalla, New York. "New Appointment For Sir Miles Thomas," *The Times*, 28 December 1956, 10; "'The Times' Law Reports," *The Times*, 25 January 1952, 8; Philip Jacobson, "Why London Looks Right Now for Arthur D. Little," *The Times*, 6 November 1967, 19.

19. McKinsey and Company, *1951 Annual Report*.

20. Patricia Tisdall, *Agents of Change: The Development and Practice of Management Consultancy* (London: Heinemann, 1982), 36–59; Henry, "Le Conseil," 48; "Management Consultants Association," *The Times*, 1 October 1956, 15; Matthias Kipping, "The Evolution of Management Consultancy: Its Origins and Global Development," in Barry Curnow and Johathan Reuvid (eds.), *The International Guide to Management Consultancy* (London: Kogan Page, 2003 [second edition]), 23.

21. Michael Shanks, *The Innovators: The Economics of Technology* (Harmondsworth, Middlesex: Penguin Books, 1967), 200.

22. This distinction was clear to British executives. For example, according to a senior executive in ICI, the British chemical giant preferred ". . . American consultants [since] they have more experience in top level management reorganization than their British competitors." Roger Ricklefs, "European Firms Turn to U.S. Consultants on Questions of Management, Computers," *The Wall Street Journal*, 30 December 1966, 5.

23. Chandler, *Strategy and Structure*, 381–2. By 1967, 86% of the 500 largest U.S. companies had adopted the multidivisional model. L. Wrigley, "Divisional Autonomy and Diversification," (Ph.D. Dissertation, Harvard Business School, 1970), 50. See also, Richard Whittington and Michael Mayer, *The European Corporation: Strategy, Structure and Social Science* (Oxford: Oxford University Press, 2000).

24. James E. Cronin, "Convergence by Conviction: Politics and Economics in the Emergence of the 'Anglo-American Model,'" *Journal of Social History*, Vol. 33, No. 4 (Summer 2000), 781–804.

25. Mira Wilkins, *The Maturing of Multinational Enterprise: American Business Abroad from 1914 to 1970* (Cambridge: Harvard University Press, 1974), 4.

26. Wilkins, *The Maturing of Multinational Enterprise*, 55.

27. Wilkins, *The Maturing of Multinational Enterprise*, 309–310.

28. Charles P. Kindelberger, "Origins of United States Direct Investment in France," *Business History Review*, Vol. 48, No. 3 (Autumn 1973), 404; "Overseas Business in U.S.: 'Important to Major Corporations,'" *The Times*, 3 January 1962, 13.

29. Peter B. Bart, "Exports of Know-How Booming: Demand Soaring for Services of U.S. Consultants," *The New York Times*, 13 January 1960, 27.

30. Jim Bowman, *Booz Allen & Hamilton: Seventy Years of Client Service, 1914–1984* (Chicago, Booz Allen & Hamilton, Inc., 1984), 65.

31. Roger Ricklefs, "European Firms Turn to U.S. Consultants on Questions of Management, Computers," *The Wall Street Journal*, 30 December 1966, 5.

32. Marvin Bower to Partners, "Extending our Practice to Europe," 8 September 1953, 3.

33. Marvin Bower to Partners, 8 September 1953, 3; Edersheim, *McKinsey's Marvin Bower*, 98–9.

34. McKinsey & Company, "Minutes of Planning Committee Meeting," April 5th and 6th, 1956, 7.

35. Edersheim, *McKinsey's Marvin Bower*, 98.

36. Marvin Bower to Executive Committee, "Observations on our International Practice," 8 May 1957, 2, [italics in the original], A2-2, "Aims and Goals."

37. Channon, *The Strategy and Structure of British Enterprise*, 115.

38. Bower, *Perspective on McKinsey*, 86.

39. Bowman, *Booz Allen & Hamilton*, 60–2.

40. Francesca Carnevali, "State Enterprise and Italy's 'Economic Miracle': The Ente Nazionale Idrocarburi, 1945–1962," *Enterprise and Society*, Vol. 1 (2000), 249–78.

41. Steven W. Tolliday, "Introduction: Enterprise and State in the Italian "Economic Miracle," *Enterprise and Society*, Vol. 1 (2000), 245.

42. Charles R. Dechert, "Ente Nazionale Idrocarburi: A State Corporation in a Mixed Economy," *Administrative Science Quarterly*, Vol. 7, No. 3 (December 1962), 340.

43. Jacobson, "Why London Looks Right Now for Arthur D. Little," *The Times*, 6 November 1967, 19; "Consultancy Success of a Multinational," *The Times*, 30 June 1975, 16; "Consultants' London Base," *The Times*, 4 March 1969, 26.

44. Matthias Kipping, 'American Management Consulting Companies in Western Europe, 1920 to 1990: Products, Reputation and Relationships', *Business History Review*, Vol. 73, No. 2 (Summer 1999), 190–220.

45. Bower, *Perspective on McKinsey*, 92. The "utilization level" is the percentage of hours in a standard 35-hour week that is billed to clients. The normal

utilization level is somewhere between 70% and 80%. See David H. Maister, *Managing the Professional Service Firm* (New York: Free Press, 1993).

46. Edersheim, *McKinsey's Marvin Bower*, 101.

47. Bower, *Perspective on McKinsey*, 92–3; "I.C.I. Divisions to Merge," *The Times*, 2 November 1963, 8; Clifford Webb, "How Dunlop Got Rid of Its Soap Factory, Cinema, Chapel, Funeral Parlour, Printing Works, and Hat Factory. It Was Revolutionizing Tyre Distribution," *The Times*, 7 March 1969, 29.

48. Michael C. Jensen, "McKinsey & Co.: Big Brother to Big Business," *The New York Times*, 30 May 1971, 1.

49. "VW Ready for Export Battle," *The Times*, 25 April 1969, 30; "KLM Airlines Undergoing Major Shakeup at the Top in Move to Halt Big Deficits," *The Wall Street Journal*, 9 January 1963, 32.

50. This is extremely unusual; Arthur D. Little, by comparison, ran initial deficits when it set up its London office in the late 1960s. See Joe Roeber, "Management," *The Times*, 30 June 1969, 25.

51. McKinsey & Company, "Trend Data: Continental Offices," Firm History Project.

52. A simple comparison between McKinsey's British competitors underscores the American firm's profitability; in 1967 McKinsey's British profits per consultant were three times those of the most profitable British consultancy, PA Consulting. Calculations based on figures from Joe Roeber, "Management," *The Times*, 30 June 1969, 25.

53. Ricklefs, "European Firms Turn to U.S. Consultants on Questions of Management, Computers," 5.

54. Joe Roeber, "Management," *The Times*, 30 June 1969, 25.

55. "Les Mercenaires de l'Organisation," *L'Express*, 18–24 October 1971.

56. As Marvin Bower, the Managing Director of McKinsey & Company and the architect of McKinsey's expansion into Europe, wrote in February of 1960, "Our *secondary* objective [after 'serving American business overseas'] is to serve European business enterprises – to the degree that they are interested in our unique services. We are *not* trying to 'sell them service' and therefore looking for what they will 'buy.'" Marvin Bower to Gil Clee, "Developing our European Practice," 5 February 1960, *Supplement to Perspective on McKinsey* (Mimeographed, McKinsey & Company, 1979), 20 [italics in original].

57. Channon, *Strategy and Structure of British Enterprise*, 239; quotation from Dyas and Thanheiser, *The Emerging European Enterprise*, 112. Unfortunately, no comparable estimates exist on the number of companies divisionalized by McKinsey & Company in France, Switzerland, or the Netherlands.

58. Rosemarie Fiedler-Winter, "Divisionalisierung als Hilfsmittel: Beratung als Assistenz – Unruhe Unvermeidlich," *Management International Review*, Vol. 14, No. 6 (1974), 96.

59. Bower, *Perspective on McKinsey*, 111–12.

60. Mauro F. Guillén, *Models of Management: Work, Authority and Organization in a Comparative Perspective* (Chicago: The University of Chicago Press, 1994), 200–1.

61. Celeste Amorim, "Spain," in Matthias Kipping and Thomas Armbuster (eds.), *The Consultancy Field in Western Europe* (Creation of European Management Practice, Report 6, June 1999), 142–4.

62. Channon, *Strategy and Structure of British Enterprise*, 239.

63. "McKinsey to Study Unilever Management," *The Times*, 14 January 1971, 17; "Unilever Board Discuss McKinsey Recommendations," *The Times*, 3 March 1972, 18.

64. Quoted in Edersheim, *McKinsey's Marvin Bower*, 141.

65. Albert Engle, "Organisation and Management Planning in the Royal Dutch/Shell Group," in Ronald S. Edwards and Harry Townsend (eds.), *Business Enterprise: Its Growth and Organisation* (London: Macmillan & Co., Ltd., 1959), 348, 353.

66. Channon, *The Strategy and Structure of British Industry*, 115.

67. Chandler, *Strategy and Structure*, 353.

68. "Shell Oil Co. President, Spaght, to Be Proposed As Loudon's Successor," *The Wall Street Journal*, 21 April 1965, 13.

69. Anthony Sampson, *Anatomy of Britain Today*, (New York: Harper & Row, 1965), 485.

70. "Going Well at Shell," *The Times*, 25 November 1969, 23.

71. Channon, *The Strategy and Structure of British Industry*, 115.

72. Sampson, *Anatomy of Britain Today*, 485.

73. "Consultants Move in to the Board-Room," *The Sunday Times*, 8 September 1963; Edersheim, *McKinsey's Marvin Bower*, 102.

74. Alfred D. Chandler, Jr., *Scale and Scope: The Dynamics of Industrial Capitalism* (Cambridge, Massachusetts: Harvard University Press, 1990), 618–19.

75. Jonathan Charkham, *Keeping Good Company: A Study of Corporate Governance in Five Countries* (Oxford: Clarendon Press, 1994), 17–25.

76. Dyas and Thanheiser, *The Emerging European Enterprise*, 114–15.

77. Alfred D. Chandler, "Comparative Business History," in D.C. Coleman and Peter Mathias (eds.), *Enterprise and History: Essays in Honour of Charles Wilson* (Cambridge: Cambridge University Press, 1984), 16; David J. Teece, "The Diffusion of an Administrative Innovation," *Management Science*, Vol. 26, No. 5 (May 1980), 469.

78. McKinsey & Company, "Profile of the Paris Office," *Month by Month*, May 1970, 15–17.

79. Edersheim, *McKinsey's Marvin Bower*, 69.

80. For a particularly detailed study of McKinsey's influence in the Dutch banking sector, see D. J. G. (Doreen) Arnoldus, "The Role of Consultancies in the

Transformation of the Dutch Banking Sector, 1950s to 1990s," *Entreprises et Histoire*, No. 25 (October 2000), 65–81.

81. Geigy subsequently merged first with Ciba and then Sandoz and renamed itself Novartis.

82. "Neue Organisation," *National Zeitung*, 17 December 1967.

83. Quoted in Susanne Hilger, "American Consultants in the German Consumer Chemicals Industry: The Stanford Research Institute at Henkel in the 1960s and 1970s," *Entreprises et Histoire*, No. 25 (October 2000), 60.

84. Von Herbert Gross, "Produktion als Hilfsfunktion: Flexible Organisation bei Geigy," *Handlesblatt*, 13 November 1968.

85. "The firm's name has even become a generic term in Britain, where contracting for a management study is known as 'doing a McKinsey.'" Michael C. Jensen, "McKinsey & Co.: Big Brother to Big Business," *The New York Times*, 30 May 1971, 1. The most recent corporate verb to enter the English language is "to Google" which means to search for information on the internet.

86. "Certainly so far as British industry is concerned the word has already passed into the language, becoming synonymous with managerial reform." Stephen Aris, "Supermanagers," *The Sunday Times*, 1 September 1968.

87. "Neue Organisation," *National Zeitung*, 17 December 1967.

88. "Consultants after Crisis," *The Times*, 8 May 1973, 21 [italics in original].

89. "British Cocoa Reorganize," *The Times*, 10 February 1967, 19; "No Need to Despair of Rolls Royce," *The Times*, 24 May 1967, 24.

90. "McKinsey to Advise British Rail," *The Times*, 14 June 1968, 21; For the records of McKinsey's work inside the BBC, see the four separate reports submitted during McKinsey's 1968–1970 survey that are available in the BBC Written Archives Centre, Peppard Road, Caversham Park, Reading.

91. Richard Casement, "Gaps in Government Use of Consultants," *The Times*, 14 November 1967, 24. In 1964, for example, an M.P., Eric Lubbock, asked the Prime Minister, "'... if he will instruct Ministers concerned to ensure that in future British management consultants are invited to submit proposals for such assignments.'" As an advisor to the Bank of England explained, "this may have been prompted by the recent announcement that the B.B.C. have engaged McKinseys [sic]." James B. Selwyn, "Consultants in the Bank: Notes for Committee of Treasury" (7 May 1968), Bank of England Archives, G39/1.

92. Quoted in McKinsey & Company, *Month by Month*, January 1969, 9.

93. "Come into my Parlour," *The Economist*, 2 November 1968, 69 [bracketed explanations are mine].

94. *The Financial Times*, 20 December 1969.

95. James B. Selwyn, "Management Consultants in the Bank" (22 July 1968), 6–7, Bank of England Archives, London, G39/1.

96. Parson's endorsement was followed, only two days later, by a conversation between James Bailey (a Director of the Bank) and J. W. Platt, the chairman

of the Foundation for Management Education, who "came down heavily in favour of McKinsey." Sir Maurice Parsons (22 July 1968) and James Bailey (22 July 1968), both in Bank of England Archives, G39/1.

97. Roy Heasman, "Management Consultants in the Bank," (30 July 1968) in Bank of England Archives, G39/1.

98. Sir Leslie O'Brien, dated marginalia (1 August 1968) in Sir Maurice Parsons (31 July 1968) in Bank of England Archives, G39/1.

99. Sir Leslie O'Brien, dated marginalia (8 August 1968) in James B. Selwyn, "Management Consultants in the Bank" (1 August 1968), and "Extract from the Committee of Treasury Minutes" (7 August 1968), both in the Bank of England Archives, G39/1.

100. "Extract from the Formal Court Minutes" (15 August 1968) and Hugh Parker, McKinsey & Company to Sir Leslie O'Brien, Governor of the Bank of England (18 September 1968), both in the Bank of England Archives, G39/1.

101. Peter Taylor, Secretary of the Bank of England, no title (11 August 1970), of England Archives, G39/3.

102. Peter Taylor, dated marginalia [15 October 1968] in James B. Selwyn, "Management Consultants in the Bank" (11 October 1968), Bank of England Archives, G39/1.

103. "McKinsey & Co." (30 October 1968) and Gordon Costello, "McKinsey & Co." (30 October 1968), both in the Bank of England Archives, ADM 10/1.

104. Bank of England, "Press Notice" (5.30 pm, 28 October 1968) in the Bank of England Archives, ADM 10/1. For the resulting coverage, see Anthony Thomas, "The Bank May Call Consultants In: Talks with McKinsey," *The Times*, 29 October 1968, 17; Kenneth Fleet, "U.S. Consultants to Check Bank of England: McKinsey invited to Threadneedle Street," *Daily Telegraph* (29 October 1968); John Coyne, "US Firm to Have Good Look at Bank," *Manchester Guardian* (29 October 1968); and Michael Gillard, "Slide Rule Men from U.S. called to the Bank," *Daily Express* (29 October 1968), all retained in Bank of England Archives, ADM 38/93.

105. "McKinsey plum chokes Britain's own consultants," *Daily Telegraph* (30 October 1968). See also Michael Blanden, "Firms upset at Bank using McKinsey," Manchester Guardian (30 October 1968); "Two McKinsey Questions for Commons," *Daily Telegraph* (31 October 1968); "Bank Probe by McKinsey Criticised," *Financial Times* (31 October 1968); and "Peer attacks Bank Choice of McKinsey," *The Times* (1 November 1968), 26, all retained in Bank of England Archives, ADM 38/93.

106. Peter Taylor, "Note for the Record" (8 November 1968), of England Archives, G39/1; "Sympathetic Bank Note," *The Times* (9 November 1968), 11.

107. "Too Little Cash, Too Much Waste in NHS," *The Times*, 9 April 1969, 2.

108. Editorial, *Manchester Guardian*, 29 October 1968.

109. Bower, *Perspective on McKinsey*, 97.

110. Allen Stewart, notes for "A McKinsey Scrapbook," to appear in *Month by Month* in 1994.

111. Douglas W. Cray, "Consulting Firms Faced with In-Between Time when Business is Difficult," *The New York Times*, 20 September 1970, 177; "The Consultants Face a Competition Crisis," *Business Week*, 17 November 1973, 72.

112. "Gloom sets in as Squeeze Hits Consultants," *Financial Times*, 5 March 1971; Hugh Parker, notes for "A McKinsey Scrapbook," to appear in *Month by Month* in 1994.

113. Jonathan C. Randall, "U.S. Abroad: New Competition," *The Washington Post*, 11 January 1970, 101.

114. McKinsey & Company, "Economics of the Firm: Meeting of New Partners, New York Office," 21 August 1972.

115. "Consultancy Boom in Public Sector," *The Times*, 12 June 1972.

116. Maurice Corina, "Consultants Stalking Whitehall's Corridors," *The Times*, 26 January 1971, 17; "Consultancy Boom in Public Sector," *The Times*, 12 June 1972, 18.

117. "Government faces new clash over 'McKinsey Study of Car Industry,'" *The Times*, 30 May 1975, 17; "Whitehall Names Management Firm for Shipbuilding Advisory Role, *The Times*, 6 June 1972, 17; "Future of the Motor Cycle Industry," *The Times*, 7 August 1975, 13.

118. Harold Wilson, *Final Term: The Labour Government, 1974-1976* (London: Weidenfeld & Nicolson, 1979), 34–5; Mark Wickham-Jones, *Economic Strategy and the Labour Party: Politics and Policy-Making, 1970–83* (London: MacMillan Press, 1996), 147.

119. "Planning Another Bankrupt State Industry," *The Times*, 1 August 1974, 15.

120. Wickham-Jones, *Economic Strategy and the Labour Party*, 99.

121. Louis Galambos and David Milobsky, "Organizing and Reorganizing the World Bank, 1946–1972: A Comparative Perspective," *Business History Review*, 69 (Summer 1995), 180 ; Martin Tolchin, "Ethics Board Asks Lindsay to Alter Consultant Pacts: Calls for Publicity in Hiring of Firms and End of Use of City Titles by Them," *The New York Times*, 10 August 1970, 1.

122. "Beame Withholds Payment to Consultant, Questioning Ethics," *The New York Times*, 3 July 1970, 1; Martin Tolchin, "City Aides and Beame Renew Battle Over Consultants, *The New York Times*, 9 July 1970, 30.

123. Bower, *Perspective on McKinsey*, 170 [italics in original].

124. House of Commons, "Dramatic Fall in British Motor Cycle Exports: Further State Funds for Industry Ruled Out," *The Times*, 1 August 1975, 8. The original Parliamentary debate is also available in *Hansard*.

125. Henry Mintzberg, "The 'Honda Effect' Revisited," *California Management Review*, Vol. 38, No. 4 (Summer 1996), 78.

126. Andrew Mair, "Learning from Honda," *Journal of Management Studies*, Vol. 36, No. 1 (January 1999), 25.

127. Pankaj Ghemawat, "Competition and Business Strategy in Historical Perspective," *Business History Review*, Vol. 76 (Spring 2002), 45–6.

128. Robert Locke, *The Collapse of the American Management Mystique* (Oxford: Oxford University Press, 1996), 164.

129. Thomas J. Peters and Robert H. Waterman, Jr., *In Search of Excellence: Lessons from America's Best-Run Companies* (New York: Warner Brothers, 1982).

130. "French Chemical-Textile Giant Retains McKinsey & Co. to Make a Reorganization Study and Recommendations," *Business Week*, 20 January 1968.

131. "Too Little Cash, Too Much Waste in NHS," *The Times*, 9 April 1969, 2.

132. This trend was noted in an article on the growth of management consulting from 1955 to 1975 in the German publication, *Die Welt*, 13 June 1975.

133. I am, of course, making an allusion to Kuhn's classic work on paradigm shifts among competing scientific theories, see Thomas Kuhn, *The Structure of Scientific Revolutions* (Chicago: The University of Chicago Press, 1962).

134. "Randnotizen zu Heberlein/Arowa," *Die Weltwoche*, 31 January 1969.

8. SELLING CORPORATE CULTURE: CODIFYING
AND COMMODIFYING PROFESSIONALISM

1. The management literature on corporate culture is vast, but several important works from the early 1990s include: Joanne Martin, *Culture in Organizations: Three Perspectives* (New York: Oxford University Press, 1992); John Kotter and James L. Heskett, *Corporate Culture and Performance* (New York: The Free Press, 1992); and Gideon Kunda, *Engineering Culture: Control and Commitment in a High-Tech Corporation* (Philadelphia: Temple University Press, 1993).

2. Historians employing the concept of "corporate culture" include John Griffiths, "'Give my Regards to Uncle Billy:' The Rites and Rituals of Company Life at Lever Brothers, c.1900 – c.1990," *Business History*, Vol. 37, No. 4 (October 1995), 25–45 and Charles Dellheim, "The Creation of a Company Culture: Cadburys, 1861–1931," *American Historical Review*, Vol. 92, No. 1 (1987), 13–44. For an economic analysis of the value of strong corporate cultures see Mark Casson, *The Economics of Business Culture* (Oxford: Oxford University Press, 1991) and David M. Kreps, "Corporate Culture and Economic Theory," in James E. Alt and Kenneth A. Shepsle (eds.), *Perspectives on Positive Political Economy* (Cambridge: Cambridge University Press, 1990), 90–143. For examples of cultural criticism employing variants of the "corporate culture" paradigm see Thomas Frank, *The Conquest of Cool: Business Culture, Counterculture, and the Rise of Hip Consumerism* (Chicago: University of Chicago Press, 1997) and the special section of *Social Text 44* from 1995 (Vol. 13, No. 3) on "Corporate Culture" introduced by Evan Watkins, with commentary by James Livingston, and featuring articles by Avery Gordon, Christopher Newfield, and Tom Moylan on topics like "The Work of Corporate Culture."

3. On the continuities between Mayo's research on human relations and the corporate culture literature, see Nora K. Moran, "'The Importance of Being Excellent:' Human Relations and 'Corporate Culture,' 1930–1995," *Essays in Economic and Business History*, Vol. XIV (1996), 229–48. For the historical setting of Elton Mayo's pioneering work in the 1930s, see Richard Gillespie, *Manufacturing Knowledge: A History of the Hawthorne Experiments* (New York: Cambridge University Press, 1991). Despite Stanley Davis' claim that he coined the term "corporate culture" in 1970, sociologist Harold Wilenky was the first academic whom I have found, to use the phrase. In 1967, Wilensky employed "corporate culture" to mean "the organizational context of work" in his article in the *American Sociological Review*. The term "corporate culture" did not, however, gain widespread currency until the 1980s, and, when the study of "corporate culture" took off, it was not as a direct result of Wilensky's pioneering scholarship. See Harold L. Wilensky and Jack Ladinsky, "From Religious Community to Occupational Group: Structural Assimilation Among Professors, Lawyers, and Engineers," *American Sociological Review*, Vol. 32, No. 4 (August 1967), 542. The fact that Stanley Davis explicitly claims that he invented the term "corporate culture," however, suggests just how important the phrase quickly became. Stanley Davis, *Managing Corporate Culture* (Cambridge: Ballinger, 1984), 1; Avery Gordon, "The Work of Corporate Culture," 6.

4. Thomas J. Peters and Robert H. Waterman, Jr., *In Search of Excellence: Lessons from America's Best-Run Companies* (New York: Harper & Row, 1982).

5. Sandra Salmans, "New Vogue: Company Culture," *The New York Times*, 7 January 1983, D1.

6. This is a particular example of a recurring, but rarely analyzed, general problem within the social sciences. Social scientists frequently create universal models based upon a particular historical, regional, or political example and later, forgetting these models' particularist origins, apply the same theories to analyze the original phenomena upon which the generalized model was based. For example, consider the inherent problems involved in using Freudian psychoanalysis to dissect the origins of Freud's own work, employing modernization theory to examine the path of Western economic development, or, as historian David Hollinger has pointed out, applying Robert Merton's sociological theories to analyze democratic society in the 1930s. See David Hollinger, "The Defense of Democracy and Robert K. Merton's Formulation of the Scientific Ethos," in *Science, Jews, and Secular Culture: Studies in Mid-Twentieth Century American Intellectual History* (Princeton: Princeton University Press, 1996), 80–96.

7. During the 1960s, organizational studies for corporate customers consistently made up one-fourth of McKinsey & Company's overall billings. Statistics derived from McKinsey & Company, "Analysis of Firm Practice by Industry, F/Y 1959–1965 Incl.," 1966, 1, and McKinsey & Company, "Dollar

Distribution of Total Billings among Industrial Categories: Fiscal Year 1966 Through 1970 Inclusive," 1971, n.p., both in Corporate Archives, McKinsey & Company.

8. Thomas C. Hayes, "McKinsey & Co., Problem Solvers," *The New York Times* (19 August 1979), D8. Michael Porter would found his own strategy consulting firm, Monitor, just three years later.

9. For a more academic formulation of Peters and Waterman's argument for which the authors give Anthony Athos credit, see Robert H. Waterman, Jr., Thomas J. Peters, and Julien R. Phillips, "Structure is Not Organization," *Business Horizons* (June 1980), 14–26. Tom Peters's later work, in turn, inspired a cottage industry of cultural criticism of his theories as the penultimate expression of postmodern society. See, for example, the analysis of Peters's writings peppered throughout Thomas Frank, "Why Johnny Can't Dissent," Bill Boisvert, "Apostles of the New Entrepreneur: Business Books and the Management Crisis," and Edward Castleton, "Post-Urban, Post-Industrial, But Never Post-Elite," anthologized in Thomas Frank and Matt Weiland (eds.), *Commodify Your Dissent: Salvos from the Baffler* (New York: W. W. Norton & Co., 1997), 31–45; 81–98; and 216–22.

10. For the links between McKinsey & Company and the initial scholarship on corporate culture, see the authors' acknowledgments in all of the following: Terrence E. Deal and Allan A. Kennedy, *Corporate Cultures: The Rites and Rituals of Corporate Life* (Reading, MA: Addison-Wesley Publishing Company, 1982), iii–v; Richard Pascale and Anthony Athos, *The Art of Japanese Management: Applications for American Executives* (New York: Simon and Schuster, 1981), 7–14; and Peters and Waterman, *In Search of Excellence*, ix-xii. Mauro Guillén, among others, describes these three books as the centerpieces of the corporate culture movement. Mauro F. Guillén, *Models of Management: Work, Authority, and Organization in a Comparative Perspective* (Chicago: University of Chicago Press, 1994), 289–90.

11. Deal and Kennedy, *Corporate Cultures*, 4. For a restatement of Bower's definition and the assertion that Deal and Kennedy's work was a "McKinsey book," see Anthony Sampson, *Company Man: The Rise and Fall of Corporate Life* (New York: Harper Collins, 1995), 214.

12. Marvin Bower, *The Will to Lead* (Boston: Harvard Business School Press, 1998), 63. Bower's remark was not simply the rewriting of history from hindsight. Even if Marvin Bower did not use the term "corporate culture," until the 1980s, Bower had indeed self-consciously reshaped the "personality" of McKinsey & Company from 1933 onward. See Marvin Bower, "Development of the Firm's Personality: Looking Back Twenty Years and Ahead Twenty," October 1953, 1–2, Corporate Archives, McKinsey & Company.

13. By the late 1990s, large corporate clients of McKinsey & Company naturally associated Marvin Bower's often-repeated definition of corporate culture with McKinsey, but not necessarily with Bower. See Peter I. Bijur, Chairman and

CEO, Texaco Inc., "Changing the Corporate Culture: A Competitive Impera-
tive," *World Energy*, Vol. 1, No. 1 (1998), 21–6.

14. Marvin Bower, *Perspective on McKinsey* (New York: McKinsey & Company,
1979), 164–5.

15. For a different perspective on the same era at McKinsey, see Amar V. Bhidé,
"Building the Professional Firm: McKinsey & Co.: 1939–68," (Boston: Harvard
Business School Working Paper #95-010, 1995).

16. Other competing management consulting firms soon began to promote their
own research on corporate culture. For the surveys performed by the Hay Group
(a large human resources consulting firm) on the "management climate" at
several hundred organizations and subsequently reinterpreted within the corporate culture paradigm, see Nancy DiTomaso, George G. Gordon, and Ted
H. Szatrowski, "Corporate Culture and Financial Performance: A Preliminary
Analysis," in Amitai Etzioni and Paul R. Lawrence (ed.), *Socio-Economics:
Toward a New Synthesis* (Armonk, NY: M. E. Sharpe, 1991), 275–90. Not
coincidentally, both sociologist Avery Gordon and cultural critic Christopher Newfield have analyzed prominent consultants to understand the broader
impact of corporate culture. See Avery Gordon, "The Work of Corporate
Culture: Diversity Management," and Christopher Newfield, "Corporate Plea-
sures for a Corporate Planet," in *Social Text 44*, Vol. 13, No. 3 (1995), 3–30;
31–44.

17. Tom Peters explicitly argued that McKinsey & Company had become the "premier role model for almost everyone else" in the emerging knowledge economy. See, Tom Peters, *Liberation Management: Necessary Disorganization for the
Nanosecond Nineties* (New York: Alfred A. Knopf, 1992), 133. Similar accounts
by other former McKinsey consultants, including Harvey Golub of American
Express, have stressed their imitation of McKinsey & Company within their
adopted organizations. Bower, *The Will to Lead*, 18.

18. On the jurisdictional battles between professionals and their maintenance
of professional fields, see the introduction to Andrew Abbott, *The System of
Professions: An Essay on the Division of Expert Labor* (Chicago: University
of Chicago Press, 1988), 1–31.

19. See, for example, John G. Neukom, *McKinsey Memoirs: A Personal Perspective* (New York: McKinsey & Company, 1975), 28–9; George S. Armstrong,
*An Engineer in Wall Street*, (New York: George S. Armstrong & Co., 1962),
5–7.

20. See, for example, the 1944 article on management consulting in *Fortune* magazine that described the varied professional fields from which the leading management consulting firms emerged, yet emphasized the overall unity of the field.
"Doctors of Management," *Fortune* (July 1944): 144–6.

21. Magali Sarfatti Larson, *The Rise of Professionalism: A Sociological Analysis*
(Philadelphia: Temple University Press, 1973), 155.

22. Richard M. Paget, "New Parameters of Professionalism in Management Consulting," *Management Consulting in the 1970s: Proceedings of the North American Conference of Management Consultants* (New York: Institute of Management Consultants, 1972), 16. Paget's comments were, in part, a barb aimed at Marvin Bower who opposed Citibank's purchase of Cresap, McCormick and Paget during the 1970s on the grounds that management consultants could not take an objective, professional stance if they ultimately had to answer to outside shareholders.

23. On the inherent compatibility between professionals and corporate hierarchies, see Kenneth J. Lipartito and Paul J. Miranti, "Professions and Organizations in Twentieth Century America," *Social Science Quarterly*, Vol. 79, No. 2 (June 1998), 301–20. Professionals not only commonly serve bureaucracy, but also employ bureaucratic forms within their own organizations – as sociologist Andrew Abbott points out, "size and bureaucracy confer competitive advantage *within*" professions. Abbott, *The System of Professions*, 153.

24. Bower, *Perspective on McKinsey*, 38.

25. Marvin Bower, the architect of McKinsey & Company's professionalization, consciously pushed his colleagues in New York to use the legislative momentum of the 1930s to the firm's advantage since Bower recognized, "how long it took older professions to get established and gain stature." Bower, *Perspective on McKinsey*, 38.

26. On the "revolt of the engineers," see Edwin T. Layton, Jr., *The Revolt of the Engineers: Social Responsibility and the American Engineering Profession* (Baltimore: The Johns Hopkins University Press, 1986), 154–72. On the attempts by cost accountants to form a new professional discipline, see Gerald Berk, "Discursive Cartels: Uniform Cost Accountants among American Manufacturers before the New Deal," *Business and Economic History*, Vol. 26, No. 1 (Fall 1997), 229–51; S. Paul Gardner, *Evolution of Cost Accounting to 1925* (University, Alabama: University of Alabama Press, 1954); Sharon Hartman Strom, *Beyond the Typewriter: Gender, Class, and the Origins of Modern American Office Work* (Urbana: University of Chicago Press, 1992), 24–35; H. Thomas Johnson and Robert S. Kaplan, *Relevance Lost: The Rise and Fall of Management Accounting* (Boston: Harvard Business School Press, 1987), 125–51.

27. On George S. May's unscrupulous sales methods, see Hal Higdon, *The Business Healers* (New York: Random House, 1969), 149–70. For a big-screen retelling of Charles Bedaux's rise from a pimp in his native France to become an influential American consultant and, ultimately, a Nazi collaborator, see the documentary film, *The Champagne Safari*, dir. George Ungar (1996), released by Field Seven Films, Inc., Toronto, Ontario.

28. Steven Kreis, "The Diffusion of Scientific Management: The Bedaux Company in America and Britain," in *A Mental Revolution: Scientific Management since Taylor* (Columbus: Ohio State University Press, 1992), 160.

29. Indeed, it was Charles Bedaux who hosted their marriage after Edward abdicated the throne in 1936 to marry Wallis Simpson. Jim Christy, *The Price of Power: A Biography of Charles Eugene Bedaux* (Toronto, 1984), 138–52.

30. Janet Flanner, "Annals of Collaboration: Equivalism," *The New Yorker* (22 September, 6 October, and 13 October 1945), 28–41, 32–43, and 32–47.

31. Janet Flanner concluded her three part article on Bedaux, quoting one of his more remarkable speeches to a group of businessmen: "[a man] is a patriot, and a sincere one, but when his money is concerned, he blissfully commits treason." Flanner, "Annals of Collaboration," 13 October 1945, 47.

32. George S. May should not be confused with George O. May, the influential accountant who was chairman of Price Waterhouse. On George O. May's career, see David Grayson Allen and Kathleen McDermott, *Accounting for Success: A History of Price Waterhouse in America, 1890–1990* (Boston: Harvard Business School Press, 1993), 66–75.

33. Perrin S. Stryker, "The Relentless George S. May," *Fortune*, Vol. 49 (June 1954), 140–1.

34. Stryker, "The Relentless George S. May," 198 [bracketed explanation from original].

35. Higdon, *The Business Healers*, 153–4.

36. Stryker, "The Relentless George S. May," 198. In recent years, as the large accounting firms have moved into consulting services, they too have emphasized that consultancies can serve not only multinationals but small, independent businesses. Firms like Andersen Consulting have marketed their services to smaller customers, in part, through sports events like the "Andersen Consulting World Championship of Golf," just like George S. May.

37. Higdon, *The Business Healers*, 153; Stryker, "The Relentless George S. May," 141. Years later, when Cresap, McCormick and Paget closed their offices in Mexico, a consultant in McKinsey & Company's office in Mexico City wrote the following addendum to his memo: "This means that we are the only major U.S. Firm with an office in Mexico. I am obviously excluding George S. May who reentered last year but has already encountered problems because of the bad reputation they left behind 10 years ago. Among other things, the local American Chamber of Commerce refused them membership." Mr. Lutz, "Cresap, McCormick & Paget," 26 April 1974, Corporate Archives, McKinsey & Company.

38. Such reminders still exist. In the 1996 ranking of the largest management consulting firms in the world, Proudfoot, PLC, the consulting firm founded by Alexander Proudfoot, who began his career at George S. May, was the 30th largest management consulting firm in the world, sitting between Michael Porter's Monitor Company and the McKinsey & Company spin-off, Mitchell Madison Group. George S. May International was ranked 33rd. *Consultants News*, "40 Largest Management Consulting Firms," 1997.

39. Eliot Freidson, *Professional Powers: A Study of the Institutionalization of Formal Knowledge* (Chicago: University of Chicago Press, 1988), 65; Theodore Caplow, "The Sequence of Professionalization," in *Professionalization*, Howard M. Vollmer and Donald L. Mills (eds.), (Englewood Cliffs, New Jersey: Prentice Hall, Inc., 1966), 20.

40. Richard M. Paget, "Management Consulting as a Profession," Presented at the "Forty Fifth Anniversary Meeting, Booz Allen & Hamilton, Chicago, Illinois," 15 November 1958, 7, Corporate Archives, Association of Management Consulting Firms (ACME), New York City; David Grayson Allen, "Bound by their Past or in Transition? An Analysis of U.S. Management Consulting Associations," *Journal of Management Consulting*, Vol. 3, No. 1 (1986), 27–35.

41. "ACME has worked out a complete program for the establishment of professional standards in management consulting. Its program would be extra-legal and would differ from state or Federal licensing or registration in that the process would be voluntary." Philip W. Shay, Executive Director, ACME, "A Look at the Management Consulting Profession," 1958, 25, Corporate Archives, Association of Management Consulting Firms (ACME).

42. Marvin Bower, "Comments," *Journal of Management Consulting*, Vol. 3, No. 1 (1986), 36 [emphasis in original].

43. Vincent Carosso, *More than a Century of Investment Banking: Kidder, Peabody & Co.* (New York: McGraw Hill & Co., 1979); Jackson Lears, *Fables of Abundance: A Cultural History of Advertising in America* (New York: Basic Books, 1994), 89.

44. Ernest Greenwood, "The Elements of Professionalization," in *Professionalization*, Vollmer and Mills (eds.), 9; Freidson, *Professional Powers*, 20–40. Interestingly, consultants' lack of a social mission – a calling – differentiated them from the ideological Taylorists and cost accountants who had previously dominated the field.

45. Joel Dean, "The Place of Management Counsel in Business," *Harvard Business Review*, Vol. 16, No. 4 (Summer 1958), 451. H. Guy Crockett, the managing partner at McKinsey & Company, echoed Dean's observation in 1945, explaining to McKinsey staff members that "We cannot call this a profession in the same sense that we think of the practice of medicine or law. It is a very young profession, comparatively speaking, unorganized, with qualifications for practice only loosely defined, with no public controls of practitioners comparable with those governing other professions, and with comparatively few people outside of its own membership understanding how management consultants work." H. G. Crockett, "Background of the Profession," 3 November 1945, 1, Corporate Archives, McKinsey & Company.

46. Richard M. Paget, "Management Consulting as a Profession," Presented at the "Forty Fifth Anniversary Meeting, Booz, Allen & Hamilton, Chicago, Illinois," 15 November 1958, 3, Corporate Archives, Association of Management

Consulting Firms (ACME), New York City; Harold L. Wilensky, "The Professionalization of Everyone?" *The American Journal of Sociology*, Vol. 70, No. 2 (September 1964), 137–58.

47. Hal Higdon, *The Business Healers* (New York: Random House, 1969), 27.

48. Talcott Parsons, "Professional Groups and Social Structure," in *Professionalization*, Howard M. Vollmer and Donald L. Mills (eds.), (Englewood Cliffs, New Jersey: Prentice Hall, Inc., 1966), 55–7; Wilbert E. Moore, *The Professions: Roles and Rules* (New York: Russell Sage, 1970), 47–9; Terence Johnson, "Imperialism and the Professions: Notes on the Development of Professional Occupations in Britain's Colonies and the New States," in *Professionalisation and Social Change*, Paul Halmos (ed.), (Keele, Staffordshire: Sociological Review Monograph No. 20, 1973), 281–310. Sociologist Magali Sarfatti Larson describes how "most studies implicitly or explicitly present professionalization as an instance of the complex process of 'modernization.'" Larson, *The Rise of Professionalism*, xvi.

49. As McKinsey's internal manual described it: "As a matter of policy, the firm approaches new engagement activities on a professional basis. This means simply that we carry on this phase of our practice in a dignified, restrained, non-promotional manner similar to that which would be employed by a lawyer associated with one of the larger legal firms." McKinsey & Company, "New Engagement and Executive Relations Guide," May 1945, 2, Corporate Archives, McKinsey & Company.

50. As historian JoAnne Brown argues: "the very vagueness and multiplicity of metaphorical meaning is what makes [professional metaphors] so powerful a social adhesive." See, JoAnne Brown, *The Definition of a Profession: The Authority of Metaphor in the History of Intelligence Testing* (Princeton: Princeton University Press, 1992), 13.

51. Andrew Abbott, *The System of Professions: An Essay on the Division of Expert Labor* (Chicago: University of Chicago Press, 1988), 99–100.

52. For example, James C. Olsen, a consultant at Booz Allen & Hamilton delivered a talk at the American Management Association in 1951 entitled "Scientific Marketing – A Vital Instrument in the Business Doctor's Kit," outlining Booz Allen & Hamilton use of "diagnosticians." As David Fox, an associate at McKinsey & Company, reported to Marvin Bower, "He developed this theme extensively with 'doctor', 'operation', 'patients', 'medical clinic', 'diagnosis', etc." David L. Fox to Marvin Bower, "Talk by J. C. Olsen before AMA 2/27/51," 1 March 1951, 3, Corporate Archives, McKinsey & Company.

53. "Doctors of Management," *Fortune* (July 1944), 143. Of course, *Fortune* magazine quickly conceded that, "many [consultants] don't like the term 'management doctors' with its suggestions of illness and bedside manners." See also, "Business Doctors," *The Wall Street Journal* (22 May 1947); "Doctors or Businessmen?" *Mechanical Engineering* (April 1947); and "What Makes

Business Call in the Doctor?" *Business Week* (11 December 1954): 66–88. The "doctor-patient" metaphor was extensively described, analyzed, and ultimately rejected in Seymour Tilles, "Understanding the Consultant's Role," *Harvard Business Review* (November-December 1961), 90–1. For the most dramatic use of the metaphor, see Edward M. Glaser, "Organizational Arteriosclerosis: Its Diagnosis and Treatment," *Advanced Management Journal*, Vol. 30 (January 1965), 21–8.

54. Paul Starr, *The Social Transformation of American Medicine* (New York: Basic Books, 1982), 13–17.

55. Thomas J. Watson, Jr. and Peter Petre, *Father, Son & Co.: My Life at IBM and Beyond* (New York: Bantam Books, 1990), 294.

56. Worse yet for management consulting has been the recurring image of the consultant as a "quack" – not just unable to save patients, but actively contributing to their demise. "Business Doctors – and Quacks," *Kiplinger Magazine: The Changing Times* (June 1947). For a more recent example, consider the title of John Micklethwait and Adrian Wooldridge's, *The Witch Doctors: Making Sense of the Management Gurus* (New York: Times Books, 1996).

57. Bower, *Perspective on McKinsey*, 164. Of course eliminating the image of sickness was not easy, see "Management Consultants: Good Medicine for Ailing Companies," *Time* (23 April 1956). For an even earlier incarnation of the "business doctor," see the regular column in *System* magazine entitled "The Business Doctor," from the 1900s.

58. Perrin Stryker, "The Ambitious Consultants," *Fortune* (May 1954), 83. Bower repeated this phrase to the other consultants at McKinsey to emphasize that they should not use medical analogies. See Marvin Bower to E. E. Smith, "Publicity," 19 October 1962, Corporate Archives, McKinsey & Company. Bower's message would eventually take hold. In 1967, the President of Booz Allen & Hamilton, Charles Bower, explained to *Forbes* magazine that he felt "cautious about [working for] sick companies. 'We work with very few companies that are on the verge of disaster.'" "The Instant Executives," *Forbes* (15 November 1967), 32. By 1970, *Barron's* would report that "rather than as healers for sick enterprises, [management consultants] are thought of as problem solvers who help healthy companies become even more prosperous." "Corporate Think-Tanks: Management Consulting Firms Have Come to Wall Street," *Barron's* (2 March 1970), 14.

59. Larson, *The Rise of Professionalism*, 155.

60. Harry Arthur Hopf, "Some Observations on the Background, Scope and Significance of the Function of the Management Engineer," *Advanced Management*, Vol. 5, No. 4 (October–December, 1940), 182–6; "Management Audits and the Outside Consultant," *Industry* (March 1950).

61. One other problem was nomenclature – licensed engineers in the early 1940s threatened to sue consultants who referred to themselves as engineers since

they were not certified by the state. "Doctors of Management," *Fortune* (July 1944), 208.

62. McKinsey & Company, *Supplementing Successful Management* (New York, McKinsey & Company, 1940), 2. On the unanimous agreement among the partners at McKinsey on the specific text of the brochure, see Bower, *Perspective on McKinsey*, 54–5. While most consulting firms emphasized their "professional" nature, McKinsey & Company was particularly likely to make an explicit comparison with the law. See by comparison the brochures created by Cresap, McCormick and Paget. Cresap, McCormick and Paget's brochures from the 1950s and 1960s declared that "Cresap, McCormick & Paget provides objective counsel to management in commerce, industry, government, and nonprofit organizations. The size, professional standing, and qualifications of the firm's staff enable it to solve a wide range of management problems." Cresap, McCormick and Paget, "Professional Counsel for Management of Hospitals, Clinics, and Health Agencies," n.d., 2., Corporate Archives, Towers Perrin, Valhalla, New York.

63. Wayne K. Hobson, "Symbol of the New Profession: Emergence of the Large Law Firm, 1870–1915," in *The New High Priests: Lawyers in Post-Civil War America*, Gerald W. Gawalt (ed.), (Westport: Greenwood Press, 1984), 3–4.

64. Consultants wanted to adopt the "scientism" of engineering, but by the 1940s, the previously common metaphorical association between "science," employed in "Scientific Management," and consulting had largely fallen out of circulation. Management consulting firms, by not claiming the "scientific method" of scientific management, sought to distance themselves from Taylorism. Thus, consultants rarely chose physicists, chemists, or biologists as reference points. A rare exception was Marvin Bower's analysis of the "challenge of problem-solving" using a quotation from the Nobel Prize winning biologist Alber Szent-Gyorgi. See Marvin Bower, "General Management Consulting," *Career Guide: A Harvard Business School Student Publication*, Vol. 2, No. 2 (February 1962), 5.

65. Edwin G. Nourse to Walter S. Carpenter, 5 October 1945, page 1, and Walter S. Carpenter to Walter G. Nourse, 18 October 1945, page 1, file: "Misc. Correspondence, 1945," box 829, acc. 542, Carpenter Papers, Hagley Museum and Library, Wilmington, Delaware. Obviously, Brandeis's famous call to make business a profession had not made much of an impression on Carpenter, see Louis Brandeis, *Business – A Profession* (Boston: Small, Maynard & Company, 1914). Interestingly, Carpenter's unwillingness to assume the mantle of "professional management" clashes with Charles Cheape's interpretation of Walter Carpenter as a self-conscious "professional executive." See Charles W. Cheape, *Strictly Business: Walter Carpenter at Du Pont and General Motors* (Baltimore: The Johns Hopkins University Press, 1995), xv–xvii.

66. Edwin G. Nourse to Walter S. Carpenter, 31 October 1945, page 1, file: "Misc. Correspondence, 1945," box 829, acc. 542, Carpenter Papers, Hagley Museum

and Library. Less than a year later, Nourse would become the first chairman of the Council of Economic Advisors under President Truman. On Nourse's role in the postwar institutionalization of economists, see Alfred L. Malabre, *Lost Prophets: An Insiders History of the Modern Economists* (Boston: Harvard Business School Press, 1994), 47–9.

67. As a writer from *Fortune* magazine explained in 1954, "Consultants, unlike doctors and lawyers, have no recognized standards of training, do not have to qualify for a license to practice, and have no professional society that can enforce standards by disbarment." Stryker, "The Ambitious Consultants," 84.

68. In accounting or law, for example, individual practitioners are assumed to have minimum levels of competence because they have been certified, even if affiliation with a prestigious firm does impart additional authority. In contrast, management consulting firms vouched for their staff through their employment within the firm. See McKinsey & Company's description of its staff in the firm's brochure: McKinsey & Company, *Supplementing Successful Management* (New York, McKinsey & Company, 1940), 15–16.

69. William J. Goode, "The Theoretical Limits of Professionalization," in *The Semi-Professions and Their Organization*, Amitai Etzioni (ed.) (New York: The Free Press, 1969), 273.

70. H. G. Crockett, "Background of the Profession: Annual Training Conference – November 3, 1945," 3 November 1945, 1, Corporate Archives, McKinsey & Company.

71. McKinsey & Company was a particularly remarkable example of an institution where professional language mattered very deeply. As Marvin Bower, the architect of the firm's postwar transformation explained, "terminology is important." Marvin Bower, "Meeting of Members, McKinsey & Company," 13 January 1945, 50, Corporate Archives, McKinsey & Company.

72. As Bower later explained, "a successful professional strategy requires building distinctiveness in the values of the firm's services...." Marvin Bower, "The Role of Strategy in a Professional Firm," in *Supplement of Perspective on McKinsey* (Mimeograph, McKinsey & Company, 1977), 67–9.

73. Marvin Bower, "Meeting of Members, McKinsey & Company," 13 January 1945, 5–6, Corporate Archives, McKinsey & Company.

74. Marvin Bower, "Meeting of Members, McKinsey & Company," 13 January 1945, 22, Corporate Archives, McKinsey & Company.

75. Richard M. Paget, "New Parameters of Professionalism in Management Consulting," *Management Consulting in the 1970s: Proceedings of the North American Conference of Management Consultants*, (New York: Institute of Management Consultants, 1972), 16.

76. Cresap, McCormick and Paget, for example, despite performing innovative studies for the legal profession, particularly the Bar Association of New York, did not emphasize "professionalism." Cresap, McCormick and Paget, "The

Inkling: The Weekly Newssheet of Cresap, McCormick & Paget," 1 May 1954, 2. Similarly, the consultants from Cresap, McCormick and Paget did not discuss professionalism in their analysis of N. W. Ayer and Son, one of the largest advertising agencies in the United States, nor in their survey of the elite corporate law firm of Dewey, Ballantine, Bushby, Palmer & Wood. See, Cresap, McCormick and Paget, "N. W. Ayer & Son, Inc.: Organizational Survey," March 1967; and Cresap, McCormick and Paget, "Dewey Ballantine, Bushby, Palmer & Wood: Survey of Office Services and Administration," March 1955, both in Corporate Archives, Towers Perrin, Valhalla, New York.

77. For an analysis of why competing firms adopt different strategies to position themselves within a market, see Michael E. Porter, "How Competitive Forces Shape Strategy," in *Strategy: Seeking and Securing Competitive Advantage*, Cynthia A. Montgomery and Michael E. Porter (eds.), (Boston: Harvard Business School Press, 1991), 22–3; Glenn R. Carroll, "A Sociological View on Why Firms Differ," in *Fundamental Issues in Strategy*, Richard Rumelt, Dan E. Schendel, and David J. Teece (eds.), (Boston: Harvard Business School Press, 1994), 271–90.

78. Jim Bowman, *Booz, Allen & Hamilton: Seventy Years of Client Service, 1914–1984* (Chicago: Booz, Allen & Hamilton, 1984), 13, 26; George L. Berkwitt, "Rise of the Service Conglomerates," *Dun's Review and Modern Industry* (December 1967), 67–8; "The Instant Executives," Forbes (15 November 1967), 38.

79. "Management Experts Thrive on Own Advice," *Business Week* (23 April 1960), 116. In the same issue of *Business Week* Jim Allen confused the professional/business distinction even further, explaining that "This is a business you live. The real professional can never get away from it." "Management Experts Thrive on Own Advice," 118. Charles Bowen, James Allen's successor at Booz Allen & Hamilton, agreed with Allen, arguing on several occasions with Marvin Bower that consulting was a "business, not a profession." Bowman, *Booz, Allen & Hamilton*, 79–80. However sharply Booz Allen & Hamilton and McKinsey & Company may have drawn the line on their differences over the importance of professionalization, it should be emphasized that Booz Allen & Hamilton stood in the middle of a continuum of professional standards with McKinsey & Company at one end and George S. May Co. at the other end. Booz Allen & Hamilton, for example, despite the lack of an explicit professional ideology, adopted a code of ethics – a typical professional device – drafted by Carl Hamilton. Bowman, *Booz, Allen & Hamilton*, viii.

80. Marvin Bower, "Meeting of Members, McKinsey & Company," 13 January 1945, 49, Corporate Archives, McKinsey & Company.

81. Neukom, *McKinsey Memoirs*, 39.

82. Marvin Bower, "Meeting of Members, McKinsey & Company," 13 January 1945, 3, Corporate Archives, McKinsey & Company.

83. Marvin Bower, "Meeting of Members, McKinsey & Company," 13 January 1945, 58, Corporate Archives, McKinsey & Company. See also, H. G. Crockett, "Background of the Profession: Annual Training Conference – November 3, 1945," 3 November 1945, 1, Corporate Archives, McKinsey & Company.

84. Bower, *Perspective on McKinsey*, 157; John Merwin, "The McKinsey Mystique: Is it Worth the Price?" *Forbes* (19 October 1987), 27; David H. Maister, *Managing the Professional Service Firm* (New York: Free Press, 1993), 310.

85. Christopher D. McKenna, "The Origins of Modern Management Consulting," *Business and Economic History*, Vol. 24, No. 1 (Fall 1995), 51–8.

86. Neukom, *McKinsey Memoirs*, 32–4, Arthur Andersen & Co., *The First Sixty Years*, 9–11.

87. McKinsey & Company, *Supplementing Successful Management*, 15.

88. As *Business Week* summarized the staffing problem in 1960, "such men are not the easiest to supervise nor to retain as members of an organization. And they're hard to find." "Management Experts Thrive on Own Advice," *Business Week*, (23 April 1960), 112. For a general discussion on professional staffing as a perennial problem, see David Maister's chapter on "Surviving the People Crisis," in Maister, *Managing the Professional Services Firm*, 189–204.

89. Robert T. Swaine, *The Cravath Firm and Its Predecessors. 1819–1948* (New York: privately printed, 1948); on the history of Cravath's system see Robert L. Nelson, *Partners with Power: The Social Transformations of the Large Law Firm*, (Berkeley: University of California Press, 1988), 71–3.

90. Marc Galanter and Thomas Palay, *Tournament of Lawyers: The Transformation of the Big Law Firm* (Chicago: The University of Chicago, 1991), 9. See also Erwin O. Smigel, *The Wall Street Lawyer: Professional Organization Man?* (Glencoe, Ill.: The Free Press, 1964), 114–15.

91. On the economic rationality of the "up-or-out" system, see Ronald Gilson and Robert Mnookin, "Coming of Age in the Corporate Law Firm: The Economics of Associate Career Patterns," *Stanford Law Review*, Vol. 41 (1989): 567–95.

92. Wayne Hobson, *The American Legal System and the Organizational Society, 1890–1930* (New York: Garland, 1986), 200.

93. Marvin Bower, "Report of Partner in Charge of Public Relations: Fiscal Year Ending September 2, 1944," 22 September 1944, 12; Marvin Bower to "Partners, Principals, Associate Managers," "The Cravath Firm," 7 January 1952, Corporate Archives, McKinsey & Company.

94. Bower, *Perspective on McKinsey* (New York: McKinsey & Company, 1977), 178.

95. McKinsey & Company, "Minutes of Planning Committee Meeting," 26 May 1954, 1–3, Corporate Archives, McKinsey & Company. As Bower subsequently explained the rationale behind this policy, "the management of any group that want to preserve and increase its effectiveness in perpetuity – e.g., the university – will separate the less effective." Bower, *Perspective on McKinsey*, 223.

96. Alfred D. Chandler, *Strategy and Structure: Chapters in the History of the American Industrial Enterprise* (Cambridge, Massachusetts: MIT Press, 1962), 14. Legal sociologist Robert Nelson disagrees with this interpretation of causality within professional firms. Nelson argues that the varied bureaucratic forms that firms adopt have had little correlation to the intensity of their commitment to professionalism. Nelson believes, instead, that external forces and internal politics have been far more important in shaping the internal organization of law firms than professionalism. Nelson's thoughtful analysis, however, does not leave room for the innovation in organizational practices – in this case innovation through imitation – that might arise because of a firm's strong ideology. See Nelson, *Partners with Power*, 120–4.

97. Marvin Bower, "H. G. Crockett: His Key Role in the History of McKinsey & Company," 5 February 1965, 4, Corporate Archives, Management Consulting Association (ACME), New York City.

98. Marvin Bower and D. Ronald Daniel, "General Management Consulting," *Career Guide: A Harvard Business School Student Publication*, Vol. 2, No. 2 (February 1962), 7. On how the faculty at Harvard Business School employed the case method in the 1950s, see Malcom McNair (ed.), *The Case Method at the Harvard Business School* (New York: McGraw-Hill Book Company, 1954).

99. Marvin Bower and D. Ronald Daniel, "General Management Consulting," 7. The masculine pronoun was appropriate since the Harvard Business School did not begin accepting women until one year later in 1963. To an outside audience, Bower's discussion of remuneration was a tad different. In 1971, when asked whether ambitious graduates who wanted to make money would be attracted to consulting, Bower replied, "If a person wants to be a professional man, he isn't capital gains oriented in the first place." See Richard A. Nenneman, "Consulting Status," *Christian Science Monitor*, 20 April 1971, B8.

100. Oral interview with Donald K. Clifford, Jr., 1994, 12, Russell Reynolds Associates, Inc., Oral History Project, Oral History Research Office, Columbia University, New York. Clifford, who was a founding partner of the executive search firm Russell Reynolds, participated in a survey of consulting firms while an MBA student at Harvard in the late 1950s (the study was published under Richard F. Amon, et al., *Management Consulting* [Boston: Management Consulting Report Associates, 1958]). Clifford joined McKinsey upon graduation because, like his classmates, he believed that McKinsey & Company "was head and shoulders above anyone else."

101. McKinsey & Company, "Firm-Wide Breakdown of Consulting Staff by Graduate School," 7 July 1967, Corporate Archives, McKinsey & Company. Over time, Harvard's dominance would decline, but as late as May 1978, of the 585 consultants at McKinsey & Company, 150 (26%) held a degree from the Harvard Business School and 430 (74%) held a graduate degree from a business school. Bower, *Perspective on McKinsey*, 180.

102. In 1961, for example, Lawrence Munson, a consultant at McKinsey, explained that Si Wareham, the director of industrial engineering at IBM, "is a loyal alumnus with a very 'warm feeling' toward the Firm." Lawrence Munson, "Intelligence and Ideas on Firm Image," 9 March 1961, Corporate Archives, McKinsey & Company. For a more recent illustration of the loyalty of alumni, see Ethan M. Raisel, *The McKinsey Way: Using the Techniques of the World's Top Strategic Consultants to Help You and Your Business* (New York: McGraw Hill, 1999), 167–78.

103. Like law associates, most former consultants at McKinsey & Company did not jump to rival firms. For example, of the forty-one "McKinsey Alumni" from the New York Office who left the firm between 1953 and 1959, only four worked in consulting firms. It was far more common to find a position within client companies as did the former consultants who worked at IBM, Hoover, Raytheon, Time, Smith-Corona, Carrier, Mobil, R. R. Donnelly, and American Airlines in 1959. See Lawrence Munson, "'Alumni' Relations Program," 6 July 1959, Corporate Archives, McKinsey & Company.

104. Lawrence Munson, "Alumni Relations," 23 July 1963, Corporate Archives, McKinsey & Company.

105. Lawrence Munson, "'Alumni' Relations Program," 6 July 1959; Lawrence Munson, "Alumni Relations Program," 3 December 1959, Lawrence Munson, "Alumni Relations," 12 March 1963, and Lawrence Munson, "Alumni Relations," 20 September 1963, all in the Corporate Archives, McKinsey & Company.

106. Consultants' success, despite their failure to achieve partnership, paralleled the experience of corporate lawyers. According to sociologist Erwin Smigel, "very few [young lawyers] leave the firm without a good position – often one paying a higher salary than the partnership they did not get." Smigel, *The Wall Street Lawyer*, 64.

107. John A. Byrne, "The Craze for Consultants," *Business Week* (25 July 1994), 60.

108. On the purchase of Griffenhagen & Associates in 1957 by John Diebold & Associates, a consulting firm specializing in automation, see Wilbur Cross, *John Diebold: Breaking the Confines of the Possible* (New York: James H. Heineman, Inc., 1965); on Fry & Associates' purchase in 1967 by ARA, a vending machine company, and the purchase of Barrington Associates by Day & Zimmerman, a consulting engineering firm, see Higdon, *The Business Healers*, 290.

109. In contrast, despite the presence of 25 partners at Cresap, McCormick and Paget, McKinsey consultants suspected that, as late as 1968, Richard Paget and Willard McCormick continued to "regard the firm as their proprietorship." One year later, the partners at Cresap, McCormick and Paget decided to sell their consultancy to Citibank. H. L. Thomas, Jr., "Notes on Cresap, McCormick & Paget," 19 February 1968, 2, Corporate Archives, McKinsey & Company.

110. This paragraph implicitly draws on evolutionary economics. For an overview of the academic field as it has matured, see Richard R. Nelson, "Recent Evolutionary Theorizing about Economic Change," *Journal of Economic Literature*, Vol. 33, No. 1 (1995), 48–90. The classic work undergirding evolutionary economics is Richard R. Nelson and Sidney C. Winter, *An Evolutionary Theory of Economic Change* (Cambridge: Harvard University Press, 1982). Nelson and Winter's work, in turn, drew heavily upon the theories of economist Joseph Schumpeter, see Joseph A. Schumpeter, *The Theory of Economic Development* (New Brunswick: Transaction Publishers, 1934), and Joseph A. Schumpeter, *Capitalism, Socialism, and Democracy* (New York: Harper & Row, 1942).

111. Marvin Bower acknowledged that "unprofessional" methods, like the employment of salesmen or advertising, were effective, profitable, *and ethical*, but "the professional approach will result in our doing better work and be more satisfying to the type of man the Firm wants to attract and hold." McKinsey & Company, "New Engagement and Executive Relations Guide," May 1945, 2, Corporate Archives, McKinsey & Company.

112. As Albert Dunn, an assistant professor at the Harvard Business School, concluded in 1951: "the reputation of the firm, the stature of the partners, their contacts in the business community seem to be vastly more important in obtaining new business than any form of sales solicitation." Albert H. Dunn, III, *Business Consultants: Their Uses and Limitations* (New York: Controllership Foundation, Inc., 1951), 3.

113. Again, this metaphor is quite intentional and reflects the importance of evolutionary economics to understand this process. See, Steven Klepper and Elizabeth Graddy, "The Evolution of New Industries and the Determinants of Market Structure," *RAND Journal of Economics*, Vol. 21, No. 1 (Spring 1990), 27–44.

114. The legacy of the 1950s as the pinnacle of the "American Century" and as the flash-point for the rebellion of the 1960s has been told in many forms including movies, television, novels, and histories both popular and academic. One recent example is David Halberstam, *The Fifties* (New York: Villard Books, 1993), ix–xi.

115. The severity of the competition would not, however, become apparent until the early 1970s. As late as 1967, for example, the senior partners at McKinsey & Company believed that their firm's "human and financial resources have grown and are growing greater every year." Gil Clee, "The Firm's Future," 23 September 1967, C-3, Corporate Archives, McKinsey & Company.

116. McKinsey & Company, "Whither McKinsey & Company? Report of the Commission on Firm Aims and Goals," April 1971, section 2, page 3, Corporate Archives, McKinsey & Company.

117. Arthur Andersen & Company, *A Vision of Grandeur* (Chicago: Arthur Andersen & Co., 1988), 95–6.

118. Arthur Young & Company, "Management Consulting – Its History and Potential: A Study of the Marketplace" (Mimeograph, Arthur Young & Company, 1982), 4–5.

119. James Newman, Vice President of Booz, Allen & Hamilton quoted in "Are CPA Firms taking over Management Consulting?" *Forbes* (1 October 1966): 59.

120. Arthur M. Lewis, "The Accountants are Changing the Rules," *Fortune* (15 January 1965).

121. John Thackray, "Winning the Game with a Hot Theory: Companies Seek Advice of Boston Consulting Group," *The New York Times* (15 April 1979), Sect. 3, 4.

122. James O'Shea and Charles Madigan, *Dangerous Company: The Consulting Powerhouses and the Businesses They Save and Ruin* (New York: Times Books, 1997), 73–108, 146–82.

123. "How's Business? Among Consultants It Depends on Whom You Ask," *The Wall Street Journal* (26 February 1976), 1.

124. For Alfred Chandler's path-breaking analysis of the impact of the large consulting firms in the dissemination of organization models, specifically the multidivisional structure, within the United States after World War II, see Chandler, *Strategy and Structure*, 381–2. On the parallel influence of consultants from McKinsey & Company in Britain, see Derek F. Channon, *The Strategy and Structure of British Enterprise* (Boston: Harvard Business School, 1973), 239; for the consulting firm's influence in France and Germany, see Gareth Dyas and Heinz T. Thanheiser, *The Emerging European Enterprise: Strategy and Structure in French and German Industry* (London: Macmillan, 1976), 120, 247.

125. Hasso von Falkenhausen, notes for "A McKinsey Scrapbook," 1994, Corporate Archives, McKinsey & Company.

126. McKinsey & Company, "Competitor Analysis Project," Montsoult, France, 18–20 March 1981, 5, 7; McKinsey & Company, "Economics of the Firm: Meeting of New Partners, New York Office," 21 August 1972, n.p., [italics in original] both in Corporate Archives, McKinsey & Company.

127. "Surprise at McKinsey: Walton Steps Down," *Business Week* (28 April 1973), 44–5; "McKinsey Manager to Step Down," *The New York Times* (27 April 1973), 49; "McKinsey & Company Names a New Managing Director," *The Wall Street Journal* (15 July 1976), 22.

128. Bower, *Perspective on McKinsey*, x–xi; John G. Neukom, *McKinsey Memoirs: A Personal Perspective* (New York: Privately Printed, 1975), 1–2; Oral History Project, Corporate Archives, McKinsey & Company.

129. McKinsey & Company, "Competitor Analysis Project," Montsoult, France, 18–20 March 1981, 3–4, Corporate Archives, McKinsey & Company.

130. Salmans, "New Vogue," D1.

131. John Thackray, "Winning the Game with a Hot Theory: Companies Seek Advice of Boston Consulting Group," *The New York Times* (15 April 1979), Sect. 3, 4.

132. Thackray, "Winning the Game with a Hot Theory," 4.

133. Pascale and Athos, *The Art of Japanese Management*, 9.

134. Peters and Waterman, *In Search of Excellence*, 11.

135. Peters and Waterman, *In Search of Excellence*, 9.

136. Waterman, Peters, and Phillips, "Structure is Not Organization," 24–5; Pascale and Athos, *The Art of Japanese Management*, 9–13.

137. For a description of Stevenson, Jordan & Harrison's earlier surveys of "excellently managed" companies, see James S. Earley, "Marginal Policies of 'Excellently Managed' Companies," *The American Economic Review*, Vol. 46, No. 1 (1956), 44.

138. "Who Can Wear a Consultant's Hat?" *Business Week* (19 June 1971), 41–2.

139. John A. Byrne, "The Craze for Consultants," *Business Week* (25 July 1994), 60.

140. Avery Gordon, "The Work of Corporate Culture," 3.

141. Terry Neill, head of services for Andersen Consulting in the U.K., cited in Mary Ackenhusen, "Andersen Consulting (Europe): Entering the Business of Business Integration," (INSEAD Case Study # 392–055–1, INSEAD, Fountainbleau, France, 1992), 1.

142. For the recent commodification of "re-engineering" by consultants see, Robin Fincham, "Business Process Re-Engineering and the Commodification of Managerial Knowledge," *Journal of Marketing Management*, Vol. 11, No. 7 (October 1995), 707–19; Jos Benders, Robert-Jan van den Berg, and Mark van Bijsterveld, "Hitch-Hiking on a Hype: Dutch Consultants Engineering Re-Engineering," *Journal of Organizational Change Management*; Vol. 11, No. 3 (1998), 201–15.

143. Malcolm Gladwell, "The Talent Myth: Are Smart People Overrated? *The New Yorker* (22 July 2002), 28–9.

## 9. WATCHDOGS, LAPDOGS, OR RETRIEVERS? LIABILITY AND THE REBIRTH OF THE MANAGEMENT AUDIT

1. Jonathan Weil, John Emshwiller and Scot J. Paltrow, "Audit Nightmare: Arthur Andersen Says it Disposed of Documents that Related to Enron, *The Wall Street Journal* (11 January 2002), A1; Adrian Michaels, "Enron Documents Destroyed after SEC began Probe," *The Financial Times* (16 January 2002), 1; Paul W. MacAvoy and Ira M. Millstein, *The Recurrent Crisis in Corporate Governance* (New York: Palgrave Macmillan, 2004), 77.

2. Michael Schroeder, "Fall of an Energy Giant: Arthur Levitt Says Enron Case Shows Need for More Curbs, *The Wall Street Journal* (11 January 2002), A4; Ken

Brown and Jonathan Weil, "Questioning the Books: How Andersen's Embrace of Consulting Altered the Culture of the Auditing Firm," *The Wall Street Journal* (1 August 2001), C18.

3. Ken Brown, "Blue Chip Companies, Blue Chip Fees," *The Wall Street Journal* (7 March 2002), C1.

4. U.S. Congress, H.R. 3763, "Corporate and Auditing Accountability, Responsibility, and Transparency Act of 2002" (the Sarbanes-Oxley Act), Section 201, 28.

5. "Professional-Service Firms are Becoming Vast Diversified Conglomerates," *The Economist* (7 July 2001); Jonathan Weil and Rachel Emma Silverman, "Consulting Unit of Accountant to Go Public," *The Wall Street Journal* (31 January 2002), A3; Robert Frank and Ken Brown, "Andersen: Just a Shadow of Its Former Self – Arthur Andersen Could Sell off Consulting Arm," *The Wall Street Journal* (30 April 2002), C1; Kemba J. Dunham, "Consulting Unit of Deloitte Plans to Go Private," *The Wall Street Journal* (7 June 2002), C5; Tom Foremski and Adrian Michaels, "IBM buys PwC arm for $3.5bn.," *The Financial Times*, (31 July 2002), 17; "Mergers Snapshot / Big-Five Consulting Firms," *The Wall Street Journal* (7 August 2002), C5.

6. Jeanne Cummings, Tom Hamburger, and Kathryn Kranhold, "Law Firm Reassured Enron on Accounting – Vinson & Elkins Discounted Warnings by Employee About Dubious Dealings," *The Wall Street Journal* (16 January 2002), A18; Ellen Joan Pollock and Kathryn Kranhold, "Law Firm Kirkland & Ellis Draws Notice from Investigators into Enron Partnerships," *The Wall Street Journal* (2 April 2002), C1; Anita Raghavan, Michael Schroeder and Jathon Sapsford, "SEC Examines Ties Between Banks and Enron," *The Wall Street Journal* (15 January 2002), C1; Jason Sapsford, "Congress Seeks Data from J. P. Morgan on Enron Deal," *The Wall Street Journal* (16 April 2002), C1; Joshua Chaffin, "How Enron Cosied Up to Its 'Best Bank' – CSFB Knew How Bad Things Really Were but Carried on Regardless," *The Financial Times* (2 December 2003), 29.

7. Rebecca Smith and John R. Emshwiller, *24 Days: How Two Wall Street Journal Reporters Uncovered the Lies that Destroyed Faith in Corporate America* (New York: HarperBusiness, 2003), 7; Dana Millbank, "McKinsey Confronts Challenge of Its Own," *The Wall Street Journal* (8 September 1993), A1; Hillary Durgin and Richard Skinner, "The Guru of Decentralization," *The Financial Times* (26 June 2000), 14; Jonathan Friedland, "Enron's CEO, Skilling, Quits Two Top Posts," *The Wall Street Journal* (15 August 2001), A3.

8. Suein Hwang and Rachel Emma Silverman, "McKinsey Held Close Enron Ties for Many Years, *The Wall Street Journal* (17 January 2002), B1.

9. "Why Honesty is the Best Policy," *The Economist* (9 March 2002); Malcolm Gladwell, The Talent Myth, *The New Yorker* (22 July 2002); Ed Michaels, Helen Handfield-Jones, and Beth Axelrod, *The War for Talent* (Boston:

Harvard Business School Press, 2001), 49–51; Richard Foster and Sarah Kaplan, *Creative Destruction: Why Companies That Are Built to Last Underperform the Market – And How to Successfully Transform Them* (New York: Currency, 2001), 148–51.

10. Hawang and Silverman, "McKinsey Held Close Enron Ties For Many Years," B1; "Enron Justice," *The Wall Street Journal* (15 January 2004), A14.

11. Hawang and Silverman, "McKinsey Held Close Enron Ties For Many Years," B1.

12. John C. Coffee, "Understanding Enron: 'It's about the Gatekeepers, Stupid,'" *Business Lawyer*, (2002), 1403–20.

13. John C. Coffee, "The Acquiescent Gatekeeper: Reputational Intermediaries, Auditor Independence and the Governance of Accounting," Working Paper No. 191, Center for Law and Economic Studies, Columbia Law School (May 2001); Burton Malkiel, "Watchdogs and Lapdogs," *The Wall Street Journal* (16 January 2002), A16; Anish Nanda, "Broken Trust: Role of Professionals in the Enron Debacle," Harvard Business School Case Study, No. 9-903-084 (Boston: Harvard Business School Publishing, 28 February 2003), 1–17.

14. Joseph Stiglitz, *The Roaring Nineties* (London: Penguin Books, 2003), 241–68.

15. Dixie L. Johnson, Chair, Committee on Federal Regulation of Securities, "Report of the Task Force on Exchange Act Section 21(A) Written Statements," *Business Lawyer*, Vol. 59 (February, 2004), 538.

16. Frank Partnoy, *Infectious Greed: How Deceit and Risk Corrupted the Financial Markets* (New York: Henry Holt, 2003), 298–308; Frank Partnoy, "Barbarians at the Gatekeepers?: A Proposal for a Modified Strict Liability Regime," *Washington University Law Quarterly*, Vol. 79 (Summer 2001), 491–546; John C. Coffee, Jr., "Partnoy's Complaint: A Response," *Boston University Law Review*, Vol. 84 (April 2004), 377–82.

17. Jeffrey N. Gordon, "Crisis in Confidence: Corporate Governance and Professional Ethics Post-Enron," *Connecticut Law Review* (Spring 2003), 1125–43.

18. James S. Trieschmann and E. J. Leverett, Jr., "Protecting Directors and Officers: A Growing Concern," *Business Horizons*, Vol. 33, No. 6 (November 1990), 52.

19. Marvin Bower, "The Merchandizing of Ideas," *Harvard Business Review*, Vol. 9 (October 1930): 26–34; Marvin Bower, *Perspective on McKinsey* (New York: McKinsey & Company, 1977), 7.

20. Marvin Bower, "Becoming a Director – A Business Honor or a Financial Boomerang?," *Harvard Business Review*, Vol. 9 (April 1931), 371–82; Marvin Bower, *The Will to Lead: Running a Business with a Network of Leaders* (Boston: Harvard Business School Press, 1997), 11–14.

21. James O. McKinsey, "Functions of Boards of Directors, Board Committees and Officers," *General Management Series*, No. 82 (New York: American Management Association, 1929): 2–20.

22. Bower, "Becoming a Director," 371.

23. Adolf A. Berle, Jr. and Gardiner C. Means, *The Modern Corporation and Private Property* (New York: The Macmillan Company, 1932), 227–32.

24. George J. Stigler and Claire Friedland, "The Literature of Economics: The Case of Berle and Means," *Journal of Law and Economics*, Vol. 26, No. 2 (June 1983), 241; Mark J. Roe, "From Antitrust to Corporation Governance? The Corporation and the Law: 1959–1994," in Carl Kaysen (ed.), *The American Corporation Today* (Oxford: Oxford University Press, 1996), 102–27.

25. William C. Warren, "Adolf A. Berle," *Columbia Law Review*, Vol. 4, No. 8 (December 1964), 1381.

26. Mark J. Roe, *Strong Managers, Weak Owners: The Political Roots of American Corporate Finance* (Princeton: Princeton University Press, 1994), 35; Stigler and Friedland, "The Case of Berle and Means," 241–3; Thomas K. McCraw, *Prophets of Regulation* (Boston: Harvard University Press, 1984), 165–70; Louis D. Brandeis, *Other People's Money and How the Bankers Use It* (New York: Frederick A. Stokes, 1914); Thorstein Veblen, *Absentee Ownership and Business Enterprise in Recent Times: The Case of America* (New York: B. W. Huebsch, 1923); William Z. Ripley, *Main Street and Wall Street* (Boston: Little Brown & Company, 1927).

27. Richard S. Kirkendall, "A. A. Berle, Jr. Student of the Corporation, 1917–1932," *The Business History Review*, Vol. 35, No. 1 (Spring 1961), 43–58; Paul J. Miranti, Jr., "Associationalism, Statism, and Professional Regulation: Public Accountants and the Reform of the Financial Markets, 1896–1940," *The Business History Review*, Vol. 60, No. 3 (Autumn, 1986), 460–1.

28. In particular, the "legal realism" movement, based on a philosophy of scientific empiricism, would play an important role in merging the new theories of corporate governance with the new regulatory initiatives. See Edward A. Purcell, Jr., "American Jurisprudence between the Wars: Legal Realism and the Crisis of Democratic Theory," *The American Historical Review*, Vol. 75, No. 2 (December 1969), 424–46.

29. William O. Douglas and George E. Bates, "The Federal Securities Act of 1933," *The Yale Law Journal*, Vol. 43, No. 2 (1933), 195; Henry G. Manne, "The 'Higher Criticism' of the Modern Corporation," *Columbia Law Review*, Vol. 62, No. 3 (March 1962), 400.

30. Chester Rohrlich, "The New Deal in Corporation Law," *Columbia Law Review*, Vol. 35, No. 8 (December 1935), 1170–1; Milton V. Freedman, "The Securities and Exchange Commission," in *The Making of the New Deal: The Insiders Speak* (Cambridge: Harvard University Press, 1983), 142; James Allen (ed.), *Democracy and Finance: The Addresses and Public Statements of William O. Douglas as Member and Chairman of the Securities and Exchange Commission*, (New Haven: Yale University Press, 1940), 175–80.

31. Jerry W. Markham; "Accountants Make Miserable Policemen: Rethinking the Federal Securities Laws," *North Carolina Journal of International Law & Commercial Regulation* (2003), 765.

32. Douglas and Bates, "The Federal Securities Act of 1933," 197; John Brooks, *Once in Golconda: A True Drama of Wall Street, 1920–1938* (New York: Harper & Row, 1969), 241–2; Bruce Allen Murphy, *Wild Bill: The Legend and Life of William O. Douglas* (New York: Random House, 2003).

33. See New York Dock Company, Inc. v. McCollom, 16 N.Y.S. (2d) 844 (Sup. Ct. 1939) in which the New York State Supreme Court held that the directors of the New York Dock Company were not entitled to be reimbursed for their legal expenses in a derivative lawsuit that was subsequently dismissed.

34. George T. Washington, "Litigation Expenses of Corporate Directors in Stockholders' Suits," *Columbia Law Review*, Vol. 40, No. 3 (March 1940), 432.

35. George T. Washington, "The S.E.C. and Directors' Indemnity: Recent Developments," *Columbia Law Review*, Vol. 40, No. 7 (November 1940), 1206; George E. Bates and Eugene M. Zuckert, "Directors' Indemnity: Corporate Policy or Public Policy?" *Harvard Business Review*, Vol. 20, No. 2 (Winter 1942), 247.

36. Bates and Zuckert, "Directors' Indemnity," 244; George T. Frampton, "Indemnification of Insider's Litigation Expenses," *Law and Contemporary Problems*, Vol. 23, No. 2 (Spring 1958), 330.

37. Roberta Romano, "What Went Wrong with Directors' and Officers' Liability Insurance?" *Delaware Journal of Corporate Law*, Vol. 14 (1989), 1–10; Colin Baxter, "Demystifying D&O Insurance," *Oxford Journal of Legal Studies*, Vol. 15, No. 4 (Winter 1995), 557–8.

38. Andersen & Co., *The First Sixty Years*, 13–14.

39. Allen and McDermott, *Accounting for Success*, 73.

40. Arthur Andersen & Co., *The First Sixty Years*, 24; Berle and Means, *The Modern Corporation and Private Property*, 309–12; Miranti, "Associationalism, Statism, and Professional Regulation," 458–9.

41. Derek Matthews, Malcolm Anderson, and John Richard Edwards, *The Priesthood of Industry: The Rise of the Professional Accountant in British Management* (Oxford: Oxford University Press, 1998), 52–5.

42. Susan E. Squires, Cynthia Smith, Lorna McDougall, and William R. Yeack, *Inside Arthur Andersen: Shifting Values, Unexpected Consequences* (New York: Financial Times Prentice Hall, 2003), 48.

43. Roddy F. Osborn, "GE and UNIVAC: Harnessing the High-Speed Computer," *Harvard Business Review*, 32 (July–August 1954), 99–107. Arthur Andersen & Co., *A Vision of Grandeur*, 99.

44. Mark Stevens, *The Big Six: The Selling Out of America's Top Accounting Firms* (New York: Touchstone, 1991), 106–9.

45. Barbara Ley Toffler with Jennifer Reingold, *Final Accounting: Ambition, Greed, and the Fall of Arthur Andersen* (New York: Currency Books, 2004), 72–3; Mike Brewster, *Unaccountable: How the Accounting Profession Forfeited a Public Trust* (New York: John Wiley & Sons Inc., 2003), 145.

46. Allen and McDermott, *Accounting for Success*, 174.

47. Thomas C. Hayes, "Accountants Under Scrutiny: Consulting Jobs Called Risk to Independence," *The New York Times* (25 June 1979), D1; Tom Herman, "Arthur Andersen & Co. Earnings Growth Rate for 1979 Fell Sharply," *The Wall Street Journal* (11 December 1979), 20.

48. Toffler with Reingold, *Final Accounting*, 73–8.

49. Allen and McDermott, *Accounting for Success*, 173–6; Gary Klott, "Uneasy Period for Andersen: Suits Beseige Big 8 Firm," *The New York Times* (23 November 1984), D1.

50. Lee Berton, "Arthur Andersen's Chief of Consulting Relieved of Role," *The Wall Street Journal* (19 May 1988).

51. Lee Berton and Bruce Ingersoll, "Rep. Dingell to Take Aim at Accountants, SEC In Hearings on Profession's Role as Watchdog," *The Wall Street Journal* (19 February 1985), 4.

52. Lee Berton, "Insurers Tell Big Accounting Concerns Liability Rates May Rise, Sources Say," *The Wall Street Journal* (8 November 1984), 4; Lee Berton, "Total War: CPA Firms Diversify, Cut Fees, Steal Clients in Battle for Business," *The Wall Street Journal* (20 September 1985), 1.

53. "Public Policy and Directors' Liability Insurance," *Columbia Law Review*, Vol. 67, No. 4 (April 1967), 716; Wayne E. Green, "Executives in Court," *The Wall Street Journal* (29 June 1966), 1.

54. The American Home Assurance Company, Full Page Display Advertisement, *The Wall Street Journal*, 6 March 1968, 9. See also Stewart, Smith & Co., Inc., Display Advertisement [quoting headline from the 29 June 1966 Wall Street Journal Article, "Executives in Court"], *The Wall Street Journal*, 4 August 1966, 4.

55. Joseph W. Bishop, Jr., "Sitting Ducks and Decoy Ducks: New Trends in the Indemnification of Corporate Directors and Officers," *The Yale Law Journal*, Vol. 77, No. 6 (May 1968), 1078.

56. Robert M. Estes, "Outside Directors: More Vulnerable than Ever," *Harvard Business Review*, vol. 51, No. 1 (January/February 1973), 107–14; Joseph W. Bishop, Jr., "Understanding D&O Insurance Policies," *Harvard Business Review*, Vol. 56, No. 2 (March/April 1978), 20–7.

57. Bower, "Becoming a Director," 372.

58. Aronson v. Lewis, 473 A2.d 805 (Del. Sup. 1984), 812.

59. Oliver Williamson, "Comparative Economic Organization: The Analysis of Discrete Structural Alternatives," *Administrative Science Quarterly*, Vol. 36 (June 1991), 106; Ronald Gilson, *The Law and Finance of Corporate Acquisitions* (Minneola, New York: Foundation Press, 1986), 741; Henry Manne, Our Two Corporate Systems: Law and Economics," *University of Virginia Law Review*, Vol. 53 (1967), 259–85.

60. David B. Hilder, "Risky Business; Liability Insurance Is Difficult to Find Now For Directors," *The Wall Street Journal* (10 July 1985), 1; Leo Herzel and Leo

Katz, "Smith v. Van Gorkom: The Business of Judging Business Judgment," *Business Lawyer*, Vol. 41 (August 1986), 1188–9.

61. Smith v. Van Gorkom, Del.Supr., 488 A.2d 858 (1985); "Trans Union Holder Sues to Halt Merger with Pritzker Firm," *The Wall Street Journal* (22 December 1980), 7. Trans Union is one of the three leading companies (alongside Equifax and Experian / TRW) that sell consumer credit reports in the United States.

62. Smith v. Van Gorkom, Del.Supr., 488 A.2d 858 (1985), 874.

63. Bayless Manning, "Reflections and Practical Tips on Life in the Boardroom after Van Gorkom," *Business Lawyer*, Vol. 41, No. 1 (November 1985), 1.

64. Manning, "Reflections and Practical Tips," 3; Smith v. Van Gorkom, Del.Supr., 488 A.2d 858 (1985), 876.

65. Jonathan R. Macey; Geoffrey P. Miller, "Trans Union Reconsidered," *The Yale Law Journal*, Vol. 98, No. 1 (November 1988), 129; 139. In retrospect, however, at least one subsequent study could not firmly establish whether the number of "Fairness Opinions" really increased or not, see Helen M. Bowers, "Fairness Opinions and the Business Judgement Rule: An Empirical Investigation of Target Firms' Use of Fairness Opinions," *Northwestern University Law Review*, Vol. 96, No. 2 (2002), 567–78.

66. Smith v. Van Gorkom, Del.Supr., 488 A.2d 858 (1985), 897.

67. Richard Koenig, "Court Rules Trans Union's Directors Used Poor Judgement in Sale of Firm," *The Wall Street Journal* (1 February 1985), 7; Fred R. Bleakely, "Business Judgement Case Finds Directors Liable," *The New York Times* (31 January 1985), D1, D4.

68. James S. Trieschmann and E. J. Leverett, Jr., "Protecting Directors and Officers: A Growing Concern," *Business Horizons*, Vol. 33, No. 6 (November 1990), 52.

69. "Corporate Liability Crisis," *The Wall Street Journal* (21 August 1986), 22.

70. Peter W. Huber, *Liability: The Legal Revolution and its Consequences* (New York: Basic Books, 1988), 135.

71. Tamar Lewin, "Director Insurance Drying Up," *The New York Times* (7 March 1986), D1.

72. "Liability Insurance is Difficult to Find Now for Directors, Officers," *The Wall Street Journal* (10 July 1985), 1; "Corporate Liability Crisis," *The Wall Street Journal* (21 August 1985), 22; Scott E. Harrington, "Prices and Profits in the Liability Insurance Market," in Robert E. Litan and Clifford Winston (ed.), *Liability: Perspectives and Policy* (Washington, D.C.: The Brookings Institution, 1988), 42–3; Ralph A. Winter, "The Liability Insurance Market," *The Journal of Economic Perspectives*, Vol. 5, No. 3 (Summer 1991), 115.

73. Roswell B. Perkins, "Avoiding Director Liability," *The Harvard Business Review*, Vol. 64, No. 3 (May–June 1986), 8.

74. "Continental Steel Corp Says its Chairman, 6 Directors Resigned," *The Wall Street Journal* (24 September 1985), 22.

75. Robert D. Cooter, "Economic Theories of Legal Liability," *Journal of Economic Perspectives*, Vol. 5, No. 3 (Summer 1991), 18.

76. Sara R. Slaughter, "Statutory and Non-Statutory Responses to the Director and Officer Liability Insurance Crisis," *Indiana Law Journal*, Vol. 63 (Winter 1987), 181–9. For non lawyers, a "tort," under the law, is when someone has been held liable for damages that are the result of an injury to a person or property that is not a criminal act nor based on a contract.

77. Lewin, "Director Insurance Drying Up," D1.

78. "Corporate Liability Crisis," *The Wall Street Journal* (21 August 1985), 22.

79. Pub. L. No. 104–67, 109 Stat. 737 (1995); Joseph A. Grundfest and Michael A. Perino, "Ten Things We Know and Ten Things We Don't Know About the Private Security Reform Act of 1995," Joint Written Testimony Before the Subcommittee on Securities of the Committee on Banking, Housing and Urban Affairs, United States Senate, 24 July 1997; William S. Lerach, "The Private Securities Litigation Reform Act of 1995 – 27 Months Later": Securities Class Action Litigation under the Private Securities Litigation Act's Brave New World, *Washington University Law Quarterly*, Vol. 76 (1998), 597–644.

80. "Businesses Struggling to Adapt as Insurance Crisis Spreads, *The Wall Street Journal* (21 January 1986), 31.

81. Reinier H. Kraakman, "Corporate Liability Strategies and the Costs of Legal Controls," *Yale Law Journal*, Vol. 93 (April 1984), 857; Matthew G. Dore, "Presumed Innocent? Financial Institutions Professional Malpractice Claims and Defenses Based on Management Misconduct," *Columbia Business Law Review* (1995), 127.

82. Timothy Clark and Robin Fincham (eds.), *Critical Consulting: New Perspectives on the Management Advice Industry* (Oxford: Blackwell Publishers, 2001); Matthias Kipping and Lars Engwall (eds.), *Management Consulting: Emergence and Dynamics of a Knowledge Industry* (Oxford: Oxford University Press, 2002).

83. Gordon Donaldson, "A New Tool for Boards: The Strategic Audit," *Harvard Business Review* (July/August 1995), 99–107.

84. Ronald D. Mallen and David W. Evans, "Surviving the Directors' and Officers' Liability Crisis: Insurance and the Alternatives," *Delaware Journal of Corporate Law*, Vol. 12 (1987).

85. QVC Network v. Paramount Communications, 635 A.2d 1245 (1993), 1255, 1270; Geraldine Fabrikant, "Delaware Court Ruling Aids QVC In Struggle to Acquire Paramount," *The New York Times* (10 December 1993), A1.

86. First Union v. Suntrust Banks, 2001 WL 1885686 (N.C.Super.), 25, 35.

87. Alison Leigh Cowan, "Caution Signal for Corporate Boards," *The New York Times* (25 November 1993), D6; Floyd Norris, "Delaware Law: From A Muddle, Owners Win," *The New York Times* (28 November 1993), F1; Carrick Mollenkamp, "SunTrust Assails Wachovia at Hearing," *The Wall Street Journal* (18 July 2001), A4.

88. John A. Byrne, "The Craze for Consultants," *Business Week* (25 July 1994), 60.
89. See, for example, Federated Department Stores, Inc., and Allied Stores Corporation, et al., Debtors, Consolidated Case No 1-90-00130, Chapter 11, Document No. 829, United Bankruptcy Court for the Southern District of Ohio, Western Division (27 April 1990). Because court cases provide a window into these often closed consultancies, James O'Shea and Charles Madigan used them extensively in their investigation of management consulting during the late 1990s. See James O'Shea and Charles Madigan, *Dangerous Company: The Consulting Powerhouses and the Businesses they Save and Ruin* (New York: Times Books, 1997). .
90. Kenneth B. Davis, Jr, "Once More, The Business Judgment Rule," *Wisconsin Law Review* (2000), 573.
91. Kenneth S. Abraham, "Individual Action and Collective Responsibility: The Dilemma of Mass Tort Reform," *Virginia Law Review*, Vol. 73, No. 5 (August 1987), 862.
92. Michael Sean Quinn and Andrea D. Levin, "Directors and Officers Liability Insurance: Probable Directions in Texas Law," *The Review of Litigation*, Vol. 20 (Spring 2001), 381–480.
93. Interview, Brian Cullen (professional liability insurance broker), Aon Corporation, New York (20 September 2004); Michael Skapinker, "Slippery Counsel," *The Financial Times* (23 July 2002), 16.
94. For one view of the risks and rewards, see Adam Raphael, *Ultimate Risk: The Inside Story of the Lloyd's Catastrophe* (London: Four Walls Eight Windows Press, 1995); Craig Forman, "Risky Business: Lloyd's of London, An Insurance Bulwark, Is a Firm Under Seige," *The Wall Street Journal* (24 October 1989), 1.
95. Lawrence A. Weinbach, "The $30 Billion Question Behind U.S. 'Litigation Crisis,'" *The Financial Times* (23 September 1993), 27.
96. "Malpractice Rates Zoom," *National Law Journal* (3 June 1995), 1.
97. James T. Clarke," Liability Reform: Keeping our Earnings; Protecting Assets," (1994) Video Tape, Box 80, Pricewaterhouse Coopers Archives, Rare Book and Manuscript Library, Columbia University.
98. James T. Clarke, "Liability Reform: Keeping our Earnings; Protecting Assets;" Statement of J. Michael Cook, Chairman and Chief Executive Officer, Deloitte & Touche before the Subcommittee on Telecommunications and Finance, Committee on Energy and Commerce, U.S. House of Representatives, 10 August 1994. Absolute numbers are difficult to establish because many of the leading accounting firms entered global settlements with federal regulators between 1992 and 1994 that distort any reliable calculation of audit firm litigation rates and costs. See Zoe-Vonna Palmrose, "Empirical Research in Auditor Litigation: Considerations and Data," *Studies in Accounting Research* #33, (Sarasota, Florida, American Accounting Association, 1999), 52.

99. "Directors Protected from Liability," *The New York Law Journal* (30 March 1992), 21; Edgar W. Armstrong, Jr., "Shrinking Coverage? Keeping Officers, Directors Protected as Insurers Pull Back," *Corporate Cashflow Magazine* (April 1992); Sara R. Slaughter, "Statutory and Non-Statutory Responses to the Director and Officer Liability Insurance Crisis," *Indiana Journal of Law*, Vol. 63 (Winter 1987), 181–3.

100. J. Michael Cook, Eugene M. Freedman, Ray J. Groves, Jon C. Madonna, Shaun F. O'Malley, and Lawrence A. Weinbach, "The Liability Crisis in the United States: Impact on the Accounting Profession" (6 August 1992), 1.

101. Eugene M. Freedman, "The U.S. Liability Crisis and Its Impact on the Accounting Profession," 8 September 1992, 1, in File 17, Box 10, Pricewaterhouse Coopers Collection, PricewaterhouseCoopers Archives, Rare Book and Manuscript Library, Columbia University.

102. Eugene M. Freedman, "The U.S. Liability Crisis and Its Impact on the Accounting Profession," 1; Eugene M. Freeman, "Suggested Message Points for Letters to Members of Congress," in File 17, Box 10, Pricewaterhouse Coopers Collection, PricewaterhouseCoopers Archives, Rare Book and Manuscript Library, Columbia University.

103. Cook, Freedman, Groves, Madonna, O'Malley, and Weinbach, "The Liability Crisis in the United States," 1–2.

104. James Boyd and Daniel E. Ingermann, "The Search for Deep Pockets: Is 'Extended Liability' Expensive Liability?" *Journal of Law, Economics, & Organization*, Vol. 13, No. 1 (April 1997), 232–4; Zoe-Vonna Palmorose, "The Joint & Several vs. Proportionate Liability Debate: An Empirical Investigation of Audit-Related Litigation," Stanford Journal of Law, Business, and Finance, Vol. 1, No. 1 (Autumn 1994), 53–72.

105. S.E.C. v. Timetrust, Inc., 28 F. Supp. 34, 43 (N.D. Cal. 1939); John T. Vangel, "A Complicity-Doctrine Approach to Section 10(b) Aiding and Abetting Civil Damages Actions," *Columbia Law Review*, Vol. 89, No. 1 (January 1989), 180–98.

106. Cook, Freedman, Groves, Madonna, O'Malley, and Weinbach, "The Liability Crisis in the United States," 5.

107. Squires, Smith, McDougall, and Yeack, *Inside Arthur Andersen*, 124.

108. Greg Hitt, "Andersen Lobbyists Work to Ease Pressure of Probes: All of Bookkeeper's Clout is Now Brought to Bear on Post-Enron Scrutiny," *The Wall Street Journal* (17 January 2002), A16.

109. Robin W. Roberts, Peggy D. Dwyer, and John T. Sweeney, "Political Strategies Used by the US Political Accounting Profession During Auditor Liability Reform: The Case of the Private Securities Litigation Reform Act of 1995," *Journal of Accounting and Public Policy*, Vol. 22, No. 5 (September–October 2003), 435, 445–6.

110. Jill E. Fisch, "The Scope of Private Securities Litigation: In Search of Liability Standards for Secondary Defendants," *Columbia Law Review*, Vol. 99, No. 5 (June 1999), 1293–7.

111. Arthur Levitt, Chairman of the U.S. Securities and Exchange Commission (S.E.C.), "Corporate Governance: Integrity in the Information Age," Speech at Tulane University (12 March 1998).

112. Alison Leigh Cowan, "Auditors Adjust to Desperate Times," *The New York Times* (5 November 1990), D1.

113. Lee Berton, "Touche Ross & Co. Buys Braxton Inc., A Large Management-Consulting Firm," *The Wall Street Journal* (4 December 1984), 14; "Price Waterhouse Buys Consulting Firm, *The Wall Street Journal* (2 April 1985), 1.

114. Mike Brewster, *Unaccountable: How the Accounting Profession Forfeited a Public Trust* (Hoboken: John Wiley, 2003), 180; "Four of the Eight Largest UK Accountancy Firms Now Receive Less Than Half of Their Fee Income From Their Traditional Core Business, Auditing and Accounting," *The Financial Times* (31 May 1988), 38.

115. Lee Berton, "Cutting the Pie: Accounting Firms Face a Deepening Division Over Consultants' Pay," *The Wall Street Journal* (26 July 1988); Reed Abelson, "Two of the Big Six in Accounting Plan to Form New No. 1," *The New York Times* (19 September 1997), A1.

116. Toffler with Reingold, *Final Accounting*, 50–2.

117. Brewster, *Unaccountable*, 166.

118. Leslie Wayne, "Departing Chief Leaves Legacy of Activism," *The New York Times* (30 January 2001), C1; Floyd Norris, "Small Firms Urged to Back Independence in Auditing," *The New York Times* (19 September 2000), C2.

119. Arthur Levitt, "Commission's Auditor Independence Proposal," Testimony before the Senate Subcommittee on Securities, Committee on Banking, Housing, and Urban Affairs, 28 September 2000.

120. For arguments of both sides of the debate in the *Accounting Review*, see Richard M. Frankel, Marilyn F. Johnson, and Karen K. Nelson, "The Relations Between Auditor's Fees for Nonaudit Services and Earnings Quality," *The Accounting Review*, Vol. 77 (2002 Supplement), 71–105 [yes, they did]; Hollis Ashbaugh, Ryan LaFond, and Brian W. Mayhew, "Do Nonaudit Services Compromise Auditor Independence? Further Evidence," *The Accounting Review*, Vol. 78, No. 3 (2003), 611–39 [no, they didn't]; and Laura J. Kornish and Carolyn B. Levine, "Discipline with Common Agency: The Case of Audit and Nonaudit Services, *The Accounting Review*, Vol. 79, No. 1 (2004), 173–200 [yes, theoretically, they do].

121. Brewster, *Unaccountable*, 210–11.

122. William P. Browne and Won K. Paik, "Beyond the Domain: Recasting Network Politics in the Postreform Congress," *American Journal of Political Science*, Vol. 37, No. 4 (November 1993), 1054–78; Andrew S. McFarland, "Interest

Groups and Theories of Power in America," *British Journal of Political Science*, Vol. 17, No. 2 (April 1987), 129–47.

123. Julia Flynn Siler, "Andersen Plans a Restructuring," *The New York Times* (29 November 1988), D1.

124. Elizabeth MacDonald, "SEC charges KPMG Violated Its Rules Covering Role as Independent Auditors, *The Wall Street Journal* (5 December 1997), A4; Michael Santoli, "KPMG Dissolves Investment Venture with Baymark," *The Wall Street Journal* (13 January 1997), B7; Carole Gould, "KPMG Consulting Arm Looks Ready to Fly Solo," *The New York Times* (13 August 2000), C1.

125. Jackie Spinner, "Accountants Won't Fight Consulting Ban," *The Washington Post* (1 February 2002), E1; Melody Petersen, "Consultants Sing the Siren Song of Wall Street," *The New York Times* (26 May 1998), D1.

126. Reed Abelson, "After Andersen War, Accountants Think Hard About Consulting," *The New York Times* (9 August 2000), C1.

127. John Tagliabue, "Cap Gemini to Acquire Ernst & Young's Consulting Business," *The New York Times* (1 March 2000), C1.

128. "Bearing Up," *Financial Times* (4 October 2002), 20; Louis Lavell, "Professional Services," *Business Week* (8 January 2001), 134; Kemba J. Dunham, "KPMG Consulting Inc. Picks BearingPoint for Its New Name, *The Wall Street Journal* (3 October 2002), B10.

129. John C. Spychalski, "Andersen's Rise in the 1930s Collapse," *The Wall Street Journal* (11 February 2002), A23.

130. Caroline Daniel, "Words of Condemnation Left Hanging in the Air," *The Financial Times* (28 June 2002), 22.

131. Smith and Emshwiller, *24 Days*, xii–xv.

132. Peter Spiegal, "Shredding Storm May Leave Enron's Defense in Tatters," *The Financial Times* (23 January 2002), 26.

133. John Plender, *Going off the Rails: Global Capital and the Crisis of Legitimacy* (Chichester: John Wiley & Sons, 2003), 165; John Cassidy, *Dot.con: The Greatest Story Ever Told* (New York: Harper Collins, 2002); Henwood, *After the New Economy*, 32–3.

134. William Powers, Jr., "Report of the Special Investigation Committee," ["Power's Report"], Enron Board of Directors (1 February 2002), 1–5.

135. Brian Cruver, *Anatomy of Greed: The Unshredded Truth from an Enron Insider* (London: Huchinson, 2002), 20–2.

136. Fox, *Enron*, 22–42. For a historical discussion of the importance of trading companies, see Geoffrey Jones, *Merchants to Multinationals: British Trading Companies in the Nineteenth and Twentieth Centuries* (Oxford: Oxford University Press, 2000), 1–3.

137. Amy Argetsinger, "Crash Course on Enron," *The Washington Post* (23 February 2002), A1.

138. "List of Creditors Holding 20 Largest Unsecured Claims," In re Enron, United States Bankruptcy Court, Southern District of New York, 2–3.

139. Joe Berardino, "Enron: A Wake-Up Call," *The Wall Street Journal* (4 December 2001), A18.

140. Jonathan Weil, John Emshwiller, and Scot J. Paltrow, "Audit Nightmare: Arthur Andersen Says It Disposed of Documents That Related to Enron," *The Wall Street Journal* (11 January 2002), A1.

141. Devon Spurgeon and Cassell Bryan-Low, "Can Andersen Partners Keep Their Firm Alive?" *The Wall Street Journal* (29 March 2002), C1.

142. Vanessa O'Connell, "Arthur Andersen Confronts Its Enron Role," *The Wall Street Journal* (17 January 2002), B4.

143. Adrian Michaels, "It's Only the Lawyers Left at Andersen," *The Financial Times* (31 August 2002), 13.

144. H.R. 3763, Sarbanes-Oxley Act of 2002.

145. Allison Fass, "One Year Later, The Impact of Sarbanes-Oxley," *Forbes* (22 July 2003).

146. Alex W. Zabrosky, "Sarbanes-Oxley: Law of Opportunity and Liability," *Consulting to Management*, Vol. 14, No. 2 (June 2003), 26.

147. Section 201, "Services Outside the Scope of Practice of Auditors,"Sarbanes-Oxley Act of 2002.

148. Edward Nusbaum, CEO of Grant Thornton, LLP, "Sarbanes-Oxley Oversight," Testimony before the Banking, Housing and Urban Affairs Committee, U.S. Senate (23 September 2003).

149. Cynthia A. Montgomery and Rhonda Kaufman, "The Board's Missing Link," The *Harvard Business Review* (March 2003), 92.

150. Armstrong, *An Engineer in Wall Street*, frontispiece.

151. Wendy Zellner, "Enron's Power Play," *Business Week* (12 February 2001) (Italics mine).

152. Smith and Emshwiller, *24 Days*, 241.

153. "Q&A with Enron's Skilling," www.businessweek.com/2001/01_07/b3719010.htm.

154. Loren Fox, *Enron: The Rise and Fall* (Hoboken: John Wiley & Sons, 2003), 33–9.

155. Robert B. Reich, *The Work of Nations* (New York: Vintage Books, 1991), 177–80.

156. Peter Temin with Louis Galambos, *The Fall of the Bell System: A Study in Prices and Politics* (Cambridge: Cambridge University Press, 1989), 1–3.

157. Andrew Abbott, *The System of Professionals: An Essay on the Division of Expert Labour* (Chicago: University of Chicago Press, 1988), 70–1.

CONCLUSION: THE WORLD'S NEWEST PROFESSION?

1. John A. Byrne, "The Craze for Consultants," *Business Week* (25 July 1994), 60; James O'Shea and Charles Madigan, *Dangerous Company: The Consulting*

*Powerhouses and the Businesses They Save and Ruin* (New York: Times Books, 1997); John Micklethwait and Adrian Wooldridge, *The Witch Doctors: Making Sense of the Management Gurus* (New York: Times Books, 1996).

2. Timothy Clark and Robin Fincham (eds.), *Critical Consulting: New Perspectives on the Management Advice Industry* (Oxford: Blackwell Business, 2002), 1–16. For the origins of critical management studies see the early edited volume: Mats Alvesson and Hugh Willmott (eds.), *Critical Management Studies* (London: Sage, 1992).

3. Matthias Kipping and Lars Engwall (eds.), *Management Consulting: Emergence and Dynamics of a Knowledge Industry* (Oxford: Oxford University Press, 2002), 1–2.

4. Even after historians began studying consulting, most industry accounts still contained significant factual mistakes. For one example of these gaffes, see Sugata Biswas and Daryl Twitchell, *Management Consulting: A Complete Guide to the Industry* (New York: John Wiley & Sons, 1999): 16–20.

5. Richard Paget, "Management Consulting as a Profession: A Talk Before the Forty-Fifth Anniversary Meeting of Booz, Allen and Hamilton, Chicago Illinois, November 15, 1958," Corporate Archives, Association of Management Consulting Firms, New York; Homer Hagedorn, "The Management Consultant as Transmitter of Business Techniques," *Explorations in Entrepreneurial History* (February 1955): 164–73.

6. Lewis Pinault, *Consulting Demons: Inside the Unscrupulous World of Global Corporate Consulting* (New York: HarperCollins, 2000), 1–5.

7. David H. Maister, *True Professionalism: The Courage to Care About Your People, Your Clients, and Your Career* (New York: Free Press, 2000).

8. Herbert M. Kritzer, "The Professions are Dead, Long Live the Professions: Legal Practice in a Postprofessional World," *Law & Society Review*, Vol. 33, No. 3 (1999), 713–59; Richard Abel, "The Decline of Professionalism?" *The Modern Law Review*, Vol. 49, No. 1 (1986), 1–41.

9. Harold L. Wilensky, "The Professionalization of Everyone?" *The American Journal of Sociology*, Vol. 70, No. 2 (1964): 137–58.

10. A. M. Carr-Saunders and P. A. Wilson, *The Professions* (Oxford: Oxford University Press, 1933).

11. Mats Alvesson and Anders W. Johansson, "Professionalism and Politics in Management Consultancy Work," in Clark and Fincham (eds.), *Critical Consulting*, 228–46.

12. Lawrence J. Fox, "MDPs Done Gone: The Silver Lining in the Very Black Enron Cloud," *Arizona Law Review*, Vol. 44 (2002): 547–58.

13. Andrew. B. Hargadon, "Firms as Knowledge Brokers: Lessons in Pursuing Continuous Innovation," *California Management Review*, Vol. 40, No. 3 (1998), 209–22; Harold Q. Langenderfer and Jack C. Robertson, "A Theoretical Structure for Independent Audits of Management," *The Accounting Review*, Vol. 44, No. 4 (1969), 777–87.

14. Association of Consulting Management Engineers, "Code of Professional Ethics," *The Journal of the Academy of Management*, Vol. 5, No. 3 (1962): 230–1.
15. Alan Ryan, Introduction for Jack Pole, "A Sociology of American Irony," British Association for American Studies, Rothermere American Institute, University of Oxford, 6 April 2002.
16. Andrew Abbott, "Professional Ethics," *The American Journal of Sociology*, Vol. 88, No. 5 (March 1983): 855–85.
17. Clarence A. Lightner, "Legal Ethics: The Canons of the American Bar Association," *Michigan Law Review*, Vol. 16, No. 6 (1918): 421–8.
18. Anthony T. Kronman, *The Lost Lawyer: Failing Ideals of the Legal Profession* (Cambridge, MA: Belknap Press, 1995); Bernard Barber, "Control and Responsibility in the Powerful Professions," *Political Science Quarterly*, Vol. 93, No. 4 (1978), 599–615.
19. McKinsey & Company, "New Engagement and Executive Relations Guide," May 1945, 2, Corporate Archives, McKinsey & Company.
20. "Booz Allen & Hamilton," *Television Magazine* (January 1959), 50.
21. Michael C. Jensen, "McKinsey & Co.: Big Brother to Big Business," *The New York Times*, 30 May 1971, 1.
22. Royston Greenwood, C. R. Hinings, and John Brown, "'P²-FORM' Strategic Management: Corporate Practices in Professional Partnerships," *Academy of Management Journal*, Vol. 33, No. 4 (1990), 725–55.
23. Jack Sweeney, "The Soul of a New Consultancy," *Consulting Magazine* (January/February 2005), 14–21.
24. Thomas J. Watson, Jr. and Peter Petre, *Father, Son, and Co.: My Life at IBM and Beyond* (New York: Bantam Books, 1990), 294.
25. Jim Bowman, *Booz Allen & Hamilton: Seventy Years of Client Service, 1914–1984* (Chicago: Booz Allen & Hamilton, 1984), 39–40; Booz Allen & Hamilton, "Report on Present Organization: RCA Laboratories Division, Radio Corporation of America, Princeton NJ," November 18, 1947, RCA Laboratories Division Collection, Box 1, Folder 1, David Sarnoff Library, Princeton, New Jersey.
26. Watson and Petre, *Father, Son, and Co.*, 294.
27. Ibid.
28. F. G. "Buck" Rogers with Robert L. Shook, *The IBM Way: Insights Into the World's Most Successful Marketing Organization* (New York: Harper & Row, Publishers, 1986); Robert Sobel, *I.B.M.: Colossus in Transition* (New York: Times Books, 1981).
29. Elizabeth Haas Edersheim, *McKinsey's Marvin Bower: Vision, Leadership, and the Creation of Management Consulting*, (New York: John Wiley & Sons, Inc., 2004), 98; Bower, Marvin, *Perspective on McKinsey* (New York: McKinsey & Company, 1979), 85–6.
30. Sweeney, "The Soul of a New Consultancy," 14.

31. For an extended version of this overwrought metaphor, see Louis Galambos, *America at Middle Age: A New History of the United States in the Twentieth Century* (New York: McGraw Hill, 1982).

32. David Grayson Allen, "Bound by their Past or in Transition? An Analysis of U.S. Management Consulting Associations," *Journal of Management Consulting*, Vol. 3, No. 1 (1986), 27–35.

33. Douglas Martin, "Marvin Bower, 99; Built McKinsey & Co.," *The New York Times* (24 January 2003), C19.

# Index